8/13

THE PRAIRIE BOYS GO TO WAR

THE PRAIRIE BOYS GO TO WAR

The Fifth Illinois Cavalry
1861–1865

Rhonda M. Kohl

Southern Illinois University Press
Carbondale and Edwardsville

16   15   14   13   4   3   2   1

Library of Congress Cataloging-in-Publication Data
Kohl, Rhonda M., 1957–
The prairie boys go to war : the Fifth Illinois Cavalry,
1861–1865 / Rhonda M. Kohl.
pages cm
Includes bibliographical references and index.
ISBN 978-0-8093-3203-8 (cloth : alk. paper) — ISBN
0-8093-3203-5 (cloth : alk. paper) — ISBN 978-0-
8093-3204-5 (ebook) (print) — ISBN 0-8093-3204-3
(ebook)
1. United States. Army. Illinois Cavalry Regiment,
5th (1861–1865) 2. Illinois—History—Civil War,
1861–1865—Regimental histories. 3. United
States—History—Civil War, 1861–1865—
Regimental histories. 4. United States—History—
Civil War, 1861–1865—Campaigns. I. Title.
E505.65th .K64 2012
973.7'3—dc23   2012017679

Printed on recycled paper. ♻
The paper used in this publication meets the mini-
mum requirements of American National Standard
for Information Sciences—Permanence of Paper for
Printed Library Materials, ANSI Z39.48-1992. ∞

To my grandmother Susan Kerston Forsyth,
who always believed in me

CONTENTS

A roster of the Fifth Illinois Cavalry,
compiled by the author, is available online at
http://www.siupress.com/downloads/excerpts/9780809332038_expt.pdf
and in the ebook.

ILLUSTRATIONS

PREFACE

When one thinks about the Union cavalry during the American Civil War, visions of glorified cavaliers on fiery horses, with swords blazing, usually come to mind. In reality, Union cavalry in service along the Mississippi River were hard-riding troopers, on poor mounts, performing tedious duty. Very few publications have been devoted to cavalry regiments originating in midwestern states; even such celebrated regiments as the Second and Sixth Illinois Cavalry lack a documented history. Ignored by scholars, and often misrepresented by historians, the Fifth Illinois Cavalry has also remained obscure, despite participating in some of the most important campaigns in Arkansas and Mississippi. What little has been written about these fighting units concentrated on the campaigns in which they participated and the men's heroic deeds during battles and skirmishes. Most regimental histories treat the regiment as a unit, an entity apart from those who served within it: a being with its own identity. Very few histories seek to understand the men that served in these regiments.

The Prairie Boys Go to War is a comprehensive military history that not only includes strategy and tactics, but also examines the men who served within it and how they influenced the Fifth Illinois regiment. Once the character and cultural heritage of the soldiers became known—who they were, where they came from, what they thought, and how they adjusted to military life—I realized the history of the Fifth Illinois could not be told without telling the story of its men. The Fifth Cavalry's military history became the soldiers' story and explains how the disparate men interacted with one another, how they solved differences within the regiment (of which there were many), and how they felt about serving with men of different belief systems and cultures. All this interaction determined how the regiment fought, how it acted within the army as a whole, and how other regiments interacted with it. Reconstructing the cultural context of Fifth soldiers led to an understanding of the internal strife of the regiment that continually ate away at the regiment's cohesion and harmony, and its fighting prowess.

Nonetheless, the Fifth Illinois fought against some of the most notorious Confederate warriors from Arkansas, Texas, and Mississippi and participated in decisive campaigns in the Western theater during the Civil War. The chronicles of the Fifth Illinois Cavalry also exposed the story of the Union cavalry that fought in the Mississippi valley. Often misunderstood, and given secondary status to the infantry and artillery, the Federal horsemen provided valuable service and often spearheaded major overland movements.

Finally, the Fifth Illinois' history is also an examination of the daily life of the soldiers, who dealt with the isolation, loneliness, and tedium of camp life. Due to the ignorance of their leaders as it related to camp sanitation, the prairie boys lived and died through epidemics of dysentery, typhoid, malaria, and murine typhus, with hundreds dying of camp diseases. They survived military incompetence, drunken officers, useless surgeons, and an army that by all appearances cared little whether a soldier lived or died. Despite all these obstacles, Fifth Illinois soldiers performed their duty admirably, and at times with great cost to themselves and their families. The men who survived the war returned to civilian life, forever changed by their military experiences. The story of the Fifth ended when the last survivor died in 1940: a witness not only to a civil war, but also to the Spanish American, and First World Wars.

Over the past ten years of researching, writing, and publishing four scholarly works about the Fifth Illinois, my knowledge of the regiment evolved as new primary sources became available. For example, my first article, published in 1998, centered on the regiment's skirmish at Mechanicsburg, Mississippi, during the Vicksburg campaign in June 1863. I wrote about the heroic deeds of the Fifth's Third Battalion as they routed Georgian cavalry of Gen. John Adams's brigade at Mechanicsburg, Mississippi, one of the regiment's highest points.

Digging deeper into the Fifth soldiers' world through primary documents, I soon discovered that in mid-1863, the Fifth was also terribly divided, with officers and soldiers battling each other for control of the regiment. Discord erupted between Republicans and Democrats, usually forming along the lines of the men's cultural heritage (Southern- or Northern- born), while men of temperance cursed consumers of alcoholic beverages. Many Fifth soldiers remained indifferent or hostile to slaves and embraced their emancipation only as a way to win the war, while others championed slavery's end as a moral necessity. The prairie boys' varied cultural heritage gave the regiment its uniqueness, but it also created an environment for internal strife. The history of the regiment, therefore, offers not only an analysis of military matters, but also an in-depth examination of how these men of disparate cultural and social backgrounds worked and fought together through the four toughest years of their lives.

Reconstructing the regiment's history required a reliance on company and regimental records from the Illinois state and national archives, as well as official correspondence and battle reports. Several diaries and memoirs written by those who served in the Fifth Illinois, and from men who served in units with the Fifth, contributed largely to the regiment's history. I allowed the soldiers to tell their own story, and as far as possible, I have also kept the original form and spelling of their statements, within the limits of readability. I have maintained the original vernacular, especially as it related to conversations recorded by the soldiers between themselves and slaves; all accounts shared assumptions about black-white differences that would be considered racist today.

I relied heavily on manuscript documents because I deem first-person accounts more reliable than published sources, for they lack the intervention of an author or editor. Some narratives contained fictitious or exaggerated accounts of a soldier's or the regiment's fighting abilities, and I considered it necessary to obtain corroboration from other primary documents, whether from the Fifth, Confederate, or other Union soldiers' accounts. If an event could not be verified, it was either not included in the narrative or so noted in the endnotes. In some cases, Fifth Illinois eyewitness accounts contradicted previous interpretations of skirmishes and battles, but all were supported by corroborating evidence from other first-person accounts.

To understand the soldiers' cultural heritage, the examination relied on demographic information provided by the Federal census from 1850 and 1860. The surveys supplied data on economic wealth with real estate and personal property values, nativity, marital status, education and literacy, occupation, and place of residence. Additional information came from letters and diaries of regimental mates, nineteenth-century biographies in the old county histories, pension files, obituaries, and biographical and genealogical information posted by Fifth descendants on the Internet and told to me through personal correspondence.

Without the aid of dozens of scholars, colleagues, and librarians in locating primary sources, the Fifth's history would not have been written. Lorilee Huffman, curator at the University Museum at Southern Illinois University Carbondale, introduced me to the Benjamin Ladd Wiley collection during my museum internship in 1984, which eventually led to my master's thesis about Wiley. The Special Collections librarians at Morris Library at SIUC (where the Wiley Collection is now housed) provided copies from the collected works of John P. Mann, second lieutenant of Company K, and the regiment's commissary. Mann left an extensive written account that chronicled not only the regiment's movements but also the views of a Republican soldier and officer. I had hoped to use only my transcriptions of original Fifth Illinois documents, but the Mann diary was, in many places, too fragile for use, and I had to rely on a previous transcription. Unfortunately, this work was authored by a person who had very little knowledge of the Civil War, thus introducing numerous mistakes in spelling, dates, and conceptions. I tried to keep as much of the original Mann diary as possible, but in many cases, was forced to rely on the transcription.

This was not the case with other primary documents written by Fifth Illinois soldiers. E. Cheryl Schnirring at the Abraham Lincoln Library in Springfield introduced me to the original diaries and letters from John W. Burke, Thadeus Packard, Francis A. Wheelock, Charles W. Higgins, Fenton Hussey, and Jonas Roe. Except for the Alonzo Payne diary, I have completed and relied on my own transcriptions of all these documents. Mary Michals and Roberta Fairburn of the audiovisual department provided many of the Fifth Illinois images from the Lincoln Library's collection.

My scholarly debts have grown considerably in the course of researching and writing this book. A number of scholars read portions of the manuscript when it was yet in the form of articles submitted to journals, and I am grateful for the guidance provided by Philip DiBlasi, Mark Christ, Terry Winschel, Edwin C. Bearss, and John Ludwickson. I also have special thanks to Sylvia Frank Rodrigue, my editor, who believed in this manuscript and guided it towards its successful publication.

This book would not have materialized without the assistance of Rebecca Kelien and Harriet Goldberg of the Jeffersonville Township Public Library in Indiana, and Dan Win of the Louisville Free Public Library in Kentucky. John Ludwickson of the Nebraska Historical Society, who patiently read my thoughts, fears, theories, and discoveries, and responded with words of encouragement and guidance. I am also indebted to all those knowledgeable people on the Civil War message boards who have answered many questions over the last couple of years. Kathryn Koldehoff, whose friendship and editing of my thesis all those years ago, started me on this journey by giving me the confidence and knowledge to write effectively. I am also indebted to Anthony Ranere, my undergraduate mentor, who taught me that cultural analysis is the key to understanding the past, and Karen Curry, whose skillful artistic talents can be seen in the beautiful portraits of Ben Wiley and Thomas Apperson. Special thanks for my mother, Shirley Kohl, who instilled in me a love of history when I was a child, accompanying me to historic homes and sites all over Pennsylvania and New Jersey; moreover, to Dave, my patient and understanding spouse, who provided computer knowledge, rescuing many a doomed chapter when programs failed, or when the operator faltered.

The Fifth's story could also not have been written without the contributions of dozens of the soldiers' descendants who came forward with stories of their ancestors. Eric Feagan published Sgt. Jonas Roe's letters on the Internet, allowing free access, and Frank Crawford, a descendant of Capt. George E. McConkey, provided materials relating to one of the best officers in the regiment. My sincere thanks are extended to all who contributed photographs, pension files, or obituaries, including but not limited to Vicki McBride, Bernie and David A. Crain, Larry Brown, Jim Albien, Tom Leach, M. Markwell, Randy Beck, Melvin McAllistor, Don Procop, Sheelee Anderson, Robert Bailey, Lucia Wilkin, Ron Coddington, Mary R. M. Nunneley, Jean Caldwell Adams, and Carol Staats. Special thanks to David Foote for finding obscure little articles and tidbits about the Fifth in the *Crawford County Argus*, and providing me with copies.

ABBREVIATIONS

ALPL Abraham Lincoln
Presidential Library,
Springfield, IL

CCA *Crawford
County Argus*

CSR Compiled
Service Records

CT *Chicago Tribune*

DO Division Order

GO General Orders

IL AGR Illinois Adjutant
General Report

JAL John A. Logan Museum

MG *Mattoon Gazette*

NARA National Archives and
Records Administration

NJ *Nashville Journal*

PFI Pension File Index

PP *Fairfield Prairie Pioneer*

RCD Returns,
Casualties, and
Discharges

ROB Regimental
Order Books

SO Special Order

Military Ranks

Adj. Gen. Adjutant General

Brig. Gen. Brigadier General

Capt. Captain

Col. Colonel

Cpl. Corporal

Lt. Lieutenant

Lt. Col. Lieutenant Colonel

Maj. Major

Q. M. Sgt. Quartermaster
Sergeant

Pvt. Private

Sgt. Sergeant

Sgt. Maj. Sergeant Major

THE PRAIRIE BOYS GO TO WAR

1

The Politics of War
August 1861 to February 1862

"We are now in the face of the enemy, and the honour of the Regt is at Stake, and not only the Regt but the State from which it hailes, to some extent, and I with hundreds of others in this Regt see with deep regret the . . . working that is going on among us," declared Capt. George W. McConkey, Co. E, Fifth Illinois Cavalry in June 1863. Leaderless after losing their second colonel to illness in January, the regiment's delicate internal cohesion snapped, and a schism formed, polarizing the officers and men into Democratic and Republican factions. Throughout the spring of 1863, Fifth Illinois soldiers wrote a multitude of letters to Illinois Republican governor Richard Yates and Adj. Gen. Allen C. Fuller espousing the disloyalty of Democratic officers or the unyielding patriotism of Republicans who sought the command. "We want a Col. whose whole Soul is in This fight," asserted Rev. John W. Woods, and one who supports the administration's "war policeys." Peace eluded the regiment until a new colonel assumed command sixteen months later. Though weakened by the internal strife and the loss of dozens of men to disease, the regiment's company officers kept the men fighting the Confederacy, and the regiment won distinction on the battlefields at Grenada, Vicksburg, Canton, Jackson, and Meridian, Mississippi, earning the regiment its sobriquet "the Bloody 5th."[1]

The internal strife of the regiment resulted from cultural differences emanating from the geographic origin of its soldiers, which led to profound religious, cultural, and political diversity. The regiment organized in southern Illinois in the fall of 1861: Northern and central Illinois contributed 1,106 men (59.9 percent), while 631 soldiers (34.2 percent) hailed from southern counties. The people who had settled southern Illinois hailed principally from Virginia, Kentucky, the Carolinas, and Tennessee. Many migrants feared freed Southern blacks would move north, disrupting the

Map 1.1. 1860 presidential voting patterns in counties that contributed men to the Fifth Illinois Cavalry. Southern Illinois is below the blackened line.

labor system, as well as initializing integration through marriage. Racism was integral to the region's history, culture, and development. So homogeneous was the culture and belief system that the area grew distinct from the rest of Illinois and became known as Egypt. Strongly Democratic, many Egyptians believed abolitionists had brought the Republican Party into being to transform their ideals into law. In the 1860 presidential election, Republican candidate Abraham Lincoln received only 19.8 percent of the southern Illinois vote: Democrats, such as Senator Stephen A. Douglas and Congressman John A. Logan, dominated the politics.[2]

Southern Illinois was closely tied to the South by its dominant Southern-born population, by the need for markets for Illinois grain and livestock, and by the Mississippi River, which took those commodities to the world market. Yet southern Illinois remained culturally and politically predicated on the antislavery article of the Northwest Ordinance and the idealization of free white labor. The African American population in the region remained small to nonexistent, due to the Black Laws enacted by the legislature in 1853, which barred any free blacks from settling within the state's confines. Fines and prison terms awaited any person who brought freed slaves into the state, while African Americans received either a fifty-dollar fine or the equivalent of time in labor. In 1862, Illinoisans adopted stricter antiblack articles to counteract any antislavery measures by President Abraham Lincoln's Republican administration.

Migrants from Northern states, who generally supported Republican principles, populated northern Illinois, but by the late 1850s, a few had settled among the Egyptians. These citizens had received a Northern education, defended antislavery proponents, and were financially more secure than the subsistence farmers of Egypt. Central Illinois became a buffer zone between the two sections. Settled by emigrants from the North and South, the population was more diverse and less conservative than Egypt. In the 1860 election, Republican doctrines began to appeal to many central Illinoisans, but the area remained strongly Democratic.

During the 1850s, two distinct and separate sets of social behaviors and beliefs coexisted within Illinois. When the slavery controversy peaked during the 1860 presidential election, Illinois mirrored the nation at large, divided along proslavery and free labor lines. The schism within the Fifth Illinois reflected the national and state divisions, with the majority of the men enlisting not to free the slaves but to save the Union.

Believing newly elected President Lincoln would end slavery in the South, slave-holding states seceded from the Union after the 1860 presidential election. The Southern origin of Egypt's inhabitants made it difficult to choose between loyalty to the section or the Federal government. While the majority of citizens supported the Union, many objected to Lincoln's use of coercion to hold the Union together and voiced their outrage in meetings throughout Egypt. Some southern Illinoisans wanted to join the Confederacy; others saw the area breaking away to form a neutral state that would mediate between North and South. Senator Douglas's words immediately following the firing on Fort Sumter in April 1861 sealed the loyalty question for Egypt: "We must fight for our country and forget all differences. There can be but two parties—the party of patriots and the party of traitors. We belong to the first."[3] With the help of Douglas and Logan, both highly regarded by Egyptians, the region not only remained loyal but also sent thousands of her men to die on the battlefield and in army hospitals, wearing the Union blue.

Lincoln's call for seventy-five thousand troops on 15 April 1861 appealed to the prospective soldiers' patriotism to "maintain the honor, the integrity, and the existence of our National Union, and the perpetuity of popular government." Secretary of War Simon Cameron requested Illinois to contribute six regiments of infantry and artillery, approximately forty-eight hundred soldiers, "for immediate service." With the Federal army's defeat at Bull Run (Manassas) on 22 July, and the prospect of a lengthy war, the president made a general call for infantry and cavalry for three years' service.[4]

On 27 August 1861, Yates authorized the organization of the Fifth Illinois Cavalry regiment. Only the governor issued commissions for commanding officers of state regiments (colonel, lieutenant colonel, and three majors), and he chose those men based on letters of recommendation and on the men's professional reputation and political inclinations. Instead of commissioning officers who were suited to command, Yates chose political allies and was known for his attempt to "Republicanize the army," which was reflected in the governor's choice for the Fifth's command: all Republicans except one. In early September, Yates issued commissions for Col. John Updegraff, Lt. Col. Benjamin Wiley, and Majors Speed Butler, Thomas Apperson, and Abel Seley. Except for Ben Wiley, none of the original general officers of the Fifth had previous military experience, but even Wiley lacked the knowledge to make this new cavalry regiment successful.[5]

As a friend and political associate, Yates issued Wiley's (1821–90) commission for lieutenant colonel in September 1861. Born to a modest Quaker family in Smithfield, Ohio, Wiley moved to southern Illinois twenty-two years later. When war broke out with Mexico, he served as a private and quartermaster sergeant in Company B, First Regiment of Illinois Infantry in June 1847. The war veteran returned to southern Illinois and settled in Jonesboro, Union County, in 1848, where he married Emily Davie, daughter of the capitalist Winsted Davie. The new family moved to Makanda, Jackson County, where Wiley established the first fruit orchard in southern Illinois, and history has credited him with establishing the orchard and winery industries in Egypt. Wiley excelled in the pastoral environment of Jackson County, but he continued his association with money lending, the law, politics, the railroad, and land speculation. His career would be greatly enhanced by his association with David L. Phillips, his partner in a real-estate firm and influential Republican.[6]

Originally a Whig, Wiley became one of the first Republicans and with Phillips helped organize the party in Egypt. He lost his bid for the Ninth District congressional seat in 1856 but served as delegate to the state and national Republican conventions in 1858 and 1860. Wiley's political aspirations made him well known in Illinois, especially within his congressional district, which covered most of southern Egypt. Wiley also helped organize the Illinois State Temperance Union and was a charter member of the Jonesboro Masonic Lodge 111. Republicans and Democrats considered Wiley to be a man of "rare qualities, that gave him a high reputation and rendered his character irreproachable." When Wiley raised the Fifth regiment in the fall of 1861, his reputation as a gentleman attracted many men who knew him from his political and commercial enterprises. Wiley believed the status of a gentleman was a social rank and a moral condition, and he took that attitude with him to the Fifth Illinois. Wiley corresponded with his wife, Emily, throughout his career with the regiment. Their letters document the trials, triumphs, and losses of a southern Illinois Republican family during the war.[7]

Leaving home in early September, Wiley joined Updegraff at Camp Butler, the new military enrollment camp near Springfield. Located on Clear Lake, six miles east of Springfield, the camp began accepting military organizations in early August. When Wiley and Updegraff arrived later that month, the grounds already held thousands of future soldiers. Maj. Hugo Hollan, a veteran of Hungarian wars, served as cavalry instructor, drilling the new equestrians on a stretch of ground just east of the Sangamon River.[8]

Speed Butler, son of William Butler and a very close friend of Lincoln, received the commission for first major in the regiment. The appointment was sheer patronage: Butler never reported to the Fifth but served on Gen. John Pope's staff during the war.

Cumberland County's Thomas A. Apperson (1818–79) received the commission for second major, arriving in camp in early September. A tall imposing man, Apperson knew the Lincoln family and became a staunch Republican. Virginians by birth, the Apperson clan moved to Coles County in 1829. Thomas eventually acquired 3,755 acres of public land in Cumberland County, becoming one of the largest and wealthiest landowners in the area. Apperson served with his father, John, Cole County's first physician, in Masonic Lodge 179. Despite his privileged upbringing, Apperson's lack of education became apparent during his tenure in the regiment. "Major Apperson is an illiterate man,—of no learning whatever,—poorly qualified for the position," declared a Democratic officer in the Fifth. As was common, a clerk wrote Apperson's regimental correspondence, but the major's private letters revealed a man who struggled with grammar and spelled phonetically. Many Democratic officers tried to use Apperson's lack of education against him, but this never deterred the Republican administration's faith in the major, nor the respect of men in the regiment. Apperson "may not be as good a Military man as some others, but he is as good-hearted a fellow as ever lived, and has done more to get the Regt up, and keep it together, than any other man, and he is allway on hands, and ready to do his duty," declared a Republican captain.[9]

Of the original volunteers, only Apperson owned a farm worth over a quarter of a million dollars. Agriculture supported the largest proportion of the men in the original regiment, with 717 identified as farmers, fifty as farm laborers, and eighteen as tenant farmers. A difference existed between property ownership in Egypt and that of volunteers from central and northern Illinois. The mean property values of landed Egyptians averaged $1,886, with an average personal property value of $423. Property owners from other parts of the state averaged over a thousand dollars more with a mean of $2,970. Personal property values for those from central and northern Illinois had a mean value of $523.[10]

Forty-seven men from the original regiment considered themselves carpenters or cabinetmakers, including 3rd Maj. Abel H. Seley (1821–86). The Vermont-born carpenter lived with his family on a $3,000 farm in Centralia, where he served as superintendent at the Illinois Central Railroad shops when war broke out. Through his involvement with the railroad, Seley associated with Wiley, and many considered him "a Moddle Man in his business transactions." Despite his prewar reputation, Seley became a controversial character due to his proclivity for gambling, convivial drinking, and card playing, and his Democratic beliefs elicited strong opposing sentiments within the regiment. While some questioned his morals and his strong Democratic convictions, others labeled him the "best Field officer. . . . [A] thoroughly practical man,—good tactician—, of the best Moral Character. . . . [N]ever lacking in judgement, Courageous and brave, and is the best man by far, for the management of this regiment."[11]

Men in the Fifth Illinois claimed foreign, Northern, and Southern family roots. Of the commanding officers, only Apperson was Southern born; all others claimed a Northern birthright or were foreign born. A demographic analysis of 1,659 Fifth Illinoisans who listed their birthplace revealed that 72.6 percent of the men were native to Northern states, with 28.5 percent native Illinoisans. Sixteen percent (265) of the men claimed a Southern birthright; only 11.3 percent or 188 men were foreign born. In Companies G, C, K, and B, foreign-born soldiers outnumbered those of Southern birth.

Despite having been raised in southern Illinois, the regiment became heavily laden with Northern-born men, who hailed from the central and northern counties of Illinois. All the companies, even those raised wholly in Egypt (Companies D, H, K, and M), claimed more Northern natives than Southern. Irrespective of their birthplace, the men enlisted to save their country, a land where many of their ancestors had fought in the Revolutionary War and the War of 1812. "[O]ur Government—the Union—," declared a Randolph County soldier, "is worth all the 'blood and treasure' in the North, and must be freely given to secure its perpetuity." Another sacrificed "Wife, Home, Life and all on Our Common Alter and this was my bleeding Sacrefice to help Save my Country!"[12]

Those with Southern roots had their own type of self-determination. According to historian David Hackett Fischer, their culture raised men to "foster fierce pride, [and] stubborn independence," which also created "autonomous individuals who were unable to endure external control." Southern-born Egyptians who enlisted in the Fifth reflected these cultural ideals. In addition, the independent spirit, forged from creating a society out of the Illinois wilderness, ran through the blood of many a Fifth Illinoisan. These characteristics hampered the regiment's ability to become a unified fighting entity.[13]

The organization of the regiment matched that of the regular Federal army in 1861. A regiment contained seven hundred to one thousand men, organized into twelve companies, containing seventy-two or more privates, commanded by three commissioned officers (captain and two lieutenants) and twenty noncommissioned officers (sergeants and corporals). Each regiment consisted of three battalions, containing four companies, under the command of a major. All three battalions were under the command of a colonel and lieutenant colonel, supported by a regimental adjutant, commissary, and quartermaster, two chief buglers, one surgeon with an assistant surgeon, and a chaplain to care for the men's spiritual needs.

The company, often containing blood relations or fellow town and county residents, became the recruits' military family. This new "band of brothers" marched, worked, slept, played, and fought together for four years of war. Captains and lieutenants remained the heart of the company, and they held the men together during battle, provided leadership in camp, and disciplined soldiers when needed. Companies suffered poor discipline and higher rates of battle casualties and disease when company commanders proved inept.[14]

At the beginning of the war, Illinois permitted her soldiers to elect their company officers, but the regimental commander certified the results and recommended the winners to the governor. The governor then issued commissions for captains and lieutenants at his discretion, with political patronage and favoritism playing large roles in his decision. As early as October 1861, one Randolph County soldier realized the inherent nature of some men to gain rank using any possible means. "The chicanery and petty tricks that are often used to procure office in the civil department of life, seem to have control of all military affairs here, and in Springfield. It is a species of corruption. . . . Merit and competency alone should be the qualification for office, both in civil and military life."[15]

Two companies of independent cavalry awaited the Fifth's commanding officers at Camp Butler; these units became Company A and Company B of the regiment. Charles Nisewanger, a fifty-five-year-old merchant from Greenup, organized Company A from Democratic Cumberland County and served as first lieutenant after turning down the captaincy. Nisewanger served as a member of the local temperance league and knew Wiley through regional meetings. Charles served with his son John in the regiment.[16]

The men of Company A elected Dr. Edward W. Pierson (1829–1916) their captain. An Indiana native, Pierson left his medical practice and family in Prairie City when he joined the ranks of the Fifth. Sixteen physicians and two druggists eventually joined the regiment, but only three served in the medical department during the war; many, however, donated time to the regimental hospital when disease overwhelmed the men.[17]

Second Lt. Gordon Webster (1833–91), from Woodbury, joined Company A "to serve my country in her hour of trial" and was "willing at any time to sacrifice my life if necessary to serve it." "[A] democrat in principle, but a loyal man . . . and a strong friend of the [Republican] administration," he achieved the rank of first lieutenant in July 1862. Lyman Clark (1839–1901) joined the ranks as sergeant but rose to second lieutenant, eventually becoming "one of the best Lieuts in the Regiment." Clark lived with his widowed mother in Neoga prior to the war.[18] The strong personalities of its commanding staff allowed Company A to become one of the most successful units in the regiment.

Company B joined the regiment in August, with men from Moultrie, Madison, and Coles Counties. Serving as the northeast border of Egypt, Madison County gave Lincoln a sixty-one vote majority in the 1860 election. Coles County in central Illinois produced a twenty-eight vote majority for the Republicans, while Moultrie remained strongly Democratic. The company did not muster until November 1861; in the meantime, the men elected Thomas McKee (1815–91) of Mattoon as its first captain. McKee worked an $8,000 farm and served with his eldest son, William, in the company. The McKees were one of forty-one father-son pairs to join the regiment; there were almost 250 other relationships of marriage or blood, including many sets of cousins. The company served as "Mounted Sharp Shooters" for the regiment.[19]

Illinois State Normal University's Regimental Brass Band escorted Normal Cavalry Company 68 to the Fifth's campground on 9 September, located in a "beautiful 'Prarie Grove' with an abundance of Wood and good Water." The forty men quickly settled into their camp. Organized by Republicans from McLean County, the soldiers elected William P. Withers (1819–98) captain after joining the regiment as Company C. McLean County gave Lincoln a 980-vote majority in 1860. Over 85 percent of the members of Company C hailed from McLean County.[20]

Kentucky-born Withers moved with his family to Illinois in 1832. After marrying, Withers tried various trades, including hemp manufacture in Missouri in the 1840s and gold mining in California in the 1850s. After he returned to Illinois, Wither purchased a $23,000 farm in McLean County and founded and managed the religious newspaper the *Illinois Baptist* in 1856, which merged with the *Christian Times* of Chicago two years later. In 1858, the citizens of McLean County elected Withers county sheriff, a position he still held when war broke out. Formally a Whig, Withers became an outspoken supporter of Lincoln and served in various capacities at the Republican conventions, hearing Lincoln's first campaign speech for the presidency in 1860. Called "one of the very best Officers of the Regiment," a man of "Strict integrity, unexceptionable character, and devotion to the cause of Sustaining the government and punishing treason," Withers became one of the Fifth's most respected and well-liked commanding officers. His exceptional command skills, and those of his line officers, gained Company C a valuable fighting reputation during the war.[21]

Despite his Mexican War service with the Fourth Illinois Infantry, James Depew failed to leave a lasting imprint on Company C, mustering out in April 1862, after being absent without proper leave. Yates then commissioned Francis A. Wheelock (1828–1904) to the rank of first lieutenant, which he filled with skill, courage, and common sense. Francis left a one-year diary for 1864, covering the regiment's participation in the Meridian campaign and the mundane and tedious garrison duty at Vicksburg and Natchez. The lieutenant gave a poignant recounting of life in the regimental and corps hospitals during his prolonged illnesses. Wheelock's personal records reveal the lieutenant's religious upbringing and his strong moral sense, chiefly when it concerned the ardent drinking of his fellow officers. A Massachusetts native and a Republican, Francis moved to McLean in 1855. Initially a mediocre farmer, he tried Californian gold mining in 1859 before moving into the mercantile sector, where he excelled. He shared his career choice with sixteen other merchants in the regiment. Wheelock became a respected gentleman and entrepreneur, serving the village of McLean as constable and sheriff before the war. His brother Clarendon (1837–1901) enlisted in Company C, and was elected corporal.[22]

"'Keep up good Courage[,] Jennie awhil[e] longer. We Shall win the day,'" heartened Q. M. Sgt. Thadeus Packard (1832–1910) to his wife, Sopronia (Jennie) Briggs. Thadeus joined Company C with his older brother William; both siblings practiced carpentry in Bloomington before the war.[23]

Immediately on joining the regiment, Packard recognized differences between the central and southern Illinois companies: "Our Regiment all but Company C are Egyptians from Southern Illinois, and they look hardy and uncouth in dress and maner." Thadeus wrote faithfully to Jennie throughout his three years of service. The sergeant had an impeccable moral sense, and his intelligence and wit shone brightly throughout his writings. He gave valuable insight about the life of the Fifth Illinois soldier: during battle, in camp, and most importantly, throughout his prolonged illnesses. He also recorded his relationship at Vicksburg with a freed African American named Ned, whom Packard taught to read and write. Ned also served as Packard's servant. The clerk's attitude towards African Americans, with whom he freely interacted, contrasted with many Egyptians in the regiment.[24]

Alonzo G. Payne (1838–1905) became firm friends with the Wheelocks and Packard. Born in Vermilion County, Alonzo married Rhoda Green in 1859 and moved to Bloomington, where they set up as farmers. Payne became a success story in the service, striving to rise above his modest beginnings and limited education. Alonzo left a six-month diary for 1865, the only daily account available for the regiment in their last year of service. The soldier struggled with writing and spelling, but he became a fast learner, and by the end of his diary in June 1865, his grammar and spelling had improved tremendously.[25]

As soon as Withers settled his men into camp, he and Sgt. Francis Wheelock left for the Bloomington Normal School to recruit additional men for the company. Mustering into the regiment did not occur until the company's ranks reached over seventy-two men. Recruiting continued throughout the regiment's four-year history, as officers periodically returned to Illinois to enroll new recruits as its ranks thinned due to death from disease and battle. During Withers's excursion, Companies A, B, and C drilled daily and participated in their first dress parade. Many learned, for the first time, how to properly saddle and command horses and to mount them with and without saddles. They also shared in Lincoln's day of "fasting, humiliation and prayer," on 26 September. Updegraff expected his Illinoisans to observe the day in camp "in a manner becoming Christian soldiers battling for a holy cause."[26]

Many early recruits to the regiment were mere boys, whose horizons had extended only a few miles from home. Their trip to Camp Butler was probably the first time away from family and neighbors for many of them. As a result, the boys took advantage of the lack of familiar oversight and discipline and exhibited and participated in licentious behavior. As was common throughout the Union army, soldiers and officers often accepted and participated in behaviors while serving that they would have rejected in civilian life. An Egyptian from Randolph County observed that some men in his company had "thrown off all restraint in regard to morals, and have abandoned themselves to the most gross obscenity." Believing these men had been raised with manners, he speculated they "were never guilty of such conduct at home." The moralist reflected that "men soon develope[d] their real character when left far from the restraints of society and men." Card playing became a standard pastime during the war, though some soldiers considered gambling a violation of religious standards. Soldiers also heard more profanity in camp than was common in civilian life. One sergeant considered the opprobrious language "the prevailing sin of the army," noting that officers often indulged in "profanity and obscene" expressions when drilling their men.[27]

The new soldiers left the simplicities and freedoms of civilian life with their families and quickly learned that military camp existed on strict rules and regulations. Indignation rolled through camp when the soldiers realized they needed passes to leave camp and could not visit home whenever they pleased. Updegraff quickly established discipline according to the Articles of War, a code of military law initially passed by the Second Continental Congress in 1775 and later revised in 1806; the colonel expected his officers to enforce strict obedience according to this uniform code. The colonel may have suffered from a bit of naïveté in expecting his men to naturally "yield a hearty obedience," for even noncommissioned officers knew "some men have to learn subordination while others 'obey' without a word of murmuring." Updegraff punished minor offences with extra duty or manual labor.[28]

Excitement ran through the newly enlisted troops in September as ten of the regiment's twelve independent companies joined the Fifth. Many soldiers lacked mounts and horse equipment, but the men practiced drill and assembly as a company and regiment on foot. "[C]avalry were all over the prarie drilling, while martial music was discoursed by brass bands, as well as fife and drum. . . . What a splendid scene," remembered a Fifth Illinoisan. During a period of recreation, one Company K soldier watched drill practice from a nearby hill: "It is no ordinary sight for an American Citizen in this country to see a regiment of troops on 'parade.' The prarie was all astir with civilians and ladies, out observing the gay and lively scenes passing before them."[29]

Drilling confused not only the soldiers, but also the unskilled officers. Not acquainted with the tactics, officers endured two hours of morning drill and then transferred their recently acquired skills to their soldiers during four hours of daily afternoon practice. This dampened the spirits of both officers and enlisted men. "Our officers being ignorant of the tactics we do not always get along as well or pleasantly as we should. The officer who attempts to teach the tactics to the men should first learn them himself so that he can drill the men without getting into confusion," complained a soldier. Since the men lacked armaments, they substituted wooden sabers and guns during drill.[30]

Some independent units that joined the Fifth had organized as cavalry; others did not choose their branch of service until they reached Camp Butler. Those who organized and enlisted as a mounted unit, such as Companies C and K, brought their horses with them to camp. Thadeus

Packard's horse, Tom, had been his pal prior to the war, and he felt great affection for his mount, an emotion reciprocated by Tom, who "was so glad to See Me [Packard]" after being separated at camp, "he fairly Kissed me." Properly equipped cavalrymen had the privilege of mounted drill, and Company C began their movements in early October. The horsemen reveled in their animals' adjustment to army life. "I put on Toms new Saddle and trappings to day," mused Packard. "You would laugh to See how [proud] he is." Though the horses adjusted accordingly, the men had their problems. "We received Our field Equipments, . . . and it was amusing to See the men looking them Over and hear the Observations." The officers of Company C became so excited about their new trappings, they abandoned their company before the daily drill. Packard, being the only company officer available, put the men through their movements under the watchful eye of regiment's lieutenant colonel. Wiley encouraged Packard with "compliment[s] for Order and presision for [his] first time" drilling the men, which were deeply appreciated by the anxious sergeant. When the delinquent officers finally returned to camp, "Lieut 'Depew and the Orderly[,] their heads were down,'" in shame at deserting their men.[31]

A great divide in pay separated the officers from the privates. A cavalry colonel received $237 per month, a lieutenant colonel $213, while majors earned $189—a very respectable salary. The men who did the fighting and dying, however, received a pittance of only $13 per month; corporals earned one dollar more, while sergeants collected $17 per month. The chief bugler, quartermaster, and sergeant major earned $21.[32]

The cavalrymen supplied their own mounts, but the government compensated the men for their horses and horse equipment with additional pay based on the horse's value. In early November, the army appraised the men's animals, usually valued between $90 and $110. Jonas Roe, Co. M, received an additional $12 for his horse, payment supposedly coming every two months. Not being satisfied with their mounts, soldiers often traded, swapped, or sold their horses to other cavalrymen. These actions prompted reprimands from Wiley, who prohibited the transactions, threatening enforcement by "the strict letter of the law" to any violators. Exchanging mounts after appraisal disrupted the pay system, forcing officers to change a soldier's salary based on the new animal's value. The camp commander also banned the men from racing and running their horses through camp.[33]

Henry A. Organ organized Company D with men from Democratic Clay and Wayne Counties and became the first company raised exclusively in Egypt. The forty-two-year-old Organ lived on a $3,000 farm and had served the Fairfield community as sheriff since 1858. Organ's personality and drinking habits conflicted with some of the command staff of the regiment. Wiley called Organ "an habitual drunkard; so much so that his faculties are bemuddled," a common problem with many of the regimental and company officers.[34]

The abuse of alcohol, with its easy access and excessive usage among the officers and men, started as soon as the men entered Camp Butler. It also affected the command staff of the regiment when Wiley and Apperson brought charges against Updegraff for "conduct unbecoming an officer and a gentleman" in September. The officers accused their colonel of intoxication in public after receiving his commission and of introducing women of "ill-fame" and liquor to the camp, often encouraging the soldiers to imbibe. Updegraff's questionable reputation often discouraged independent companies seeking a regiment: "Updegraphs [regiment] is not full, but, we don[']t want to go in that one, for he has not got a very good reputation, & he has a rough set of men, they have to keep a guard around his camp to keep his men in, so they cant get drunk," declared William Skiles, whose independent unit eventually joined the Fifth as Company G.[35]

Captains also had difficulty keeping liquor away from their men and often rejected or dismissed volunteers before their mustering due to "drunkenness and riotous conduct." Some captains even confronted the "groceriekeepers" in town and forbade them to sell whiskey to the soldiers. Liquor became available a number of ways: in packages sent from home, through sales from a sutler, or smuggled into camp by soldiers. An enduring battle ensued between officers and men over whiskey, which continued every day during the war. Alcohol became a point of contention between those who imbibed and those who did not, with many temperate officers believing alcohol kept the Fifth Illinois a second-rate regiment.[36]

After the court dismissed Updegraff on 22 October for conduct unbecoming an officer, Wiley received orders to "assume command of the 5th Regt of cavalry until further orders." Wiley immediately posted extra patrols and guards around the camp to keep new recruits in and spirituous drinks and unwanted persons out. The governor spent two months deciding on a new leader for the regiment; in the meantime, the commissioned officers of the Fifth petitioned Yates to appoint Wiley as their colonel. "His strict attention to all the duties . . . his constant personal supervision of all that pertains to the comfort and efficiency of the men, and his industry in perfecting them . . . justifies us in making the above request," declared the petition, signed by Apperson and Seley and every captain except for the commanders of Companies B and I (who may have been on recruiting duty).[37]

Gentleman farmer Samuel J. R. Wilson (1816–93), from Wayne County, served as first lieutenant of Company D. Most of Samuel's soldiering had been done as second lieutenant of Company F, Third Regiment of Illinois Infantry, fighting at Vera Cruz and Cerro Gordo during the Mexican War. The lieutenant was one of fourteen Fifth soldiers who had served in the Mexican War. Wilson hailed from Kentucky but had moved to Wayne County in 1822 and considered Illinois his native state. He lived with his fourth wife and children on a $9,000 farm in Fairfield, serving as county judge who adhered to Republican principles and believed in prohibition.[38]

The Mexican War experience of Tennessean farmer Calvin Schell (1824–1900) assisted him in obtaining the commission for second lieutenant in Company D. Schell lived with his family on a $5,000 farm in Long Prairie. Farmer and Republican Lawrence P. Hay (1827–1906), another old pioneer of Wayne County, became quartermaster sergeant. Packard called Hay a "great big Strapping Six footer," with a bit of a temper, who picked fights with fellow soldiers.[39]

Company E organized in Coles County under the efforts of George W. McConkey (1820–1912) and Francis M. Webb. Coles County gave Lincoln and the Republicans a mere twenty-eight vote majority in 1860. The men of the company unanimously elected McConkey captain, John J. Adams first lieutenant, and Republican Madison Glassco as second lieutenant.[40]

McConkey had joined Company H, Fourth Illinois Volunteer Infantry, participating in fighting on the Rio Grande, Vera Cruz, and Cerro Gordo during the Mexican War. After returning from service, McConkey became a successful farmer, wisely speculated in land, and soon held several local offices, including chairperson of the first board of supervisors representing East Oakland Township. A Virginian by birth, McConkey joined the Republican Party in 1860. The captain served with his company through all four years of the war and was considered one of the best officers in the regiment.[41]

John W. Woods (1815–98) enlisted as a private in Company E but received the commission of chaplain of the regiment in October. A Hoosier by birth, Woods became a preacher in the Presbyterian Church in 1837, and a full minister two years later. Woods lived with his wife and six children in a substantial home in Mattoon, where he became instrumental in building the town's church. Before Woods's appointment, many soldiers complained of the lack of religious services in the regiment: "There is no

Sabbath here. All is noise and bustle as if the world had forgotten the command 'Remember the Sabbath Day to keep it holy.'"[42]

Horace P. Mumford (1841–64) organized Company F, accepting men from Crawford County; later recruits (15 percent) hailed from Richland County. Standing at four inches above six feet, the captain maintained a strong presence and was a natural leader. The eighty men Mumford brought to the regiment elected him captain, along with Francis M. Dorothy as first lieutenant, and William Wagenseller as second lieutenant. Located north of Egypt, Crawford County gave the Democrats a 463-vote majority in the 1860 election. Mumford remained a die-hard Democrat throughout the war, and his beliefs clashed with some Republican officers, but no one questioned his loyalty. Horace was born of Scotch Irish decent in Knox County, Ohio, but moved to Cumberland County in the late 1850s. He established the Democratic newspaper *Crawford County Bulletin* in July 1860. When war broke out, Mumford's newspaper "strongly advocated the prosecution of the war for the preservation of the Union."[43]

Hoosier-born Francis M. Dorothy (1834–88) moved to Illinois as a mercantile sales clerk, living in the Buckingham Hotel in Robinson, Illinois. William Wagenseller (1820–1903) entered military service as second lieutenant but rose in rank to captain by May 1863. The native Pennsylvanian owned a $2,000 farm in Hardinville. Despite losing both parents, his spouse, and a brother to illness during the war, Wagenseller stayed with Company F until he resigned in July 1865, four months after his wife's death.[44]

Central Illinois counties, in particular Democratic Pike, Christian, and Shelby Counties, contributed their men to fill the ranks of Company G, commanded by Capt. John A. Harvey, 1st Lt. William N. Elliott, and 2nd Lt. Amos H. Smith. Harvey was an unmarried civil engineer from New Salem, who did not leave a lasting impression on the company.[45]

Kentucky-native William Elliott (1818–72) worked a small farm in Oconee, Shelby County, when he received the lieutenant's commission. Elliott had previous military experience as a private in Company A of Capt. A. Dunlap's independent company during the war with Mexico. His oldest son, Wesley, enlisted with Company G in December 1863. Second Lt. Amos Smith was a native Pennsylvanian but worked as a farm laborer in New Salem prior to the war.[46]

"I hope you are not turning copperhead & getting above writing to a Soldier. [B]eware of the disease for it will prove fatal," Pvt. William A. Skiles (1842–1916), Co. G, warned his parents in Pana, Christian County.[47] Skiles wrote forty-one letters during his war service, recounting the regiment's participation in skirmishes in Arkansas and Mississippi, and his suffering with scrofulous ophthalmia (also called sore eyes, it was a contagious inflammation of the eye) through most of 1864. Skiles supported the Republican administration after his enlistment, but his father held strong antiblack and Democratic tenets. Skiles viewed the war through the eyes of a common person, who learned that his parent's negative beliefs about Republicans and blacks were not conducive to the spirit of the Union cause. William's letters document his desperate attempt to educate his parents about the fine qualities he found in the newly freed slaves and later African American soldiers.

Located in the heart of upper Egypt, and held tightly by the Democratic Party, Washington County supplied the ranks of Company H. The company's first commanding officer, farmer Joseph A. Cox (1826–1907), and 20 percent of its members hailed from Republican-dominated St. Clair County. A Mexican War veteran from the First Illinois Foot Infantry, Joseph originally gained the commission as first lieutenant in Company D of the Ninth Illinois Infantry, before serving as captain in the Fifth. The Cox family contributed three members to the company, as did the Nelson family from Nashville, including William, who served as second lieutenant, with his brothers John and Robert enlisting as sergeants. Washington F. Crain (1835–75), also from Nashville, gained the commission for first lieutenant and held that position until he became captain in March 1863.

Company I contained men from strongly Democratic Cumberland County, but Republican counties of McDonough and Coles contributed almost 11 percent of the original members of the company. The heterogeneous quality of the company may have caused problems within the command structure, which destroyed the company's cohesion. As was custom, companies voted for their command when the unit reached half its full complement of men. With Company I, however, Wiley and Apperson validated a temporary election of officers, with less than twenty men of the company present for the election. The field officers promised the men an election for permanent company officers when the unit reached its full complement. Cpl. James Pease appealed to Adjutant General Fuller in December 1861, after the soldiers' attempt to "get up a petition in favor of our rights to an election" was shot down by the company's temporary commanding officers, who "forebid us to say or do any thing about an election." Pease's complaint went unheard, until "the banefull influences" demoralized the company to a point that it became "almost a disgrace to the regiment."[48]

The soldiers of Company I elected carpenter Bartholomew Jenkins (1837–81) as their captain. Jenkins lived on a small farm with his wife and three children in Mattoon. Edwin S. Norfolk (1833–84), a merchant with a wife and three small children, secured the commission for first lieutenant, while John F. Smith, a farmer by trade, became second lieutenant; both hailed from Majority Point. The command structure of the company changed many times until a reliable captain took control in 1863.[49]

The people of Liberty, Randolph County, lined the streets on 9 September to witness the Randolph County Rangers leave for the war. "All were sad and many were in tears, for it is a terrible calamity to go to scenes of blood and strife from peacefull happy homes," recounted one soldier. The twenty-five men from the town met other recruits from Sparta, Jones Creek, and Chester at St. Louis before becoming Company K of the Fifth Illinois. Situated along the eastern banks of the Mississippi just south of St. Louis, the county recorded a healthy Republican vote (1,382) during the 1860 presidential election but remained Democratic (1,815 votes). Company K was a true Egyptian company, raised almost exclusively in Randolph (78 percent), with later 1864 recruits from Cook and Will Counties. Company C and the Randolph Rangers became two of the strongest, most cohesive, and most homogeneous units in the regiment.[50]

Dr. James Farnan (1830–77), a Sparta Republican and acquaintance of David L. Phillips and Wiley, organized the Rangers in August. Phillips, a United States marshal appointed by Lincoln, gave Governor Yates a rousing recommendation for accepting Farnan's company into the Fifth: "He [Farnan] has a good Company, and will give a good account of himself." A handsome man of almost six feet, with brown hair and blue eyes, Farnan would be one of three physicians who held commissioned posts in the company. Having graduated from St. Louis Medical College in 1853, Farnan moved with his wife to Sparta, where he practiced medicine. Despite the support of the Republican administration, the men of the company had reservations in his competency to lead: "I see nothing about the Captain to make me think him fit for the place he has been elected to fill in the company. He was elected with the full understanding that he was to go into the Medical Department. . . . He is pettish and hasty, and lacks the judgment necessary for one in command of men," lamented a noncommissioned officer of Company K. Two years later, the commissioned officers in the regiment reflected the same sentiments: "While nothing can be said against Major Farnan as an officer, yet he is a very vindictive, malicious, & mischievous man, a low trickster and wise worker."[51] During his service, Farnan became a man driven by desire for fame, social acceptance, money, and rank. His history of promoting his claim, albeit through others' voices, to a higher rank, often at the expense of fellow officers, turned the entire regiment against him; even his friends from Randolph County considered him unscrupulous.

Dr. Charles J. Childs (1827–99) gained the rank of first lieutenant in Company K, after gaining valuable military experience as a private in Company B, Second Illinois Infantry in 1847. Charles attended the St. Xavier Catholic College in St. Louis, then the Eclectic Medical Institute of Cincinnati, finishing his medical training at the St. Louis Medical College in 1848. Childs practiced medicine in Chester, where he lived with his wife and four children. Beginning as a Whig, Childs was one of the earliest Republicans in Illinois, being a delegate to the first Republican convention in Randolph County in 1856. Due to his Republican beliefs, Childs knew Lincoln, Wiley, and Yates before the war.[52]

Dr. Calvin A. Mann (1832–1902), a six-foot, blue-eyed medical practitioner from Liberty secured the commission for second lieutenant. Forty-one men in the company objected to the commission and did "not consider him competent to fill the office." A petition to Yates voiced their opinion, but Dr. Mann held onto the rank, even gaining the captaincy in July 1862. A year after graduating from the St. Louis Medical College, Calvin married Emily Young in 1859 and moved to Liberty, where he opened his first medical office. The people of Randolph County considered Dr. Mann "one of the most able physicians who ever practiced" in the county. His son was only a year old when Calvin joined Company K.[53]

The Manns were ardent Republicans of strong Presbyterian structure, with a tradition of upward mobility prevailing in the clan. Calvin's older brother John Preston (1822–1908) also enlisted in Company K. John owned Liberty's grocery and dry goods store before he entered military service as a private, then quickly rose to sergeant major of the Third Battalion.[54]

During his three turbulent years of service, John Mann kept a personal record and wrote faithfully to his wife Nancy, outlining in detail the actions of his company and regiment. Mann meticulously documented the political and religious strife in the regiment, which lead to the cooling of relationships in 1862 between officers and men over the moral standing of the Union cause. John also delighted in recording verbatim conversations between himself and Southern sympathizers, and between those within the regiment whom he considered unpatriotic, chiefly Democrats. John Mann "possessed an unusually talented mind," where "the frivolous and the unworthy and the vulgar" had no place.[55] The lieutenant considered himself a fair-minded and moderate man, a friend of liberty, and a defender of the Christian way of life. His diaries and letters expressed his opinion about everyone and everything and reflected his growing impatience and disenchantment with his commanders, principally those who did not share his principles. Mann would take a tough, defiant posture against all the commanding officers, but particularly against Abel Seley, the consequences of which would haunt Mann's reputation for the rest of his life. He was extremely self-righteous, had a strong moral code, and was not afraid to voice those convictions in person or on paper, but he was also very peevish, endlessly complaining about the service. His diary gave the impression of someone who was very confident in his own superiority, chiefly where it concerned morals and ethics. Despite his moral code, Mann's diary became a running record of the Randolph Rangers' plundering by himself and his messmates. Often hypocritical in his writing, Mann nonetheless gave a poignant view of a soldier's life: his dreams for his future and of the family he left in Illinois, his fears of disease and battle, and his religious and patriotic beliefs.

Mann conflicted with Farnan and Childs, whom he considered incompetent, and with other commissioned officers of the regiment, whom he considered immoral drunkards. Thomas H. Barnfield (1835–1920), a close friend of John and a merchant from Liberty, joined Company K in early October. John mentioned Barnfield and their army life together so often in his memoirs that he referred to his friend simply as "THB."

A loner who wanted to see the country, New York native John Burke (1841–1935) had been farming in St. Clair County when he joined the Randolph Rangers. A traveler at heart, Burke had a difficult adjustment to camp life, and if it "were not for the tiresome motony of Camp life I could enjoy my self very well."[56] Burke wrote sporadically to his sister Ellen Hudson in New York, but those few letters reflect Burke's optimistic outlook on life and his indomitable spirit and delicious sense of humor, even through his devastating fight with malaria, hepatitis, and dysentery. The private was very fair minded, of good moral judgment, but not a fanatic. Burke remained a private until 1864, when he received promotion to sergeant. He was one of the soldiers who lacked faith in Calvin Mann's ability to lead the company, an opinion that probably saved his life in June 1863.

The women of Randolph County sent their men off to war carrying a guidon—a swallow-tailed flag that was half red and half white, dividing at the fork, with the red in ascendance. The red section carried the letters "U.S." in white, while the white section carried the letter of the company ("K") in red. Army regulations allowed each regiment a silken standard and each cavalry company a silken guidon. The regimental standard bore the arms of the United States, embroidered in silk on a blue background, with the regimental name and number on a scroll beneath the eagle; the names of the battles the soldiers fought in appeared at the end of 1862.[57]

Attorney Henry Caldwell (1825–1902), "a true man to his country and a good and valiant officer," organized Company L in Democratic Effingham County. A Virginian by birth, Caldwell left his two motherless children in Teutopolis under the care of family members in April 1861, when he enlisted for three months in Company G, Eleventh Illinois Volunteer Infantry. On his return to the prairie state, Caldwell received a captain's commission to raise a company for the Fifth Illinois. Henry's two brothers, Samuel and Amos, also joined the regiment; Amos was elected sergeant.[58]

Printer Harrison H. Brown (1837–1921), an Ohio native, secured the rank of first lieutenant. Joining Caldwell and Brown was William N. Berry (1840–1909), from Majority Point. William initially enlisted as a private in Company B, Twenty-First Illinois Infantry, and fought in the battle of Fredricktown, Missouri, in October. For his service and valor during the fighting, Berry received the commission for second lieutenant of Company L. He joined his younger brother James, who enlisted as a private.[59]

Patriots from Wayne and White counties enrolled in Robert Schell's Company M. Located along the eastern edge of Egypt, the two counties remained Democratic, giving the party a huge majority in the 1860 presidential election. Schell (1811–70) kept a hotel in Fairfield before organizing for the war. Despite his age, Schell "deserved great praise for the energy he displayed in getting up and organizing his company." Schell belonged to a select group of men that included Hall Wilson and Jacob Baker, who developed the town of Fairfield in 1856. Afterward, Fairfield retained Schell as street commissioner, while Baker served on the board of trustees.[60]

Company M's 1st Lt. Samuel Burrell and 2nd Lt. Albert S. Robinson were dismissed from the regiment for desertion: Robinson in July 1862 and Burrell in April 1863. Despite the actions of its original lieutenants, the company produced many honorable soldiers, including Alexander and Robert Jessop, brothers who resided with their Irish parents in Wayne County. Alexander (1839–1923) enlisted as a private and served Company M for almost a year before becoming its captain in September 1862. Younger brother Robert (1840–1915) enlisted as a private in January 1863 but quickly rose to the rank of first lieutenant.[61]

"My country calls for me and I leave all that I hold dear upon Earth and freely go to her assistance[,] conscious that I embark in a holy and righteous cause," declared Dr. Jonas H. Roe (1819–73) in his first letter to his third wife Celina. Roe, a New Jersey native, had moved to Clay City, Illinois, after participating in the California gold rush. The medical professional entered the service as a private but achieved the rank of commissary sergeant. Roe's letters expressed the sergeant's strong religious and patriotic upbringing, as well as his Republican tendencies.[62]

Still in command of the regiment in early November, Wiley had the men on a strict daily routine of mounted and dismounted drill. The cavalrymen's day started at five in the morning, "all aroused in the morning by sweet swelling notes of "'Hail Columbia'." The men answered roll call with "every expression of joy that a man can [express:] cat calls, chicken crows, wolf howls, yells, [and] whooping." While the officers learned their drill, the soldiers spent their time currying, feeding, and watering their mounts, which continued until the men had squad drill from nine to eleven in the morning. After dinner, the boys continued their squad drill until three, then "march[ed] over to drill parade" before Wiley, "quite formal, but of short duration—20 minutes." After the evening meal, the men answered another roll call at 8:00, then serenaded "to dreamland by cheering Yanke[e] Doodle, Dixie, Sweet Home, or [Bonaparte's] Retreat."[63]

Army-issued clothing arrived in November and each soldier received blouse, pants, shirts, drawers, cap, blanket, and poncho. The Illinois adjutant general's office was so well organized that the Fifth received their winter clothing before the Illinois winter arrived. "Drew our overcoats—a good article for such cold weather and needed very much. We are well clothed at present and only need a few blankets and gloves to be comfortable. The boys are generally well pleased with their outfit," declared an Egyptian. Surprisingly, the men did not complain about the food either. "We have good quarters[,] plenty of food for man and beast[,] good bacon[,] Beef[,] sugar[,] coffee beans[,] rice[,] potatoes[,] molasses[,] salt & pepper, &c for the men." Even the horses received excellent treatment: "Good hay[,] oates corn & Salt for the horses," Roe declared.[64]

The prairie boys complained very little during drill practice in the warm autumn air, but when sleet and cold weather visited the camp in late November, the grumbling became a roar. Wiley received the brunt of their anger when the "wind blowing a gale," he insisted on daily drill. An astute observer remarked that his fellow soldiers were "inclined to find fault because things are not so comfortable as at home" anymore. The Egyptian believed his fellow cavalrymen would soon "learn how comfortable they are [in camp] after they leave here and get into enemy country." As some men kept up their constant bickering, others "keep their spirits by freely indulging in fun and anecdotes to while away the hours."[65]

With the last of the companies mustered into service on 8 December, the regiment reached its maximum of 1,086 soldiers. This allowed the governor to appoint a new colonel to the regiment, and with General Orders No. 248, Maj. Hall Wilson, Twenty-Seventh Illinois Infantry, received the commission. Many of the company officers had known Wilson prior to the war, and they respected the Englishman as a man of honor and integrity. Wilson became the leader the Fifth needed: one who had the knowledge, experience, and personality to hold together a disparate group of men with cultural and political differences.[66]

An unseasonably warm, pleasant day greeted the Fifth officers as they waited for their new colonel to emerge from Wiley's tent on 15 December. Hall Wilson (1831–69) exhibited a "fine personal appearance" and gave a good address to the officers of the regiment. Many considered the colonel a "gentleman and a soldier," who carried with "him the best wishes of all who know him," but some Egyptians had their doubts as to his ability to lead. "Hope he will prove a good and efficient officer, as, our Reg't has a good deal of 'raw material' in, that needs to be worked over. It is not all good men that make efficient officers," reflected Mann.[67]

An Englishman by birth, Wilson traveled to New York in 1835, when he was five years old. He ventured to California for the gold rush in the 1850s and then settled in Wayne County, Illinois, in 1856, helping to establish Fairfield with Schell and Baker. Wilson held the office of tax collector and acquired almost four hundred acres in his first year of residency in the county. In 1857, he joined Jesse K. Dubois's state auditor's office as a clerk, a position he maintained after the war. Privilege and political associations opened doors for Wilson as a major in the Twenty-Seventh Illinois Infantry in August 1861. Three months later, Wilson participated in the battle at Belmont under Ulysses S. Grant, "where he made himself conspicuous by his bravery and won his 'Eagles,'" and earned the colonel's commission in the Fifth Illinois. On 17 December, Wilson assumed command of the prairie boys, while Wiley remained lieutenant colonel.[68]

Away from their families over the Christmas and New Year's holidays, the men determined to add something special to their holiday meals. The nearby farmers took the brunt of the misguided holiday spirit. Andrew W. Vance (1831–65), a blacksmith from Randolph County, "'jayhawked' a couple of chickens and some cabbage" for the mess that John Mann attended in the Randolph Rangers. "We had a fine meal upon the 'stolen' articles," confessed the sergeant major; he "had some conscientious scruples about eating the ill-gotten meal[,] but feeling like it was more joke than fact[,] got along with the meal very well." Soldiers easily justified their stealing by calling it "jayhawking" or "a joke." For the New Year's Day celebration, other Fifth soldiers stole and killed a hog owned by a nearby farmer. Mann hypocritically found "such conduct is bad as we have plenty of provission and no necessity exists for taking from the country people." Stealing from the local farms became such a habit that when Company D boys brought in some chickens, their actions "were Check Mated . . . by a Company of Infantry Patrolls with loaded Muskets." The patrol, designed to deter thefts, marched Organ's men straight "to the guard House." Jayhawking continued throughout the war, and the Fifth became quite famous for their theft of edible commodities in both Arkansas and Mississippi.[69]

The holidays came and went without much fuss, and many considered it "a very dull affair, having always made it a custom on that day to make merry with our friends." Very few of the men complained, however, for they considered the holiday a sort of novelty at being away from home for the first time. Holiday boxes sent from family members arrived late for the Company H boys, but when opened they revealed to the men "a most bountiful supply, consisting of 4 turkeys, 5 geese, 73 chickens, 51 apple pies, 37 peach pies, 7 custards, 148 sweet cakes, [and] 13 pound cakes." Company H sent invitations to all the regimental officers to "partake once more in life of a good feast, and we truly had a good time of it." Robert M. Laney, who would enlist in the regiment in 1864, had sent his Wayne County friends some good cigars for the holidays, and the boys enjoyed the smokes while all listened to "good addresses delivered" by Reverend Woods, Captain Cox, and several other officers. The evening left a hearty feeling with all the men, and they believed "we shall often recall this day when far away from here and remember it as one of the happiest we have yet spent in Camp Butler."[70]

Holiday packages also brought news from home and reports about the activities of the Knights of the Golden Circle (KGC) in southern Illinois. The secret organization was founded primarily to promote the interests of slaveholding states but also spread into areas with strong pro-Southern populations, such as southern Illinois, Indiana, Ohio, and Missouri, after 1861. During the war, the members of KGC became Peace Democrats or Copperheads, their main agitator being Clement L. Vallandingham, an Ohio politician. *Copperhead* was a derogatory sobriquet applied to members of the Democratic Party who criticized Lincoln's war policies and who sought an armistice with the Confederacy. Considered treasonous by

Northern soldiers, Copperheads used constitutional freedoms of speech and the press to undermine the war effort and nurture disloyalty. "It is outrageous that while so many of us are off preparing to fight for our homes and loved ones," declared Mann, "that such a set of villians should be plotting treason while we are absent and pitting the community with discord. . . . Traitors at home deserve double punishment for while they try to pass for Union men, by using words of deceit[;] they try also to stab our country by plotting treason where such things are so little expected."[71]

Opposition to the Lincoln administration's war policies began in early 1862. The movement had many economic elements, including agrarian discontent due to an economic depression caused mainly by the closing of the Mississippi River. Low farm and produce prices and excessive freight charges by the eastern-based railroads fueled midwestern Copperheadism. As the Lincoln administration passed war measures and policies to insure a Union victory, the conservative element in midwestern politics came into play. "The constitution as it was" became a rallying cry for those who did not want to see a consolidation of power in the Federal government, an end to slavery, or the violation of civil rights. Southern Illinois' negrophobia, an extensive and powerful prejudice, fueled the Copperhead movement in the region, for many wanted to keep the area for the white population. The Copperheads' actions caused uproar among the prairie boys, prompting the passage of pro-administration resolutions in the regiment and a letter-writing campaign to Northern newspapers denouncing their actions in early 1863.

As winter closed in on the recruits, disease spread among the soldiers. Dr. Charles W. Higgins aided the Fifth's men in their transition from civilians to army soldiers. The men needed his services and those of his assistant, John B. Ensey, as soon as they arrived in camp. Hospital stewards supported the commissioned surgeons and cared for the sick and injured. Many, though not all, had medical training, such as William Watts (1819–90), who entered the service as sergeant of Company F. Within days of his enlistment, Watts transferred to the noncommissioned staff as a hospital steward of the Second Battalion. When the War Department discontinued the battalion formation in September 1862, the military dismissed Watts from the service. Not wanting to lose his valuable services, the governor issued a second lieutenant's commission (Company M) to Watts in October 1862. By June 1863, Watts had earned an assistant surgeon's ranking and served in that capacity until the governor commissioned him as the regimental surgeon in January 1865. Col. Hall Wilson labeled Watts "a man of education and ability—both as a medical & military man" and "one of the most valuable officers in the regiment."[72]

The Fifth's six months of training became their seasoning period, where soldiers, particularly those from the rural areas, were exposed to unfavorable epidemiological environments, in which spread such diseases as measles, smallpox, and typhoid. Rural recruits were more susceptible to these diseases because they lacked any prior exposure during childhood. Sammel Blakely, Co. F, who died of typhoid, became the first regimental death on 24 November 1861. Typhoid, a highly infectious disease of the intestinal tract caused by the bacterium *Salmonella typhi*, spreads quickly throughout a population living with poor sanitation. Once infected, survivors become immune and often become carriers of the disease, spreading the bacterium through water or food contaminated with feces. Typhoid became the scourge of troops in both the Union and Confederate armies and would eventually devastate the Fifth at Helena, Arkansas, within a year. Initially, though, the men succumbed to measles and its subsequent pneumonia. Only eleven men died during organization and training; Company D suffered the most with measles, losing three men. Dr. Roe reported in December that "measles are very bad in our regiment[;] several men have them. Among them Joseph Allen. [H]is eyes are also very sore. [H]e has broken out well and I think he will soon recover." Allen recovered from his measles, but his sore eyes worsened, and he obtained a disability discharge in March 1862, having never left Springfield. Camp diarrhea also quickly spread through all barracks, hitting almost everyone, and turning healthy individuals into walking corpses. Diarrhea and dysentery killed more Fifth soldiers than any other disease and continued to cripple the men when they reentered civilian life after their service. The regiment witnessed a higher prevalence of human wastage due to illness and exhaustion during its four years of service, mainly due to ignorant officers who did not follow basic sanitary rules. Overall, 386 men succumbed to disease, and 227 soldiers received disability discharges during the war.[73]

Some officers learned that sickness followed slovenly behavior, but nineteenth-century concepts of sanitation did not include daily bathing. Science had yet to discover germs and their connection to the origin of disease. Bathing, as one soldier noted, "makes one feel fifty percent better," but it was never considered a sanitation measure. The army regulated bathing to "once or twice a week," with the feet gaining more attention with twice a week washing.[74]

By late January 1862, some Fifth companies had been training for more than five months, and "[h]ad we known that we would have remained here so long most of our company would have enlisted where the service was more active." Expectations ran high at the end of the month, as rumors spread through camp that the regiment would finally leave Springfield. Lacking any arms, the cavalrymen doubted the rumors: "We are not armed yet nor does there appear to be any prospect of leaving here soon," lamented a soldier. Within those five months at camp, however, Wiley and Wilson took men of independent and frontier spirit and molded them into an effective fighting force, ready for battle. When word arrived of Ulysses S. Grant's successes against fortified Confederates in Tennessee, the cavalrymen's spirit soared. "Glory to God," Packard declared, "[Fort] Donaldson is Ours!" Mann also appealed to God to "speed the Union course until the last traitor had been subdued, and peace restored to our land again." The urge to get to the front strengthened the resolve of the Fifth soldiers.[75]

"Reports thicken in camp that we are soon to be sent South into active Service," declared John Mann in mid-February. Soldiers hoped they would be allowed to visit their families before shipping out, but the paymaster had yet to appear, and many lacked funds for a trip home. Finally, marching orders arrived, and the men had just hours to pack their bags for the front. Newspapers, which declared the regiment "splendid . . . composed of the flower of this portion of the State," informed the soldiers' families of the impending move, disclosing the regiment's new mailing address.[76]

The boys finally donned their uniforms and drew dragoon sabers, "which is the first arms we have received yet." Skiles believed his saber came from a "fine lot . . . lighter & finer than some of them. There was only about 7 of them in the company." Leaving behind their little dog tents, the boys drew "new large ones [Sibley] for 16 men to a tent with a stove." Songs prevailed through camp as the men prepared to leave the prairie state on Thursday, 20 February.[77]

Emotions ran high as the boys anticipated action in the field. Many believed Colonel Wilson would serve them well under enemy fire: "He is an officer who has won the esteem of all," and who had "made several great and advantageous improvements for his soldiers." Cpl. Richard Rainforth, Co. H, declared Wilson was "made of the right stuff for a commander," a man who sets an "example in managing military matters worthy of following." The prospect of participating in battle, however, did not leave everyone happy. Pvt. Clarence D. R. Goulden, Co. E, deserted the regiment on 15 February. Guards captured the wayfaring soldier and brought him back to camp, but four days later, he deserted again. The clerk of Company E expressed the sentiments of all soldiers concerning deserters when he officially recorded in the company's morning report that Goulden had "gone to the Devill," after his second desertion. Many deserters returned to southern Illinois, hiding out in the woods and valleys "skulking around in various parts" of Cumberland County. During the summer of 1863, Federal officers hunted down five deserters from the regiment, killing William Fulfer in July 1863.[78]

2

The Springtime of War
March to July 1862

The day dawned warm, the western breeze carrying the scents of a change in the seasons: perfect weather for marching through Illinois. At nine in the morning on 19 February, 1,055 men of the Fifth Illinois, along with their horses and twenty wagons, rode away from their training camp, heading south. The prairie boys marched off to war with light hearts, anticipating the adventures and glory that lay ahead. Joyous citizens met the boys at various villages and towns. Evidence of "genuine outburst[s] of real Union sentiment and are much enjoued by the troops," declared John Mann. None gave a reception like Springfield, where cheering crowds honored the soldiers' departure with waving handkerchiefs and American flags. Most towns along the route to St. Louis commemorated the cavalrymen's arrival, including Fairfield, Illinois, hometown to Col. Hall Wilson and two companies of the Fifth. The *Prairie Pioneer* held the regiment in highest regards: "This is one of the best regiment[s] yet sent from this State, being composed of stout, able-bodied men, excellently mounted and equipped. . . . As for winning 'Eagles,' just give them a chance and eagles will be no name for it."[1]

After eight days of marching though Illinois, the regiment crossed the Mississippi River into Missouri, camping near Benton Barracks, about five miles from St. Louis. The army built these barracks on the old fairgrounds in August 1861, and the site quickly became the launching point for troops moving into the Western and Trans-Mississippi theaters. Benton Barracks served as a troop cantonment, a prisoner parole camp, a military hospital, and a camp for refugee and contraband slaves during the war.

As with every winter season in the Midwest, the warm weather yielded back to the last tastes of winter, with cold rain drenching the prairie boys' camp at Benton Barracks, turning it into a spreading sea of oozing mud.

In early March, the men earned their first pay, which covered only from mustering to December 1861. They also received their arms, including French Lefaucheux revolving "pin-fire" pistols that took six 12mm cartridges. Wilson believed these pistols were of "inferior quality, entirely insufficient for effective service," and he continued to press Governor Yates for replacements. Only three companies, one in each battalion, drew rifles that William Skiles identified as "Short Mississippi rifles." Originally called United States rifles, model 1841, they gained their Mississippi nickname after being used by Confederate president Jefferson Davis's unit during the Mexican War. These percussion-cap rifles took a .54 caliber bullet and had a short range of about one hundred yards. Some of these rifles were refitted in 1861 to shoot the standard .58 caliber, but the Fifth still had the old model. Mann considered the revolvers "pretty good articles but the rifles are to[o] heavy." While at St. Louis, soldiers purchased personal items from sutlers and businesses in the city, and many had their photographs taken and sent home. Skiles also purchased a six-dollar bulletproof vest, "arranged so . . . that I can take the iron out of the vest, and wear it that way."[2]

With pistols in their belts, the Illinois cavalrymen gladly accepted their orders to march for Pilot Knob, Missouri, on 3 March. The Fifth became part of Henry W. Halleck's plan to secure Missouri and Arkansas for the Union. The same day the regiment received their orders, Halleck informed Brig. Gen. Frederick Steele of his plan to capture Helena, Arkansas, on the Mississippi River. Capture of the port town secured the mighty river and its vital transportation for the Union and cut off steamboat communication with Confederate-held Memphis, Tennessee. Halleck gave Steele command of all troops in southeastern Missouri, west of the St. Francis River, and ordered him to move quickly and drive back the Rebel forces along a route that eventually led to Helena. Steele was certainly the officer to implement Halleck's plan. He graduated from West Point in 1843 and served in the Mexican War and the western territories until 1861. Steele became brigadier general of volunteers in January 1862, after serving as colonel of the Eighth Iowa Infantry. He quickly secured the command of the District of Southeast Missouri.[3]

The boys not only rejoiced at finally getting some action but also felt confident in Colonel Wilson, who "has done more for the Regiment in the past two day[s] then all the rest of the Officers put together since the Regiment was Organised." Packard believed that if Wilson was as "cool on the battlefield" as he was in pitching camp, he was the right man to lead the regiment. The men finally began to understand "what Kind of a man it takes to fill" the position of commander.[4]

After loading their horses and gear, the Fifth boarded cars of the St. Louis and Iron Mountain Railroad for the journey south. After a bumpy, uncomfortable sixteen-hour trip, the regiment reached the Arcadia Valley, home to the small ore-mining towns of Pilot Knob, Arcadia, and Ironton. Mountains of the St. Francis range surrounded the six-mile-long valley, creating some of the most spectacular scenery in southeast Missouri, a fact not lost on the prairie boys. Despite the splendor of the area, many soldiers had apprehensions about their first foray into Secesh territory: "This is the Commencement of hard Knocks in Dixie: it is the roughest part of MO. [T]he Scenery is so wild around here that what inhabitance there is left[,] look at us with a Sort of Scarey Suspicion. [T]hey say they was Sesesh Once but Union now!"[5]

The true sentiment of the inhabitants became clear to the Fifth when they learned that enemy fire hit the camp's pickets the night before their arrival in the valley. On 7 March, the prairie boys set out their own guards, which produced "Some Sober faces" among the new soldiers. All returned the next morning "each of course had Met with Some adventure [in the night] to relate" to their regimental mates. One guard from Company C shot a "Secesh Cow," while another unsuspecting soldier was "badly [scared] by a Mule that Came up Suddenly." While the picket guards battled it out with the Secesh farm animals, the rest of the regiment tried to gain some warmth from fires, for the weather in the valley had turned bitter cold, and snow covered the ground. Since the Fifth was new to the area and had yet to build a camp, Wilson ordered his men to sleep "on the Cold ground at the Side of Our Horses," with arms at the ready; their only comfort being a wet wool blanket.[6]

The Fifth established camp one mile west of Bald Knob near the Sixteenth Ohio Battery of Independent Artillery. Colonel Wilson commanded the post of Pilot Knob. When Steele arrived on 11 March, he ordered Wiley with Companies A, B, C, K, L, and M to station at Greenville on the St. Francis River, about forty miles south. This move lengthened the Union army's front and extended Steele's supply line from St. Louis through Pilot Knob and Ironton. Steele left garrisoned posts throughout southeast Missouri and northern Arkansas to maintain his supply line as he moved into Arkansas; the Fifth played a major role in guarding this lifeline. Packard commanded the advance guard of the column, which left Pilot Knob on 13 March. Wilson took precautions in case of attack by ordering Wiley's detachment to leave with "Our Sabers ground Sharp" and four hundred rounds of ammunition per company.[7]

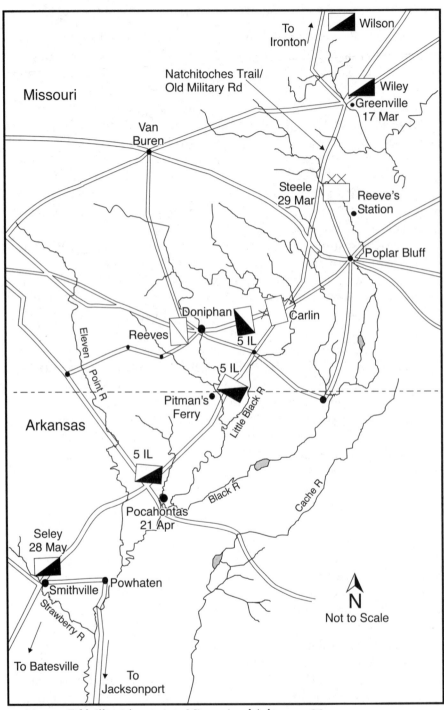

Map 2.1. Fifth Illinois' route into Missouri and Arkansas, 1862.

Heavy rains drenched the countryside on 12 March, turning roads to slush, and filling the cavalrymen's "boots half full of Water" before they even loaded up their horses. Wiley's detachment slowly marched through soggy, undeveloped country, reaching Big Creek by evening. The next day brought the men to Patterson, where Wiley camped "at the Side of the River, in the Swamp," contributing to another uncomfortable, cold night's rest.[8]

By Monday, 17 March, the skies cleared, and the warm sun dried out the cavalrymen's clothes and equipment. Twenty-nine miles later, "with hard tack and Salty Side Meat to Subsist uppon," the column reached the St. Francis River, swollen from the recent rains. A flatboat, previously "used by the Rebels," ferried the men and horses, except for Hoosier-born Jonathan Glimpse (1840–1904) and Illinois native George McLaughlin, who decided to swim their mounts across at a more convenient crossing. When the current strengthened "they began to flounder & Struggle," and eventually floated downstream to a small island. Wiley sent the boat to retrieve the rash cavalrymen, who "felt thankful to get onto dry land again."[9]

Wiley's horsemen camped on the east bank of the St. Francis River a few miles from Greenville in a small apple orchard with "two rows of Apple trees to a Company." The Fifth joined Capt. William T. Leeper's Company B, Twelfth Missouri State Militia (MSM) Cavalry, and Captain Mitchell's MSM Cavalry, guarding the Federal supply depot. As senior officer, Wiley commanded the post at Greenville. His first order forbade the cavalrymen from disturbing local citizens and their property. The Fifth relieved the Thirty-Eighth and Twenty-First Illinois Infantries, which moved farther south to garrison Reeve's Station on the Black River.[10]

The countryside and its residents did not impress the prairie boys. "I have traveled in rough Countries and have Seen Some of the world," remarked Packard, "but this goes beyond all of my Expectation. I Cannot See what in the name of Common Sence we are Sent down here for. . . . It is not fit for any Man that is half sivilized. 'Just a fit place for [Brig. Gen. M.] Jeff Thompson,' [Sterling] Price and [Brig. Gen. Ben] McCulloug[h]."[11]

Mann told his wife, Nancy, that the boys in his company would "never speak against Jackson Co. [Illinois men] after seeing some specimens of the natives here. They appear to know little of the world, out of Wayne Co. Mo." The beautiful, mountainous countryside showed "[m]arks of desolating effects," with burned-out or vacated family farms. Mann believed those who held slaves "fled at the approach of our troops, going south, because 'Lincoln wanted their <u>niggers</u>.'"[12]

The cavalrymen had not yet seen any hostile Confederate bands, but the sentiment of the Greenville citizens became evident, even though they loudly professed "love for the Union." One soldier judged the sentiments of a person by whether or not they freely sold provisions to the cavalrymen: "The Union men are all glad to sell, but the <u>Secesh</u> have none to sell. But they do <u>spare considerable</u>." Mann referred to the Fifth's habit of plundering Secesh property; though against orders, looting became common practice for the prairie boys, who drew "many things they need[ed]" from the local farmhouses.[13]

Despite soldiers' apprehensions, life at Greenville quickly dragged into monotony. The men practiced drill routines, foraged for food at Rebel farms, cooked their meals, scouted the countryside for guerilla bands, and became adapted to life in Secesh territory. Their main duty centered on accepting Southerners into camp to take the Oath of Allegiance, a written and oral pledge of loyalty and allegiance to the Union. These recently declared Unionists sometimes provided valuable information on Confederate troop movement. One such report on 26 March alleged that five hundred Confederates, under Jeff Thompson, approached Greenville. Rumors caused alarm and confusion in the Fifth's camp all day, especially for Wiley, who, Mann maintained, was "Scared out of his boots!" To determine the rumor's validity, Wiley sent out three scouting parties from the Fifth; each unit left Greenville on a different road. After scouring the country over "Hills, mountains & through valeys & Streams," the parties found no evidence of any Confederates.[14]

Wiley's unease became further inflamed when he learned that local bushwhackers had cut the post's telegraph wire. That same evening, concealed Rebels drove in the Fifth's pickets, with firing quickly becoming general and steady. Wiley ordered two companies to mount up, while the remainder "formed to fight on foot." Despite the pickets' constant firing, the anticipated battle never materialized, and by two o'clock in the morning, Wiley dismissed the men. Many felt their first real taste of battle fear. Packard, the "first on Horse," and with "a revolver in One hand," took charge of the Second Battalion of the Fifth detachment. The sergeant remembered his fellow soldiers' reactions: "The Pickets and Men in Camp was badly [scared]. Some of the boys was So frightened You Could hear them vomitting and Some their Sickness Seamed to turn the Other way till I was realy <u>ashamed</u>! I must Confess I was Some what Startled when the fireing was near. . . . The 1st Order I gave My Men was not to Shoot themselves and Stand by me[,] trust in God and Keep their powder dry 'till we were attacked.' Then let the bulletts fly."[15]

Mann found the whole encounter and the men's reaction compelling, as each man "seemed to have a way of giving expression to his feelings" at the time of battle. The Randolph County merchant observed that some soldiers became so excited they did not know what they were doing, while others exhibited fright beyond comprehension. "Each man holloed, sang, laughed, swore, or whistled, just as the impulse of the moment directed and one man, in particular, was singing . . . at the top of his voice," as he readied himself for battle. Wiley's handling of the affair brought doubts about his competency to lead. "Wiley is in command of this post [at] present but I regret to say [he] is i[n]competent to the task. 'Old Bean Belly' as the 'boys' call him is not popular nor do I think him fit for his post," confessed Mann to his wife. Wiley's moniker referred to his corpulent physique, which had not diminished with active military service. Believing a person's weight reflected his social standing, Wiley had cultivated his considerable girth since his return from the Mexican War and had worn it with pride.[16]

The arrival of the Thirteen Illinois Cavalry at Pilot Knob freed Wilson's detachment of the Fifth Illinois to move south, closer to Arkansas. Wilson ordered Wiley to meet the remainder of the regiment in two days at Reeve's Station, fifteen miles south of Greenville on the Black River. A battalion of the Thirteenth Cavalry took over garrison duty at Greenville, guarding Steele's supply line as the army moved south. On reaching the rendezvous point on 29 March, the prairie boys joined the Thirty-Third, Thirty-Eighth, and Twenty-First Illinois and the Eleventh Wisconsin Infantries, the First Indiana and Ninth Illinois Cavalries, and the Sixteenth Ohio Battery of Light Artillery. The massing of these regiments produced a force seven thousand strong and became the Division of Southeast Missouri, commanded by Steele. The Fifth served in the Third Brigade with the Ninth Illinois and First Indiana Cavalries with their four small steel rifled guns that the boys called "the little bulldogs." For the march south, however, the Fifth served in William P. Carlin's First Brigade with the Thirty-Eighth and Twenty-First Illinois Infantries and Sixteenth Ohio Artillery. Carlin had graduated West Point in 1850 and had served in various expeditions and campaigns in the west. He received his colonel's commission to the Thirty-Eighth Illinois in August 1861.[17]

As Steele's troops moved south into Arkansas, Samuel R. Curtis's Army of the Southwest moved east, following the retreating Confederate Army of the West under Gen. Earl Van Dorn. After Curtis defeated Van Dorn's troops at Pea Ridge (Elkhorn Tavern) in early March, the Confederate leader moved his army from Van Buren east to Des Arc, Arkansas.

Unknown to Union forces, the Rebels expected to cross the Mississippi River to assist Albert Sidney Johnson against Ulysses S. Grant. By the end of March, Confederate forces, including Jeff Thompson's Missouri state guards, occupied Pocahontas, Jacksonport, and Batesville, Arkansas. Steele's move south toward Doniphan, Missouri, and Pitman's Ferry was to stop these Confederate troops from entering Missouri.

Doniphan was the county seat of Ripley County and populated with Confederate sympathizers and slaveholders. Strategically, the county contained the only all-weather roads into northern Arkansas, passing through either Doniphan or slightly southeast of the town. The Natchitoches Trail, also called the Old Military Road, led from St. Louis, through Greenville, southeast of Doniphan and then crossed the Current River at Pitman's Ferry and into Arkansas, ending at Little Rock. All troops either leaving or entering southeast Missouri used this main thoroughfare for travel, making Ripley County and Doniphan strategically significant for both armies.

Carlin's troops started for the Ripley County seat at the end of March. These forces became the advance guard of Steele's army as it moved into Arkansas to connect with Curtis's army. Steele ordered Carlin to secure supplies at Doniphan, and then take possession of Pitman's Ferry, just south of the Arkansas border.[18]

On Monday, 31 March, Companies A, B, and C of the Fifth took the advance of Carlin's column as it marched southwest toward Doniphan, taking about two days for the twenty-five-mile journey. The boys moved through gentle "pine clad hills" bisected with little streams. The flattened landscape allowed larger and "better improved" farms, "softened by the large fields of corn, and abundance of horses, cattle, hogs, and sheep." Rough log cabins housed the farmers and their families, but Mann noted that an "air of negligence" pervaded the scenery. The troops encamped on the Little Black River, twenty miles from Reeve's Station after their first day on the road. Early in the morning of 1 April, again in the advance, the Fifth marched down the Little Black–Doniphan Road, "over a pretty good road for this country." By mid-afternoon, the Fifth encountered pickets from Timothy Reeves's Company of Independent Scouts about four miles east of Doniphan. The Fifth horsemen drove the Rebel scouts through town and across the Current River, taking possession of the county seat "without firing a gun," and capturing three prisoners.[19] Reeves commanded a company of independent cavalrymen out of Doniphan, which was attached to Confederate general John Sappington Marmaduke's cavalry.

Since Carlin and the infantry lagged behind the Fifth, Wilson ordered his pickets to the Current River bottom to guard against a Rebel ambush. Within minutes, however, Reeves's men opened fire from across the waterway. Wilson sent an orderly to Carlin and the infantry informing them of the presence of Confederates. He also ordered Captain Withers of Company C to ascertain the Rebel strength. Taking the lead with Lt. Gordon Webster, the officers appeared "'Donntless and fearless'" as they led Companies C and B into the fast flowing river. When they were half way across the "25 rods Wide" river, Reeves's men again opened fire "from ambush[,] good point[-]blanck range" from the southern shore. The "lead fell thick and fast."[20]

Fifth sharpshooters fired a volley across the river, trying to give Withers's men much-needed coverage. Instead, the volley frightened the horses, causing them to panic and bolt, dislodging several cavalrymen. Sgt. Edward W. Beath (1838–91) and Cpl. Manalcus (Gray) Keeran (1842–1918), Co. C, lost control of their terrified mounts. Beath fell but managed to hold on to his bridle reins. His close friend, Thadeus Packard, grabbed the horse's reins "while the bullets were Whising" past and managed to guide Beath and the horse to safety. Beath suffered a dislocated shoulder from being "tred on and badly jamed in the Stampeed." Keeran fainted during the panic after his horse ran over his legs, but his fellow soldiers managed to rescue him and guide him to shore before he drowned. Despite the pain, it was discovered that Keeran suffered only minor injuries to his legs. Packard's small flask of "4th proff B[r]andy" provided comfort to both men.[21]

The Rebels' obstruction of the ford with felled trees and brush successfully stopped Withers's charge. The Bloomington captain regrouped on the north bank and, after being joined by Wilson, moved three hundred yards upriver to a wider and deeper, but passable ford. Wilson ordered Company B as mounted sharpshooters to cover the crossing, and he plunged into the water ahead of Companies G and C. The Fifth cavalrymen rode defiantly through the rough current, as the Rebels fired on them from ambush. Skiles described the second crossing in a letter to his parents: "When we heard the firing we were all excitement & eager for the fray. When the Col. come up he said forward Co. G & we went dashing after him. . . . [W]e plunged into the river[,] our Capt [John Harvey] at our head & he led by the Col. [T]he Col. crossed[,] junped off his horse waist deep in water hollered come on boys and help pull . . . these trees so we can get up the bank and we rode up, Scoured the brush but could not find them. . . . I tell you it is fun."[22]

A lucky shot from a Fifth sharpshooter wounded Reeves, who fell from his horse on impact. Unfortunately for the horsemen, the Confederate partisans rescued their leader, leaving only a bloody stain on the ground as evidence of his wound. After pursuing Reeves for a couple hundred yards, Wilson gave orders to return to camp: The Illinoisans' horses were too jaded from the march from Reeve's Station for a long pursuit. As Wilson's horsemen recrossed the river, the Sixteenth Ohio arrived and shelled the northern bank to discourage Reeves's return. The Fifth killed one Confederate lieutenant and wounded several others and captured five Rebel soldiers plus camp equipage, horses, mules, and small arms. Wilson's cavalrymen survived without any battlefield casualty, and "every body [felt] jolly over the Bloody 5th['s] first fight."[23]

Carlin's brigade arrived after the skirmish. In his memoirs, the general asserted his participation in the Doniphan encounter. "As soon as we arrived at Doniphan, I determined to secure the south bank of the river and posted some of my troops on the north bank to cover the crossing. This done, Colonel Hall Wilson, with his regiment, plunged into the river to ford it. . . . Captain Tim Reeves's company was hidden. They opened fire on Wilson's cavalry. . . . The infantry on the north bank returned the fire, and Wilson effected a crossing."[24]

This was the Fifth's first battle: their first exposure to whistling lead, the first time they had seen the damage a bullet did to the human body; and Carlin tried to take their victory away from them. First-person accounts from the Fifth Illinois contradict Carlin's memoirs and do not mention any infantry involvement. Furthermore, regimental records from the Twenty-First and Thirty-Eighth Illinois Infantries of Carlin's brigade lack any reference to a skirmish on 1 April, but they do confirm the regiments' arrival at Doniphan on that date. The Twenty-First Illinois entered Doniphan at 3:30 in the afternoon, hours after the Fifth's foray. William Elwood Patterson, Thirty-Eighth Illinois Infantry, remarked, "the cavalry, who were in advance, had a skirmish in the town with a guerrilla band" but made no mention in his diary of his regiment's involvement. The historian for the Sixteenth Ohio Battery maintained that after receiving Wilson's orderly, who carried word of the skirmish to Carlin, the column "all hurried forward with the hope soon to be in our first engagement. . . . All our hurry was for nothing," declared the Ohioan; "the cavalry had put the enemy to flight."[25]

The prairie boys established camp between Doniphan and the second terrace of the Current River. A violent spring storm, so common in Missouri, broke over the camp that night, drenching the soldiers and destroying many of their tents. Frightened cavalry horses fought their riders as they tried to calm their mounts; many were already worn out from the long march over muddy roads. Packard's horse, Tom, who was recovering from distemper, was "worn Cleer down and is not fit for duty. [I]t takes a tough Horse with a Strong Constitution to Stand this Bush-whacking business."[26]

The cavalrymen's duty at Doniphan included scouting, picketing, for-aging, and accepting the Oath of Allegiance from the citizens. "We are Civilizing them as fast as possible," declared Packard; "some have already taken up arms for the Union." During the 5 April scout to Pitman's Ferry, ten to fifteen miles south on the Current River, Farnan's Randolph Rang-ers and Company H captured the contents of the Confederate post office, along with Dr. Peyton R. Pitman, the ferry operator and Confederate postmaster. The confiscated letters provided entertainment for the boys, who learned of the "various opinions, hopes, feelings and fears of many citizens and soldiers of the rebel states." The boys were especially happy to read that many Rebels believed "the Confederacy was about to go up 'Salt River.'"[27]

Other scouts and foraging expeditions uncovered hundreds of pounds of bacon, oats, corn, wheat, guns, horses, mules, and buggies from neigh-boring Secesh homesteads. Though most of the Confederates had moved south to Jacksonport by early April, a few irregular troops remained to hassle the Federals at Doniphan. On one scout, a Confederate bush-whacker shot Isaac M. Jones, Co. C, in the leg. In another incident, Reb-els captured John P. Brower (1836–71), Co. G during a scout on 2 April. Packard was not impressed with the Confederate bushwhackers' appear-ance. "You ought to see the Butternut Kansas Jay Hackers," the sergeant announced to his wife Jennie, "They are not half Civilized, but they are beginning to get their Eye teeth cut."[28]

The people that settled southeast Missouri and eastern Arkansas hailed from the states of Georgia, the Carolinas, and Tennessee, and most were of Scotch-Irish descent. These groups, according to historian David Fischer, had their own system of justice, which they brought with them from Scot-land, northern England, and Ireland. Societal order was maintained by "a system of retributive violence," often perpetuated by individuals who believed he was the guardian of his own interests. During the Civil War, these men, called bushwhackers by Union soldiers, turned to a form of guerilla warfare, with retributive violence feeding the cycle of attack and counterattack. "Rebel Butternut bush whackers" found pleasure in firing on Federal pickets at night, and the soldiers were often awoken by the long roll of drums sounding the alarm. Soldiers "[S]prang to their arm[s] with a Yell of joy for a fight." After lobbing a few shells over the river to discourage an attack, the boys returned to their tents, and "all was quiet again along the banks of Current River." The prairie boys fought these partisan bands many times while in Arkansas.[29]

An exchange of fire during the night of 6 April provoked reflective insight by Mann. "The flash and roar of [t]he musketry and guns, the whirring of the shells, as they passed near where we were and the bursting beyond, all combined made up one of the grandest sights I ever witnessed in my life, and seemed to one unused to such scenes as if all nature was reveling in its own ruin. . . . In an hour after we arrived not a sound disturbed the quiet slumbering of the camp. The excitement, confusion, and noise now yielded to a darkness almost 'felt,' and a stillness that was nearly 'profound.'"[30]

"Glory to God!! Island No. 10 is Ours!" declared an exuberant Packard. For almost a month, the Fifth and the rest of Steele's troops listened as John Pope's forces "pound[ed] away" at the Confederate stronghold on the island and on nearby New Madrid, Missouri. Andrew H. Foote's navy flotilla added extra gun power to the bombardment, but it was not until Grant's victory at Shiloh on 6 April, that the Confederates found their position on Island No. 10 untenable and surrendered on 7 April. With these victories, and the lack of organized Confederate troops in Arkansas, Halleck instructed Steele to move his army south of Pitman's Ferry in the direction of Salem and the White River to connect with Curtis.[31]

Horace Mumford's Company F participated in a reconnaissance to Pocahontas to determine the feasibility of moving Steele's army south and to confirm the withdrawal of Rebel troops. The horsemen not only verified the paucity of troops in the area, but also captured the editor of the local newspaper, with his press "already boxed up for the removal," which the Fifth brought back to camp. Within a few days, the prairie boys printed and sold newspapers at five cents apiece to their fellow soldiers. The press made its rounds of the regiments, eventually falling into the hands of an "independent Cavalry Co.," that printed for profit with "all 1 side Just the same, and not much on the other." The cavalrymen sold the papers for ten cents but soon "ran the thing in[to] the ground." With the lack of evidence of any organized Rebel resistance, Halleck ordered Steele to take possession of Pocahontas and Jacksonport.[32]

On 10 April, the prairie boys gladly mustered for their pay covering January and February 1862; many sent the money home to their families through either the mail or a courier. Seven days later, the regiment left Doniphan, moving slowly south through the muck and mud of the Old

Military Road. Spring had finally landed in southeast Missouri, but the weather remained "cold, wet, and disagreable." The column crossed the Current River, "the most beautiful stream of water I ever saw," acknowledged Mann, "it being so clear we could distinctly see the smallest pebbles at its bottom." As they passed through a cedar forest, Wilson punished a private from Company K for insulting a Missouri woman at a farmhouse the regiment had passed. Wilson relied on public degradation to discipline the soldier and tied the offender's hands behind his back and made him walk unassisted at the rear of the train.[33]

Rain, and the subsequent mud, followed the men as they moved out of Missouri and into northern Arkansas. Progress slowed as both men and horses pulled along the mired-down wagons, and all got "out of humor at being ordered out when it was so disagreable." Along the way, the more adventurous men left the column and found whiskey; one Fifth soldier got so drunk he had to be rolled into a wagon and hauled away. Finally, on 21 April, Wilson halted the regiment fourteen miles from Pocahontas. Establishing camp in the timber on a high ridge, the prairie boys awaited the arrival of the rest of the brigade, who lagged miles behind the cavalry.[34]

After pitching their tents, Captain McConkey sent out a squad from Company E to locate badly needed horse feed for the company. Eight men scoured the soggy countryside, looking in barns and houses for any available forage. The boys had just dismounted at a small house, when a "band of Secesh" rode onto the property. The Fifth held their fire, confusing the guerrillas with Indiana soldiers due to the similarity of their light-colored clothes. During the Illinoisans' confusion, the Rebels took the opportunity to shoot and kill Joseph Sell, who had separated from the main group. Company E boys "r[a]llied[,] drove them, and took in . . . [Sell's] body." The twenty-six-year-old private from Coles County became the first casualty of the regiment killed by enemy bullets.[35]

On Tuesday, 22 April, Wilson sent Apperson and three companies to Powhatan to locate any Confederate troops between Pocahontas and Jacksonport. Wilson expected the scout to return in the evening, but the terrain and high water delayed Apperson's arrival. Not hearing a word from the major and fearing the worst, Wilson sent out two more companies the following morning. When an orderly arrived with word that Apperson pursued Archibald MacFarlane's Fourth Missouri Infantry between the Eleven Point and Strawberry Rivers, the colonel ordered the remaining companies out in support. MacFarlane's newly formed Missouri infantry was poorly armed and contained only four hundred men from the Springfield, Missouri area.

Apperson never came in direct contact with MacFarlane, and soon returned to the Fifth's camp on the afternoon of 25 April. On the scout's return, Spartan-native William Keith, Co. K drowned while fording the Eleven Point River. Farnan attempted a rescue, as did William Packard who threw in a large rail for Keith to grasp, but to no avail. The boys retrieved Keith's body for burial back at camp. The regiment suffered two losses within days of each other, putting a sad note on the affairs at Pocahontas.[36]

Steele arrived at Pocahontas on 27 April, and within two days ordered the Fifth to take post at that place, with Wilson commanding. Companies A and B rode back to secure Pitman's Ferry, while Mumford's Company F became Steele's bodyguards. After securing his column's rear and his tenuous supply line with these movements, Steele, Company F, and Carlin marched to Jacksonport. When Carlin left with his brigade, he also took all the provisions, leaving the Fifth with nothing to eat. Carlin's actions created an atmosphere of disrespect among the prairie boys: "Col Carlin acted very badly towards our regiment and has exhibited a bad spirit for an officer of his standing and rank." According to another member of the regiment, Carlin's actions arose from some disagreement on a military matter between Carlin and Wilson—quite possible Carlin's insistence on his participation in the Doniphan skirmish. This altercation resulted in the regiment's return to the Third Brigade and out of Carlin's command. Packard stated bluntly in his memoirs, "[Carlin] don[']t like the bloody 5th." Steele gave Wilson permission to make "every exertion to procure supplies of forage and provisions," from Rebels and peaceable citizens, the latter getting vouchers from the government, redeemable for money.[37]

Wilson contracted dysentery and typhoid fever while at Pocahontas, and became debilitated enough for Wiley to assume command of the post. For the first time since entering the war, the Fifth was "in our enemies country surrounded with those who would take our lives by any means in their power." Life for the majority of the men at the town, however, became dreary, and the men rapidly "tired of the inactive life and would rather be moving farther south." With very little to do, the men spent their time playing cards, drinking alcohol, or raiding the property of both Rebels and Unionists. Unauthorized foraging became such a favorite pastime that the unpopular lieutenant colonel used a chain guard to keep the men in camp. The regiment, Mann recalled, developed such a state of mutiny at this action that Wiley lifted the chain guards, but increased the number of roll calls. This incensed the men even more, especially when the bugler sounded the roll call one night, and the men "[sent] up such a shout that the bugle could not be heard." Many men believed Wiley had "not judgment to command the regiment"; quite a drastic change from October 1861, when the Fifth requested the Illinois governor to give Wiley command of the regiment.[38]

By the end of May, however, the Fifth exceeded Steele's foraging orders as their actions turned to plundering and stealing from all citizens in Randolph County. When Wilson returned to active duty, he appealed to all the "honest men of the regiment to aid him in enforcing the laws" to save the good name and reputations of the men and the regiment. The distraught colonel believed if the stealing did not stop immediately, this lawlessness would "make the once fair name of this regiment a disgrace." Wilson faced an irremediable situation, for he struggled not only against thievery, but also with his soldiers' belief system. The men who did the fighting knew before the Federal government that they fought the Confederate army and its support system—the slave owners. Destruction of the support system weakened the Confederate army. Mann wrote extensively about the subject: "I do not think the rebels should be protected in the possession of their property. . . . We cannot expect to end the war by coaxing and persuading rebels to be loyal, but should punish them, and make them feel war untill they are subdued. Many of the boys are angry because of the leniency shown to rebels around here."[39]

It was during their stay at Pocahontas that the prairie boys developed, what might be labeled, as four unspoken rules for plundering in enemy territory. According to soldiers' writings, empty houses announced the owners as enemies and all property subject to confiscation. Aggravated plundering of property was reserved for those citizens who showed impudence or resisted Federal troops. Soldiers also viewed all property owned by enemy combatants as booty subject to legal confiscation. Finally, in order to keep the peace, families who had stayed in their homes would not be stripped of all possessions, but left enough to survive through the next season. The Fifth adhered to these principles throughout the four years of war, though their stay in Arkansas stretched the limits of this undeclared policy.

The health of the regiment also suffered during this inactive period. John Burke confessed to his sister that he hoped the regiment moved soon and "not be kept inactive long for it is not very healthy here and inactivity will produce more sickness than any thing else. [T]here is considerable sickness in camp now and we are losing men every day." Many contracted diarrhea, dysentery, or typhoid; all three assaults the intestinal tract, leaving the patient weak from the inability to digest nutritional food;

in the worst cases, the severe diarrhea causes the victim to suffer from dehydration, which eventually leads to death. Eleven men died of these diseases while stationed at Pocahontas, a town many believed was "one of the last places, to be sick, with nothing to eat, but just fat bacon, & corn meal, salt & water, fried up in strong fat." Others blamed the foul tasting spring water as the source of the diarrhea, believing the limestone-filtered water contained minerals that caused the water to taste "bad," thus rendering it unhealthy.[40]

As illnesses took the lives of some men, others became debilitated enough for the army to grant a disability discharge. March through May witnessed thirty-two men leaving the Fifth's service due to their health, because of sore eyes, pulmonary infections, and general debility. Many carried money home to the families of regimental mates, for the soldiers received payment for their services for March and April.

The regiment also lost two commissioned officers in April. The incompetent Captain Jenkins, Co. I resigned for the good of the regiment, instead of being court-martialed. Jenkins, according to Apperson, "was a traitor" who would "not attend to the welfare of his Company." James Pease, who had previously complained about the lack of good leadership in the company, again appealed to the governor to appoint someone "not in any way conected with the regiment," and one chosen only by the governor. Nevertheless, Yates promoted Benjamin Glenn (1831–1905), Co. E to the captaincy of I, reinforcing Pease's assertion that all the commissioned officers of the company "are not competent in any respect to fill the places." In civilian life, Glenn owned a $1,200 farm in Mattoon, Coles County, and had recently lost his wife to disease. He assumed command of Company I on May 8 and served as captain until his resignation in December 1862.[41]

"I hope and pray We may be Called away from this Stinking Town dead! Men! Dead Horses dead Hoggs and it is almost unbarable Morning and Evening," declared Packard. Even the horses suffered from the lack of good food, and many died from Texas or cattle fever, transmitted by ticks carrying *Babesia protozoa* (bovine babesiosis). Highly contagious, the disease destroys red blood cells, causing dramatic weight loss, muscle tremors, bloody urine, and an extremely high fever. Packard's beloved horse Tom looked "like a traviling Skeleton," but rest at Pocahontas allowed the horse to regain strength, and he was soon "in good heart," getting fat on good grazing.[42]

Arkansas was the first place the Fifth soldiers came in direct contact with slaves and their owners. Runaway slaves eventually entered the

Fifth's camp, and the Illinoisans employed them in messes and as laborers. George Washington, a slave once owned by Confederate Col. William O. Coleman of Missouri, had been sent to the Hunter plantation in Pocahontas for "safe keeping" while Yankees occupied Missouri. George slipped away from the plantation and made his way to the prairie boys' camp, eventually becoming a cook for some of the Randolph Rangers' commissioned officers. Within a few days, Hunter appeared in camp, claiming George as his property. Approaching Calvin Mann, Hunter demanded the runaway slave's return, but the lieutenant replied that slaves of traitors were free. Hunter then appealed to Wiley, but the Quaker informed the slave owner that returning runaway slaves was not part of his duty. Hunter then tried to persuade George to return, but the freed slave decided to remain with the Yankees. After Hunter left camp, Wiley sent out patrols expecting a rescue attempt in the night, but none materialized. In a later incident, Wilson confronted a slave catcher who tried to remove a runaway owned by Judge Crenshaw. Calling the man a "filthy ruffian," Wilson informed him that Federal troops did not come into Arkansas to "catch 'niggers,'" and ordered the man out of camp. Mann believed Wilson's anger and "indignation was so great that [Wilson] almost laid violent hands on this Arkansas specimen of 'Southern Chivalry.'" The colonel announced that "any man that would 'catch slaves' for the masters was 'no better than a dog.'"[43]

With Van Dorn's Confederate troops east of the Mississippi River, Arkansas was left open for occupation, and Curtis and Steele easily moved through the state. Curtis reentered Arkansas on 29 April, dashing south along the eastern bank of the White River and entering Batesville on 2 May. The First Indiana Cavalry in Steele's column took Jacksonport on 1 May, with the rest of Steele's division-sized force occupying the town within three days. In mid-May, Halleck ordered Steele to Batesville to combine his forces with Curtis, with the intention of capturing Little Rock.

At this time, however, Pierre Gustave Toutant Beauregard, who assumed command of the Army of Tennessee after the Confederate defeat at Shiloh in April, appointed Thomas C. Hindman to command the Military District of the Trans-Mississippi. During Hindman's short reign as commander in Arkansas, he declared martial law, enforced the unpopular Confederate conscription act, and commandeered all Texas cavalry troops passing through Arkansas en route to Mississippi. He also issued General Orders No. 17 in mid-June calling on all citizens to organize into "independent companies" and "at once commence operations against the enemy without waiting for special instructions." Hindman ordered these partisan rangers to attack Federal pickets, scouts, and foraging parties.[44]

The general's strict enforcement of the Confederate conscription act also had immediate consequences for the prairie boys. Throughout the month of June, fleeing conscripts inundated the Illinoisans' camp at Pocahontas and brought news of Hindman's partisan rangers that quickly spread among the men. "The retreating Corinthians are found in Bands of all sises up to 2,000 between Crowley[']s Ridge and Little Rock, Ark. [T]here is something of a Skirmishing going on, all the time," declared Packard. By late May, Fifth officers were receiving daily information from Union men that partisan bands prowled the countryside.[45]

With their men gone to answer Hindman's call, the Secesh women remained behind to care for family and farm, and deal with the Federal army. The wives, daughters, and mothers of Confederate soldiers used "all their talents and bewitching smiles" on the Fifth's officers "to secure protection to the property of traitors." John Mann condemned the officers as "<u>weaker</u> than the women who bam[b]oozle" them. He believed Colonel Wilson the only one capable of repelling "all their soft appliances and machinations."[46]

Those who answered Hindman's call often tried to reach their families in Federally held territory for short visits. In May, the prairie boys captured three Rebels trying to visit their wives: James Martin, Peter Aik, and a man named Phelps. Peter Aik tried to visit his wife who had been "playing 'widow'" to Sgt. Jacob M. Cullers (1838–1909), Co. A. The unmarried Cullers "was evidently attentive to her, untill he learned our boys had found her husband." Her devotion to Cullers probably stemmed from his rank as one of the Fifth's commissary sergeants and his access to fresh supplies. A week later, Calvin Mann and twelve Randolph Rangers, silently escorted the prisoners to Pilot Knob, the secrecy necessary to avoid "an attempt to rescue them by their [Secesh] friends."[47]

Mutiny visited Company K in late June when a few of the boys spent the night out drinking and consorting with local women. When they returned to camp, Farnan ordered the two miscreants to extra labor, cutting down trees and chopping up stumps. The men refused, causing the captain to restrain the men by tying their hands to a tree. Sgt. James McQuiston, Cpl. James B. Gordon, Tobias Boudonot, and Thomas S. Morrison went to the captives' rescue. Inciting Farnan's Irish temper, the captain pulled his pistol on the four, who, in turn, pulled their guns on the captain. Company mates talked the men down, and all walked away without any injury. Mann believed Lt. Charles Childs was behind the mutineers, for he coveted the captaincy and wanted Farnan out of the company. Within a few days, Wilson had McQuiston and James Gordon reduced in ranks. Farnan, however, pursued the matter, and eventually brought the men to court-martial. No records exist as to the court's findings.[48]

Company C also saw its share of insubordination when food became scarce in late June. The boys had been living on half rations for some time, and "five refused to do duty," until they procured meals at a local hotel. Withers declined their request and ordered their return to duty. When the hungry men ignored the captain's orders, Withers reported their disobedience to Wilson, who sent a "Squadd of Men and arrested them." No one was court-martialed, but the boys suffered "in the Old Stinking Guard House Seven days." Wilson's disciplinary actions emphasized humiliation and physical discomfort, with the occasional courts-martial relegated for harsher offenses.[49]

On 26 May, Steele released Mumford's Company F from personal guard duty and sent it to Smithville, where they met Companies D and L, under Seley. The detachment's duty included establishing a Federal garrison twenty-five miles south of Pocahontas. Smithville sat at the strategic junction of major roads, and a branch of the Military Road ran through the small town, connecting it to Batesville and Jacksonport. Partisan irregulars under Wiley C. Jones used Sharp County for forage and recruiting. Jones was a prominent Smithville citizen who commanded Company E of Col. William O. Coleman's Regiment of Missouri Cavalry, newly raised under Hindman's Partisan Ranger Act.[50]

Seley's men connected with Mumford just outside of Smithville on 28 May. Children from the Hillhouse School lined the Smithville-Evening Shade Road and watched as the prairie boys entered their town. Seley's men looked magnificent on "the finest horses," the children had ever seen and people commented on the "decorated bridles, saddles and saddle blankets" that covered the mounts. Some of the children stood in awe of the Union soldiers, while others became so scared, they "tried to hide under the [desk] seats."[51]

On the afternoon of 17 June, Seley sent out his most experienced soldier in the detachment: Lt. Samuel J. R. Wilson, with fifteen men from Company F to collect cattle and assist a Union family's move into the Federal campground. The Mexican War veteran completed his orders and started toward camp when a woman emerged from a nearby house to inform Wilson that one-hundred Rebel guerillas planned to attack his force. The lieutenant immediately sent a messenger to Seley for reinforcements while the balance of the men headed for shelter at James McKinney's farmhouse, nine miles west of Smithville on Osborn's Creek. On receiving Wilson's desperate message, Seley sent the remaining men under Captains Organ, Caldwell, and Mumford. Seley also requested more reinforcements from Wilson at Pocahontas, who promptly forwarded Company E, one of four rifle companies in the regiment.[52]

Organ and the reinforcements rode quickly to the McKinney farmhouse through a driving rainstorm. Unknown to Wilson's rescuers, Jones's guerillas had already surrounded the McKinney house, and were concealed in nearby log structures anxious to attack. Not considering the situation before he took action, Organ drove his men recklessly into the ambush, where Jones's men poured a volley into the unsuspecting Federals. The Fifth was surprised, but unfazed and quickly regrouped, charging Jones's guerillas. Unfortunately, the bushwhackers' trap backfired: the heavy rainstorm quickly made Osborn's Creek area untenable, which trapped the Rebels between the farm and creek. Organ quickly exploited Jones's error, and the Fifth rapidly surrounded the partisans, capturing Jones and fourteen of his Missourians, and also killing one and wounding two Confederates.[53]

Seley commended the officers and men in his official report for "the courage and bravery displayed . . . as the circumstances were perplexing and [the men] knowing nothing of the strength of the enemy," as they entered the battle. The Fifth had two men killed and five slightly wounded in the engagement. A shot to the head killed Marvin Welker, Co. L, while Wyatt J. Mills, Co. F, received a mortal wound to the bowels. Lt. Francis M. Dorothy, Co. F, received a knee injury but survived. The injury plagued him for months before he finally resigned in January 1863. Four other Illinois cavalrymen received slight wounds.[54]

Seley learned from his Rebel captives that Coleman's Missouri regiment planned to attack his detachment. The major relished the idea of another attack and planned on "giv[ing] them a warm reception if they come." Wilson sent further assistance in the form of Companies K and M, but no attack materialized. The companies remained at Smithville for a few days, returning to Pocahontas by 23 June.[55]

While the Fifth had whiled away the time in northeast Arkansas, Curtis and Steele worked their way toward capturing Little Rock. Curtis moved toward the state capital on 20 May but soon discovered that his attenuated supply line from St. Louis was stretched to the breaking point. The Army of the Southwest could not move forward without supplies, and Curtis's three divisions became thinly strung out between Searcy, Jacksonport, and Batesville. To make matters worse, Hindman's partisan

rangers clashed with Federal troops as they foraged the flooded countryside for much-needed supplies. Finally, Curtis recognized the futility of
his advance and withdrew back to Batesville, requesting a water-borne
rescue. Halleck immediately ordered the navy to send boats up the White
River to resupply Curtis. After a heated battle at St. Charles on 17 June,
Charles Henry Davis's Federal flotilla chugged up the White River only to
be stopped at Clarendon by low water. On learning of this development,
Curtis severed his overland supply and communications lines to St. Louis
and marched his army down the east bank of the White River to meet
the navy flotilla at Clarendon. This was the first time in the war that an
army would completely subsist on the countryside for food and supplies.

Rebel irregulars constantly harassed Curtis's troops as they moved
through the countryside, prompting the general to call forward his troops
from northern Arkansas, including the Fifth Illinois. Before the regiment
moved toward Curtis, however, the men suffered another loss, when John
F. Heath died from typhoid and chronic diarrhea. "Another patriot is gone!
Death has struck a blow near our hearts . . . we have lost a valued friend,
the country a brave warrior and his company an efficient officer," declared
an Illinois newspaper in Heath's obituary. Heath had been a teacher prior
to the war and was only twenty-five years old when he died.[56]

On 26 June, the men heard the news of their move to Jacksonport.
Wilson ordered all able-bodied men to pack up for the march, while
those soldiers too ill to march remained in the hospital at Pocahontas,
under the care of Sgt. Phillip A. Kemper (1832–92), Co. E, who had been
a physician in civilian life. When the column moved out, Confederates
captured the four debilitated Fifth soldiers and their physician on 30 June
but paroled them a month later.[57]

The excitement of moving forward aroused the soldiers to overindulge
in "debauchery and drunkiness," resulting in many hungover soldiers
marching through the rocky hills and broken roads of northern Arkansas;
fortunately no one went missing, and the regiment crossed the pontoon
bridge over the Black River and arrived at Jacksonport four days later.
The Fifth became part of Steele's First Division, Army of the Southwest.
Eugene A. Carr commanded the Second, and Peter J. Osterhaus led the
Third Division of the army, all under the command of Curtis. There was
no rest for the men when they joined Curtis's army, for the next day found
the regiment moving toward Augusta.[58]

In a desperate move to stop Curtis, Hindman requested aid from the
people of Arkansas. Local newspapers published Hindman's 24 June proclamation calling for the people to "press upon the invaders . . . attack[ing]

him day and night" by lying "in ambush," to "surprise his detachments."
Hindman also wanted the roads filled with felled trees, the bridges burned,
and all forage destroyed.[59]

On 1 July, Curtis's fifteen-mile column of bedraggled and weary soldiers encountered their first obstacles just south of Jacksonport, but
troops easily cleared the road of fallen trees. The Fifth protected the
rear of Steele's division, where the dust suffocated men and horses, and
the few wells and cisterns provided little water for the parched cavalrymen and their mounts. Wilson, still incapacitated by diarrhea, rode in
an ambulance, while Wiley controlled the active operations of the regiment. The Makanda colonel sent out foraging parties, who found plenty
of corn, horses, mules, and beef at nearby plantations. The Fifth again
received a reprimand for their foraging activities from their commanding general when they "'gobbl[ed]' a field of oats that [Steele] wanted for
his 'body guard.'" As punishment, Steele did not invite the regiment to
the Independence Day celebrations at Augusta on 4 July. Instead, the
men gathered at Wilson's headquarters to celebrate and hear speeches
by Wiley, Apperson, Reverend Woods, and others.[60]

The army spent 4 and 5 July resting at Augusta and getting ready to
resume the march. During the army's intermission, Confederates built
large timber blockades over narrow, water-lined roads leading to Clarendon, making it impossible to pass around the barriers. According to
one cavalryman, the Rebels laid "along side the road, in the edge of the
brush, so they can fire from their cover, and run before, we can open a
road through the fallen timber, to charge on them." The only way to move
forward was to cut through the blockades. Curtis met this challenge by
creating a pioneer corps of soldiers and former slaves who cut through
the trees so rapidly Curtis's army never lost momentum.[61]

After working their way through one of the largest and densest barriers, Curtis's troops reached James's Ferry on the Cache River in the
afternoon of 6 July. The pioneers quickly hacked through the tangled
mess, allowing the army to continue its march with the loss of only half
a day. Early the next morning, Curtis directed Steele to establish a strong
bridgehead on the east bank of the Cache. Steele gave the task to Charles
E. Hovey, who sent Charles Harris with detachments from the Eleventh
Wisconsin and Thirty-Third Illinois Infantries, and First Indiana Cavalry, with one of their 2.9-inch rifled steel cannon. Harris encountered a
thousand Texas cavalry, including the Sixteenth and Twenty-First under
William H. Parsons at the intersection of the Clarendon and Des Arc
Roads, just south of the Parley Hill plantation. A brisk skirmish ensued,
ending in the routing and defeat of the Rebel cavalry.

During the skirmish, the Fifth helped save one of the First Indiana's steel guns when "2 Comps of our Reg. Charged them with sabres, which they [Confederates] could not stand. [T]hen we emptied our pistols at them." A battalion of the Fifth under Apperson later joined William P. Benton's reinforcements, pursuing the fleeing Confederate forces toward Des Arc. Late in the afternoon, Benton reached the lower crossing of the Cache and directed his artillery to shell the opposite shore. When the Rebel failed to respond, Benton returned to James's Ferry. The Confederates' attempt to prevent Curtis's Army of the Southwest from advancing toward Clarendon and their supplies ended in a decidedly Confederate defeat at the Cache River.[62]

3

THIS GODFORSAKEN TOWN
July to October 1862

Curtis's march through central Arkansas became known as "one of the most arduous and fatiguing of any made during the [C]ivil [W]ar." Newspapers in Chicago and New York described the horrible conditions the soldiers endured while moving through the state, where Confederates blocked roads, using slave labor to fell trees across narrow passages to hinder the army's progress. Plantation wells, the only source of cool, fresh water for the troops, were filled up or poisoned with dead animals. The Federals fought and cut their way through cypress swamps and cane breaks, where the Rebels took every opportunity to harass and delay the Union army's advance.[1]

At Bayou de View, the Confederates fired the bridge, "but our boys drove them off and put out the fire," allowing the prairie boys to reach the eastern shore on 8 July. As they moved through the bottomland swamp, where tupelo and cypress grew to enormous heights out of chalk brown water, the men caught their first glimpses of Spanish moss and cypress knees. On reaching the high ground near a plantation two miles south of the bayou, Wilson established camp. Swarms of mosquitoes attacked the men, exposing the vulnerable soldiers to malaria. Their only hopeful thoughts were of the supplies and transports awaiting them at Clarendon, twenty miles south on the Cache River.[2]

Already on half rations, and "nothing but 'swamp' water to drink and it most wretched," the weakened Federal soldiers remained vulnerable to Rebel attacks. A sweltering sun greeted Curtis's seven-mile-long column of troops on 8 July, and humidity from waterlogged ground weakened both infantry and cavalry, with the former causing more problems to the foot soldiers due to the dust created by the horses. Officers often moved the cavalry off the main road, taking long detours so as not to suffocate the infantry.[3]

The heat and the dust created such suffering as only a drink of cold water could alleviate, but the men found nothing to quench their thirst. "Oh how we Suffer[ed] for want of Water," wrote Packard, "and provisions on the long Marches. I Sucked water through the mud where the tadpoles were all Sort[s] & Sises and nothing in My Haversack to Eat but a few cracker crumbs for three days." John Burke described a more desolate picture for his sister:

On our march we suffered mor[e] for water than anything else. [O]n every plantation there is generely two or three wells which might have afforded us tolerably cool water[,] but our enemies would . . . fill up the wells with logs and dirt on our approach leaving only the muddy swamps and Bayous along the road. [T]his water was perfectly hot and almost putrid for the [S]ecesh would drive hogs and cattle into these places and then shoot them and leave them to season the water for us to drink[,] but it was the only chance for us and it was rendered palatable by a burning sun and dust that flew so thick that sometimes we could not see the horses on which we rode.[4]

The horror of the march faded for the Illinois cavalrymen near the junction of the Military and Cotton Plant Roads, where they "passed through a very small prarie, and the boys set up a shout of joy as if they had found an old acquaintance."[5] Taking the Military Road, the column moved slowly toward Clarendon, and what the Illinoisans thought would be provisions and water. The men reached the outskirts of the little river town by the evening of 9 July and went into camp, falling asleep as soon as they dismounted.

The army entered an area of Arkansas known for black, sluggish bayous that appeared out of nowhere. Often clogged with logs and weeds, the banks overgrown with tangled vegetation, the mournful spots became breeding ground for mosquitoes and alligators. Clarendon rose out of the brambles on the east bank of the White River near the mouth of the Cache River. The town thrived as an important river port and overland trading center, and it quickly became the focal point of both Confederate and Union armies. The Fifth visited the town often while stationed at Helena.

When the prairie boys woke the next morning, they learned that the navy's boats had not deposited any supplies but had left Clarendon due to low water and moved farther south on the White River. The Illinoisans rested in camp all day and joined thousands of their fellow soldiers as they bathed in the White River, washing away thirteen days of dust and grime of the road. Steele also reorganized his divisions, with the regiment serving with the First Indiana Cavalry under Col. Conrad Baker in Steele's Fourth Brigade.[6]

Due to the lack of supplies, Curtis turned his attention to Helena, Arkansas, a small town on the Mississippi River, sixty-five miles south of Memphis, Tennessee, and 140 miles north of Vicksburg, Mississippi. Like Nashville and Vicksburg, Helena had gained its wealth from slave labor, plantation agriculture, and steamboat transportation. By capturing Helena and establishing a Federal post, the Union army would have a permanent water-borne supply route and a staging area for Union forces participating in operations to open the Mississippi River to New Orleans.

In the afternoon of 10 July, Curtis detailed Col. Cadwallader C. Washburn, Second Wisconsin Cavalry, with three thousand cavalry to capture Helena and secure the port for the rest of Curtis's army. Wiley reported with five hundred Fifth Illinoisans, joining detachments of the Tenth Illinois, Fifth Kansas, and Second Wisconsin Cavalry regiments and ten pieces of light artillery as the advance of the army.[7]

The bugle sounded reveille at two in the morning on 11 July. After a meager breakfast of "three crackers to each man," Washburn's advance hit the Little Rock Road at half past four in the morning. The cavalry traveled all day, stopping only once to feed and water the horses. An afternoon rain shower relieved the heat, and the boys "hailed [the rain] as a blessing although it [soaked] us through [every] stitch for a little time the burning sun was shut from our sight and we had no more dust the rest of the march." Rain also provided drinking water for the parched horsemen; though it was muddy, the men were glad it lacked the "smell of Carrion." After traveling all night, Washburn arrived at Helena at 9:00 A.M. the next day "much to the surprise of the inhabitants."[8]

Being some of the first troops in Helena, the regiment had choice locations for a campsite. Wiley secured ground near a dried cypress swamp on the Clarendon Road, one mile from Helena and Confederate general Gideon Pillow's plantation, in St. Francis Township. Most of the men collapsed with fatigue and heat prostration, falling from their horses on reaching camp and sleeping until the next morning. Those that stayed awake, like Mann, took advantage of the situation and explored the nearby Isa M. Lamb plantation, in St. Francis Township, "'[j]ayhawk[ing]' some corn for my horse and a side of bacon for our mess." By mid-afternoon, even Mann became fatigued and fell into a deep sleep. The camp lay quiet until the next morning. Many expected the supply boats to be at Helena when they awakened, but when none appeared, the Fifth boys, and other regiments, used local plantations as supply depots, confiscating food for themselves and their horses. This was the first time during the march the regiment expropriated Southern property for their use without prior approval. Federal supplies finally reached the troops four days later.[9]

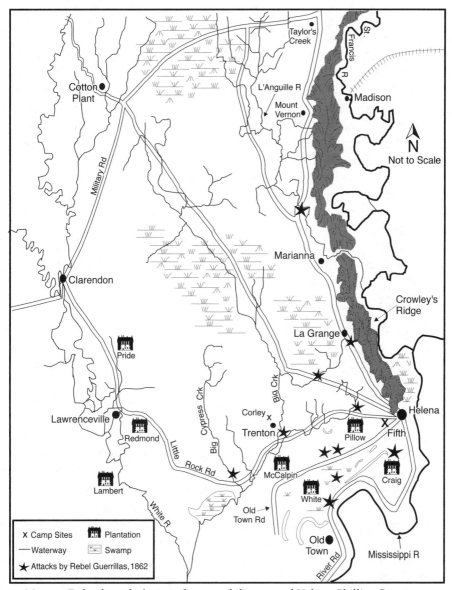

Map 3.1. Federal cavalry's area of responsibility around Helena, Phillips County, Arkansas, July 1862 to May 1863.

Curtis's main army traveled a few days behind Washburn's column. More than two thousand slaves who sought freedom with the Federal army followed Curtis. "The [N]egroes flock in thick, [and] the Plantations, are considerably larger down here," declared Skiles; "some Planters have from 60 to 300 [N]egroes.... [They] would tell us where their massas had their Mules, Corn, & Bacon hid in the cornfield, or the woods." After the battle at Cache River, three slaves belonging to one of the Confederate soldiers killed in the foray joined Curtis's column, "each [slave] took a good mule ... and came with us."[10]

Mann, an abolitionist at heart, speculated as to the slaves' fate. "What is to become of the poor creatures, and whether the Government will care and provide for them?, are questions that is yet unknown. To drive them out of camp would practically send them back to their old masters." The sergeant believed the freedmen should be treated "[kindly] and some care be exercised over them" for the slaves were not in rebellion against the Federal government. He supported Curtis's controversial action to give certificates of freedom to all slaves who were forced to work on Rebel fortifications.[11]

Between July 12 and 14, the Federal army trickled into Helena. John Burke was thrilled finally to see "the broad Mississippi.... It seems naturall to be where we can hear from our friends again or at least it seems more pleasant than what it does back in the Swamps and Cane Brakes of Arkansaw, where for the past six weeks I have heard nothing but our drums and Bugles." An intestinal illness caused by drinking contaminated water dampened Burke's joy. "[T]he weather was very ... hot and I drank water that before I entered the army[,] I would have been ashamed to offer to a hog." The private barely stayed in his saddle as he rode into Helena, but after getting supplies and fresh water, Burke began to mend; however, he remained weak for many weeks. Packard had expected to endure "all Kinds of hardships," but "being harrassed by the Gurrillas" made service almost unbearable. The prospect of being part of the army, instead of outpost duty, however, satisfied the sergeant, who found it "rather Scarry Sometimes before we joined the main Armey."[12]

Within a few days the heat and the effects of the march debilitated the Federals, and sickness quickly spread. Packard succumbed within a few days of his arrival at Helena. The Bloomington clerk believed his illness, and that of about one-third of Company C, came from drinking poor water and breathing foul air. "The Miasma that has arisen from that Cypress swamp, which has been Called Lake Wiley[,] has given the boys the ague Chills & fever. ... I have been reporting ten or a dozen every morning at the Hospital, with that old acheing head & bones." Malaria also hit Skiles, who "had a touch of the Chills, & Fever, had 3 shakes, 1 every day."[13]

Lake Wiley referred to the Fifth's first campground, chosen by the regiment's lieutenant colonel. The dry summer weather and the large oaks and cypresses made the area look inviting for a campground. The Illinoisans had settled into camp for about four days, when they experienced a torrential rain on 16 July. "[T]he winds blew and the floods Came, Rushing down every 'branch[,]' . . . 'Ravine & Hill' til[l] it was Knee deep, some of the Boys Stuck to their tents by [tying] themselves up on Chunks [of] wood, when all at Once they took a Stampeed Shoulder[ed] their heavy wet blankets and Started for the Hills above. Yelling as they went Lake Wiley!!" By the next morning, the boys used boats to gather up personal items, sabers, guns, and saddles floating in the bayou. The deluge left a stinking mud hole that Packard believed would lead to "Ague that will Shake us out of our boots if we Stay here long."[14]

The waterlogged terrain in and around Helena created an unhealthy environment for the soldiers. Helena sits on the alluvial plain of the Mississippi River, just ten miles below the mouth of the St. Francis River. An inadequate levee protected the town's eastern border from the Mississippi; high ground and numerous hills dot the area just west of town. To the north sits Crowley's Ridge, a continuous area of upland that runs from Helena to southern Missouri. Creeks, sloughs, bayous, and swamps, including a large cypress swamp at the base of the ridge, ran around the town. Due to the high water table of the alluvial plain, the secondary streams often overflowed, flooding the town from the west and south.

The Illinois troops, along with all the other Federal soldiers at Helena, lacked experience and camp discipline, which resulted in the soldiers paying a terrible price for their officers' ignorance of sanitary measures. The army polluted their camps and fouled their water supply, and with the high water table around Helena, fecal material quickly spread throughout the camps. The result was an outbreak of dysentery, typhoid, and other enteric diseases, with simultaneous infections of murine typhus and malaria. Murine typhus visited soldiers crowded together in filthy camps with poor sanitation. Spread through the fecal matter of bloodsucking fleas, the disease had similar symptoms as malaria and typhoid, and physicians often confused the three diseases.

By the last few days of July, the Fifth had dozens of men in the hospital, and many applied for leaves to recuperate at home. Though Colonel Wilson left on 17 July for an extended sick leave (his second) to recuperate from chronic diarrhea, the army refused to issue furloughs for privates and noncommissioned officers. Even a disability discharge became difficult to obtain. Packard tried for months to obtain a discharge for his brother William, who suffered from a lung infection since Camp Butler. Spending more time in a St. Louis hospital than with the regiment, William eventually rejoined Thadeus, improved, but lacking in strength and fortitude. William's health again waned after the long march through Arkansas, and with the dust weakening his lungs further, "he coughs constantly nights." With the regimental surgeon on sick furlough, Thadeus believed his brother would have to stay in the army for a few more months. Packard alleged the government did not care about its soldiers: "They had rether give a fellow his death warrent then his discharge any time." Halleck curtailed any hope for a leave of absence or furlough when he ordered the cessation of leaves, believing absentee soldiers destroyed the army. The sick, Halleck maintained, recovered sooner at camp than if sent north to a hospital or to convalesce at home. Thousands of men died at Helena because of Halleck's shortsightedness.[15]

A few men healthy enough for duty sought entertainment outside camp. Lt. John Smith, Co. I, led seven drunken prairie boys to Pillow's plantation and "abused and maltreated" the female slaves on the night of 21 July. Since the white overseer had fled when the Federal army arrived at Helena, there was no one at the plantation to protect the women from outside mistreatment. Later, a brave slave arrived in the Fifth's camp and informed Wiley of the rapes. Smith, a Kentucky native, and the other attackers, had voiced their hatred of abolitionists and their fear that Lincoln would "adopt the policy of 'nigger equality.'" In Mann's opinion these men, whom he called "ruffianly white men," were "far inferior to the poor unprotected slaves they so wantonly abused."[16]

At the end of July, Curtis sent the Fifth Illinois and twenty-five hundred cavalrymen on a scout to find Rebel partisan bands south of town. "[Q]uite a large body of troops [had been] seen in that vicinity, just before night," and Curtis wanted his southern flank protected. The troops headed for Old Town, a dilapidated old landing, located twenty miles south of Helena on the banks of Old Town Lake. Hovey, with his infantry, had secured the area, which served as a port for steamboats shipping out cotton or bringing in supplies for the surrounding estates. Companies F and G of the Fifth served as Hovey's bodyguards while at the landing. The Illinoisans participated in various cotton-acquisition scouts in Arkansas, though one "went over into Miss[issippi] after cotton, got 130 bales, staid 1 night, & came back." Wiley, however, "did not like to lose 2 such good

Companies" and recalled F and G. The scout found no evidence of Rebels in the area and quickly returned to Helena.[17]

The area was devoid of Confederates because Hindman had withdrawn his weakened infantry to Little Rock, leaving behind only William Parsons's regular cavalry and partisan rangers to harass the Federal army at Helena. New Jersey–born Parsons had organized the Twelfth Texas Cavalry in August 1861 and moved to Arkansas seven months later. When Theophilus H. Holmes assumed command of the Confederate Trans-Mississippi Department on 30 July, he gave Parsons free reign to scout independently around Helena. Headquartered near Clarendon, Parsons organized his own brigade by early August, which contained the Twelfth Texas, George Carter's Twenty-First Texas, Nathaniel Burford's Nineteenth Texas, and Joseph Pratt's Tenth Texas Field Battery. Several partisan bands also joined the brigade, including Alfred Johnson's Texas Spy Company of Cavalry, Francis Chrisman's Arkansas Cavalry, and Charles Morgan's Texas Battalion. Many of these bands had hindered Curtis's march through Arkansas, but by the end of July, their sole duty centered on patrolling Phillips County to harass Federal foraging parties, kill Federal pickets, and ambush scouts.[18]

The Confederate cavalry became the only body of troops between the Federals at Helena and the Confederate army at Little Rock. As matters stood in August 1862, the Confederates in Arkansas were drastically outnumbered in men and supplies, so the Rebels adopted a war of attrition and refined their guerrilla tactics to deal with the Northern invaders. On 3 August, Parsons's Twelfth Texas and Johnson's Spy Company ambushed a supply train at L'Anguille Ferry, just thirty miles north of Helena, resulting in the death of fourteen and the capture of twenty-five Wisconsin cavalrymen.[19]

In response to Parsons's bold ambush, and believing that the Texans planned an impending assault on Helena, Steele ordered Hovey, now commanding the Fourth Division, to make a demonstration toward Clarendon. Mann described the new general as "a quick spoken, fierce looking little man" and hoped his looks reflected his fighting style. Hovey's troops consisted of four infantry regiments, the First Indiana Cavalry, and their battery of steel guns; the Fifth Illinois (350) under Wiley; and the Fifth Kansas Cavalry, all commanded by Col. Graham N. Fitch, Forty-Sixth Indiana Infantry. Mann described Fitch as an "old political 'foggy'" who did not make a "favorable impression upon the mind of a practical soldier." The sergeant maintained that "old politicians make very poor military men. They deal in pompous humbugs, rather than stubborn facts." The cavalry left Helena at nine in the evening of 3 August, heading southwest on the Little Rock Road. Packard, who did not accompany the scout, hoped "Our Boys will have a Chance to Show their Mettle, this time."[20]

The column traveled through the hot stifling night, reaching Trenton midday on 4 August. Fitch learned of a camp of Texas Rangers in Patterson's Deadening, about two miles south of "'Uncle Billy [Baily] Kendall's'" property, located west of Big Creek, and sent in a detachment of the Fifth, supported by the First Indiana artillery. Dismounted, the cavalrymen closed in on the property, but the "underbrush was so matted together with Cane and Biers that it was impossible to charge," let alone see any Rebel troops. Shots from the First Indiana's steel guns towards the Milton Norton house dislodged the Texans, who hastily withdrew. The Fifth drew up in line to apprehend any who might attempt an escape, but the Texans eluded capture.[21]

That evening at their camp on Big Cypress Creek, the Fifth received a visit from a plantation owner who had lost his slave. He had also missed a mule that the "boys had 'appropriated' . . . for the U.S. Service." Mann conversed with the Southerner about slavery, arguing that confiscation of slave property was one way of winning the war. The slave owner called the Illinoisans "ungenerous" and took a religious perspective on the "war and slavery," stating that "Slavery was justified in the Scripture." Mann, a devout Presbyterian, knew the passage but reminded the slaveholder of another passage that stated man should "enjoy the good of all his labor, it is the gift of God."[22] The sergeant insisted the Southerner remained a traitor to his government and left the man by the side of the road still proclaiming the religious justification for the peculiar institution.

The Federals marched through a cool, cloudy morning, arriving at Clarendon by 9:00 on 7 August. After establishing camp, Captain McConkey, Co. E, commanded a foraging expedition to William S. Pride's plantation, in Duncan Township, seven miles below Clarendon. The Northerners were appalled to see the condition of the plantation, where the "feeble[,] decrepit, old man," who had no Caucasian wife, had used his female slaves to produce "numerous mulatto children." Mann believed Pride had little intellectual capacity or culture. The boys drew freely from Pride's cultivated fields, filling their wagons full of "watermelons, peaches, honey, poultry, and bacon." During the expedition, the Federals lived well off the provisions from "the best the land could afford," stripping plantations owned by Confederate sympathizers. "When everything is abandoned by the owners[,] our boys seize it as contraband. Treason is enjoying its reward." After confiscating a supply of young chickens and frying them for dinner, Mann entertained the notion that "this [was] the bright side of a soldier[']s life."[23]

During its stay at Clarendon, Hovey's detachment received hundreds of escaped slaves into camp. Hovey later employed them as teamsters, freeing the Federal soldiers detailed for that purpose. The prairie boys learned from a slave that owners took their chattel to southern Arkansas and northern Texas to elude Federal confiscation of their property. Many owners told their slaves that if they ran away to the Federal lines, Lincoln's men would hang or kill them. Mann, surprised by this statement, asked the slaves if they truly believed this falsehood. The freedman answered, "[we] lets on dat we b'lieve all dey say but we do'nt." The naïve battalion officer learned that "slave 'property' is <u>peculiar</u>, and <u>thinks</u> for itself sometimes."[24]

Wiley again relied on McConkey, one of the ablest officers in the regiment, to command a scout sent to Aberdeen and Harrison's Ferry, to gather cattle for the expedition; both locations sitting four to six miles southwest of Clarendon on the White River. A few days earlier on 9 August, the First Indiana used their steel cannons to shell the woods opposite the ferry, scattering the partisan band that used Aberdeen as a base. Unaware of the Rebels' return, the overheated and exhausted Fifth rode sluggishly down the bank of the White toward town. Suddenly the Rebels opened fire with "at least one hundred shots . . . from the other side of a small creek or Bayou." McConkey ordered his men into the timber opposite of where the Rebels concealed themselves, with one company dismounted, "secreted at the bank to await a nearer approach" of the enemy. The men dove for cover, but nothing was worse than waiting for another volley from the enemy—that was when panic and terror gripped the soldiers, making the heart pound and the hands shake with anxiety. Finally overwhelmed by angst, the boys fired their first volley before the Rebels moved within firing range, causing the Texans to mount their horses and escape. McConkey did not pursue because of their horses' fatigue. The Fifth killed two Texans, while not sustaining any injury, though some of the boys boasted about the holes they received in their clothing. Burke had his "bridle rein . . . cut [in] half in two within an inch of my hand[,] and a buck shot struck the Brass guard on the front of my saddle but glanced off doing no harm." On returning to Clarendon, the Fifth received orders to march the next day for Helena, and "joy reign[ed] throughout the camp" that night, for soldiers "enjoy a march much better than laying in camp."[25]

Hovey had his men on the road by four in the morning of 14 August, with McConkey and four companies of the Fifth in the advance. Ten miles from Clarendon, Fitch took McConkey's command and left the main road to capture Francis P. Redmond and B. Joel Lambert, both suspected guerilla captains, but Fitch found both plantations abandoned. McConkey's men moved down to Big Cypress Creek and established camp. They immediately searched nearby houses for contraband and were rewarded with arms and horse equipment owned by men of the Fifth who had been captured a few weeks earlier. Hovey's column arrived later in the day. As the entire command moved out the next morning, Rebel guerrillas shot and killed Robert T. Larne of Company A. The vengeful Fifth requested permission to pursue the scoundrels, but Hovey refused until ten in the evening of 16 August. By then it was too late, but McConkey and a small detachment made an effort. Riding back almost four miles, they surrounded several houses, but they found no one at home except women. Mann believed "the villians too cunning to be found at home when Yankee [force] is in the vicinity."[26]

Along the route to Helena, the soldiers encountered angry slave owners demanding the return of their property. In one incident at Trenton, a juvenile slave approached Mann while he drew water from a well. The boy wanted to join the Yankees, but an "old rebel citizen" tried to grab the child to return to his master. Mann, of course, came to the child's rescue and threatened the old man with bodily harm if he touched the "juvenile 'chattel.'" Surprise crossed the man's face, for he believed that the Federal army had a policy of "returning the slaves that ran away from their masters." After informing the Southerner of the Fifth's policy, Mann took the newly freed slave and rode away believing that "there are a good many more crazy men in the south. . . . it is a disease prevailing in the south called, 'nigger on the brain,' but is easily cured, by blistering the patient severly with a plaster made of 'Lincoln hirelings.'" The regiment reached their main camp at Helena the next day about noon and "indulged in a good sleep [in the] afternoon."[27]

On returning to camp, Wiley succumbed to bilious fever (malaria or typhus). Rheumatism extended his prostrations, forcing Wiley to command from his sick bed while Wilson remained in Illinois. Rumors passed through camp that Wilson planned on resigning due to poor health. The thought of Wiley becoming colonel with Wilson's resignation created anxiety among the rank and file. John Mann, who seemed to possess an acute ear for camp scuttlebutt, heard that Captain Cox and Dr. Charles Higgins had circulated and presented to Yates a petition requesting Seley for the colonelcy over Wiley. "Very few of the officers or men in the regiment would be in favor of Col Wiley getting the appointment. . . . The regiment does not like Col Wiley and [has] very little respect for

Major Apperson, and if Col Wilson leaves there will be a bad state of feeling among both the officers and men." Packard knew and respected Seley from Bloomington, a feeling, the lieutenant noted, that was held by almost all the commissioned officers. "Major Seley is quite a favorite with the men. He is Keen and is always on the alert, and always out with his Men." Though the rumors about Wilson's resignation proved false, the petition against Wiley and Apperson created animosity between the commissioned officers, which festered until the summer of 1863.[28]

Disease and sickness quickly spread through all the regimental camps. By the late summer, nearly 44 percent, fewer than sixteen thousand men out of the army's total aggregate of twenty-eight thousand, were available for duty. Curtis's grand Army of the Southwest became an enervated military body held in abeyance by environmentally induced pathogens that medical science was incapable of diagnosing, treating properly, or curing. To relieve the situation, the War Department ordered all sick men at Helena sent to Northern hospitals. Roe described the worsening situation to his wife, Celina: "Curtis's Army is laying here yet. [A] large amount of his men are sick and they are dying off fast[;] several are burried every day. . . . It is very sickley here now[,] and in consequence of its being so sickley our Army has been laying still . . . nearly one half of all of our Regiment is now sick and many are dying."[29]

During the Civil War, no one understood the etiological cause of disease (germ theory) and the relationship among sanitation, the environment, and health. Federal troops at Helena became further victims of this ignorance on 24 August, when the army decided that brigades should camp together. The Fifth belonged to Washburn's First Brigade, Third Division, under Fitch, who moved his troops to Long Lake, three miles south of Helena, in the river bottom, where soggy ground harbored cesspools for mosquito breeding, and fecal matter mingled with drinking water. The brigade's six cavalry regiments spread out around the lake, with the Fifth making camp on land between two of Pillow's plantations, and were "feeding [their] horses out of his extensive cornfields of green corn." Mann believed the place was "not suitable for a camp of cavalry" and would increase rather than decrease the number of sick men. Packard initially thought the campground agreeable and the lake water "the best of any water I have seen in the State."[30]

Within a few days, however, Packard revised his opinion. "My health is as good as I Can Keep it considering the Locality and Surroundings of this Briggade. They are dieing off fast with billious fevers and Chills. [S]ince we Mooved Camp the Regiment has lost five Men in four days & two out of Co. D." Packard named this new locality "Camp of Death." Within four days of the move, Mann's prediction, unfortunately, held true. "There are two hundred and eighty seven men reported sick in the regiment to day. This is a very large number and will if the sickness continues soon reduce the [r]egiment materially. One or two are dying daily. We should be moved to some place where there is better water. I do not wonder at the large number [of] sick for the water we <u>are compelled</u> to use is enough to make any one sick."[31]

The Federal army was also stricken with malaria immediately upon arrival at Helena. In the 1800s, people believed malaria to be an environmentally induced and atmospherically transmitted disease caused by vegetable decomposition. When vegetable matter decayed, it produced a noxious, yet subtle gas (miasma) that people then breathed into the human body through the respiratory tract, producing illness. Today we know mosquitoes spread malaria, which debilitates the patient by destroying human hemoglobin and is characterized by a cycle of fever, chills, and sweating. The cycle begins with a shivering cold, rapid pulse, and vomiting of blood that may last up to an hour. This stage is followed by a high fever. During the final stage of the cycle, the fever breaks, the vomiting stops, the headache eases, and the patient sweats. The stage may last up to four hours, allowing the patient to sleep before the entire cycle begins again. As the disease progresses the spleen swells and anemia develops as does jaundice with liver damage. Frequent relapses are a common characteristic of the disease, and a person can be re-infected, and carry multiple infections simultaneously. Malaria, with its recurring bouts of chills and fever, affected the fighting strength and effectiveness of not only the Fifth, but also the entire military body at Helena.

Quinine quieted the fever/chill stages, but many soldiers hated taking the drug because of its bitter taste and its side effects of severe diarrhea and the shakes. Packard asked Dr. Higgins for an alternative treatment, but he had none. The Vermont-born sergeant, however, had no faith in either the drug or the physician; instead, he preferred to use homeopathic medicines, but his had "lost Much of its Strength." He hoped to resupply when his wife Jennie sent a package from Illinois, believing he could not obtain any while in Arkansas, for "Homeopaths are scarcer then hen[']s teeth in the armey." As a last resort, Packard "was Oblige[d] to resort to the Horse Doctor for Medicine."[32]

Wilson told his company officers he would move camp away from the miasma as soon as possible for the sickness would deplete the regiment of able-bodied men. Packard cursed the brigade officers for making the

initial move solely for the benefit of gathering the regiments in one loca-
tion. "[T]hey had better let the brigade go to thunder; then let the Men
All die in the Swamp. . . . God send More Wisdom to our Commanders,"
Packard prayed.[33]

Relief finally came to the brigade on 4 September when Wilson took
command of the Second Brigade, Fourth Division, Army of the Southwest,
upon Fitch's resignation. Command of the regiment fell to Apperson, for
Wiley confined himself to his sick bed. Wilson's first action moved the
Fifth to Beech Grove, a lovely shaded spot at the foot of Crowley's Ridge,
about two miles southwest of Helena. The Fifth also received many ame-
nities because of Wilson's command. Skiles bragged to his parents that
"[w]e have first rate times here now, plenty to eat, ice water to drink, & also
1 ration of Whiskey in the morning & plenty of horse feed. Corn, Oats,
& hay." During the thirteen days the Fifth had camped with the brigade
at Pillow's plantation, ten men from the regiment died from malaria,
typhoid, or murine typhus. "So they drop for want of locality and Care.
I have Seen them all, and my heart has bled to See men die for want of a
'Kind Friend' and propper Care," confessed Packard.[34]

For the prairie soldiers, who had enlisted in the Union army spoiling for
a fight, the romance of war and their dreams of glory came close to van-
ishing as they languished away in Helena hospitals. The Fifth's regimental
hospital quickly overflowed with sick soldiers, resulting in the establish-
ment of brigade and post wards. When these also filled to capacity, soldiers took their sick and sometimes dying friends to local homes. Francis
Wheelock quickly succumbed to a fever in late August, and Packard took
his friend to a "private House down by the River," where another soldier
from Company C convalesced. Ed Beath, who had been a recipient of care
from his friends after his injury during the Doniphan skirmish, cared for
the popular lieutenant. Those that held medical diplomas, but had not
enlisted in the army's medical department, spared considerable time to
the sick during this period. Roe and Calvin Mann moved between private
homes and tents administering to the convalescents. Despite the additional medical assistance, the Illinoisans constantly "hear[d] the Soldiers
death Knell! and all is O[']er as though nothing had happened."[35]

Packard succumbed to intestinal problems, but he believed he was quite
well compared to "Some of Our boys that look as though as their Warfare was about over." By late September, with the hospitals overflowing
and dozens of men dying daily, the medical director of the department
permitted regimental surgeons to furlough one man from each company.
Packard spent the rest of the month trying "to get the Sickest of the Invalids

off to the North with discharges and Furloughs." Other patients, if they were able to get aboard a boat, were sent to Northern hospitals. Packard described the scene: "[There] is three thousand Sick going up the River. . . . I tried to get Frank Ingles [Ingalls] on board the transport with his baggage but there was such a crowd and he was So weak that I could not lug all on board. . . . There will be many poor Suffer[ers] on this trip. Some was dieing! while going onboard of the boat, and Such a Scene I have not Often Witnesses!" Ingalls (1843–1914) survived his illness and spent two more years serving with the regiment.[36]

With so many men sick during September, the regiments could not rally enough soldiers for scouts and expeditions. The standard for the summer and fall of 1862 was to combine small healthy detachments from numerous regiments. For William Vandever's (Ninth Iowa Infantry) expedition to Lawrenceville and St. Charles in mid-September, only three hundred men from the Fifth Illinois, under Apperson, accompanied the troops. The remaining twenty-five hundred troops consisted of detachments from eight other cavalry regiments.

The object of the expedition baffled its participants as they rode fast throughout the humid night of 9 September, resting only once, past a "beautiful little prarie" to a "charming spot [by] a little creek," where the men halted for an hour to feed and water. Jumping back in the saddle, the troops passed through several more prairies "more lovely than the first," and "clothed in all the primitive beauty of unchanged nature." Still they kept their horses at a gallop, hitting the Cotton Plant Road, and riding through heavily timbered areas, finally reaching Clarendon during a heavy thunderstorm at eight in the evening, marching one hundred miles in twenty-four hours. "The rain, darkness, and excessive fatigue occasioned by the long and tedious ride without rest, caused the men, with few exceptions, to lie down and sleep as soon as the column halted" at Clarendon. The ride was so intense that Mann had difficulty rousing company officers to detail men for picket duty.[37]

The men followed the long night's sleep with a "good breakfast of fresh meat and sweet potatoes," before Vandever saddled up the exhausted soldiers. A side trip to the Redmond plantation produced an encounter with Rebel pickets hiding in the brush on the west bank of the Maddox Bayou. Guns from the horsemen dispersed the enemy into the dense underbrush. With little else to do, the Illinoisans decided to quench their appetites from Redmond's plantation. Food became easy pickings for the Fifth, as the "boys slaughtered the old rebel[']s beef, pork, mutton, chickens[,] geese, ducks, and took his sweet potatoes, corn, honey, pots, kettles, buckets and everything they could render useful, leaving his household effects alone unmolested." Samuel N. Wood, Sixth Missouri Cavalry, provost marshal for the expedition, encouraged the boys to loot: "'Boys it is our right to take everything from the rebels that is useful to us, or them, nothing else.'" According to Mann, the prairie boys "followed this rule pretty closely" where it concerned "this rebel guerilla chief."[38]

A steady slow walk two days later brought the troops to Helena in time for supper. Mann had a very poor opinion of Vandever's handling of the mounted troops, believing the infantry colonel had "no proper idea how to move cavalry. . . . Few Infantry officers are qualified to command cavalry." The entire scout, Mann announced, lacked any merit or objective and was barren of results. The sergeant major wondered if Vandever would "be promoted for this brilliant scout?"[39]

With Wilson in command of the Second Brigade, Wiley suffering from fever, and Apperson taken ill during the expedition, regimental command fell to Seley. From his sick bed, Wiley had sought an extended leave of absence to recuperate at home but had failed. The Makanda Quaker was also afflicted with a "keen mental anguish" on learning his two sons had contracted "Scrofulous Ophthalmia of a severe type," from a wounded soldier who had convalesced at the Wiley farm. "Johny says I wish pa was here to night and I expect the poor boy did for he has been blind with sore eyes since [F]riday evening. I have to feed him & lead him where he goes[,] but that is not much for he lays down most of [the] time," Emily informed her husband.[40]

Finally, Wiley obtained a disability certificate signed by regimental surgeon Charles Higgins, who claimed Wiley suffered from a "protracted attack of bilious fever . . . [and] chronic Rhumatism . . . aggravated by exposure in the service." Wiley tendered his unconditional resignation, which Seley accepted and signed, and supposedly sent the paperwork through the official channels. With his twenty-day leave and passes in hand, Wiley boarded a steamboat and left for Jonesboro, Illinois, on 26 September. The position of lieutenant colonel was now open, and members of the regiment began intriguing for the position, pitting field officers against one another.[41]

Further complicating the internal structure of the regiment was the promotion of 1st Maj. Speed Butler to colonel in the regular army in June 1862. With Butler gone, Apperson moved up to first major, while Seley filled the second major's position, leaving the third position open. The jockeying for higher rank became a source of bitter wrangles and enmities, threatening the unity of the regiment and the solidarity of the command structure. By August, "there seem[ed] to be no lack of aspirants for the position. Many of the Captains and some of the Lieutenants, are trying to get the appointment." Many, Mann believed, were "totally incompetent for the place, and not any too well qualified for the positions they now occupy in their companies." Three major contenders vied for the rank: James Farnan, Joseph Cox, and Edward Pierson. Wilson believed he could sway the appointment through an election by the commissioned officers; the winner received his endorsement to Yates. After three ballots, the results favored Cox, but in the end, Farnan received the commission to third major, which had unknowingly been issued by the governor prior to the election. Cox's supporters angered at the results, with blame squarely falling on Wilson, who "should never have ordered the election as the Govenor of the State is alone the proper person to appoint the officers." Due to the bad feelings the voting generated, Wilson prohibited any further election of field officers, relying instead on seniority and merit for promotions.[42]

In August 1861, Congress passed the First Confiscation Act, allowing the Federal army to seize the property of all those openly participating in the rebellion. The act essentially reaffirmed internationally recognized laws of war allowing the seizure of property used by an adversary to aid the war effort. By the end of the year, with the Federal army's defeat on the battlefields, public outcry against the Confederacy demanded a more vigorous approach to curtail Southern activities. Introduced by Lyman Trumbull, but toned down by the Thirty-Seventh Congress, the Second Confiscation Act permitted the Federal government to seize all the real and personal property of anyone in arms against the government, of anyone directly aiding the rebellion, or of anyone offering aid or comfort to the insurgency. To enforce this act, the Federal army confiscated slaves and cotton, commodities that directly fed the Confederate army. By mid-1862, cotton acquisition had become the paramount goal of the Union army at Helena and in other Federally held territory in the Western theater.[43]

Cotton speculators flooded Helena, and Curtis tried to regulate the market by issuing permits allowing traders access to the commodity. Under Curtis, some army officers joined in the market, and many soldiers believed that their commanding officers' interests lay more in acquiring cotton and profit than in the welfare of their troops. Fortunately, neither Wilson nor Wiley ever became involved in cotton profiteering, but the Federal army eventually removed Curtis from Helena on 29 August due to his suspected involvement with the cotton trade. The command of the Army of the Southwest fell to Steele. Rumors abounded as to Steele's loyalty, since he was "a Southern[-]raised man," whom many thought "sympathizes too much with the rebels." Much of the speculation centered on Steele's rejection of Curtis's liberal approach to slaves, which included allowing freed slaves to sell their previous owner's cotton to earn money. Curtis had given refugees currency for food and clothing and permitted regiments to employ the freedmen as teamsters, cooks, and servants. When Steele assumed command of Helena at the end of August, he passed ordinances that restricted freedmen in their liberty and ability to earn a living, forbade Federal officers to employ contraband as servants, and banned freedmen from selling cotton.[44]

Lincoln held a contrary view to Steele's handling of the slave situation. Following the Federal army's victory at Antietam, Maryland (September 1862), Lincoln formally alerted the Confederate states of his intention to free slaves in rebellious states if they did not rejoin the Union by 1 January 1863. This war measure outraged conservative Democrats and Copperheads who suspected that the president's intentions all along centered on emancipation. Two days after his announcement, Lincoln suspended the writ of habeas corpus, which led to the imprisonment without trial of thousands of suspected traitors and war protestors. Copperheads declared Lincoln's proclamation unconstitutional and the suspension of the writ a violation of civil rights.

To appeal to as many people as possible, Copperheads added a racial element to their protests, cultivating the inherent ethnic prejudices found in southern Illinois and the Midwest. Secretary of War Edwin M. Stanton complicated matters on 18 September, when he ordered the northward transport of freed slaves from Arkansas and Tennessee being temporarily held at Cairo. Coming just prior to Lincoln's preliminary proclamation, Illinoisans connected the northward movement of African Americans into their state as a consequence of the proclamation. Democratic antiwar newspapers charged the Republicans with changing the character of the war from one conducted to save the Union to one waged in favor of black equality.

As a result, the Copperheads gained in popularity during the fall elections of 1862, sending a Democratic majority to the Illinois legislature and placing Democrats in many local and county positions. Every Illinois congressional district (7th through 13th) that sent men to serve in the Fifth remained solidly Democratic. The racist quality to the Copperhead's protest resounded with many of the Southern-born people of Egypt, and the political movement established a stronghold in the small towns and villages. To the soldiers, however, the peace rhetoric resonated with treason, and they alleged the Copperheads undermined their efforts in the field and prolonged the war. The movement widened the wedge within southern Illinois society: pitting neighbors against one another, and soldiers against civilians and family members.

Issued on 22 September, the Illinoisans learned of the preliminary Emancipation Proclamation from letters and newspapers. "In a letter from My Wife, She States The President has just issued His proclamation freeing! All! Slaves in the United States!! to take Effect on January 1st 1863," declared Vermont-born Thadeus Packard. Not all Fifth Illinoisans initially accepted the proclamation, but before the foliage turned that second autumn of the war, the attitude of most of the Southern-born prairie boys changed, and they began to view the slaves as men who lacked personal liberty.[45]

The preliminary proclamation, however, did not negate Illinois' Black Laws. Moving through Cairo on his way into Illinois, Wiley assisted freedmen into the state, giving them employment on his farm. Farm laborers became extremely scarce during the war, and many Republicans withstood local sentiment and welcomed African Americans onto their property. Within months of his resignation, the state charged Wiley with "importing blacks with the intent of freeing them from slavery," a violation of the Illinois Black Laws.[46]

Although the war and Stanton's order made the Black Laws legally insignificant, public opinion toward African Americans still echoed hostility. "The policy pursued by the President and Congress will have the effect to deluge the northern border states with a flood of the slaves liberated in the south, and those states must either submit to inundation, or in defense of their interests, make laws to prevent it," cried a Jonesboro, Illinois, newspaper. Organized resistance manifested into violence as people tried to maintain Illinois for the white race. Several months after Wiley's arraignment, a hostile group confronted Emily Wiley, insisting the freedmen leave her employ. A frightened Emily informed Ben that the laborers expected to leave soon but their direction remained uncertain. "Th[e]y have not decided which way th[e]y will go. [They] are afraid if th[e]y go north the[y] could not get to stay and it would cost them just that much more. Th[e]y are talking some of going to Cairo." The Fifth's reaction to Egypt's antiwar sentiments manifested into a regiment-wide writing campaign to Illinois newspapers in January 1863.[47]

As matters stood in the fall of 1862, the Confederates in Arkansas were outnumbered in men and supplies to the point where their only option was fighting a war of attrition. Rebel bands in eastern Arkansas skirmished with Federal foraging parties, snatching up supplies, wagons, and horses; sniped at pickets; and nibbled constantly at Helena's defensive perimeter. The Rebels organized themselves into small parties, usually of fewer than fifty men, that infiltrated the thick dense woods around Helena, where they would attack, take prisoners, and then disappear into the endless swamps of the countryside. This tactic worked well, keeping the Federal army isolated at Helena, where, as one Confederate soldier admitted, "they ... have quit stirring much to keep their men from being 'bushwhacked.'" The Federal soldiers retaliated by plundering and burning plantations and small farms wherever they believed the citizens secretly supported the Confederate cause.[48]

The Fifth became particularly concerned when Rebel partisans attacked and captured a party of First Indiana Cavalry only sixteen miles from the Fifth's camp. "The guerrillas are becoming more bold in this vicinity and if any other man except Gen Steele was in command, they would be severly punished," believed one Egyptian. Steele's willingness or naïveté to accept a landowner's loyalty created a situation in which Southerners professed allegiance while secretly assisting Rebel bands. Soldiers suspected that "loyal" landowners helped the Confederates by harboring them and providing the Rebels with supplies purchased in Helena. Property owners who professed loyalty often requested guards from Steele to protect their estate from Federal scavenging. In one such incident, Steele granted protection to plantation owner Claborne McCalpin after he took the Oath of Allegiance. Steele placed guards around the estate located six miles south of Helena on the Old Town Road. McCalpin's loyalty became clear, however, when Rebels attacked and captured all the guards during their first night's watch on 22 September. When word arrived at Helena of the soldiers' capture, Steele arrested McCalpin and placed him in the guardhouse. Mann's words expressed his feelings of betrayal, "Our boys were very angry about it [the capture of the guards], and will destroy his plantation if they get an opportunity." A few days later on 27 September, Mann's messmates redressed the wrongs inflicted by McCalpin. The Illinoisans "brought much provision in[to] camp from the plantation of McAlpin . . . and we are having plenty to eat."[49]

To control the guerrillas, Federal cavalry spent early October scouting Phillips County. "After being in the Saddle 4 days without much rest[,] I take this opportunity to inform You I am not dead Yet," declared Packard to his wife. The Fifth had just returned from pursuing "One thousand Texas Rangers out on the St. Francis River," after they attacked a detachment of Second Wisconsin. The Fifth and Ninth Illinois, First Indiana, and Sixth Missouri Cavalry regiments, with two batteries, "Started out in hot persuit." A few shots from the First Indiana's steel guns sent the Texans on a "Skedaddle for the Woods," the first night, but the Federals lost them in the dark. Moving onto La Grange, "a Strong Sesesh hole," the troopers "made it Our <u>Quarters</u>." The boys "Killed Some <u>Contreband</u> Chickens and Pigs," and took advantage of the well-stocked homes to fill their empty bellies.[50]

After a "Sweet nights Sleep, on a Stack of Corn fodder" and a healthy breakfast of "Fish & Chicken," the boys rode after the retreating Texans. Passing through the "fine Oak bottom land," and through several plantations, the Fifth found an old slave who guided them to a deserted Texan camp. The boys resumed the saddle, heading for one of the largest plantations in the area. There the Illinoisans "pertook of a few delicases . . . good Sweet Milk, good butter, 'Butter Milk' [and] Honey[.] [I]t was truly a god Send to the perishing!! After being Starved So long in the Old Stinking Camp." With a full stomach, they hit the saddle again, only to find "a [Squad] of Rangers in the Brush." Company C deployed as skirmishers, and was picking up steam to a full gallop, when Lt. Jonas A. Lawrence "run his head plum into a wild grape vine" that nearly dismounted him. Packard, second in command of the company, came to the rescue and managed to keep Lawrence on his horse. The commotion allowed the Texans to escape, and the embarrassed McLean County boys returned to the main column, heading toward Helena. When they returned to camp, the boys mustered for pay, receiving badly needed funds for their service in June and July.[51]

Federal attitudes changed in October when Eugene A. Carr replaced Steele as commander of Helena. Many in the Fifth believed that a change in commanders initiated a policy of no tolerance toward Southern sympathizers and partisan bands. According to Mann, " [Carr] is [a] much better officer than Gen Steele, and has no sort of sympathy for the rebels, but does everything he can to subdue the rebellion, and help the Union cause. He 'treats them as enemies,' and destroyers of our fair land and peaceful homes, that should be whipped instead of coaxed."[52]

Under Carr's direction, officers immediately set out to curtail partisan activity in the marshes and swamps south of the Federal lines. Intelligence reached Hovey that two Confederates named White and Pruit resided at the White Plantation on Long Lake, one of the many small bodies of water scattered throughout the swamp. Hovey ordered two hundred men from the Fifth to proceed to the estate, capture the Rebels, and send them into exile across the Mississippi River. Hovey ordered the large contingency to counter any possibility of surprise by the small Confederate bands that prowled the area. He may also have anticipated trouble with the reported forty armed slaves that guarded the two suspected Confederates.[53]

The following day, 19 October, a Fifth detachment, commanded by McConkey, left Helena on the Old Town Road. They headed toward the lowlands south of Helena, where boggy little streams led from nowhere to nowhere, and where partisan bands held sway. During the rainy season, the area became a large swamp that stretched almost twenty miles to Old Town. The waterlogged ground supported tall cypress trees, whose huge bell-shaped black trunks reached down into the spongy earth. Cane breaks bordered the swamps, and everywhere, even in mid-October, the men heard the buzzing of mosquitoes; some soldiers even spotted alligators in the waters. On higher ground, plantation owners cultivated corn and cotton.

McConkey navigated the Fifth through the swamp without incident until they reached the White plantation, located a few miles north of Old Town. There the soldiers found Pruit, held captive by the armed slaves, but White had escaped to the John A. Craig plantation, near the McCalpin estate. The only other Caucasian at the White estate was the overseer, Lynch. Being held by armed slaves terrified Lynch, and he pleaded with McConkey to leave Pruit or his life would be forfeited. Mann had no sympathy for Lynch and wrote reflectively on the situation in his diary.

> I told [Lynch] we could only leave him to his fate, for our orders were imperetive to set the young man across the river, and that if his life was in danger[,] it was his misfortune (the misfortune of being so closely connected with the institution of slavery, and this the treason of the slaveholders) and he must do as he thought best under the circumstance[:] leave the slaves to their freedom or remain with them <u>untill</u> <u>they freed themselves.</u>
>
> What a strange state of affairs? Here was a man, who: just at the last moment, trembling and Pale with fear, when he saw the real situation he was in, and began to realize the relation he held towards the fifty slaves he h[a]d so long kept in subjection, was ready to cry out for help from the 'abolitionists,' or any one else who could relieve him from the torture of his own victims.[54]

McConkey allowed the slaves to keep their guns, and after searching the plantation, the Illinoisans rode away with Pruit as prisoner, leaving the overseer's fate to the freedmen. By allowing the ex-slaves to remain armed, the captain initiated a policy that the Federal government would not embrace until spring 1863, when the Federal army actively recruited blacks for military service.

McConkey's horsemen rode to the Craig plantation, the largest estate any of the men had seen in Arkansas. One Egyptian soldier recalled his astonishment at seeing such a rich estate in the quagmires around Old Town: "[Craig's] splendid, palatial, brick mansion, surrounded by a lawn and yard, well adorned with trees, flowers, shrubbery, and all the appliances that nature an[d] art could combine. . . . The long row of neat, whitewashed and comfortable, looking 'quarters' for his slaves, added much to the <u>interest</u>, if not the beauty of this fine 'patriarchial' estate."[55]

The cavalrymen, looking bedraggled and frayed after their march through the swamps, halted in Craig's yard; the men promptly dismounted and began their search for the suspected Confederate. McConkey and Mann walked to the main house, where the "Lady of the Mansion" awaited them. Though the woman exhibited "no little degree of trepidation and anxiety" at their approach, Susan Craig greeted the Northern invaders cordially. After she called for her husband, John Craig and White joined the Union officers in the front hall of the mansion. White admitted his identity, "while a shade of anxiety and fear flashed on his face," as McConkey explained that he would be arrested and escorted across the Mississippi River.[56]

Susan Craig declared White to be loyal and a nonpartisan in the war. She explained that many rumors about a person's disloyalty were not true, especially if slaves had supplied the information. Mann's obdurate response startled Mrs. Craig, "The [N]egroes are all the loyal people we find in many places in the south, and we are compelled to look to them for information and depend upon our own judgment as to whether it is correct or not." Mann witnessed Mrs. Craig's mortification that the slave's word was held in higher esteem than her own. The Southern matriarch continued to express her loyalty by claiming friendship with Curtis and Steele, but that only cemented Mann's belief in the Craigs' disloyalty. McConkey paroled White and Pruit and ordered them to stay at the Craig plantation until he obtained further instructions from Carr.[57]

Unknown to the Fifth Illinois or the commanders at Helena, three Partisan cavalry companies had infiltrated the swamps between Old Town and the Federal lines in mid-October. They used the woods around Trenton to hide when Federal columns moved through the area and often ambushed isolated soldiers at the rear of the column. First to arrive was Samuel Corley, whose independent cavalry became Company C in Francis Chrisman's battalion in July 1862. Corley received orders to move toward

Helena to weaken the Federal army "by attacking his pickets and cutting off his foraging and other parties" whenever an opportunity arose. Corley left Cotton Plant on 13 October with approximately fifty-five men and rode toward Trenton, where George W. Rutherford and his fifty-three Arkansans joined the group.[58]

Corley and Rutherford's men navigated through the Arkansas swamps undetected by the Federals for almost a week but could not gain an advantage over a Federal party. On 20 October the partisans encountered Johnson and fifty-seven men of his Texas Spy Company near Trenton. When Corley informed Johnson of his plan to proceed to Old Town "and there lie in wait till [he] could strike a blow," Johnson "expressed his willingness and pleasure to act in concert." The Fifth Illinois had encountered these pestiferous partisans several times since the occupation of Helena three months earlier. The Confederates' combined forces totaled approximately 150 men.[59]

Early in the morning of Wednesday, 22 October, 150 men of the Fifth Illinois left their Beech Grove camp to plunder the rich cornfields at the McCalpin estate. Each company contributed only a few men to the foraging party, due to illness and disability. The more able-bodied soldiers of the Fifth, under Apperson, had left on 20 October for a two-day scout. Not only did the prairie boys lack sufficient men for the foraging detachment, but the regiment also had an inadequate number of experienced, healthy officers to command the men.[60]

With the regiment lacking a senior officer, Hovey appointed the command of the foraging party to Lt. William Elliott, Co. G, which may have been the lieutenant's first solo command. Considering the Confederate activity in the area, and the constant state of alertness needed at the time, Hovey's decision to send the foraging detachment out under the command of a single rookie lieutenant proved unwise.

The Illinoisans saddled up at daylight and moved out on the ridge road with light hearts, anticipating the adventure that lay ahead. They rode south until the column hit the road to Old Town. A wet, heavy fog drifted along the swamp deadening the sound of the wagons, horses, and men, and obscuring the road ahead. A cold autumn mist permeated the air and carried with it a hint of the winter weather to come. Though the fog obscured their line of sight, the Illinoisans rode with confidence and ease, not suspecting that three companies of Confederate cavalry scouted within a few miles of their location.

By chance, Corley and Johnson chose to use the same road the Fifth followed that fateful Wednesday. With fog obscuring his movements, Corley positioned pickets in the cane breaks, while the remainder of his men concealed themselves in the bordering woods. By ten in the morning, pickets informed Corley and Johnson that a Federal column approached their position. The Rebels counted the horsemen and wagons as they passed, and Johnson estimated the foraging party consisted of thirty-two wagons, guarded by 236 Federals: easy pickings for the experienced bushwhackers. The Rebels waited thirty minutes, then withdrew from their concealment and cautiously pursued the Federals down Old Town Road. This tactic placed the Illinoisans in a vulnerable position: isolating the regiment and impeding, if not fully obstructing, their only avenue of escape.

The Fifth's column rode slowly down the pike followed by their heavy wagons until they reached McCalpin's farm. The prairie boys dismounted and, thinking they were safe, left their horses and weapons at the edge of the fields. Teamsters parked the wagons in two of McCalpin's cornfields, while the boys scattered over the two acres. Not expecting trouble, Elliott posted only two pickets on the road by McCalpin's farm, one small group of armed guards in the yard, and a third small group at the edge of the cornfields. None of the guards had a line of sight with any of the other sentinels. According to Roe, "the guard was very small," and Elliott exacerbated the situation by disarming and accompanying the soldiers into the field to gather corn. Another staff officer complained that had Elliott "remained with the excort and have rallied the whole of our boys together[,] they could have checked the Rebels."[61]

The Rebels moved quietly down Old Town Road, so silently that they surprised the first and second set of Illinois pickets, who did not recognize the Rebels until it was too late. The Confederates took the Federals prisoner without firing their guns. From the road, the Rebels witnessed the third group of Illinois pickets at the mouth of the lane leading to the cornfields, and watched as the cavalrymen leisurely gathered corn; their horses pastured near the guards at the field opening. Both Federal parties remained unaware of the Rebel approach. The Confederate captains took a few minutes to outline the plan of attack. Johnson detailed seven men to charge the pickets, while the remainder would advance on the soldiers in the field, with Johnson in the lead.

It was a beautiful and quiet Wednesday morning. The sun had finally risen above the cypress, dissipating the mist, and the boys of the Fifth were enjoying their time away from camp. As they leisurely filled the wagons with corn, many chatted with comrades. They had been at their task for almost an hour when the Rebels attacked. Few Illinoisans considered themselves in danger and consequently, only a few took side arms into the field; many left their weapons, uniforms, and other possessions on their horses while they worked. The peaceful scene was suddenly shattered with shouts from the Texas and Arkansas cavalrymen and the sound of shotgun blasts. As the Rebels rushed into the field, blazing away, many Illinoisans bolted for cover, but a few took a stand, shooting wildly, but with deadly aim. The Fifth wounded two Texans, and one Illinoisan came close to killing Johnson when he shot and killed the captain's old war-horse, Copperhead. The whole field was a pandemonium of gun smoke, shouting men, and the screams of wounded soldiers.

Roe, an unarmed corn gatherer, had anticipated action that morning. Though he took no arms with him into the field, except a pocketknife, he had "expect[ed] an attack & consequently I was not taken by surprise. I told several that mornin[g] that our train would be cut off some of these days & perhaps it would be taken today." When Roe heard the shotgun blasts, he was "not at all excited & consequently I knew that the only chance to escape was [in] running to the thick Kain & hiding [in] the cane[,] wa[s] about 1/4 of a mile off so I ran for that and hid until a Relief came from Helena."[62]

Many Illinoisans did not reach safety and were shot down by Rebel cavalry. Joseph T. Voorhees, Co. F, died instantly when fifteen buckshot pierced his body. The twenty-seven-year-old constable had lived with his newlywed wife in Hutsonville, Crawford County. James B. Martin, Co. M, died of wounds he received in the back while fleeing the attacking Rebels. Surgeons failed to remove all the buckshot, and Martin's wounds mortified, killing him six days after the ambush. Jonathan D. Dryden, Co. E, from Charleston in Coles County, received a wound to his right arm, which crippled him enough to be taken prisoner. Fortunately, Dryden escaped and later received medical care from Federal surgeons; however, his stay in the hospital made him vulnerable to disease, and Dryden died at Jefferson Barracks in St. Louis in January 1863. Leroy P. Kilgore, Co. A, died seven days after being shot in the chest with buckshot.[63]

The strangest story of the ambush involved Rodney Adkins of Co. A. The private claimed Corley shot him in the arm after he had surrendered and was under Confederate guard. Apparently, Confederate surgeons could not remove the spent ball in his arm, and Adkins received a disability discharge for his wound after returning to the regiment in February 1863. John W. Roberts, Co. G, received wounds to his neck and the small of his back. The twenty-two-year-old farm laborer from Oconee, Shelby County, lived but also received a disability discharge in December 1862. By April 1863, the government considered Roberts an invalid, and he received a disability pension for his wounds.[64]

The Confederate attack was flawless—the Illinoisans knew nothing of the Rebel approach. When Corley and Johnson entered the fields, the Fifth boys scattered, "each trying to escape the best way he could and taking care of himself." Corley boasted about the action of his men, many of whom had never seen battle: "So perfectly unsuspecting did they [Fifth Illinois] seem, they did not move till we were within 200 yards of them, when they simultaneously made a general stampede, our troops pursuing; not withstanding their perfect surprise, a few of them fought bravely, but it was to no purpose." The Confederate captain praised all his officers and men who participated, especially the new soldiers, where "there was not a pale cheek" among them.[65]

W. A. Crouch, Rutherford's company, an untried soldier before 22 October, described his baptism of fire in a letter to his wife. "Severel minnie balls came singing near my head, but we kept charging along the lane beside the field untill we came to the gap where they [Fifth Illinois] had gone in the field, and we plunged in right into the midst of them. Some of them fought, but the most of them surrendered or ran off. . . . The most of us did not fire a gun, for we so completly surprised them, that they surrendered without fighting."[66]

Of the 150 Fifth Illinoisans ambushed, eighty-one, including Elliott, became prisoners, while the rest made "a regular skedaddle," narrowly escaping Rebel buckshot or capture. Many, like Roe, escaped their captors by hiding in the cane breaks; eventually a few found their way back to the Fifth's camp at Beech Grove.[67]

The attack lasted only a few minutes, and when the gunfire died away, the Rebels hastily gathered up their prisoners and wagons and retreated toward St. Charles on the White River. Corley knew the Federals would launch a rescue, and he wanted a good head start. A few of the escaped Illinoisans reached the Fifth's camp by one o'clock in the afternoon. Lt. Col. Simeon D. Swan, Fourth Iowa Cavalry, marshaled the rescuers, composed of about one hundred Fifth Illinoisans and detachments from the Fifth Kansas and Fourth Iowa Cavalries, and a battery of artillery, totaling two to three thousand men. The column intercepted Apperson and his detachment returning from their scout, and the number of rescuers increased by one hundred.[68]

The column reached McCalpin's within an hour of the attack. The men were dismayed to see the burnt wagons, the injured and abandoned horses, and their wounded and dead friends left unattended in the fields. Within a few minutes, the prairie boys hiding in the canebrakes broke out of concealment, eager to participate in the rescue. Swan, however,

wasted thirty minutes placing the column into line of battle, "to no visible good purpose," except to ease the lieutenant colonel's belief that the
Confederates planned a second attack. Swan, finally satisfied that the
Rebels had left the area, got the rescue party moving; unfortunately the
Rebels now had at least a ninety-minute head start. The column rode
rapidly for about twelve miles, hoping to catch the Rebels and rescue
their friends. In another misguided moment, Swan ordered a slower pace
to ease pressure on the artillery and their horses and then stopped early
to camp. Fifth officers argued vehemently to continue pursuit through
the night, but Swan refused to continue the search. Mann later observed
Swan and the quartermaster imbibing from a liquor bottle the colonel
always carried with him.[69]

The rescuers started early the next morning, but within an hour, Swan
ordered a countermarch to Helena. Again, Fifth officers remarked about
Swan's lack of effort, but to little effect. Mann penned the feelings of many
Egyptians: "I felt chegrined to think we were compelled to obey such an
incompetent and inefficient officer as Col Swan and thereby allow our
captured comrades to suffer in confinement when a little activity and
energy on our part would have relieved them."[70]

As the last of the twilight melted into darkness, many soldiers considered the fate of their friends and family members, lost or wounded
during the attack. Mann expressed his grief in a letter to his wife Nancy:
"O my dear wife could [you] have realized the feeling of us all when we
got the news of the loss of our train and escort. War is terrible indeed
and its scenes hardens all hearts to cries for pity." Fortunately, Mann
found solace with his messmates Henry Gilbreath (1841–1924) and Jacob
Hooker (1831–1915), who managed to escape, but Mann felt the loss of
his best friend, Thomas H. Barnfield, who could not be found after the
ambush. "'T.H.B.,' my friend, the life of our mess and of the company, was
among the missing. Was he wounded or taken prisoner without being
hurt?, were the questions often passing through my mind, unanswered."
Many Fifth Illinoisans contemplated the same uncertainties, for at least
thirty captured cavalrymen shared their service in the regiment with a
blood relative.[71]

Early Thursday morning, 23 October, McConkey organized seven companies of the regiment to head back to the McCalpin plantation to retrieve
the abandoned wagons and search for more survivors. They found several
wagons, mired in mud, at the Johnson plantation. The boys exacted retribution, burning every building at the estate; the same fate McCalpin's and
other plantations in the area suffered the day before by a rancorous party

of Fifth Illinoisans under Captain Mumford. According to Mumford, Apperson ordered his party to "burn every plantation on the road," and the captain carried the orders out to such an extent, the authorities arrested and tried the captain by court-martial for the destruction. According to witnesses, Apperson also ordered Mumford to "hang every White man [or] overseer" found in the neighborhood of the ambush. The country, an Egyptian diarist described, was laid to "waste with [the] desolation of war. Such a scene of devastation I had never before witnessed. Splendid mansions, large cotton barns, stables and meat and carriages, houses were all in ashes. . . . Chared remains and smoking ruins is all that [is] now to be seen of those once stately edifices. The comforts and luxury of peace, have been exchanged for the devasting scenes of war."[72]

The troops carried off anything from the homes that would be useful in camp. Mann believed "the citizens who induced the attack and capture of our forage trains have been severly punished, in fact they are ruined. 'Those who draw the sword, must perish by the sword.'" The soldiers spared nothing except the slaves' quarters, "showing how fully [we] sympathize with these creatures, who are the only friends we find here."[73]

Corley and Johnson took their prisoners to Little Rock, where the Illinoisans were confined, but treated well, "or at least as well as it was in their power to treat them." The prisoners ate parched corn, fresh beef, and corn bread, but, to the chagrin of some, no coffee or tea, just cold water. The prisoners received paroles quickly, and by early November 1862, many returned to the Beech Grove camp. On 29 December, the prisoners moved to a parole camp at Benton Barracks in St. Louis and remained there until they could be exchanged (on paper) for paroled Confederates. Thomas H. Barnfield returned to his messmates in good health and received a promotion to second lieutenant in March 1863. Some twenty-four Fifth Illinoisans did not travel to St. Louis but instead considered themselves out of the war and returned home for an unofficial extended furlough. Many did not return to the regiment until March 1863, and consequently, regimental authorities listed these men as absent without leave.[74]

A healthy Hall Wilson, lugging .52 caliber Cosmopolitan carbines, returned to his depleted regiment four days after the ambush. The only person he held responsible for the debacle was Hovey for "Sending out an ineficient force to forage." Though Wilson's superiors looked for accountability within the regiment, no evidence exists to suggest Federal authorities punished Elliott and Apperson for their poor judgment. This may have been due to two reasons: Elliott remained a paroled prisoner until March or April 1863, and no one, not even the Fifth's brigade commander, Cyrus

Bussey, knew who commanded the regiment that fateful October day. Elliott remained with the regiment as first lieutenant of Company G, but his actions at McCalpin's plantation caused many officers to question his abilities. When the captaincy of the company became available in January 1863, due to Harvey's resignation, Wilson recommended Sgt. Benjamin Hopkins (1838–1925) in a letter to Fuller because Elliott's actions on that day "reflect strongly against his efficiency as an officer."[75]

Hopkins superseded Elliott to the captaincy. An Englishman by birth, Hopkins had crossed the Atlantic at age fourteen, landed at New Orleans, then taken a boat for Pike County, where he settled in Griggsville. In his letter of recommendation, the Fifth's colonel labeled Hopkins a "man of great energy & industry," who would "fill the [captaincy] . . . efficiently."[76]

Kendall B. Peniwell (1835–1903) received the captain's commission for Company B in October after Thomas McKee resigned due to poor health in July. Peniwell, an unmarried farm laborer, lived with his father and two sisters in Moultrie County before the war. He had served only three months as second lieutenant of the company when Yates promoted him to captain. Peniwell remained with the company until his term expired in February 1865. Company B also received Ohio native Clement March (1836–90) as its new first lieutenant, after Alfred Thayer resigned in April due to health issues.[77]

The regiment lost more men at the end of October due to General Orders No. 126 issued by the secretary of war, dated 6 September 1862. The army streamlined regiments, mustering out all supernumerary and noncommissioned battalion officers. The regiment lost seventeen soldiers, including John Mann. "After part[ing] in sorrow" from his brother and the Randolph Rangers, Mann was "Homeward Bound," to his wife and three young daughters.[78]

4

Under Grant's Command
November 1862 to May 1863

When Withers and Farnan returned to Helena in November, they brought new recruits from Illinois. Including the sixteen who joined in August 1862, the regiment received forty-seven new souls: twenty-nine from Egypt, fifteen from central Illinois, one from Maryland, and two from unknown parts. These men replaced the sixty-three prairie boys who had died of disease during the summer and fall epidemics at Helena. The regiment also witnessed the advancement of two others within the regiment. Alexander Jessop received the captaincy of Company M, while the governor gave Calvin Mann the captain's commission for Company K after Farnan's promotion to third major. Steele also returned to command the Helena troops on 8 November.[1]

On 26 November, the Illinoisans saddled up for their first foray into Mississippi against the Mississippi Central Railroad. This move coincided with Grant's thrust into central Mississippi against Van Dorn's army. After the Confederates' disastrous defeat at Corinth, Van Dorn retreated to Holly Springs and Grand Junction on the Mississippi Central Railroad. By the second week of November, Grant was moving his army south, dislodging the Confederates as they retreated south of Holly Springs and the Tallahatchie River. Grant's swift move caused John C. Pemberton, new commander of the Department of Mississippi and East Louisiana, to fortify behind the Tallahatchie, near Abbeville.

When Curtis learned of Grant's movement, he formulated a plan to use the Helena troops, under Steele, to cut off the Confederate retreat by destroying major railroad bridges behind Confederate lines at Grenada. This small Mississippi town occupied a strategic position where the Mississippi Central met the Mississippi and Tennessee Railroad, on the south bank of the Yalobusha River. Federals at Grenada would essentially trap

Pemberton's army between themselves and Grant's Army of the Tennessee moving down the Mississippi Central Railroad. With the destruction of any organized Confederate resistance, Grant would be free to capture Vicksburg and open the Mississippi River to the gulf.

Steele's forces under Hovey, with seven thousand infantry and artillery, and nineteen hundred cavalry under Washburn, were tasked with a quick strike against the railroad at Grenada. Hall Wilson commanded the First Brigade, which contained 212 men from the Fifth Illinois under Seley and detachments from the First Indiana with their four steel guns, the Ninth Illinois, and the Third and Fourth Iowa Cavalry regiments. The Second Brigade contained detachments from the Second Wisconsin, Sixth Missouri, and other cavalry regiments.[2]

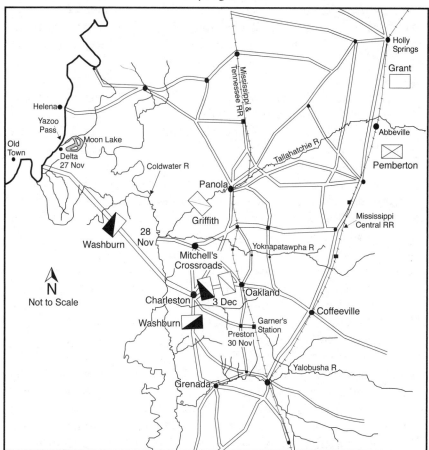

Map 4.1. C. C. Washburn's Grenada, Mississippi, expedition, 27 November to 5 December 1862.

Boarding transports, Washburn's horsemen arrived at Delta, Mississippi, on the afternoon of 27 November, disembarked, and encamped. The next morning, Washburn moved his forces toward the confluence of the Coldwater and Tallahatchie Rivers, where they encountered a group of sixty Rebels across the waterway. Shells from the First Indiana's steel guns, supported by the cavalry's carbines, urged the Rebels to flee "with the utmost precipitation," leaving behind arms and horses strewn over the ground. The Federal horsemen crossed the Tallahatchie by daylight, connecting with Hovey and the infantry.[3]

At daybreak, Washburn pushed his troops hard, following the road along the south bank of the Yoknapatawpha River (Yokna). Resistance occurred at Mitchell's Crossroads when the Sixth Missouri skirmished with pickets from John S. Griffith's Texas Cavalry Brigade on the Panola Road. After dislodging the Confederates, they headed south to Preston, a small town only sixteen miles from Grenada and four miles west of the Mississippi and Tennessee Railroad, early 30 November. After failing to capture the train at Hardy Station, Washburn ordered two hundred men from the Second Wisconsin and the Fifth Illinois to ride to Garner's Station and destroy bridges and the telegraph, and if possible, capture the northbound train. The raiders succeeded in destroying about one hundred feet of the railroad bridge but were unable to reach the Mississippi Central due to dense underbrush around Jonathan Perry's Creek. The disappointed raiders quickly caught up with Washburn, where they found the exhausted column resting in camp four miles southeast of Charleston.[4]

A rainy 3 December opened with rumors of a concentrated Rebel line on the road to Oakland. The Fifth "marched there about 1½ miles," but before the regiment reached the field, "our advance was attacked by a Texas Reg. No. 12[,] who had formed in line of battle." After an hour-long skirmish, in which the Texan "Charge was [a] desperate one," the Rebels made off with one of the First Indiana Cavalry's little steel guns. Washburn's cavalry eventually pushed the Texans through Oakland.[5]

Believing that Washburn had damaged the rail lines, Steele ordered Hovey's return to Helena. Washburn's column of two thousand horses quickly churned the soggy roads into thick viscous ooze, making the march that much more difficult for the exhausted horses and their riders. After slogging through thick, cold mud for a day and a half, the exhausted Federals finally reached their transports at Delta, boarded, and rode back to Helena, entering their camps on the night of 7 December. The cavalry destroyed a few bridges and downed telegraph lines in Mississippi, but the damage was minimal and temporary. Confederate forces had the rail line running again within twenty-four hours. The prairie boys had a "fine time exceptt some wet weather," with "plenty of chickens[,] sweetpotatoes, &c" to eat. Washburn's column rode deep into Confederate territory and defeated Texas cavalrymen in several intense engagements, causing the Confederates to abandon their fortified line on the Tallahatchie and withdraw to the Yalobusha River. Any sense of victory the Federals felt for the Confederate's retreat, however, was soon overshadowed with the loss of Grant's supply depot at Holly Springs a few days later.[6]

Curtis again removed Steele from command at Helena and replaced him with Willis A. Gorman on 3 December. Many believed Gorman would "make a better administrative officer than General Steele." Others hoped the general would supplant Steele's decidedly favorable policy toward slave owners, and that there would be no more freedmen returned to their masters. Newly promoted 2nd Lt. John Mann, who reenlisted in the regiment in December, called Gorman "an 'old blow'" who was prone to folly.[7]

On 15 December, Washburn assumed command of the cavalry at Helena. His horsemen considered him the "best cavalry officer in the Southwest," who combined solid character, talents, and honesty. The Wisconsin general organized his cavalry division into two brigades. Col. Conrad Baker commanded the First Brigade, which contained the Fifth Illinois, the First Indiana, and detachments of the Tenth Illinois and First and Sixth Missouri Cavalry regiments. Col. Cyrus Bussey, Third Iowa Cavalry, commanded the Ninth Illinois and detachments of the Third and Fourth Iowa, Second Arkansas, Fifth Kansas, and Second Wisconsin in the Second Brigade.[8]

December also witnessed an escalation in hostilities in the incendiary region of Phillips County, with the bold and brazen Confederate guerillas often attacking pickets just outside the Helena lines. John Burke complained that, "the Guerilas around here are getting very troublesome." When Steele and his division of thirteen thousand joined Grant in Mississippi on 22 December, he again depleted the Federal garrison. Gorman claimed that the Helena stronghold had became "so weak in forces now that it invites attack."[9]

During one December week, Rebel guerrillas terrorized freedmen near Helena, ambushed and captured twenty-four guards at their outpost, and bushwhacked forty Federals near Jeffersonville. In response, Gorman sent out detachments of the Fifth Illinois (under Farnan), the Fifth Kansas, and the First Indiana on an offensive to hunt down and capture any Confederate cavalry around Helena. Leaving on 17 December, the cavalry, with the First Indiana's three steel guns, commanded by William Wood, rode northwest toward La Grange. Men from Company M served as the column's three advance guards and six support guards. The advance guards "whent a head about two or three hundred yards about the same distance behind them were six more & the same distance behind them came the advance of the main column," explained Roe. Wood gave the prairie boys strict orders concerning contact with the Rebels: "keep a good look out and if they saw [anyone] to fire and fall back if there were over two or three enemy[;] if there were not . . . [to] rush on them kill or take them [prisoners]." If the advance fired, Roe, commanding the six support guards, would "rush to their rescue as soon as possible to fire upon the enemy[,] and fall back upon the main Column."[10]

Within ten miles of Helena, the advance, consisting of Indiana native Isaac Pritchit (1841–73) and Tennessee native George Jerdan (1837–1912) and Ohio native Frank Burton (1842–1923), came upon a Rebel picket, "sitting on a Log" and oblivious to the Federals' approach. After looking down the barrels of three guns, the picket saw the futility of his situation and immediately surrendered. After sending the prisoner to the main column, the advance encountered a picket of twenty Rebels about a mile down the road. These soldiers were a bit livelier for they "sprang upon their horses, fired at our advance & turned to run." Pritchit and Jerdan returned fire, but Burton's gun failed. The Fifth managed to hit two horses, causing one to fall into a gully on top of its rider and seriously injure him; the other was thrown from his horse. The Egyptians took both Rebels prisoner.[11]

The terrified Texans swiftly rode over the upcoming hill and out of sight of the guards. The Fifth advance combined their forces and "put off after the retreating Rebels as fast as our horses could run." A running fight ensued, with the prairie boys "[shooting] at them 50 or 100 times," and the Texans "occasionally would turn & shoote at us." The Egyptians saw blood from injured horses and Confederates splashed over the road for six to eight miles during the pursuit. They chased the Texans "all day & part of the night," capturing about eleven men and the same number of horses. Wood brought his men and jaded horses to Helena the following day.[12]

Nothing special occurred for the men on Christmas day. The command did not provide a special dinner, nor did the majority of the men commemorate the holiday. John Mann reflected on the war and its progress. He had once speculated, as did many soldiers, that the war would end by the beginning of 1863. The lieutenant now believed he could not "pretend to form any correct conclusion about the war from the present state of its progress. That it will be much longer than we at first expected is very plain but nothing definite as to the end is to be seen. It may be in a few months or it may last years."[13]

Gorman ordered Baker's cavalry back in the saddle at the end of December to hunt down Johnson's Texas Spy Company, who had been ambushing Federals near La Grange. Baker moved out on the St. Francis Road, with Calvin Mann commanding the detachment of the Fifth, consisting of Companies I, K, and L. The men camped at Dick Anderson's plantation, just past La Grange, taking advantage of the estate's resources, "eat[ing] up all his corn, Bacon, Pork, Sugar Molasses, chickens, sweet Potatoes, [and] turkies." Despite Baker's orders to stay on high alert, Johnson's men managed to kill a Second Wisconsin picket, only 150 yards from the sleeping Federals. The next morning, the Wisconsin and Missouri regiments returned to Helena, while the Fifth Illinois and First Indiana reconnoitered the six miles to Marianna, returning to Anderson's plantation within a few hours.[14]

Pickets rode in during the evening meal announcing the presence of a group of Rebels at La Grange. Baker sent Calvin and Lt. Harrison Brown, Co. L, to their saddles, the boys riding off full speed with Brown's squad in the advance. They quickly "coaxed up a 'Reb,'" and a squad under Sgt. Joseph Neville (1841–1900) chased the Confederate through town and into a swamp in the timber, "and were soon out of sight." Soon Calvin and the detachment heard shots fired in the direction of the wetland and "had us to fear they were ambushed." The captain ordered his men to support and they dashed off in the direction of the shots, only to find Neville and his squad bringing in a prisoner. "After a laugh," the boys returned to Marianna without further incident.[15]

A second encounter with the pickets occurred shortly after Calvin's return. Baker placed his force in line of battle, as a detachment of the First Indiana "dashed out to reinforce the pickets." The Hoosiers brought their steel guns to bear and fired a few shots at the Rebels, who soon "skedadled in double quick." The affair made for "an exciting time, over which [the boys] had a good laugh." For the first time, though, Lt. John Mann felt the burden of responsibility of command: "the safety of many good men depended upon my action. I felt equal to [the] occasion, but a volly of leaden missiles might have changed the whole aspect of affairs."[16]

Scouts to the La Grange area continued throughout January; most of the time the Federals saw a few Confederates but had no significant fight with them. John Mann believed that the Federals should scout more often, and use the resources available on the plantations, "for our boys will eat and destroy anything around the country, so that the rebels cannot live."

After the La Grange Road pickets had been fired on nightly for a week, Gorman sent three regiments of cavalry and four of infantry to reinforce the guards. They stayed only overnight, lying on their arms, and returning to camp the next morning. Again, Mann voiced his discontent: "It is a shame that so many men are kept up all night, when one regiment could repulse all the rebel[s] near this place if they were concentrated and made an attack."[17]

The new year also brought the fruition of plans to capture Arkansas Post (Fort Hindman) on the Arkansas River, and then Little Rock. The newly completed Confederate fort posed a great threat to any Federal plans against Vicksburg, for the Rebels could easily cut communication lines, capture supply boats, and threaten Helena from the new stronghold. A few weeks earlier, Gen. John C. McClernand and Gorman had formulated plans to secure the post with William Tecumseh Sherman's troops, while Gorman and the Helena forces moved up the White River, capturing Confederate strongholds to DeValls Bluff, the terminus of the railroad to Little Rock and Des Arc. After Arkansas Post fell, Gorman would carry the war into central Arkansas and capture the state capital.[18]

The plan to take Little Rock had been foremost in the mind of every general commanding Helena since July 1862, but the lack of able-bodied soldiers at Helena hampered any interior movement of troops. In mid-January, however, Clinton B. Fisk arrived from Memphis with six infantry regiments, a detachment of the Tenth Missouri Cavalry, and a battery of the First Missouri Light Artillery. Fisk also came with enough steamboats to carry the Helena troops to their destination on the White River.

On 10 January, the prairie boys received orders to pack up and move out, with the intention of permanently leaving Helena for another destination. Many men hoped their objective would be Vicksburg, but unfortunately, they joined Gorman's ill-fated offensive up the White River. Most of the regiment traveled on horse, but a small detachment of the Fifth under Packard accompanied the regiment's baggage on board the *New Sam Gaty*. They shared the boat with sharp shooters from the Twenty-Fourth Iowa Infantry, who were there to "pick off Bushwhackers along the River Banks." A gun from Fort Curtis signaled departure and with the *New Sam Gaty* in advance, the fleet of thirty-two boats left the little river town and chugged downriver. The squadron "Made one of the Grandest Sights My Eyes Ever beheld on Water," remembered a delighted Packard.[19]

The rest of the Fifth Illinois, along with the Fifth Kansas, Ninth Illinois, Second Wisconsin, Fourth Iowa, and First Indiana Cavalry regiments, totaling fifteen hundred men, rode out of Helena on the Lower Little

Rock Road, heading toward St. Charles on 11 January, under the command of Powell Clayton, Fifth Kansas. The Little Rock Road wandered southwesterly through the low swampland, crossing numerous minor and major streams, before veering north, paralleling the White River toward Clarendon. Clayton and the cavalry trudged through knee-deep mire and muck, taking two days to reach three miles west of Big Creek, where they made camp.

The weather dawned warm and muggy Tuesday, 13 January, causing many men to throw away their heavy coats and blankets. In spite of the bad roads, the men rode twenty-five miles and encamped at the plantation of "a rich old rebel where we got plenty of corn, pork, and salt meats." An Egyptian captured a "ragged old 'Butternut' with a shot gun," took him prisoner, and brought him to Calvin Mann. The Rebel's ludicrous appearance prompted the captain to send him to Colonel Wilson as "one of the rebel General Hindman[']s 'body guard.'" Wilson was quite amused at the joke and set the old man free to return to his home.[20]

Rain started during the night and turned the ground into a quagmire of mud by morning. The horses inched along with cold water up to their bellies, and some disappeared in the sloughs; others were lost to sheer exhaustion. The area around the White River, as one soldier described it, was "a more dreary and desolate region." The flat terrain leading from the river allowed the banks to overflow quickly, flooding a countryside populated with canebrakes, vines, and heavy timber "as far back as the eye can see into the forest." As the rain fell in torrents, water rose from nearby swamps and streams and made shallow lakes of the fields. The baleful sky brought with it a cold front, and the men rode through rapidly dropping temperatures, finally making camp at a large plantation three miles from Clarendon. The prairie boys pitched camp, while their commissioned officers quartered in nearby houses. Rain turned into snow by three o'clock in the afternoon, making picket duty a cold, miserable watch. Within hours, the snowfall turned into a regular blizzard, with over a foot on the ground by sundown and turning the air fearfully cold. Both men and horses suffered through the bleak night. Officers had difficulty finding their pickets in the blinding snow and often discovered the posts "by the noise of the horses['] teeth shattering against the bridle." Besides the cold, the men were out of rations, with nothing to eat but sweet potatoes they confiscated from pantries and cellars.[21]

Clayton's cavalry woke to a damp, cutting cold that chilled the soldiers to their weary bones. With snow still falling Thursday morning, the horsemen trudged toward Clarendon, the rendezvous point for the cavalry and Gorman's infantry on the flotilla, arriving around noon. The Fifth's wretched march through the snow was alleviated when they passed a house that had a chained pet bear in the yard. Wilson allowed the regiment to stop and watch the animal's antics, and many conversed with the women who had moved to the fence to watch the column ride past. Putting aside political differences, the two groups intermingled, and all laughed at the "Bar [Bear] Show." When Wilson finally reached Clarendon, he found all the available homes "full of soldiers, & horses" and moved the regiment a mile further down the road to Pikeville. Dusk came early, and the bitter weather turned even colder, but the men found shelter in vacant houses. Tearing down fences rails, the frozen horsemen built large fires in the hearths, and the boys were "able to get our wet clothes dried as well as our blankets and saddles."[22]

Gorman and the boats soon arrived at Clarendon, bringing word of the capture of Arkansas Post by Sherman, along with soldiers' rations of "crackers, coffee, sugar, and salt." Mann also detailed James Nesbit with obtaining meat for Company K, and he returned with "two beaves [beef] and a hog," taken from nearby farms. Frozen, miserable soldiers in the morning turned into soldiers "full of joy and song, as well as, 'grub' in the evening. . . . Good quarters, good fires, and plenty of provision makes us very comfortable although it is very cold."[23]

The men on the boats suffered from severe cold even more than the cavalry. Soon after the crowded boats left Prairie Landing, the heavy rain commenced, soaking the soldiers on deck. As the temperatures dropped overnight, the decks turned into ice rinks, and the men lacked warm accommodations below the decks. When the flotilla arrived at St. Charles on 14 January, accompanied by Commander John G. Walker and his gunboats, many men were on the verge of freezing to death. After disembarking an occupying force, Walker, Gorman, Packard, and the rest of the flotilla continued upriver to Clarendon.

After unloading the much-needed rations at Clarendon in the afternoon of 15 January, Walker and Gorman ascended the White, heading for DeValls Bluff, where they found a "Small Garrison of Rebels there. And they commenced a hasty retreat." Gorman recaptured the Columbiads taken from St. Charles, arms and ammunition, and seventy prisoners, mostly in tattered clothing and barefoot. The cavalry, including Packard and a squad from the Fifth, penetrated the countryside for seven miles along the Little Rock Road, rounding up stray Confederates, though most had escaped by rail. Even hampered by deep, frozen mud, the prairie boys apprehended twenty Rebels. Walker captured Des Arc on 17 January, but unable to pursue any further, Walker returned to Clarendon the next day.[24]

Sunday marked the end of Gorman's advance into Arkansas. With Grant's recall of McClernand, Sherman, and Fisk's brigades to Napoleon, Gorman would be unsupported in his attack on Little Rock. Also, Gorman's mobile arm, Clayton's cavalry, remained powerless and ineffectual at Clarendon due to the flooded countryside. With little to do except picket and guard duty, the Fifth boys passed the time stealing edible commodities and liquor from area plantations. Mann sent out one squad for pork, and the boys, headed by Isaac Castell, "Came in with a hog weighing 200 [lbs] tied to a Butternut Horse[']s tail dragging in the snow . . . and it tasted all the better by coming right after one or two days Short rations." The cold weather and a foot of snow hampered any good feelings for the expedition. "I saw more than one brave fellow have the tears on his cheeks with the cold," confessed Mann.[25]

By 19 January, the cold weather broke, and the horsemen found themselves marching from Clarendon on snow packed "roads very full of water and miry." Horses and soldiers sank deep into thick sucking ooze; every step became a struggle as riders tried to stay on horses that slipped, fell, and sometimes disappeared into mud holes. They finally arrived at Big Creek just after noon on 21 January. The Illinoisans tore down a large log house and carried the logs two hundred yards to the creek and built a bridge. "The men [worked] with a good will, and in great glee," completing the structure in two hours, allowing several regiments to cross by nightfall. One soldier observed that "if the rebels burn the bridges[,] we soon make others out of their houses."[26]

During the meal break at Big Creek, the prairie boys spent their time visiting nearby farmhouses looking for food. When one Egyptian approached a crib to obtain corn for his horse, "a respectable looking [lady] of sixty" came out of the house and told the soldier that "God would not smile on such conduct." The soldier, touched with guilt, started to turn away but quickly changed his mind remarking that his horse needed the corn and he would be obliged to take it. Mann, who witnessed the incident, believed the Illinoisan had some misgivings "as whether it was right to take from such a pious old lady." Another soldier had no reservations when he called at a house and asked for bread. The mistress replied she had none to give, but the soldier "not liking to be 'did up' so completly" pushed his way into the home and found a "large 'pone' of cornbread, which he cooly 'confiscated' and started out eating." This angered the woman, who accused the cavalryman of visiting her before and borrowing her coffee pot with the promise to return it when he was done. The soldier confessed he had not returned the pot because "I'm not done with it yet. I make coffee in it every day." Mann witnessed as the woman "swept into the house with the air of an offended queen, muttering something about 'Yankee thieves.'"[27]

The long shadows of winter greeted the disheartened and discouraged soldiers at their Beech Grove camp, where the men found their warm and cozy shanties, or "what there is left of [them]," either torn down for their resources or occupied by freedmen with smallpox. Many soldiers suffered through the cold winter night without quarters, and the worn-out horses without food or shelter. The men rejoiced, though, when they received packages and mail from loved ones back home. Skiles, who had been plying his parents with tales of packages received by other soldiers, finally received his. "I have recieved the box," he delighted. "It contained 1 Turkey, 1 piece of Beef, 1 can Peaches, 1 roll Butter, 1 big Cake, & some small ones[,] 4 mince pies[,] 4 apples . . . Pop Corn & Ginger Bread. The Turkey was nearly spoiled, all the rest was in fine order." Even after the long exposure on the expedition, he assured his parents that he "was in fine order to eat & enjoy them."[28]

Gorman declared the expedition a success, having captured three Confederate strongholds, 125 prisoners, large numbers of stores and forage, ammunition, railroad cars; and having destroyed track, bridges, and telegraph lines. Fisk, however, concluded the expedition "has not been productive of great results," for nothing of military significance resulted from the expedition. Gorman's assumption that the Confederates had fled eastern Arkansas was proven wrong when the Fifth Kansas discovered a camp of two hundred bushwhackers just outside the Helena lines on 24 January.[29]

The extreme weather conditions led to unbearable hardships during the expedition, and to death and disease once the troops settled back at Helena. Measles, pneumonia, diarrhea, typhoid, bronchitis, and murine typhus (transmitted by fleas) swept through the troops, depleting the number of men available for service, and killing and permanently disabling hundreds more. Many blamed exposure on the boats, especially Fisk, who complained that the men in the two hundred new graves at Helena had been "murdered outright by crowding them into dirty, rotten transports, as closely as slaves. . . . It was a crime against humanity and Heaven, the packing of our brave soldiers on the White River expedition."[30]

The prairie boys did not escape the rampaging diseases. During the trip, Thadeus Packard became racked with diarrhea and weakness, which continued for weeks afterward. Learning that his shanty had been partially torn down and all his furniture and stove stolen while away from camp, Thadeus felt he was living through "the roughest Servise I have Seen Since I Started out." Feeling low and depressed from illness, Thadeus requested of his wife to pray for him while he remained "in bondage." The sergeant relied on his "One true Friend . . . my 'right boner' and firm Friend Sargt A. G. Payne." The sergeant called Payne "the truest bravest Soldier I have Met Yet in the Service" and relied on him to help him get well. Eating a diet of "'been Soup' and 'hard bread,'" which Thadeus considered a "very nourishing diet," he was soon "in the assendancy again." Mann also became ill and feverish, sending him to bed where he was unable even "to sit up." He dreamed of home, where the "kind, soft hand" of his wife smoothed his pillow during his fever. "How sweet is home and friends to us, when we are paralized with disease, and scorched with fever," reflected the lieutenant.[31]

Company K lost 1st Lt. Charles Childs, who resigned due to poor health, but gained Illinois native James Nesbit (1835–65) as first lieutenant. A Spartan house painter, Nesbit became one of the Randolph Rangers' and the regiment's best officers.[32]

The greatest loss for the regiment was the resignation of Colonel Wilson, who never fully recovered from the typhoid and diarrhea he had contracted in the summer of 1862. Wilson struggled with his decision to resign: "My heart is as much in the cause as when I first volunteered, and every consideration of patriotic and personal duty, prompts me to remain where I am, but my judgement plainly points me to the present course, as the only thing left for me to do." The War Department accepted his resignation, and he left the regiment on 10 February. Mann felt the regiment had lost its leader: "His discharge is much regretted by all those who have the good of the Service at heart, as he was such a good officer, and kept the regiment well disciplined and in a high state of efficiency. His general judgement was very correct." The lieutenant noted Wilson's reluctance to leave the regiment when "the hour of departure arrived" and told everyone he would return if his health allowed it.[33]

At the beginning of the war, what could be called the rhetoric of common cause—Save the Union—brought men of disparate backgrounds together to form the Fifth Illinois. As is so common with causes, the original cohesion or enthusiasm eventually wanes, especially with the loss of a leader, and disagreement emerges. Without Wilson to hold the group together, the distrust and suspicion fueled by social and cultural differences of the men's heritage grew, and the internal cohesion of the regiment snapped as the political entities vied for control. According to Mann, "a scramble will now commence among the officers, for the position vacated" by Wilson.[34]

The regiment did not remain leaderless for long, as Ben Wiley returned to the regiment eight days after Wilson traveled north. The Fifth soldiers did not offer the unpopular lieutenant colonel a welcomed return, but as Mann remarked, "he [will] be respected and obeyed." The animosity toward Wiley was "caused by the influence of officers, who wish to drive him out, so they can be promoted," and may have been the reason for the loss of Wiley's resignation. Whoever "lost" Wiley's paperwork wanted the lieutenant colonel gone from the regiment and discredited.[35]

While caring for his sons and nursing his own health in Makanda, Wiley had expected an acknowledgement from Washington about his resignation, but he received no notification. As his health improved, Wiley had second thoughts about leaving the service, and he "wish[ed] to return to my old position and see the end of the war, should God Spare my life." In November 1862, Wiley wrote to his superiors, officially withdrawing his resignation; unfortunately, no one had received it. An ineffectual search of the records of the Departments of Missouri and Mississippi at St. Louis led Wiley to conclude that his resignation had never been received or accepted. The Makanda colonel immediately returned to the regiment on 18 February and requested an official inquiry into the loss of his paperwork. A court of inquiry at the Fourth Iowa Cavalry headquarters convened in early March, with Conrad Baker, First Indiana Cavalry, as judge advocate.[36]

February also witnessed the number of sick increase to such an extent that regiments could no longer properly care for their soldiers. The army took over all the unoccupied houses and buildings in Helena for use as hospitals and "similar government purposes." Buildings were in such high demand as infirmaries that Benjamin Prentiss, who assumed command of the Helena forces on 18 February, permitted only division and brigade commanders to "occupy buildings for their quarters." Diseases spread by unsanitary conditions seemed to be the prevailing illnesses in the camps: High waters of the Mississippi and local creeks sent latrine contents and animal excrement over the landscape, contaminating everything in its path. The thousands of horse, cow, and pig corpses surrounding the camps for miles around became a haven for rodents, which carried fleas infected with *Rickettsia mooseri* bacteria. The fleas spread to human hosts, causing murine typhus, but physicians could not distinguish the disease from malaria or typhoid.[37]

Observing the unhealthy conditions at Helena prompted Prentiss to issue new guidelines for sanitation. "Since Genl Prentice took Command here," observed Packard, "quite a different Order of things Exist." The general directed the burning of all animal and vegetable decay in and around camp, and that "Company Commanders are to Keep their Quarters in a Cleanly healthy Condition." Seley, who commanded the regiment while Wiley waited in court-martial, instructed the men to remove all animal carcasses and burn all "decomposing matter of any kind" before the warm weather. To Packard, the new standards "Suite me to a T," for he could now "get around Camp without holding onto My nose with one hand."[38]

By the beginning of February, Mississippi floodwaters covered much of the bottomland, "the water being up within a few hundred yards" of the Beech Grove camp, creating havoc throughout the town and the camps of the soldiers. Everyone, including horses and mules, struggled through the muck, and the prairie boys had a difficult time rebuilding their shanties and horse stables in the rain. Many men hired freedmen to assist in the building, "with our colored boys getting timber to build stables for our horses." Mann and Nesbit worked out in the woods "in the silent [solitude] of the forest away from the noise and bustle of the camp, where the mind can roam wild and free." A good day of hard work, according to Mann, "is quite a relief to the mind."[39]

The winter months also witnessed the first cases of smallpox at Helena. Smallpox, a highly contagious disease caused by the virus *viriolae*, killed, scarred, and blinded hundreds of millions of people before the advent of immunization in 1796. The War Department during the Civil War provided inoculations in the form of crusts from lesions of infected infants, but many soldiers went untreated. By isolating smallpox patients and caring for them with only inoculated or previously exposed hospital stewards, the medical department at Helena avoided widespread epidemics. The Fifth Illinois suffered seventeen cases of smallpox during the spring of 1863, including Capt. Alexander Jessop. Seven men in the regiment died of the virus. Smallpox affected all regiments at the flooded river port.[40]

As preparation for the campaign against Vicksburg materialized, Grant incorporated the Helena forces into McClernand's Thirteenth Army Corps, Department of the Tennessee on 21 January. The horsemen at Helena became the Second Cavalry Division under Washburn in Grant's Army of the Tennessee. The Fifth served in Baker's First Brigade along with the Tenth Illinois, First Indiana, and Sixth Missouri Cavalry regiments, together with the mountain howitzers and steel guns. Prentiss continued as the commander of the District of Eastern Arkansas throughout the spring of 1863, but the command of the post of Helena changed hands numerous times, due to ranking discrepancies and order changes within the department. By 4 March, Gorman was back commanding Helena, but two days later, Prentiss assigned Hovey to the position. Within ten days, Gorman took command of the post only to be superseded by Washburn on 2 April. Four days later, Washburn was assigned to duty in west Tennessee, with Hovey returning to the command position, only to be relieved by Leonard F. Ross, who assumed command on 9 April.[41]

Though the incessant rain made life miserable for the men at Helena, the continual high waters in the Mississippi River assisted Grant in his preparations to capture Vicksburg. At the end of January, Grant inaugurated several plans to get either behind or below the Confederate army and its fortifications in Mississippi. While James B. McPherson worked to cut the levee at Lake Providence, providing a way to get below Vicksburg, Grant sent engineers to Mississippi, opposite Helena, to examine and open a way through Moon Lake and the Yazoo Pass. In the past, an inlet provided access to Moon Lake, which in turn, flowed into the Yazoo Pass, then to the Coldwater River. From there river traffic entered the Tallahatchie River at Polkville. At the Yalobusha, both rivers merged to form the Yazoo River, which then flowed southwesterly, and emptied into the Mississippi, nine miles above Vicksburg. If Grant opened the inlet into Moon Lake, the Federal army could use the interior rivers to attack the Gibraltar from the rear.

On 2 February, Federal engineers cut the Moon Lake levee, allowing the flooded Mississippi to increase the water level in the Yazoo Pass, and inundating the bayous and countryside between the Mississippi and the Coldwater. Hearing rumors of the Federal's plan, Confederates obstructed the pass with felled trees to block passage into the Coldwater River. After Confederate cavalry harassed and attacked Federal infantry as they removed the driftwood barrier, Prentiss sent detachments from the First Indiana, Fifth Kansas, and Fifth Illinois Cavalries under Lt. Col. William Wood, First Indiana, to guard the troops. Due to his reputation for excellent leadership and bravery, Seley gave Calvin Mann command of the sixty-man Fifth Illinois detachment, despite the captain's grief for the recent death of his only child. Calvin commanded twenty-five men from Company A under Jacob Cullers, and thirty men under Peniwell from Company B, plus a small detachment from Company K.[42]

Wood's three cavalry detachments entered the bayou at Moon Lake and disembarked at Dowd's plantation on the morning of Wednesday, 18 February. The horsemen advanced down the bank of the Yazoo Pass, crossing several bayous, finally bivouacking at Chism's plantation on the pass's north bank, where they built rain shelters from rails and straw. Washburn's boats with the infantry appeared two days later. The general ordered the Kansans to guard the infantry as they cleared out the pass, while the Fifth Illinois and Hoosiers scouted the vicinity for Rebels.[43]

Six miles from camp, on the south side of the pass, Wood's cavalry came across two hundred men of Aaron H. Forrest's Sixth Battalion Mississippi Cavalry, also known as the Sunflower Rangers, an independent cavalry company organized in August 1862. Aaron was Nathan Bedford Forrest's younger brother. Cullers, with Company A, started skirmishing immediately, while Wood ordered Captain Mann to "'take [his] company round through that field on the flank of the enemy and attack them.'" Company K quickly rode off with the Hoosiers serving as support and reserve. Calvin, leading the sweep against the Rebel flank, advanced on the Sunflowers to within long range of the Fifth's Cosmopolitan carbines. The Randolph Rangers formed in line of battle and fired, causing Forrest's men to retreat across the swamp and reform "in line behind some fallen timber," intending to "'hold the post' and 'die in that <u>timber</u>.'" Captain Mann again advanced his men to within 150 yards, reformed his line, with each man firing his carbine as he stepped into formation. Forrest's Rangers fired "from their shot [guns] and squirrel rifles" at the Egyptians, making "the shot rattle all over them in the timber." As the shooting heated up, Calvin yelled at the Hoosiers to get ready to advance, and within minutes, the captain yelled, "Charge Boys!" and "into the fight went 'K' with a yell such as never before resounded within those usually quiet woods."[44]

Believing the Federals dared not cross the swamp, the Sunflower Rangers waited confidently behind fallen trees. With Captain Mann leading, followed closely by Andrew Gordon (1835–1913), Henry Gilbreath, Andrew "Whit" Vance, Company K rushed through the swamp on the "'double quick.'" Stunned, the Sunflower Rangers fired a few ineffectual shots before "they broke and fled each man trying to escape in his own way," in "every direction <u>pell mell</u>." Company K captured many of Forrest's Rangers as they attempted to mount their horses, but a few escaped, and participants could hear sounds of "'Halt,' 'Surrender,' mingled with shots[,] rattle of sabers[,] and the running of horses" from every direction in the woods. The chase continued for almost a mile, described by John Mann as "a death struggle in which all vigor and energy of man[,] both mental and physical[,] is employed." As the sound of battle died in the distance, an "awe-inspiring stillness . . . followed," broken only by the "smothered laugh of the victors, and the sighs and groans of the wounded and dying."[45]

Nesbit relayed stories of the prairie boys' victory when he returned to the Fifth's camp at Helena on 23 February to restock the detachment's ammunition. In one instance, James Gordon ordered a Rebel trying to mount his horse to surrender. When the man refused, Gordon pulled the trigger of his carbine, but the gun misfired. Luckily, Gilbreath and Nesbit witnessed the scene, and both fired simultaneously at the "stubborn traitor," who reeled and bit the dust, with his cocked pistol in his hand. In the end, the Federals killed six, wounded three, and captured fifteen of Forrest's Sunflower Rangers. John Mann noted that Alex Jamison received a "spent shot on the leg" that did not even break the skin. A ball "about as larg[e] as [a] five cent piece," grazed Boyd Cashen's (1838–1905) hand, while Harrison Barnes's horse threw him at the beginning of the skirmish. Unhurt, Barnes captured and confiscated one of the Confederate's horses for his own use. All enjoyed the scene, and as Whit Vance exclaimed, "'it was a half hour[']s enjoyment that equaled any half hour' of this life." Mann's men stayed in Mississippi until the fleet cleared Yazoo Pass and moved into the Coldwater, returning to Helena on 2 March.[46]

When Calvin Mann and the boys returned to Helena, they found the town flooded due to a broken levee. The incessant rain for the previous two weeks had put too much pressure on the small, ineffectual soil barrier. The flooded town wrecked havoc on it citizens and the army. Traveling became dangerous as the mud grew thicker and deeper, and in one instance caused injury to Captain McConkey when his horse slipped in the mud and fell on him, injuring his back and legs. Despite his injury, McConkey stayed on duty, being treated in his tent by the regimental doctors. Skiles complained, "the rain seems unusually wet here. [I]t is so muddy in town that mules get drowned, people stuck, & the streets are blockaded, with broken wagons." Regiments abandoned the low ground around Helena and established camps on Crowley's Ridge, fighting with the infantry for the valuable real estate. Within just a few weeks, the crowded conditions on the high ground created a very unhealthy environment for both animals and soldiers, and Prentiss's new sanitary guidelines became obsolete.[47]

By February, the Federal army owed the prairie boys salary for half a year's service, but when the paymaster arrived in March, the men received only two months' pay. The Fifth grumbled about the unavailability of funds and the hardship on their families. "It is pretty hard on the men that they get only two months pay when there is six due them and they are so much in need of all of it," complained John Mann. Roe, on receiving his pay, discovered he drew less than what he owed the sutler and could send only ten dollars to his wife, Celina. He promised her that he would pay the family's rent when he received his next pay and told her not to worry, that he would "send . . . enough to live upon." The scarcity of funds was not just hard on the soldiers' families, but caused the men to become indebted to the many sutlers plying their wares around Helena. According to Skiles, some soldiers' indebtedness amounted to over a hundred dollars.[48]

In early March, the court found Wiley guilty of being absent "without proper cause" and sent their recommendations to Washington for approval. The Makanda colonel returned to duty on 11 March, and he immediately wrote to Fuller in Illinois, fully confident that the War Department would reverse the "finding of the Court—as it was one selected with Care." He also wanted Fuller to inform his friends in Illinois that he was "once more in My old place . . . the 5th Cav is loyal to the Core." Wiley told his wife, Emily, that he was anxious to have the "matter straitened up soon" so that he could "either stay at home honorabley or remain in the service."[49]

Prentiss changed the social and economic landscape at Helena when he closed the lines around the town in early March, permitting only those citizens who had taken the Oath of Allegiance before the provost marshal to enter. Any Southern male over eighteen years old who refused the oath was arrested and placed outside the lines. The Fifth, on picket duty "every third night," dealt with many irate Southern women who wanted to shop in Helena or visit family. Skiles informed the women of the new rules and recalled their reactions to his parents: "You ought to have seen them turn their noses. One Mrs. King said she would not take the Oath to save Old rotten Government, not to save Old Abe Lincoln[']s neck." The prairie boys quickly recognized Mrs. King as the owner of a home where they had captured a few Rebels, and the officer of the day told her "if she ever came inside of our lines, We would send her up the river a while." By 11 March, Prentiss sealed off Helena even further when he ordered the cessation of all trade with the countryside and stopped traffic except for people with official passes.[50]

The new commander also kept the cavalry busy with constant scouts in search of the remaining Rebels in eastern Arkansas. On 6 March, the ever-popular Maj. Samuel Walker, Fifth Kansas, commanded detachments from several cavalry regiments in search of Texans operating near the White River. As Walker headed south, Farnan took 150 Illinoisans acting as a "reer force" on the Cotton Plant Road, heading west with orders to connect with Walker at a prearranged rendezvous point. Alonzo

Payne, on his "notorious Steed Wild Bill," a horse from the "Wilds of Kansas," acted as advance guard and came across a "Rebel Spy" just east of Lick Creek. Packard described the spy as about "20 Years Old[,] well dressed[,] good looking Young Man" on a fine horse, who had come close to the Federal lines a few nights past and counted the outpost pickets. Payne lost no time in running the spy down, firing his revolver as he rode, until the two reached a muddy creek. Here the spy's horse refused to jump the impediment, and with Payne close on his heels, the Rebel quickly raised his hands and shouted "Surrender." Immediately Rebels appeared on the opposite bank, and a two-hour skirmish ensued, the Rebels firing double-barreled shotguns, while the Fifth had the advantage with their .52 caliber Cosmopolitan carbines. During the altercation, the Confederates abused the white flag, prompting Farnan to send volunteers across the creek to deal with the bushwhackers. With the Fifth lining the bank for support, volunteers headed directly for a house where most of the firing had originated, but the bushwhackers had vacated it. The regiment quickly rode to a nearby hill just in time to see the Rebels "Skeddle out of sight." After crossing back to the eastern bank, Farnan rode to the rendezvous point, but Walker, whom Packard described as "the best & Coolest Commanders in this Service," failed to appear, and the regiment made camp for the night. Packing up early, the Fifth rode back to Beech Grove, accomplishing nothing except the killing of a few Confederates and the capture of a spy.[51]

In mid-March, Washburn assigned Wiley, as senior officer, command of the First Brigade, Second Cavalry Division, a position he held until the regiment left Helena in late May. According to Packard, "Old Ben L. Weley takes Command of the Brigade. We are not Sory." Since Apperson served on a board of court-martial, command of the regiment fell to Seley.[52]

With very little luck in clearing out the Rebels lurking around the lines of Helena, Washburn formulated plans to scout near Cotton Plant, the once-stronghold of Parsons's Texan cavalry. Washburn sent twelve hundred cavalry from both his brigades, supported by two cannon, under Clayton, Fifth Kansas. Seven companies of Illinoisans commanded by Seley accompanied the expedition. The men anticipated a fight with the estimated three thousand Confederate troops, who "have Said Several times They would fight us if we would go there [Cotton Plant]." As dawn broke over the horizon on 20 March, a green landscape and the sweet scent of new spring growth greeted the exhausted men. The men rode out about twenty-five miles before finally stopping for a meal break, and, as usual, sixty Confederates attacked the pickets. However, this time, the

Federals remained vigilant, and "when the [Secesh] come in range of their guns[,] they fired upon them killing the Captain dead." Supposedly, the captain had been wounded nine times prior to facing the prairie boys; his last injury came from an Egyptian rifle with "the Ball [passing] through his Heart, poor fillow."[53]

The Rebels made a second and third charge; "the [Secesh] fired & retreated as before with the same success as before." Finally relinquishing the field, the Rebels retreated, and the Federals mounted up, moving toward Cotton Plant. They reached their destination by the second day, "but nobody to fight," as the Rebels had scattered into the countryside. Local citizens claimed the Rebels had moved nineteen miles "farther up White River." Packard believed "they [were] nightly Scattering in Ark," to avoid "Meeting these 'two' Fifths Boys! [Fifth Illinois and Fifth Kansas]." With rations giving out, Clayton turned back toward Helena, arriving in camp on Tuesday, 24 March. The men found the trip enjoyable, but their horses suffered from the muddy roads and hordes of buffalo gnats. These wretched insects emerged with warm weather and swarmed over the horses, getting into the eyes and nose, and eventually being sucked into the animal's lungs, causing inflammation, and later death. The Fifth Illinois lost over one hundred horses on the march, due to gnats and fatigue.[54]

Spring also welcomed many of the officers' wives to camp. Thadeus Packard had been expecting his wife, Jennie, since November, when he had "erected . . . an Arkansan 'Shanty for . . . [Jennie] to Winter in,' if you are in the notion of Coming." The sergeant had "every thing fixed up," though he warned her "it may not look inviting to You but it is Comfortable be it Ever so humble." He assured Jennie that "We Can Make it Home! for a Season," and if the Rebels did appear, "we Can Make good our retreat under the Cover of 'Our Gunboats.'"[55]

Packard finally welcomed his Jennie in late February, and after a week-long visit, she left for Illinois, towing Packard's horse, Tomey. The horse fared the worst during the White River expedition, and he became "worthless for the Service." Tomey's condition broke Thadeus's heart: "You Cannot think how bad I feel to See him [Tom] So crippled down and Spoil[ed] by Such hard usage. [T]he cordaroy Bridge Spoil[ed] him 'he goes half biped.'" The loss of Jennie and Tom left Packard "so lonesome" and feeling low, but he believed "there [was] no use of Complaining[;] I must take things as the[y] come." He asked Jennie to "Take good car[e] of 'Tomey' and Make him get well."[56]

With three small children, Nancy Mann could not visit her husband, John; instead, he sent his wife "a likeness of your Cavalier" and hoped the photograph would be acceptable to her and their little girls. Mann hoped that "if you love the original well enough, you may place this likeness in your bosom, and allow me the sweet pleasure of thinking my own heart nestles there. Such toys are gems when we are so far from each other from necessity."[57]

Not all men found solace and support in wives and girlfriends, and many suffered the heartbreak of broken relationships. Edward T. Gullcross, Co. G, received a letter in March from "the 'girl' he left behind," learning of her unfaithfulness. Though the distraught and depressed private had survived the ambush at McCalpin's plantation, imprisonment under the Confederates, and months in parole camp, the twenty-nine-year-old Gullcross's will was broken, and he committed suicide by slashing his own throat. Thomas Williams, Co. K, received an anonymous letter informing him of his wife's infidelity and her plans to sell his property and leave him. In the same mail, he received confirmation from his wife, Sarah, who informed Williams that she intended to move to California with his children and the other man. Williams bore the message with dignity, prompting John Mann to express his feelings of regret for the misfortune of "a Steady, quiet, honest man."[58]

A prank at the picket post caused the death of Henry Mansker, when a friend accidentally shot the private in the femur as he faked a saber charge. The ball crushed the bone, but physicians decided not to amputate the leg due to the mortality of the wound. Mansker lingered in the hospital for three weeks before succumbing to a massive infection on 14 April. His brother, his sister-in-law, and Sarah T. Crain, a close friend who had "more than an ordinary interest" in Henry and who had "not forgotten him while in the Service," traveled from Illinois to Helena and stayed by his beside until he died. Burdened by their loss, the trio conveyed the body to Jones Creek, Illinois, for burial.[59]

When Lincoln released the Emancipation Proclamation in January 1863, he changed the character of the war by freeing the slaves in seceded states and welcoming them into the armed services. On the warm spring morning of 6 April, Helena soldiers gathered at Fort Curtis to hear Adj. Gen. Lorenzo Thomas explain the government's new policy for the raising of African American regiments. The soldiers announced their immediate approval with "a Shout of approbation . . . that was such a yell as soldiers only can make." Packard expressed Company C's viewpoint: "we harkly Concur with the President[']s proclamation, and endorce all Measures that go to put down this Rebellion." Wiley knew the proclamation was an important step for the government: "Negro slavery has gone up. You can never make slaves of them after useing them as soldiers & I am glad of it. I hope the war will abolish the institution every where & forever—the more I see of slavery the less I like it."[60]

Guessing the reaction on the home front in Egypt, Fifth soldiers responded with words of praise for the new policy in letters written to home newspapers. With these treatises, the soldiers tried to comfort their friends and family, who feared a society in which the free black laborer would impinge upon white status and citizenship. For many of the men in the Fifth, the proclamation remained only a war measure and was not a move toward African American equality.

Skiles's father, a devout anti-Negro adherent, believed the Emancipation Proclamation caused an influx of freed slaves into Illinois, but he also refused to support the antiwar Democrats. William tried to convince his father that Lincoln was correct to free the slaves, for only then would there "be no slavery questions to agitate, & after the war is over there will be plenty of ways & propositions to dispose of them. . . . [T]he negroes would rather be in the South than North anyhow, & when the war is over[,] they will flock South." The arming of freed slaves became a "Military necessity," for it "weakens the enemy that much, . . . & at the same time help[s] us, instead of the enemy." Skiles believed African Americans "make good soldiers," who "can whip the rebs as well as us & at the same time save our blood."[61]

Robert M. Nelson, Co. H, sent his clarion call to the *Belleville Advocate* and his hometown newspaper the *Nashville Journal*. At the beginning of the war, Nelson recalled, he did not believe in "taking anything from the secession inhabitants," but due to the Rebels' guerrilla tactics, he endorsed the president, even though he was a Democrat. "I close," declared Nelson, "still in favor of the Union and the Constitution."[62]

In his letter of affirmation to the *Nashville Journal*, Washington Crain not only wanted Negroes free and armed but also supported arming anybody or anything "even to a jackass, if he could use a musket." The Egyptian could not understand why some Northern men believed the army "mus'nt touch their negroes . . . The niggers are the main stay of the rebellion, and it is our duty, if we are in earnest, to deprive them of that mainstay." Crain favored the arming of contrabands, but he viewed the proclamation as nothing more than a war measure, which would not lead to racial equality. If he could, he would "hang the rebels; and the negroes I would put to the jumping off place; then kick them off and let them go—'root hog or die.'" As far as Crain was concerned, the men who opposed the proclamation were "a cowardly set of copperheads in Illinois who are trying to discourage our brave boys." The Egyptian's declaration included his support for peace, "but I am for getting it in the right way, and so it will be durable."[63]

Many commissioned officers also sent public statements north to counteract the Copperheads' denunciations of the proclamation. Apperson, an avid Republican, addressed the Copperheads directly in his public statement to the *Mattoon Gazette*: "The boys all endorse the Proclamation and are in favor [of] arming the negro. If a few of your Illinois Coppersnakes had been here they would have showed such a disposition 'to stand from under,' as would have done all loyal hearts good." Apperson warned the Copperheads that if they "don't like it, they had better make up their mind for a 'trip up Salt River' when the boys get home."[64]

Protests against the Copperheads and in support of Lincoln and the proclamation came also from Fifth Democrats. Gordon Webster thanked God "that while I am still one of the true Democratic party, that I do not belong to the damnable faction" of Copperheads. The Company A lieutenant believed he owed allegiance first to "my God, second to my bleeding country," but he owed "no allegiance to traitors." Those who claimed the Emancipation Proclamation made "the nigger the soldier's equal" told "a falsehood." He would rather "fight side by side with a loyal negro" than "stay at home and associate with traitors." Webster warned the Copperheads that the Fifth watched their actions and that they had "provoked the just indignation of the soldier." Eventually the Fifth would call upon all traitors for "public account."[65]

When friends from Randolph County brought news of the "Copperhead traitors" in the region, they incurred the wrath of John Mann. "Just let one single Union man's blood be spilled by them," he declared, "and not one of them will be left to desecrate the loyal State of Illinois." The lieutenant believed the "villianous sneaks" had already been "too base for a soldier already," and if they made "a show of resistance to the Conscript Law," he promised, a "terrible doom awaits them. . . . A Rebel with [a] gun in hand is a gentleman by the side of the sneak at home who strikes at your back." Mann advised his wife to stay at home, guard his family's lives, and leave it to the state militia to take care of things "untill we get there." The Egyptian lieutenant hoped the Union men at home kept up a "bold front" towards the traitors; only then would they "soon cease their treasonable acts and words."[66]

With the local Illinois elections in April, many feared the Copperheads would gain more political power and validation in their hometowns. The men became so agitated with the Peace Democrats' treasonous rhetoric during the election that they met in Apperson's tent to discuss their actions. After hours of debate, the prairie boys developed a set of resolutions, announcing their rejection of the Illinois antiadministration Democrats, whom they labeled "'Copperheads,' 'Sympathizers' and traitors." The soldiers' resolutions were reminders to the Democratic legislature of its duty to support the soldiers and Lincoln's administration; others viewed the resolutions as interference in state politics.[67]

Some Democrats in the regiment, especially Seley and Mumford, believed the language of the regimental decrees pulsated with anti-Democratic sentiments and refused to sign the documents. Mann, supported by Captain Cox, argued against revising the resolutions, each speaking with "feeling, earnestness, and fluency." Eventually the Republicans in the regiment won, and on 24 February, all the commissioned officers, including those initially opposed to the resolutions, unanimously adopted the statements. According to Mann, "the pressure of public sentiment in the regiment was great, that Major Seley and other conditional patriots among the officers were compelled to [sign] the resolutions or lose caste with the appointing power in Illinoi[s]." Democrats who remained loyal to their party, especially those in command positions, like Seley, paid for their allegiance in the form of strained relationships with their regimental mates. These political divisions within the regiment demoralized the men and denied them the strong leadership they needed to be a successful regiment.[68]

With the passage by Congress of the Enrollment Act in March 1863, the Copperhead movement gained strength. The Federal government, with this act, enrolled every able-bodied male between the ages of eighteen and forty-five into Federal service, thus supplying fresh bodies for the Union army. An eligible individual could also pay a substitute to serve for him, or he could pay three hundred dollars not to serve at all, thus padding the war coffers. The draft changed the character of dissent, and the substitution and commutation clauses made the war a poor man's fight.

When the Copperheads complained about the constitutionality of the draft, Richard Rainforth, Co. H, called them on their hypocrisy: "When we left home . . . they favored our cause," but "now it is one long continual whine about arrests, and rights denied them; one continual complaint and threats against those we are protecting and continue to protect." The lieutenant warned them that "their attempt to instill their poison into our men will prove a miserable failure." Rainforth declared the Fifth would never "join in their hellish treason."[69]

As the Copperhead voices grew louder, they rankled and scared many Fifth wives, left alone at home, probably with children, to tend to the family's affairs. When Jennie Packard fretted about the Peace Democrats in Illinois, Thadeus reassured her that the state would never "come under the Yoke & rule of those black[-]headed villians!" Packard claimed the thought of traitors back home caused his "blood to boil and Each particular hair to Stand on End, like So Many bayonets that would Stab to the heart [of the] cowards." The big-hearted sergeant reassured his wife: "By the <u>Great 'Eternal God'</u> this will never do for them to lift their Copperheads now and thrust their fangs into the very hearts of our <u>Dear Ones</u> at <u>Home</u>. No! God Forbid! They Must Come to judgement, though it Should take one third of the Soldiers back that they may wipe out Such Traitor[s] from off the face of the Earth. 'All we want is for the Govenor to Say the word' and the Praires will Swarm with the brave and the true, that cannot and will not let the traitors go unpunished."[70]

Wiley's wife, Emily, whose relatives were strong Democrats and sympathetic to Copperheads, spent the early part of 1863 informing her husband of the Federal deserters lurking in Union County, of the Copperhead meeting in the local school house, and of the Anna riot in April. "The KGC [Knights of the Golden Circle] are getting pretty numerous as I have lately heard that some of our neighbour[s] belong. . . . the soldiers are still arresting citizens and deserters almost eve[r]y day," alerted Emily. Wiley responded with words of encouragement: "Those foolish people in our part of the country who think of opposing the war & the Government do not know what danger they are in. The powers at Washington are getting their places all ready to punish <u>traitors</u> at <u>home</u> as well as in the rebel states. Officers & Soldiers are now at work gathering up deserters & those who befriend them & a great many of the former are being brought back in irons & plenty of them will be shot to let people know that it is death to desert the army, or be a traitor." Wiley told Emily to keep the "'<u>Stars</u> & <u>Stripes</u>' floating over our home," for he intended to have "the Old flag . . . wave over my house as long as I live."[71]

Within two days of Thomas's announcement, cavalrymen witnessed the drilling of two companies of African Americans and saw several recruiting officers working their way through the freedmen community at Helena. Roe described the new soldiers as "a more jovial & happy people[;] their rights are respected . . . their wives & children are clothed & fed." Newly promoted 2nd Lieutenant Packard encouraged his men to seek commissions in black regiments: "Dig out every Mother['] s Son of You and be Officers, and give Old Rebel Jeff Davis the devil in Shape of black clouds, which is an arm of the U.S. Government handled with White Mussal going to the rescue now on the double Quick." Packard never doubted the bravery of newly freed slaves, and he warned Confederates, "Stand from under Ye Slave holders, Ye Southron Aristacracy. Glory to God!! The nigers are all coming right front into line from the Atlantic to the Pacific. Old Jeff Davis m[ight] be flanked by his own Children." Six men from the regiment gained commissions in African American regiments: Marion Brashares, Joseph Hale, Charles S. Mumford, Ziba G. Brown, St. John Vanarnum, and John Breese.[72]

The prairie boys became personally involved in African American recruitment throughout April, scouring the outlying estates for "able bodied negroes and induc[ing] them to enlist." Farnan, with nine companies of the Fifth, set out toward Clarendon, stopping at Eliza Thomson's plantation for a meal. The widow demanded guards from Farnan, who "politely declined" and informed the woman that they would be removing her fifty slaves, taking them to Helena for military use. The slaves, continued Farnan, would be "'arm[ed] . . . and sen[t] . . . out in the country for your protection.'" Eliza assumed an air of defiance and indignation and cried, "'Why sir, you would not set the slaves to fighting those who have raised them, and been so kind to them, would you'?" Farnan's response pleased only his fellow soldiers, "'Loyal negroes are better than white traitors.'" Mann sent a young boy to fetch the slaves from the woods where the mistress had secreted them, and they came in and "got ready to leave their kind mistress and go with us, as free persons." Thomson tried to regain possession of her "property" the next week, but Fifth pickets refused her admittance into the Helena lines.[73]

Within minutes of the slaves' appearance, a messenger from picket, Thomas Barnfield, rode in and informed the major of the presence of Confederates in the woods just beyond the plantation. Companies I and K rode out for battle, and soon the men heard the first volley of fire. The whole command spurred to the rescue but learned Corley's men had fled at the first volley. Farnan broke up the command, sending Capt. Horace Mumford with four companies to La Grange, while he and the rest of the detachment "followed the trail of the rebels for a few miles." A short insignificant skirmish occurred in the evening with about twenty-five of Corley's men, but Companies A and K "thunder[ed] down upon them," scattering them into the woods. The Illinoisans bedded down for the night at a local plantation.[74]

Farnan saddled up early on 10 April and, after connecting with Mumford, rode toward Helena, stopping at homes along the way to confiscate horses and induce the slaves to enlist. A woman objected when an Egyptian led her horse away from its barn, and she screamed at the man to return her riding mare. When that proved unsuccessful, she brandished an eighteen-inch knife and again demanded her mare. The woman's appearance did not help her achieve her goals. Chewing tobacco had turned her mouth black, "while a streak of a darker hue adorned the circle of her mouth, adding immensely to her ludecous appearance." Lieutenant Mann believed that if she "had been less masculine, and more womanly in her display of her feelings, she would have received the respect and attention due her sex, but exhibiting such a disposition to assume masculine <u>airs</u>, she met with the attention due her assumption."[75]

The scout brought in almost one hundred freedmen for the new regiments, thus depriving the Secesh in Phillips County the means to carry on a living. Without their labor force, and denied the use of equine labor, plantation owners were unable to plant crops for the 1863 growing season. White officers drilled recruits for the new African American regiments, and by the end of the April, the first African American regiment performed picket duty at Fort Curtis.

On 7 April, the Fifth Illinois, First Indiana, and Fourth Iowa Cavalry regiments escorted Washburn as he left Helena for the last time for other duties in Tennessee. Col. Cyrus Bussey, Third Iowa Cavalry, became the new cavalry commander of the Second Cavalry Division, Army of the Tennessee. Wiley still commanded the First Brigade, while Apperson led the regiment. The Fifth also lost four veteran captains and their chief surgeon, Charles Higgins. Caldwell resigned in April under questionable circumstances that may have been the result of political differences between him and Seley. According to Apperson, Seley, a strong Democrat, filed a false, damaging report to the War Department about Caldwell, resulting in the captain's dismissal. All the commissioned officers of the regiment signed a petition to Lincoln to have Caldwell's dismissal revoked and him reinstated to command, which occurred in November 1863. Apperson reaffirmed his belief that Caldwell was "a true man to his country and a good and valiant officer."[76]

Seley also had differences with Joseph Cox, which resulted in Cox tendering his resignation in March. Seley, in a last attempt to tarnish Cox, endorsed the letter and charged the captain with "frequent utterance of disloyalty sentiments before his enlisted men, and disgust for the service." This endorsement resulted in Cox's dismissal "without pay and allowances." The controversy over Cox's dismissal erupted in Illinois newspapers. Apperson, Wiley, and Farnan, all Republicans, publicly endorsed

Cox against Seley, stating of Cox: "a more loyal man I don't think God ever made." According to Mann, "Major Seley acted mean in the affair, and took advantage of his position while in [temporary] command [of the regiment], to injure the Captain." Cox never regained his commission in the Fifth, though his dismissal was revoked to honorable discharge in 1866.[77]

Henry Organ resigned 23 February but requested reinstatement to his previous position in April. Wiley requested Organ's absence from the regiment to be permanent, due to the captain's habitual drunkenness, causing injury and demoralization in Company D. When Benjamin Glenn resigned his captaincy of Company I in December 1862, Yates promoted Edwin Norfolk to the command, but "unfortunately he also followed much in the footsteps of Capt Jenkins." February 1863 brought charges of "conduct unbecoming an officer and a Gentleman" against Norfolk, for drunken behavior on the streets of Helena. The captain pleaded guilty to all charges without a trial, forcing the army to dishonorably discharge him on 18 March.[78]

Apperson believed the captain of Company I needed to be "a man, good, true, with energy and determination," and recommended James Balch (1833–69) from Company E. The governor concurred, and Balch received promotion to captain in May 1863. The Balch family, originally from Tennessee and Kentucky, moved to Coles County about 1820, becoming early pioneers of the state. James, a farmer with a wife and two children, worked a $2,400 farm in Cumberland County and served with his two brothers, William and John, in Company E before attaining the captaincy of Company I.[79]

Edward Pierson, Co. A, resigned in January, and Wiley recommended Ohio native Jacob Cullers due to charges against Gordon Webster for "embezeling the money known as Co savings . . . [and] for selling Contraband Horses, & Mules for Money." Wiley accused Seley, who recommended Webster for the position, of overstepping his privileges as temporary commander of the regiment: "the officer in Command [Seley] . . . is inclined to assume large powers, & not at all inclined to Consult with the other field Officers in matters of this kind." The lieutenant colonel requested information about Seley's recommendations and requested the adjutant general to convince the Illinois governor not to confirm Seley's choices. Webster, a Democrat, had the support of Seley and Mumford, while Wiley and Apperson supported Cullers, who became captain in January 1863. Webster received the captaincy in January 1865, after Cullers mustered out. The smoldering enmity that existed within the regiment over political differences crept into all aspects of the regiment.[80]

In May, 425 Illinoisans under Farnan rode with Powell Clayton to stop Marmaduke's forces from reestablishing the Confederate position in eastern Arkansas, after his failed raid to Missouri. To do this, Clayton had to destroy Confederate property and forage in Phillips County, and, if possible, intercept and capture Marmaduke's men on their way to Cotton Plant and Little Rock. Clayton's cavalry also contained detachments of the Fifth Kansas commanded by Wilton Jenkins, and the First Indiana Cavalry, with their three steel cannon, under Thomas Pace.[81]

On the expedition, the Fifth participated in some of the most demoralizing destruction of private property in Phillips County during the war. Traveling along the Little Rock Road, the prairie boys burnt all the corn, forage, and bacon the horsemen found, "and as far as we went our instructions were Carried out as well as fire could do it." A member of the Twenty-First Texas Cavalry, who shadowed Clayton's column, reported that the Federals "were leaving behind them land & water, & nothing else. The people were turned out of their houses—not being permitted to remove their household goods—and their houses set on fire & burned to the ground."[82]

The destruction continued along the Military Road, until Clayton's forces reached Seaburn's Bridge, the only causeway over the L'Anguille River in the area. Clayton divided his forces at Seaburn's, retaining the First Indiana with their artillery and Company B of the Fifth Illinois to hold the bridge as an escape route. The rest of the troops, including three companies of the Fifth (K, G, F), and the Kansans under Jenkins, rode east to Taylor's Creek in search of Archibald Dobbin's cavalry, and to determine whether Hughes' Ferry remained a viable crossing point for the expedition forces.

A little after sunrise on 11 May, Clayton repelled an attack by Marmaduke's cavalry and initially drove back the Rebel advance past Taylor's Creek, to the woods just north of the town on the Wittsburg Road. When Marmaduke pressed forward with his artillery, Clayton realized he was about to be overwhelmed and quickly retreated to the bridge. The Federals held Seaburn's and their avenue of retreat west along the Military Road, guarding it with their small steel guns.

Jenkins, with the two Fifth regiments, left Taylor's Creek about six in the morning, missing Marmaduke's attack by hours. Destruction continued along their route, with the cavalry capturing a Confederate recruiting station and flourmill at McDaniel's mills. The Federals "drove out 30 [Rebs] . . . burned the mill . . . as well as all the corn in the vicinity," about fifty to sixty thousand bushels. The prairie boys also captured the mill owner, a Confederate captain, and several others prisoners. Here Jenkins received word that Marmaduke had attacked Clayton, and had laid plans to cut Jenkins off from Clayton. He ordered the Illinoisans to backtrack to the Widow Hinton's plantation to feed their horses and eat their evening meal. The Kansans passed the Fifth about 4:00 P.M., and Jenkins ordered the Illinoisans to finish their meal and quickly follow.[83]

Within an hour, Jenkins and the Fifth Kansas struck Confederate skirmishers from the Nineteenth and Twenty-First Texas and Charles Morgan's cavalry at Mount Vernon. On hearing these opening shots, Jenkins instantly sent word to the Illinoisans that he desperately needed reinforcements. While waiting for the Fifth, Jenkins fought off two assaults from the Texans. During the Rebels' second assault, a freedman, named Buck, who accompanied the Federal column, stood in the thickest fray, and when a Kansas private received a bullet in the thigh, Buck picked up the fallen Sharps rifle, threw off his hat, and "faught as brave as the bravest[.] [W]as known to have shot at least one of the Rebels," noted an Egyptian. The shocked Federal soldiers witnessed for the first time how ex-slaves fought for their freedom. In a letter that recounted Buck's brave stand, Roe confessed, "the blacks are our only friends here."[84]

The Rebels attempted a third charge but came only part way before seeing the futility of it and retreating to their line of battle. As darkness fell over the battlefield, the prairie boys galloped into view, shouting, yelling, and eager for the fight. The Kansans greeted "with almost as loud a cheer as came from the Texans," the Confederates answering with a few shells from their artillery. Farnan "spoke of [Company] 'K' taking the Battery," but Jenkins immediately ordered them to take cover behind the trees and await developments. Realizing the superiority of the Confederate forces, Jenkins called a retreat.[85]

Jenkins ordered Farnan, with "2 rifle Co's," to cover their withdrawal and burn all the bridges behind them, to retard Confederates' pursuit. Farnan got his wish when Jenkins also ordered him to "charge & take that battery if they press you to[o] closely." The Irish major placed his old Company K in the rear of the column, while the Kansans led the advance of the rapidly retreating cavalrymen. "[T]hen commenced our silent[,] sullen but rapid retreat. . . . As we skedaddled down the valley the whole road was lighted up by the burning corn, and barns, and mills, we had fired but a few hours before. Should . . . we fall into their hands[,] we'd fare but midling," prophesied Mann.[86]

Jenkins arrived at Hughes' Ferry, but with no boat in sight, the horsemen built a floating bridge, crossing over by dawn. The horsemen rode to the Jones plantation, where the planter's "corn, bacon, lard, meat & flour as well as beef, pork, chickens, milk butter, turkeys, all contributed" to the prairie boys' comfort. The horses even "fared well with hay, fodder, & grass." Mann speculated that the planter had been a rich man "when we came but we left him poor . . . after eating all we wanted." The boys even "pulled his beautiful roses and flowers," angering the man's "two indignant daughters." In the morning, the Federals set fire to Jones's corn pen; took his horses, mules, and other supplies; and freed his slaves.[87]

Leaving the plantation at noon, the Federals marched directly for Helena, where they found Clayton's troops. The Hoosier forces and Company B held onto the Seaburn's Bridge until evening, when Clayton deemed it safe to abandon their position and retreat to Helena. The Fifth Illinois suffered no casualties, though Confederates captured two privates from Company B: Langston Richards (1832–93) and Lt. Edwin Harrison (1840–1920). The Federals claimed to have destroyed one hundred thousand bushels of corn, fifty thousand pounds of meat, and tons of hay and fodder. The local population also lost to fire thousands of dollars worth of personal property, including a mill from which the Rebels drew their supply of bread. As Roe noted, the troops "brought off all the mules and Negros that we could find."[88]

After returning to camp at Beech Grove on 14 May, the Fifth received orders to move to Germantown, Tennessee, as soon as transportation became available. Prentiss countermanded the order the next day as encouraging rumors entered camp concerning Grant's army at Vicksburg. Mann, in his new position as commissary officer for the regiment, hoped for a quick move away from Helena, where he believed "the rebs . . . are pretty well used up and subdued. Another winter will find them in starving condition for we have destroyed most of their corn and they cannot raise another crop this year. They are whipped." On 29 May, Special Orders No. 148 sent the men to Vicksburg, called by the Confederates the Gibraltar of the West, for the city's command of the Mississippi. After making accommodations for the thirty men too sick to move to Vicksburg, Wiley had his command ready for transport on 30 May. The Fifth also lost Rev. John Woods, who remained behind to manage the contraband camp at Helena; he would not reunite with the regiment until 1864.[89]

5

Redemption at Vicksburg
June to August 1863

Throughout May, the soldiers at Helena heard the encouraging rumors of Grant's victories in Mississippi. "News from Vicksburg is quite cheering and indicate the complete success of Gen Grant. Vicksburg is probably now in his possesion," declared an impassioned John Mann. After leading his army through Mississippi, and winning victories at Jackson and Champion's Hill, Grant invested Vicksburg, sealing Pemberton's Confederate army off from supplies and reinforcements. The Federal army twice assaulted the formidable Confederate works, only to be repulsed in both attempts. Finally, Grant realized the futility of his efforts and settled in for a siege. The Federal commander needed additional soldiers to watch his army's rear, observe the enemy, and prevent the Confederates from rallying a force strong enough to attack. Grant requested from Prentiss to send him all the available forces he could spare and still maintain his parity in Arkansas. Though the loss of infantry would make Helena vulnerable to attack, Prentiss informed Grant that he took "pleasure in being able to say in reply thereto that I shall send you the Fifth Illinois Cavalry."[1]

Leaving Helena on 30 May, Wiley's prairie boys chugged downriver on four transports, escorted by two gunboats. Mann reflected on the regiment's future: "Never shall I forget the 10½ months we have spent in and around Helena. New places and new scenes are before us. May God protect us and give us victory [over] the enemies of our country as we march forward with our armies." The prairie boys carried superior munitions with them, including three hundred new Cosmopolitan carbines.[2]

Wiley reported to Federal authorities when the flotilla reached Young's Point, Madison Parish, Louisiana on the last day of May. The Federal army captured this important little town located opposite the confluence of the Yazoo and Mississippi Rivers in December 1862. After receiving instructions, the Fifth rode up the Yazoo River, landing at Chickasaw Bluffs on 1 June, where Wiley reported to Grant. There the Illinoisans disembarked and wandered between the "shot & shell" from Sherman's ill-fated attack the previous December. "[T]he Boys are bringing in Shells as big as my hat that neve[r] bursted. [G]ood joke on the Southron Confederacy," recalled Packard. After lying in the woods all day, the prairie boys moved to Snyder's Bluff, where they bivouacked for the night. The men spent a delightful evening visiting friends and family members in the Eighth and Thirtieth Illinois Infantry regiments. Those with an enhanced curiosity soaked in the wonders of their new surroundings. "The Sun is just Sitting[,] looking like a large ball of fire. The Moon just rising to relieve it seamingly right ove[r] Vicksburg. . . . Truly this is a Splended Scene never to be bloted from My Memory unless a big Bom[b] Shell Strikes Me," wrote Packard.[3]

Wiley had his men in the saddle early, riding to Haynes' Bluff, nine miles north of the Gibraltar of the West. After reporting to Frank P. Blair, Wiley assumed command "as the Senior Cavalry Officer present" of all the cavalry detachments at the bluff, amounting to some fifteen hundred men. Wiley's men encamped at Roach's plantation, four miles above the bluff. As John Burke explained to his sister Ellen, "Our Position is on the extreme right and our camp is in the rear of Sherman's Army Corps. We are continualy changing our Camp and though we hold materialy the same Position[,] we do not occupy the Same ground two days at a time[,] but we are in the saddle more than half the time." The day after the Fifth made camp at the Roach plantation, Grant ordered Wiley to pack up his brigade for an expedition to Mechanicsburg, forty-five miles northeast of Vicksburg.[4]

Grant's principal goal centered on preventing Joseph E. Johnston's Army of Relief, then concentrating at Canton and Jackson, from reinforcing Pemberton. Twice before, the Illinois general sent Federal forces to destroy the Way's Bluff Bridge, which carried the tracks of the Mississippi Central Railroad over the Big Black River, north of Canton. This rail service supplied Johnston's army with soldiers, food, and equipment. Both attempts failed, but the May excursion destroyed forage and supplies in the Mechanicsburg Corridor, the northern route into Vicksburg.

By early June, John C. Breckinridge's infantry division and William H. Jackson's cavalry joined the Confederate Army of Relief. This gave the Confederates approximately thirty-one thousand men against Grant's army of fifty-one thousand effectives. With these reinforcements hovering around the outskirts of the Federal army, Grant "determined to send a garrison up there [the Yazoo], using Satartia as a base of supplies."

With assistance from Rear Adm. David Porter's Mississippi squadron, Grant devised a movement that included Joseph A. Mower's brigade, Nathan Kimball's infantry division, and Wiley's cavalry.[5]

Mower's troops would clear the area of Confederates, while Grant tasked Kimball with obstructing all roads leading to the Big Black River and the destruction of the area's forage and transportation. Wiley's cavalry served as the infantry's eyes and ears, watching every avenue Johnston could use to penetrate south, especially all river crossings, but the cavalry's main task remained the destruction of the Way's Bluff Bridge. Wiley commanded the cavalry and a battery of artillery during the expedition, receiving instructions directly from Kimball.

Wiley and his troops moved out on the Oak Ridge Road, heading east. According to Packard, the post commander gave Apperson command of two cannon from Ezra Taylor's Battery, First Illinois Light Artillery. At Oak Ridge, Wiley split his cavalry, sending part up the Benton Road, while the majority, including the Fifth with the artillery, headed for the Lower Benton Road. On reaching Bear Creek, the Illinoisans encountered pickets from Walter A. Rorer's Twentieth Mississippi Mounted Infantry of John Adams's brigade, in William H. T. Walker's cavalry division. A short skirmish ensued, resulting in Rorer retreating and disappearing into the woods. After they cleared the area of Rebels, Wiley camped for the night at Bear Creek.[6]

The next morning emerged hot and humid, but Wiley had his horsemen in the saddle before dawn. Packard believed he would never forget "how sharply the bugles of the Fifth Cavalry rang out the reveille. We knew the early call meant business. . . . And in a moment four hundred veterans, their skins bronzed, almost black through years of exposure to the southern sun, glistening with health and vigor in the morning light, were in the saddle, riding out on the Lower Benton Road. The cavalry entered the morass of forest, swamps, and cypress breaks between the Yazoo and Big Black rivers."[7]

When the summer sun broke over the tall swamp trees, the heat and humidity thickened the morning air, and the men rode "carefully and leisurely" so as not to tire. Wiley's advance guard struck Rorer's troopers again about nine in the morning: "first the sharp crack of the rifles from their pickets; here and there through the scrubby timber we could see the glint of their guns and the flash of their swords." Warily the cavalry advanced "towards the smoke of the enemy's rifles." Packard believed this "'feeling of the enemy'" was the most exciting business one could engage in. "Just ahead of you is the enemy, who signify their interest in

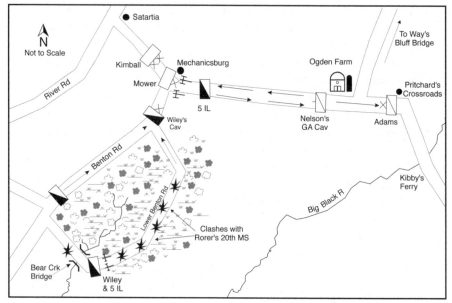

Map 5.1. Fifth's charge against Nelson's cavalry during the Mechanicsburg expedition, 4 June 1863.

you with various little pellets of lead, and huge chunks of iron thrown in your direction." The morning skirmishes resulted in a leg wound for Tennessee native Thomas Williams (1816–88), Co. K. Surgeons removed his leg at Mechanicsburg, "it being necessary to save his life." Williams received a disability discharge and an invalid pension by the end of the year and returned to his small Randolph County farm.[8]

Wiley gave Farnan command of the troops skirmishing with Rorer. The ambitious Irishman pushed his men forward, "and quite a sharp spell of firing was had before they [the Rebels] fell back." The horsemen traveled just a short distance when "we met them again and as the brush was too thick and the ground to[o] broken for horses, we dismounted and took it afoot after the regular Bushwhacking style and kept driving them before us." Finally, Apperson brought forth the cannon, and shells fell where before the men had seen the smoke of the enemy's rifles. The Mississippians quickly withdrew, but not before the prairie boys captured two cannon and a number of men. Rorer never retreated, though, and for almost eight hours, the Confederates fought a delaying action, with "their rear guard fighting our advance."[9]

As the cavalry slowly made progress towards Mechanicsburg, Mower's infantry disembarked at Satartia and moved unimpeded through the village, with the Eighth Wisconsin Infantry in the advance. The opposing forces met between Satartia and Mechanicsburg, with severe fighting developing as the Federal infantry slowly advanced. Kimball's troops arrived about eleven and joined the Eighth Wisconsin between the two villages. A few shells from Battery B, First Illinois Light Artillery, dislodged Adams's troops and allowed the infantry to advance to Mechanicsburg. On reaching the little Yazoo River village, the infantry discovered James A. Hoskins's Brookhaven Artillery unlimbering, but Federals rushed the Rebels so quickly they retreated through Mechanicsburg without firing a shot. The Federal infantry slowly worked their way through the village only to be stopped by two other guns from the Brookhaven Artillery, supported by Adams's main cavalry force. The Federal infantry occupied the ditches in the rear of the town and held their ground for almost thirty minutes until the Federal guns dislodged the Rebels from their stronghold. The Confederates started their final retreat about three in the afternoon.

Wiley's cavalry column reached within four miles of Mechanicsburg concurrently with the Rebels' final retreat. On hearing the boom of artillery, Wiley and his staff rushed forward and reported to Kimball, who had assumed command, as senior officer, of the whole force when he arrived at Mechanicsburg. Kimball directed Wiley to send five hundred men "by a right hand road to strike the Big Black [R]iver at Kibley[']s ferry," thus destroying the Rebels' eastern avenue of retreat. The Makanda colonel also ordered the Fifth to charge the Rebel battery.[10]

Wiley gave Apperson command of the prairie boys' attack against the Rebels east of Mechanicsburg. The major took the Third Battalion, containing only one hundred men from Companies K, L, M, and I forward, while Seley and the Second Battalion stayed in support. The daft Republican first major, "mounted on his famous black charger," gave the forward command. "Our Maj Apperson led the Charge and right Manfully did Our Men follow." As Apperson passed Kimball, the Hoosier told the major, "Boys I will give you fifty dollars to take that Battery." Apperson flatly replied, "My men do not fight for money," and the men started out "at first a gentle trot, then a gallop and finally a run. Our bodies leaning forward in line with our horses' heads at an angle of forty-five degrees, and sabers at front point, ready for the shock." Just as the column rode off, Apperson's horse stumbled, throwing the major "headlong in the sand and dust." Apperson immediately ordered Withers and Packard to lead the men. The first major remounted and tried to regain momentum to reach his battalion, but to no avail. John Mann later claimed the major was very "prudent in regard to the safety of his person." Charges of cowardice from the Third Battalion accused the major of "Shamefully, wilfully, and Cowardly halt[ing] his horse," turning back toward the rear lines, leaving the Third Battalion "to Charge in upon the enemy without any immediate Commander."[11]

The lane on which Withers led the men stretched straight through to the Rebel battery, and they saw the Confederates retreating. Adams's men fell back "in good order" for almost two and a half miles before he realized Thomas N. Nelson's Georgia cavalry had not retreated as quickly as the main body of troops. As the Fifth bore down on the Georgians, Adams turned his men around and tried to reach Nelson before the Fifth's barrage, but Adams arrived too late. Lewis F. Levy, in Nelson's company, who served in the first battle line, described the Fifth's onslaught: "Suddenly about two or three hundred yards behind us appeared a regiment of Federal cavalry, only the heads of the men and the bright gleam of their sabers as they flashed in the sunlight being visible above the dense clouds of dust which enveloped them as they rushed headlong upon us." The Georgians quickly gave the Illinoisans the "best reception we could; but our line was too weak to resist the onslaught from such a superior force, and they broke through it like a whirlwind, sweeping along with them our shattered and disorganized remnant. . . . [S]ome luckless horse and rider went down, which caused others in turn to fall; and wildly leaping over such piles of men and horses, the balance of the cavalcade swept madly on, leaving . . . our men . . . prisoners in the hands of the enemy."[12]

The hot, dusty environment created the most horrifying scene, for the Illinoisans were "enveloped in a thick cloud of dust which rendered marksmanship by the enemy impossible." The obstruction did not hinder the rifles of the Rebels, who fired on the advancing cloud, but fortunately, they fired high, missing the charging Illinoisans. The Fifth's column, radiating the confidence and esprit of an experienced unit, "went on like a whirlwind in a mad onward rush." Packard believed the charge succeeded by "its own momentum."[13]

The noise and uproar of the Fifth's battle charge became deafening for those waiting for the attack. "The discordant sounds of officers and men, and the sharp crack of the rifle and the thunder of hoofs; the agonizing cry of horses and men . . . all unite[d] in an overwhelming horror." Just in front of the Confederate line stood a three-foot trench, "as a protection against attack," but it "was no defense to a cyclone like this." "[W]ith a yell of triumph," the Illinoisans blew down on the Georgians "like a whirlwind and swept over them as if they were men of straw." Many horses refused to jump the ditch, but others cleared the impediment, rushing forward to capture the fleeing Rebels. Sgt. Zennius (Bean) Bradshaw, Co. M, on his celebrated racehorse Dog Legs, had the highest count with six captured Confederates. A prisoner told Packard that "after being run fifteen Mile and then run Over by the damd Yanks was a little more th[a]n they bargained for."[14]

After scattering the Georgians, the Fifth headed toward Adams's troops, who had tried to form a second and third line at the Ogden farm, but each time, the Illinoisans "came down upon them waving their pistols & sabers over their heads like a whirlwind, Shouting & yelling—breaking their lines." The Confederates tried to stop the Fifth with "leaden balls pass[ing] through the air like hail stones in a hailstorm." Again they failed, and the prairie boys rounded up Rebel prisoners. A few Confederates, discouraged and frightened by the Fifth's charge, rushed to Scott's Ferry on the Big Black River and reported that Adams and his troops had all been captured or killed.[15]

The Confederate main column continued to retreat. The heat, however, took its toll on the Fifth's horses and men, leaving only thirty soldiers participating in the last charge. Though his horse had fallen twice, John Mann urged his brother Calvin to rally the men "as the <u>Major</u> [Apperson] <u>was far in the rear</u>." Lieutenant Mann spurred his horse severely and shouted at the remaining prairie boys to "'keep closed up,'" while he silently uttered a "sincer[e] prayer . . . 'God grant us victory [over] our enemies.'" In their last attack, the Fifth met Adams's troops secured behind fencing at Ogden farm. The Rebs fired a volley into the charging column, which wounded three and killed Pvt. Emanuel Thomas, Co. K. On they surged, though, breaking the last Confederate line, killing two, wounding five, and capturing fifteen to twenty Rebels. While Lieutenant Mann tried to get to the front, he "saw our boys take dozens of the <u>rebs</u> prisoners. I saw two wanting to find some one to surrender to, when I ordered them to go to the rear and left them <u>going that way</u> in a hurry." John believed the charge completely "routed the rebs and if the whole Reg't had Kept up[,] we would have taken two or three hundred prisoners. Most <u>men</u> are timid about starting into a battle but when in they <u>know no fear</u>."[16]

The last confrontation was more punishment than Rebel flesh and blood could endure, and Adams's beaten and demoralized soldiers retreated to Pritchard's Crossroads, from where Adams reported that the Fifth Cavalry "pressed me so closely that I had to fall back here." After a chase of three miles, the Fifth headed slowly back toward Mechanicsburg. The horses had stirred up so much dust that it "was impossible to tell friend from foe" until ordered to surrender. Reporting to Apperson at

Mechanicsburg, John Mann heard Apperson swearing at Seley for failing to support the cavalry charge. Apperson, flustered in his belief that his command had been "cut all to Hell," finally calmed when Mann informed him that "his army [Apperson's battalion] had cut the Rebs and scattered them completely." The commissary officer added acerbically that this was accomplished without the major's knowledge or leadership. The Fifth lost only one man killed and three wounded. John Burke expressed surprise at the low casualties in the Fifth: "it is a wonder that we did not lose more men for the [S]ecesh held their fire until their powder would burn our hands as we rode through them[,] but the dust was so thick that I suppose was one cause of our coming off as well as we did."[17]

By twilight on that bloody 4 June, the Fifth hunted down and captured sixty Confederate soldiers. After the sweaty, exhausted, dust-covered prairie boys gathered up their fallen soldiers, fagged and broken-down horses, they marched their prisoners back to Satartia. According to Skiles, the Rebels "don[']t like the 5th Ills nor their sabres." Even after fourteen hours in the saddle and the exhausting attack, the Fifth provided for their enemies. Confederate Lewis Levy remembered the grace shown him: "Our captors proved themselves as kind and generous toward us in defeat as they had been brave and fearless in action, showing us numerous little courtesies and attentions."[18]

Soon fires blazed and the men settled in for the evening meal. Many talked about the afternoon excitement, while others wrote to loved ones back in Illinois. Mann admitted to his wife, "I have not enjoyed myself better since my enlistment." The prairie boys accepted the praise from fellow soldiers and listened to the boasting by the infantry of the cavalrymen's charge. Packard bragged, "The bloody 5th has Imortalized itself." Apperson's battalion later received a commendation for its charge at Mechanicsburg.[19]

Heat and humidity permeated the early summer air the next morning as Wiley's cavalry recuperated from the exertions of the previous day. Company K attended the funeral of Emanuel Thomas: "Poor Thomas is no more. Bravest of the brave, he fell at the head of the column in the charge," lamented Mann.[20] In the evening, the Confederates penetrated the Federal's left and lobbed a few shells on the transports, but mostly the day remained quiet. Prisoners from Adams's brigade informed Kimball of Johnston's growing army near Canton, with Walker's troops at Yazoo City. This essentially closed the avenue for the cavalry to Way's Bluff Bridge, and with word from the navy of the drop in the water level in the Yazoo River, Kimball lost all hope of a successful mission.

After torching Mechanicsburg, the cavalry rode out on the Lower Benton Road around noon on 6 June in the intense heat, riding slowly southwest, stopping often to water themselves and their mounts. The steamy June day was unmitigated torture for the soldiers, who marched in heavy wool uniforms, and for their mounts, which carried the soldiers and their equipment. As the temperature rose, the horses gave out, and several were abandoned. Wiley allowed his soldiers to march only ten miles before they made camp and found relief from the burning sun. Another sweltering day followed, the trip made more miserable with the constant sniping of Rebel cavalry on the rear of Wiley's column, but no general engagement developed. The Fifth reached their camps at the Roach estate before noon on 7 June. Two days later, C. C. Washburn took command of the Sixteenth Army Corps.

Wiley retained command of the cavalry until 10 June, when he received his dismissal from the service from the adjutant general's office, for being absent without leave in 1862. The befuddled Wiley immediately sent a letter of consideration to Illinois Adj. Gen. Allen Fuller. Wiley relied heavily on Republican patronage to save his reputation.

> I did hope that I should not now at this late day be dismissed in this manner. Maj Gen'l Washburn who commands the forces at this place was very much asstonished at the result & immediately prepared a strong letter to the 'Sec of War' in which he was cordially joined by Gen'l Kimball under whose immediate command I have been since my arrival here, asking to have the order revoked. Gen'l Grant told me yesterday that he had forwarded the letter to the War Department. . . . I feel as every loyal Officer should, the disgrace of being dismissed when in the face of the enemy, & deeply desire to avert it.

Wiley entrusted the department would not fill his position for he expected to have the decision reversed.[21]

Many officers in the regiment delighted at Wiley's dismissal. "He never was a very good officer and few of the men or officers like him," commented Mann. High-ranking Democrats in the regiment rejoiced to the point of getting "on a drunk," including "Major Seley, Surgeons [John B.] Ensey & [William] Watts and Capt. Mumford. Poor an officer as Col Wiley is, he is every respect their superior as man and officer."[22]

As soon as Wiley left the regiment, the commissioned officers developed a petition supporting the colonel's dismissal and requesting that Wiley not be reinstated to his position. The appeal identified Wiley as a coward who did not have the qualifications to lead the regiment. Many of the accusations against Wiley had no foundation in fact but were per-petrated by those who wanted the Fifth to be officered by Democrats. Even Mann refused to sign, believing Wiley's disgraceful dismissal was sufficient and should not be followed with a document that he considered excessive in its accusations.[23]

The Fifth Illinois was now leaderless. When Wilson left the regiment in the spring, the majors had clamored for the position, many request-ing promotion over Wiley. The governor's office in Illinois had been deluged with letters of recommendation for Apperson (Republican) or Seley (Democrat); protests against a candidate took the form of written remonstrance from almost every commissioned officer in the regiment. While still at Helena, Rev. John Woods, an earnest Republican, wrote in favor of Apperson for the colonelcy and related to the governor how men in the regiment had circulated a secret petition favoring Seley, which received only nine signatures. Seley, a Democrat, was not completely in support of Republican war principles and had to be coaxed to sign the 1863 spring resolutions denouncing Copperheads. Apperson's support, Woods claimed, never wavered, and he had been instrumental in making the regiment a top-notch fighting machine.[24]

Horace Mumford, an ardent Democrat, supported Seley and wrote to Yates expressing why the major should be considered for the position. Though Mumford believed Wiley was "a gentleman of high moral stand-ing, . . . as a military commander, he has not the responsible qualifica-tions" to be colonel. Apperson, according to the captain, was illiterate, and a poor tactician who still did not know how to drill the men. Seley maintained Mumford "is the best Field officer we have. He is the choice of the regiment both officers & men. . . . good tactician, of the best moral character," who is "never lacking in judgement, Courageous and brave, and is the best man by far, for the management of this regiment."[25]

Wiley's dismissal in June created a power vacuum that reverberated throughout the regiment for almost a year. With both commanding of-ficers gone, Apperson believed he would receive the colonel's commission, with Seley as his lieutenant colonel. Writing to Yates, Apperson expressed his concerns: "We as a regiment feel the great necessity of having our Regiment properly officered. As first or ranking Major I have been in command of this regiment most of the time for the last few months and I feel that the position of Colonel is due me. Major A. H. Seley has been active and efficient and I would . . . gracefully request that he be appointed Lieut Colonel,—and in the appointment of Majors that they be made from our Captains according to their respective rank."[26]

John Mann supported Farnan for the colonelcy and developed a petition to Yates. "Major Farnan is the only man in the Reg't that is qualified
for the position of Col. Majors Apperson and Seley are both aspiring to
the position[,] but neither of them are qualified." Mann and Farnan's association had begun during their civilian lives, and Mann respected the
major; however, many of the line officers did not support him. Farnan
constantly sought betterment for himself, often to the detriment of fellow officers. Farnan's ambition, and the extent he would go to achieve
his goals, became controversial, and many would soon turn their backs
on the once-popular captain.[27]

The writing campaign probably had a deleterious effect on Yates's decision. Receiving dozens of letters from soldiers accusing one another of
unpatriotic beliefs caused Yates to question the loyalty of all who desired
the position. In his quest to "Republicanize the army," Yates appointed
known Lincoln supporter John McConnell, late major of the Third Illinois Cavalry, to the position of colonel, while Apperson became lieutenant colonel. McConnell had resigned his commission with the Third
Illinois in March 1863 due to poor health. He was still unfit for duty
when he received the commission to the Fifth and would not join the
regiment until May 1864. The governor made an excellent choice, for
McConnell had proven his abilities while serving with the Third and
had even received commendations for his bravery during the battle of
Pea Ridge. His appointment did not sit well with either the field officers
or the men of the Fifth, who considered McConnell an outsider and a
civilian. Mann had only one word of comment concerning McConnell's
appointment: "<u>Shame</u>."[28]

Seley moved up to first major, with Farnan holding the second major's
position. Yates gave the third major's commission to Mumford, contrary
to the wishes of the new lieutenant colonel. Mumford actively sought this
position, even writing to Curtis for a recommendation. Apperson, however, questioned Mumford's honesty and twice asserted that Mumford
"obtained his commission, as 3rd ranking Captain, by <u>false representation</u>
and <u>false 'Morning Reports.'</u>" Mumford, according to the charges, bor-
rowed men from Company E to muster in October 1861, when in actuality,
his company did not reach its full complement until December. The major
also believed Mumford's personality lacked the needed requirements for
the rank. Company F also preferred charges against their captain in July
1862 for violating Article 15 of the Articles of War (false muster).[29]

With Apperson commanding the regiment, the Fifth moved their camp
to the Snyder's Bluff batteries and breastworks and joined a provisional

brigade of cavalry with the Third Iowa and Second Wisconsin regiments, commanded by Cyrus R. Bussey, Third Iowa Cavalry, under Washburn. On 17 June, John G. Parke, with the Ninth Army Corps, arrived at Snyder's Bluff. Parke ranked Washburn and took overall command of the forces at the bluff. Responsible for securing Grant's rear lines, the Fifth shared scout duty with the Iowans, often patrolling the area between the Yazoo and Big Black Rivers, as far north as Mechanicsburg. Between scouts, the horsemen built roadblocks and spent endless hours on picket and guard duty. Mann admitted, "We are having more active times now than ever since being in the service scouting, picketing, & blockading."[30]

The regiment's heroic exploits at Mechanicsburg and Calvin Mann's leadership convinced Washburn and Grant that the prairie boys would be successful in destroying all railroad transportation in southern Mississippi on a planned raid in mid-June. The raiders' goal was to cut the New Orleans, Jackson and Great Northern Railroad at Broovkhaven to stop any troop transfers to or from Johnston's or Frank K. Gardner's invested troops at Port Hudson. The raiders' second objective focused on the railroad bridge of the Mobile and Ohio Railroad over the Bucatunna Creek at Winchester, cutting off supplies from Mobile. Additional targets included the Alabama and Mississippi Railroad at Lindon, the

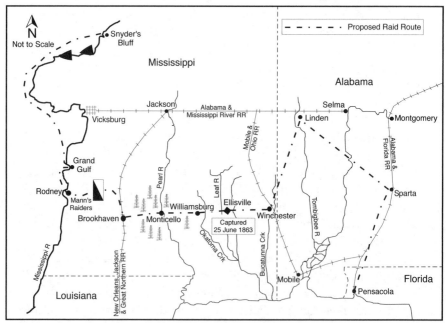

Map 5.2. Calvin Mann's ill-fated raid in Mississippi, 22–25 June 1863.

Alabama and Florida at Sparta, and all the standing bridges over major waterways. The design of the raid was simple: ride rapidly and destroy as much property as possible, avoid a fight, and "escape all dangers by flight & <u>Strategy</u>."[31]

Capt. Calvin Mann spent the afternoon searching for forty volunteers for the raid. He began with the Randolph Rangers, where he got eleven men, but John Burke refused to volunteer. The young New York farmer believed "the expedition would be Captured," especially under Calvin's leadership. Lt. William N. Berry, Co. L, served as second in command. After being informed of the raid's goals, the men obtained ten days' rations of hard bread, sugar, salt, and coffee and then went to bed early. Apperson questioned John Mann as to his brother's motives for taking on such a risky mission. John proudly defended Calvin: "Gen Washburne had . . . desired him to take charge of the expedition[,] and being thus singled out by the Gen, he felt it to be his duty to go." Proud brother John added that Calvin "would not expose himself to danger foolishly[,] yet he would take all necessary risks and dangers to fulfil[l] his duties to his country."[32]

June 22 dawned warm and pleasant as Calvin and his men reported to Washburn's headquarters. Seeing his brother off at Snyder's Bluff, John Mann believed that the "whole party started off this morning in fine spirits & full of hope in regard to the success of their hazardous undertaking." The raiders acquired water-borne transportation to Rodney, Mississippi, where Calvin's raiders disembarked, then rode east through dense forest and underbrush. Around noon, they hit their first destination: Brookhaven, and the New Orleans, Jackson and Great Northern Railroad. So far, they encountered no opposition to their raid.[33]

Confederates maintained a conscription and training camp at Brookhaven, and on the afternoon of 23 June, its commander, Lt. Col. William S. Lovell, Twenty-Third Louisiana Infantry, sent Capt. John Tonkin, Forty-Third Tennessee Infantry, to scour the countryside in search of deserters from the camp. Ignorant of the Federal raiders' approach, Tonkin collided with the Illinois raiders eight miles north of Brookhaven, which resulted in the Rebel captain's capture. After paroling Tonkin, Calvin misled the Rebel by telling him that he commanded the advance of the Fifth Illinois, who were just then passing through Gallatin.[34]

Calvin Mann forced Tonkin to ride with the raiders to Brookhaven; thus, the Confederate camp had little warning of the impending danger. The Federals' timing of the attack at 1:00 P.M. caught the Rebels off guard, and they scattered from their interrupted dinner. The raiders rode through town without opposition and, within minutes, burned twelve railcars, half the number of cars below Jackson. The Illinois raiders left the railroad track and other property undamaged. In their haste to flee Brookhaven, the raiders also left the telegraph wire intact.[35]

A delighted Lovell took advantage of the raiders' mistake and dashed off messages informing Confederates east of Brookhaven of the Egyptians' foray. After leaving the conscription camp, Calvin headed east and kept his raiders riding hard on the Monticello Road. Their next stop, the bridge over the Pearl River at Monticello, was an arduous twenty-three miles away.

Lovell's pursuit was hampered due to lack of ammunition, men, and superior mounts. During the four anxious hours the Illinoisans used for their escape, Lovell recruited townsmen, home guards, and conscripts, securing horses and ammunition for the majority of the volunteers. Lovell placed Lt. William M. Wilson, Forty-Third Tennessee Infantry, in command of the twenty-two-man squad. The Confederate posse, armed and on fresh horses, raced after the raiders.

The Illinoisans rode hard through the Piney Woods area toward Monticello, where they reached the Pearl River late in the afternoon of 23 June. The raiders crossed the muddy waters on flat boats and then cut the ferry loose to hamper Confederate pursuit. The rapid pace of the mission and the intense heat of a Mississippi summer day took its toll on both the men and horses, but Calvin sped his men toward Williamsburg.

Wilson's Confederates reached Monticello three hours after the Illinois raiders crossed the Pearl. Heartened when they learned they were closing the gap, Wilson became frustrated at the recruits' refusal to continue the pursuit. The lieutenant again wasted valuable time enlisting fresh troops, rounding out his thirty-five-man squad with old men and boys from home guards of Lawrence, Covington, and Jones Counties, and a few regular soldiers from Terrell's Dragoons of the Fourth Mississippi Cavalry. Wilson received news that the Illinoisans were only a few miles ahead.[36]

The Egyptians' fagged horses soon slackened the raiders' pace, and even though the soldiers took fresh horses from civilians, their mounts sorely needed an extended respite. Confident that he had outdistanced his pursuers, Calvin rested his men on the main road, east of the Leaf River. Instead of following Grant and Washburn's instructions for constant motion, Mann allowed his forty men to relax.

Thundering into Williamsburg, Wilson was forced once again to recruit men and horses, delaying his pursuit by a few hours. Forging ahead about dusk, the Confederate posse, now consisting of detachments from the Twenty-Third Louisiana and the Seventh Mississippi Infantry, reached an impasse at Okatoma Creek, where the raiders had destroyed the bridge. Turning south, the Confederates detoured to the Leaf River Ferry. Riding through the night, Wilson's posse hit the main road some six miles from the river and two miles west of Ellisville, where he learned Calvin had yet to pass. The lieutenant destroyed the Rocky Creek Bridge to cut off the raiders' eastern avenue of escape, then hid his Confederates along the main road and waited.

The refreshed Illinois raiders appeared within an hour, riding boldly down the avenue in the early morning light of 25 June. Wilson waited until the prairie boys were within a few yards of his guns before his men fired. The single, destructive volley announced the end of the Illinoisans' raid and Calvin's military career. The Confederate barrage killed four raiders and wounded four. Company E lost Smith Lamm and Hiram Landrus. Sanders M. Earl, Co. H, and Co. B's John Arrington also died in the ambush. Frightened by the assault, Calvin's horse reared, throwing the Randolph County physician into the custody of the Confederates. The remainder of the raiders dove for cover along the main road. Wilson compelled Berry to surrender his force, and within an hour, a flag of truce appeared for the forces to determine the number of dead and wounded. Soon another flag appeared, and the entire Illinois raiding party surrendered without firing a shot.[37]

Wilson's posse quickly unhorsed and unarmed the raiders and left the wounded Egyptians in Jones County, hoping to obtain medical assistance. Two of the soldiers—Pvt. Michael O'Neil (1841–1922), Co. C, and Pvt. John Webster (1843–99), Co. A—received paroles due to their wounds. The other Illinois raiders remained in the custody of the Confederate provost marshal at Jackson, Mississippi. Southern newspapers reported Calvin's mortification and humiliation at surrendering to mostly old men and boys, and to troops that numbered less than his own. The Confederate authorities sent the captives to Richmond, Virginia, where they arrived in early July. The authorities paroled all the privates and noncommissioned officers, and the lucky raiders returned to their regiment throughout August, September, and October.[38]

The commissioned officers, however, spent time at Libby Prison in Richmond. Union cavalry raids forced the Rebel authorities to send Calvin Mann to a new prison in Macon, Georgia, in May 1864, and later to South Carolina, when Sherman's troops marched through the Peach State. The captain escaped in late November 1864 and reached Knoxville, Tennessee, on 30 December. Ironically, not knowing of her husband's flight to freedom, Emily had written to Confederate authorities in early December, requesting Calvin's exchange, stating, "he has been a prisoner for near 19 months[,] had several opportunities to escape with others but has trusted he might be honorable exchanged." She did not learn of her husband's return to Federal lines until January 1865, when he reported to the Military Department of the Mississippi. Calvin mustered out in February 1865, due to the expiration of his term. Returning to his medical career, he became one of the most "able physicians who ever practiced," serving various communities in Missouri, Kansas, and Illinois after the war.[39]

During the raid, Farnan and the regiment patrolled the area north of Vicksburg and participated in a scout aimed at destroying hidden gun enclaves along the Mississippi. During the latter, the prairie boys witnessed the brutal side of Southern bigotry at Lake Providence. When Grant's army invaded northern Louisiana, many Southern plantation owners abandoned their estates and moved inland with their slaves. The government then began a program to lease these abandoned farms to loyal white men, and in some cases to freedmen. As Skiles explained to his parents: "where uncle sam is farming on confiscated plantation[s,] the negroes [are] doing the work" and being paid by the Federal government. Many Confederate soldiers abhorred this system, which materialized in William Parsons's Texas Cavalry attack on the plantations and Federal garrison at Lake Providence on 28 June. Parsons attacked the First Arkansas Volunteers (African Descent), who manned the garrison, capturing approximately twelve hundred African Americans, sending them back into slavery.[40]

Farnan's soldiers arrived the day following the assault and helped secure the area from additional attacks. Skiles, whose parents remained racists, accompanied the horsemen and was appalled at the Rebels' treatment of the freedmen: "they burned every thing, Cotton Gins, houses, & negro quarters, killing negroes, & burned several. [W]e could see their skulls, & Jaw bones laying around." Farnan maintained that the surviving freedmen told him that the "<u>rebels</u> locked some of them [freed slaves] in their houses and others were too sick to get out of the flames and they <u>burned them alive</u>." Even the commander of the expedition could not describe the Rebel atrocities committed against freedmen, for "the pen fails to record in proper language."[41]

By 4 July, the Fifth encamped at the Methodist campground, one and a half miles from Harris's plantation on the Benton Road, and closer to the other cavalry regiments in their brigade. In one respect, nothing had changed that Independence Day: The morning dawned hot and humid with the men anxiously awaiting news about the fall of Vicksburg.

According to John Mann, the "whole army here are in fine spirits—sanguine & determined" to whip Pemberton and Johnston. By early afternoon, the prairie boys heard rumors that Pemberton and Vicksburg had surrendered to Grant. All the regimental diarists recorded their feelings concerning the surrender. "Vicksburg is ours this time for certain," Skiles exclaimed to his parents.[42]

Mann, as usual, reflected the emotions many soldiers expressed that day. "Glorious 4th of July. All the camp is in high state of excitement & joy at the triumph of the Union army over the traitors. What a day of rejoicing it would be if the assembled thousands in the north could get the news of the fall of Vicksburg to day. Such a shout of joy would ascend that would reach the four corners of the globe."[43]

Unknown to Pemberton, Johnston's Army of Relief had moved toward Vicksburg to rescue the besieged Confederate army on 28 June. Over the next three days, William Walker's, William Loring's, and Samuel French's divisions reconnoitered the area around Birdsong's Ferry, while John C. Breckinridge's division held Edward's Station. While Johnson examined Sherman's impenetrable exterior lines on Independence Day, Pemberton surrendered to Grant. News of the surrender reached Johnston that evening, and he began his retrograde movement simultaneously with Sherman's thrust toward Jackson. Grant instructed Sherman to destroy Johnston's Army of Relief "as effectually as possible" and charged the Ohioan with driving the Confederates away from the railroads, especially the Mississippi Central Railroad, and to "do the enemy all the harm possible." As soon as Pemberton surrendered, Sherman moved into action, and within two days he had all his forces near the Big Black River, ready to cross and begin a new campaign.[44]

Bussey's cavalry brigade consisted of all available men from the Third and Fourth Iowa, Fifth Illinois (under Seley), and Second Wisconsin regiments. The horsemen crossed the Big Black River and overtook Steele's Fifteenth Army Corps at Messenger's Ford. The cavalry rode to the front of the column and took the advance on the Bridgeport Road. Due to the extreme heat, the horsemen slowly pushed toward Confederate president Jefferson Davis's plantation on 7 July, where they met a small force of John W. Whitfield's horsemen, consisting of the Third, Ninth, and Twenty-Seventh Texas Cavalry regiments, from William H. Jackson's brigade. Johnston had tasked Jackson with screening the Army of Relief's retreat, resisting the Federal advance to allow Johnston ample time to retreat to the state capital. The Federals easily brushed aside the Texans and reached Bolton by one in the afternoon.

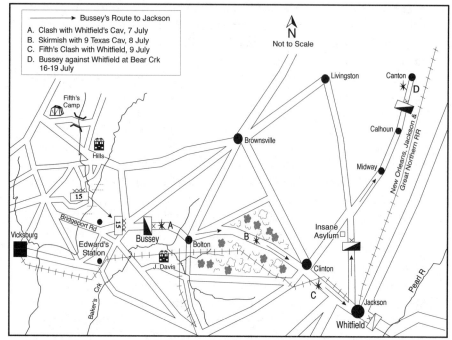

Map 5.3. Sherman's move on Jackson, July 1863.

A heavy rainstorm at dusk brought an early evening for the soldiers, who slept on the ground in the hot, wet air. Mosquitoes plagued the men from both armies. Before the storms hit, though, the Illinoisans visited Bolton, sightseeing and reading the local newspapers. John Mann learned the fate of his brother Calvin and the other forty raiders from a local newspaper, but John "hope[d] the account exaggerated." Not everyone in Company K was saddened by Calvin's capture. John Burke hoped his captain found "Libby prison quite congenial" and wanted the physician to continue to "board there during the rest of the war."[45]

The night storms brought in cooler air and gave the men a reprieve from the hot, dusty march. The Federal cavalry stayed in camp near Bolton until 2:00 P.M. on 8 July and then moved onto Clinton, eight miles to the east. Heading out on the Bridgeport Road, with the Third Iowa Cavalry under Maj. John W. Noble in advance, they encountered pickets from the Ninth Texas two miles east of town. The Third Iowa charged, driving the Texans four miles and into the main body of Confederate cavalry, three miles west of Clinton. "[S]trongly posted in the woods and behind a fence" stood a squadron of the Ninth Texas Cavalry, supported by the Twenty-Seventh Texas Cavalry (First Legion).[46]

Bussey formed his cavalry into line of battle at the edge of the woods. The Iowa colonel detached one company of the Third Iowa and the beleaguered Company I, Fifth Illinois, under Capt. James Balch, led by Lt. Col. John Henry Hammond, of Sherman's staff. Hammond moved to the right of the road to flank the Texans, while the main body of cavalry, with Companies K and L, under Seley, in the advance, pressed forward on the main road. Hammond moved to the Texans' left, to a fence, which the cavalry threw down "under a heavy fire," and fired their carbines.[47]

Companies K and L confronted the Texans, "[c]harging upon the flying rebs using the pistol and Carbine freely[,] not getting close enough to the saber." The Fifth drove the Rebels about a mile, "through a skirt of timber," and came "to a field where the rebs were in force in line." Here the regiment received a "severe lesson" from the Texans, who wounded Robert King, Co. K, and another man in Company L. Two other privates lost their horses to bullets meant for their riders. As the Texans formed another line, "our men scattered somewhat," as Seley ordered a halt until reinforcements arrived, but none came. The Fifth stood in line "in the edge of the field in full view of, and in range of the rebs['] fire," receiving two volleys from the Texans, but "not one man got struck." Mann believed this moment was the most incompetent his company experienced during the war. Bussey ordered neither a retreat nor a charge, and the Fifth "boys became raving mad because they had to stand under a severe fire." Without orders, Seley took his men out of the line of fire and into a hollow, finally gaining some relief from Texas lead.[48]

The flanking movement by Hammond checked the Texans' progress, and they withdrew to Clinton. The incident in the field prompted Hammond to chastise the men of the Fifth. Mann believed Hammond "rendered himself very obnoxious to our 'boys,'" by calling some "D——d Cowards & boasting of his own bravery." After suffering the affront, Illinois native Cpl. Wallace C. Tuthill (1842–1931), Co. K, told Hammond "'to get Col [Bussey] to order a charge instead of keeping [them] there to be shot at where they could do nothing & he would soon see who ware cowards.'"[49]

The morning of 9 July dawned sweltering hot and humid. The cavalry, with the Fifth in advance, passed easily through Clinton but ran into trouble four miles east of town, where they slugged it out with the Third and Ninth Texas Cavalry regiments. The Texans "skirmished carefully and stubbornly," hampering the advance of the Federal cavalry for several hours. Both sides put their men into position, but the dismounted Texans slowly retired to Jackson. About sunset, Parke's Ninth Corps arrived, and both sides opened up with artillery. This was the first time the prairie boys "was ever under

Cannon fire[,] but their Shells made more noise than any thing else for all they done was to Cut down plenty of timber over our heads." Burke explained to his sister that" it would be an old story to tell about the roaring of Shell[,] but I Can assure you that I have heard Sweeter Music than they make and have seen nicer Sights than an Eight inch shell burst about thirty feet above our heads." No one from the regiment received injuries. With the loss of daylight, the Confederate cavalry retired to Jackson.[50]

Moving out on the Livingston Road the next day, Bussey traveled north to the Jackson Insane Asylum on the Canton Road. A nice breeze tempered the heat and humidity as the men rode through the once-lush countryside that still showed evidence of the Federals' occupation in May. "War[']s dread desolation is to be seen all around us and this people once so [happy] are now miserable and turn stricken, reaping the bitter fruits of their own folly and wickedness. No earthly power can restore what they have lost by their treason to the Government." The Federal forces converged on Jackson from three sides, investing Johnston's army. Bussey, with Parke's Ninth Corps, served on the Federal's left flank from the Canton Road to the Pearl River. Steele's Fifteenth and Edward Ord's Thirteenth Corps comprised the center and right, respectively. Johnston's only avenue of retreat lay to the east, across the Pearl River, toward Alabama.[51]

Settling into camp, the cavalry boys expected to spend the next day in leisurely pursuits but instead received Bussey's instructions to move out just before supper. Loud protests followed the men as they packed up their horses for the scout. Six miles from the asylum on the Livingston Road, the cavalry turned east at Battle Springs. Riding about five miles, the men hit the New Orleans, Jackson and Great Northern rail line, just south of Midway. Bussey dismounted the Iowan cavalry, charging them with the destruction of one-half mile of track, while the Fifth Illinois and Second Wisconsin served as guards. The cavalry completed the rail destruction by midnight and then saddled up and moved to a few miles north, where the exhausted horsemen encamped at 2:00 A.M.

Riding out before daylight, Bussey arrived at Calhoun by six in the morning. The cavalry burnt two locomotives and twenty-five cars and destroyed the depot, including one hundred bales of cotton. They also tore up another half mile of track. With the destruction complete, the Iowan moved his cavalry on to Canton. A few miles south of the town, at the crossing of Bear Creek, the Federals found George B. Cosby's brigade of Mississippi cavalry behind entrenchments in the woods surrounding the creek. The Confederates guarded "a valuable wagon train" of supplies for Johnston's army as it tried to cross the Pearl River at Canton.[52]

Pickets from both sides exchanged a few shots, and Federal cavalry-men soon discovered whom they fought, prompting Bussey to withdraw. Mann criticized Bussey's leadership: "The Col (Bussey) would not move on into the place [Canton], but turned the column west and stopped for dinner. . . . Col Bussey is not fit to command a troop and should quit." Skiles echoed the same sentiment and thought Bussey "incompetent." The Federal column rested at Beattie's Ford on the Big Black River until the heat dissipated, then moved toward Vernon, where they bivouacked that night at ten o'clock. Bussey allowed his troops to rest until half past three in the morning and then headed south along the Brownsville Road. The cavalry moved in a zigzag pattern to confuse any Confederate pursuit. Mann described the country as "pretty level" and under cultivation that was "all under fence." The movement not only slowed the horsemen's progress but also, owing to the nature of the countryside, did not conceal the cavalry's path of escape. They did not arrive back at the asylum until late in the afternoon of 13 July.[53]

General Orders No. 141 sent Bussey's cavalry, Charles R. Woods's brigade of infantry, and Clemens Landgraeber's four 12-pound howitzers from the Missouri Horse Artillery on a second attempt to take Canton. The foot soldiers received instructions to destroy at least forty miles of rail track, while the cavalry provided support on the infantry's flanks. Once at Canton, however, the horsemen were tasked with the destruction of the Way's Bluff Bridge, while the infantry demolished the rail network. Though Woods commanded the infantry and artillery, the cavalry remained under Bussey, who would be available should the troops encounter any resistance that required a "concert of action."[54]

At daybreak on 15 July, the two columns moved from their respective camps, rendezvousing at Grant Mills' Ferry on the Pearl River, about ten miles north of Jackson at 9 A.M. The advance of the column skirmished with a squad of Cosby's cavalry, causing the Confederates to retreat to the east side of the Pearl River. Woods burned the ferryboat and two canoes, while the cavalry destroyed a large lot of lumber. Having completed their tasks, the column moved on to Calhoun Station.[55]

Col. Edward F. Winslow set off with the Fourth Iowa and Fifth Illinois with instructions to destroy the two bridges over the Pearl at Madison-ville. The detachment rode at high speed through the hot and cloudy summer morning, reaching both bridges without being discovered and destroying their targets. Heading into Calhoun about dinnertime, the cavalry detachment witnessed the infantry destroy the railroad track by piling up a "good portion of the iron on the ties, and setting fire to them."[56]

With the destruction complete, Woods and Bussey moved out on the Canton Road just after six in the morning. Three miles south of Canton, the Second Wisconsin advance encountered Whitfield's Texas Cavalry Brigade, plus Wirt Adams's Mississippians, returning from their raid to Clinton, where they attempted to destroy Sherman's ammunition train. After two hours of skirmishing, the Federals found the Rebel battle line "extended from Bear Creek west on the Beattie's Bluff road as far as we could see—about a mile—and commanded the Canton road." Bussey also became aware of a movement to the Federals' left, which intended to cut off and capture the column's seventy-five wagons carrying extra ammunition and the precious water supply.[57]

Bussey, as senior officer, took command and consolidated his forces, deploying two regiments of infantry and one section of Landgraeber's artillery to the left and right of Canton Road. He also sent Farnan's battalion and one gun from the Missouri battery to deal with the Rebel's flank movement. The Illinoisans rode hard down the Livingston Road, encountering Texans only four hundred yards from the wagon train. The Fifth moved through a thick hedge and into a cornfield and opened fire at short range with their carbines, emptying saddles, but they were greatly outnumbered. A few shells from the artillery checked the Texans' advance, but the Confederates concentrated more troops near the valuable wagons. Bussey, seeing the vulnerability of the Fifth, sent reinforcements from the Third and Fourth Iowa, who deployed to the left of the Fifth in the cornfield. The Seventy-Sixth Ohio, a detachment of the Twenty-Fifth Iowa, and another gun from the Missouri battery served as support, while Seley and the rest of the Fifth held the right. The cannon opened fire with shell at short range, pushing the Texans back in great disorder through the cornfield. The Federals witnessed as the Texans rallied and advanced a second time, but a charge by the Iowans on the left, and a few more shells from the artillery, halted the Texans' advance. Finding the Federals "too strong for us," the Rebels "were ordered to retire" and moved to Shallow Ford, where they crossed the Pearl River. Bussey believed his troopers caused a great loss of men, for he witnessed a number of Confederate ambulances moving toward the area of engagement and retiring on the Beattie's Bluff Road.[58]

Meanwhile, on the Canton Road, Col. Charles Woods met Col. Wirt Adams's Mississippians positioned in the dense undergrowth of Bear Creek. Woods eventually flanked the Mississippians, causing the Confederates to disengage and withdraw toward Canton. Bussey called a halt because he deemed it not "prudent to attempt to enter [Canton] at so late an hour." The exhausted Federals camped by the waterway for the night, while the Rebels crossed the Pearl River without any pursuit.[59]

Bussey posted guards "at all the street corners, [who] were also detailed to protect private property when asked for." While Woods's infantry destroyed every vestige of railroad equipment at Canton, Bussey sent a cavalry force under Winslow to the Way's Bluff Bridge. After four attempts, the cavalrymen destroyed the structure, along with all the rail property of the Mississippi Central at the site. The Confederates estimated the monetary loss at both Canton and Way's Bluff at two million dollars.[60]

The Federal column started for Jackson mid-morning on 19 July. Having traveled only eight miles, Bussey rested his horsemen, allowing time for dinner, then into the saddles for five more miles of travel. As the heat rose, the horses and men suffered from lack of water. Bussey finally stopped and rested his men until the heat dissipated with the sunset. Reaching camp near the insane asylum, the men learned of the Confederates' evacuation of Jackson three days earlier. The Confederates retreated through Brandon, with Johnston finally stopping and concentrating his forces at Morton. Steele's brigade followed the Confederates to Brandon, but Sherman deemed pursuit beyond his army's endurance and ordered its retreat to Vicksburg.

The horsemen had been in the saddle a few hours when they felt the Mississippi sun rise hot and deadly on 21 July. The intense heat caused the men to take it slow and easy, camping only eight miles into their retrograde march. At Bolton Station on 24 July, Company G lost five men while they foraged the countryside: Thomas Taylor, Thomas C. Craig, James McAllister, William R. Thomas, and Albert Willets, together with their horses and equipment. Taylor died while a prisoner at Andersonville in July 1864. Overall, Bussey's cavalry lost only nine men during the entire expedition, with the Fifth losing three wounded at Clinton and five missing on the return trip to Vicksburg.[61]

Federal victories in other areas of the country followed in the wake of Pemberton's surrender and Johnston's retreat. "Good news from 'All Points.' Port Hudson taken by Maj Gen Banks. Lee whipped in Penn (at Gettysburg) by Gen Meade. Price repulsed at Helena with heavy loss. [Braxton] Bragg driven back in Tenn to Chattanooga. . . . the whole camp is rejoicing," noted Mann. Packard believed that Price's ill-fated attack at Helena "show[ed] they did not dare to Make the Attack while the bloody 5th [Illinois] was there." The still-fevered lieutenant thought "the news is Glorious and is as good as Several doses of Medicine." Roe declared "now we have complete possession of the Mississippi River & I have no doubt of what we will keep it." The Clay County physician believed the Federal army, with the help of the "God of Heaven," would soon destroy the "Rebel & Copperhead Traitors." Many hoped the victories would bring a quick resolution to the fighting.[62]

Hundreds of men became victims of heat stroke, malaria, and camp diarrhea during the Vicksburg and Jackson campaigns. The area around Vicksburg is part of the Mississippi delta country, with the landscape interspersed with numerous waterways, bayous, and swamps—ideal breeding grounds for the mosquito. With the lack of sanitary conditions during the Vicksburg siege, many men relieved themselves at their convenience, allowing typhoid and dysentery bacteria to spread into the scarce water supply, then throughout the army. Murine typhus also became an issue for the men in the trenches, where fleas flourished on the grimy soldiers, who were unable to cleanse themselves properly without exposing themselves to enemy fire. By early July, fevers of all types ravaged the ranks of Grant's army.

Sherman knew his men's health suffered while fighting Johnston and believed pursuing the Confederates east of the Pearl would ruin the army. Even Grant ordered his friend to "take your own time returning" to Vicksburg, to preserve what little health the men had left. Within a few days of the army's return, Grant allowed the sick to obtain thirty-day furloughs on a surgeon's certificate, but only if the soldier would not be fit for military duty during that time. All others suffering with illness would be discharged or sent to the newly formed invalid corps.[63]

When the prairie boys returned from the Mechanicsburg expedition in early June, the men who participated quickly weakened from heat stroke, exhaustion, and malaria. With the heat and humidity on the rise throughout June, many soldiers became prostrated, unable to regain their strength quickly. Convalescent camps, such as Milldale Church, located three miles from Haynes' Bluff, serviced many of the sick, including those from the Fifth. The camp quickly reached its capacity, forcing the ill to languish in overcrowded regimental hospitals or their tents. Though many Fifth soldiers obtained immunity to typhoid at Helena, murine typhus and malaria quickly spread through the regiment, with four out of the five regimental chroniclers prostrated with illness during the summer.

Many soldiers, like Thadeus Packard, did not recognize the symptoms of the mosquito-borne disease, and he misdiagnosed his illness. "Taken with a Severe pain in head[,] think I took a Sunstroke after getting wet the night befor[e] while on picket." After being "crazy for Several hours" with a "raging fever," Dr. Ensey, who did recognize the disease, administered quinine to the ailing lieutenant. When Packard picked up his pen again to write in his diary a week later, he concentrated on the health of friends in his company. "Capt. [Withers] dangerously sick with Billious fever [typhus or malaria]. . . . Geo [McLaughlin] very Sick with a fever. M[ost] of Company C and some other companys Sent to Convalesent Camp at Mill Dale. 2/3s of the Men Sick and I am Still Suffering," lamented Thadeus. He eventually convalesced at Milldale Church, his "head paining me Still Severely," though he continued his duties obtaining furloughs for fellow soldiers. Jonas Roe, who contracted a severe case of "Camp Diarhea & chills," joined his fellow soldiers at the hospital camp, where he estimated there were at least five thousand sick in early July.[64]

According to Packard, the majority of the soldiers of Company C in early July occupied sick beds, and "Some of them [are] just getting looking like human [beings]. . . . Only 20 available Men an[d] an Officer was Able to start out on a large 15 days Scout [Jackson]." With Captain Withers convalescing at a local house, and Lt. Francis Wheelock too ill for duty, Packard tried to attend to the company during the Jackson campaign. Seriously ill with fever, the lieutenant nevertheless mounted up, with his friends assisting him into the saddle on 6 July. The boys had not gone far when Apperson called a halt and ordered Packard back to camp, which the lieutenant determined "was luckey for Me for I had a burning fever and Came Near fainting Several times." Packard suffered from malaria and its subsequent hepatitis, and even though he was "So poor You Can hear my bones fairly rattle," he believed George Secrease and William Glimpse, also from Company C, were "at the point of death . . . , and were not Expected to live." The lieutenant credited the illness to "Southern fever [malaria]. They are taken Chilly & Vomiting and fever." Being sick brought out the loneliness and hopelessness of his situation. "I am in a tent all alone and I feel So Strange & lonely in this camp of death! When You Can hear the Burial Volley every few hours. I do hop[e] we Can be permitted to go up the river Soon."[65]

Packard relied on homeopathic medicines his wife sent him, using them "as Skillful[ly] as I know how," but they quit working, and he resorted to heavy doses of quinine. When the malarial medicine ceased to help him, the lieutenant resorted to calomel (mercurous chloride), which caused him to "See Stars all the time." The mercury in Packard's system eventually sent him spiraling into hallucinations where he saw his mother, who "handed Me the Most delicious Apple I Ever Ate." As the lieutenant recovered his senses, he began to record his thoughts again in his diary. "God pity the Sick here, for all the relief they receive from Sanitary [Commission] sources. The Big Officers get all of that, and not a Scrap do the poor Sick Boys get. . . . this is the poorest Country on God[']s Earth for Sick peoples. . . . This is the Most Godforsaken place I have Seen Yet." Packard remained "as Weak as a rag," but he still dragged himself "around to See the Sick boys" and tried "to Encourage them!"[66]

Finally, on 9 August, Packard received a thirty-day furlough, but the trip caused emotional turmoil for the stricken lieutenant. Crowded together with hundreds of other invalids on board the "Splendid Hospital Steamer *City of Alton,*" Packard noticed that some men were "dying from dred to day," after seeing all the occupied coffins onboard their transports. The psychological trauma to men already weakened by diseases cannot be comprehended, for many knew their ship also carried "Em[p]ty Coffins for Some More of us" who would perish on the trip north. The lieutenant survived the journey and arrived home to his beloved Jennie on 15 August, where he found "Open Arms an[d] hearts to Receive my Carcuss." Even under Jennie's care, Packard's health did not improve, and he extended his furlough sixty more days, based on two surgeons' certificates. While convalescing in Bloomington, he attended the funeral of another stricken Fifth Illinoisan, thirty-six-year-old John Cowan, Co. C, who died of chills and diarrhea on 19 September. By the end of October, Packard still suffered from diarrhea and "pain in my head," but his strong sense of duty compelled him to return to the service. "To Keep . . . My vows and Concience Clear," the ailing lieutenant made arrangement to return to the regiment. The brave lieutenant never fully recovered his health.[67]

Roe did not even attempt to accompany the regiment on the Jackson campaign, for he was stricken with something he called "Bilious Diarhea," probably typhus and malaria with complications from quinine overdoses. Roe believed he had suffered from the same malady while at Helena; the chills and diarrhea more reminiscent of remittent fever (malaria) than dysentery. The private hoped he could get a furlough to recover at home, but he advised his wife Celina "not [to] make any calculations about seeing me soon [so] you will not be disappointed," if he could not obtain one. Roe finally received his furlough in early August, which he extended for another thirty days, returning to the regiment in early October.[68]

Those who did accompany Sherman fared even worse than those who convalesced at Milldale and Oak Ridge. During the Confederate retreat, the Rebels contaminated the few wells and cisterns between the Big Black River and Jackson, causing a shortage of potable water on the long, hot, dusty march. The lack of water, combined with the intense heat and with sleeping outdoors exposed to mosquitoes, destroyed the health of many soldiers, including John Mann and John Burke.

Mann became incapacitated with tertian malaria on 19 July, suffering through the chill, fever, and vomiting cycle every other day. His health became so prostrated he returned from the Jackson campaign with the convalescent train, under the care Dr. Roger W. Pease. He joined nine others from the Randolph Rangers, in the tent he shared with Thomas Barnfield at their main campground. These men also recuperated from illnesses, especially diarrhea, that "is pretty hard to get clear of," when serving in the military.[69]

So many soldiers and officers received furloughs after Jackson that many regiments and divisions lacked commanding officers. Before his sick furlough, Packard had not received pay in five months because he could not "get Muster[ed] [as 2nd Lieutenant]: No Office[r] here to do it." Sherman believed that each division should retain at least one general officer, a regiment needed one field officer, and a company should have at least one commissioned officer. The Ohioan feared that "if we don't look [out], our army will take leave en masse." Mann believed at least one hundred desperately ill prairie boys became part of the first group of furloughed soldiers.[70]

During the late summer, Mann also suffered greatly from diarrhea, "which keeps me too weak to Stir much. In fact it is very hard for one to get up in this climate when once reduced." The diarrhea, more than likely, resulted from the large quinine doses Mann took for his malaria. The lieutenant tried to quell the diarrhea with blackberry cordial, a homeopathic tonic. Whatever the cause, diarrhea became debilitating enough for the commissary officer to apply for a leave of absence, but when that failed, Mann resigned. Unfortunately, the Fifth's commanding officer, Major Seley (whom Mann openly detested), denied his resignation. By the end of August, Mann informed his wife that his health had improved a little, but being forced to recuperate in the unhealthy air of Milldale would keep him down a long time. He lamented to his wife, "The obstacles thrown in the way of going home or resigning are So numerous that if I was out . . . of the army once[,] nothing but the Conscript Law would get me in again." If he had his health, John told Nancy, he would stay in, but now that he felt weak and unable to perform his duties, he would try repeatedly to get home. His chances improved when men returned from the original thirty-day furloughs in late August. Mann finally received his thirty-day furlough in mid-September.[71]

John Burke, however, never received a furlough, and he languished in his tent for over a month with an illness he never specified to his sister. He stayed on duty, for he was not sick enough to be confined to bed, yet he was "so weak that I am not able to sit in the Saddle an hour without turning Perfectly Blind." When his company left for a scout to Grenada in August, Burke became overwhelmed with the isolation, for he had never missed duty before. "I feel [so] . . . lonesome that I hardly know what to do," he told his sister. Burke survived the summer, but his health never improved while he remained in the service.[72]

In August, Apperson applied for a twenty-day leave to recuperate from a body ravaged by malaria. Physicians also diagnosed the major with chronic diarrhea and jaundice, resulting in general debility. Apperson's alleged cowardice at Mechanicsburg never became common knowledge within the regiment, and many believed his furlough to Illinois was to make arrangements to bring the Fifth home to curtail treasonous activity, and "to keep the Traitors down." Skiles actually anticipated fighting Northern Copperheads, for he "would ten times rather fight them, & learn them the value of Uncle Sam[']s protection." According to the private, when his friend Allen Johnson was on furlough in Illinois in August, the fellow Company G private "carried his revolver all the time. [I]f the Copperheads had insulted him," Skiles believed, "they would have got their dues."[73]

Within two months of his furlough, Apperson resigned because of poor health; those who served with him at Mechanicsburg believed he left the service to avoid charges of cowardice, incompetency, and misconduct. Part of the charges against Apperson covered his supposed orders to Mumford to burn plantations and execute white overseers in October 1862 in response to the ambush at McCalpin's estate. The men also alleged Apperson visited and kept a whore at Helena, and that he commanded the regiment while intoxicated. There was nothing in Apperson's character to suggest this type of behavior, but the charges were signed by two majors (Seley and Farnan), four lieutenants (John Mann, Harrison Brown, William Berry, and Gordon Webster), and six captains (Mumford, Cullers, Peniwell, McConkey, Calvin Mann, and Alexander Jessop), many of whom were Democrats. Surprisingly, Captain Withers, who led the charge after Apperson's stumble, and Lieutenant Packard, who accompanied Withers, did not sign the specifications, suggesting that the charges were politically motivated. Farnan, according to Seley, became obsessed with humiliating Apperson, all in the name of gaining a higher rank, and "exerted all the influence he could against [Apperson]." Seley named Farnan "the worst enemy that Apperson had in the whole Army."[74]

With Apperson gone, Farnan took matters into his own hands and sought the lieutenant colonelcy over Seley. The second major informed

JUNE TO AUGUST 1863

Governor Yates how Farnan had circulated a petition among some of the officers to "supercede me as [Apperson's] Successor." He requested quick action against Farnan and "in strict accordance with justice to the Soldier." Through all the political wrangling, officers eventually brought court-martial charges against both majors: Seley for drunkenness and Mumford for false muster. Two of the Fifth's surgeons, Ensey and Watts, also had charges preferred against them for the excessive use of alcohol. All charges against the officers would eventually be dropped. In spite of all the solicitations, Yates failed to appoint a lieutenant colonel; Seley remained a major but gained the rank in July 1864, after Col. John Mc-Connell recommended him for the position.[75]

6

WINSLOW'S CAVALRY
August 1863 to January 1864

In early August, Bussey lost command of his cavalry brigade at Vicksburg. The Fifth whispered of the Iowan's incompetence and believed
the rumors that alluded to his arrest and subsequent loss of command for
his inaction at Canton. In actuality, Grant transferred Bussey with Steele's
troops to Arkansas. Bussey's promotion to brigadier general astounded
John Mann: "[Bussey] makes a poor Col and how . . . could he be appointed
Brig Gen on merit. If he is fit for a Brig [Gen], I am more fit for a Major
Gen." A detachment of Bussey's Third Iowa remained at Vicksburg and
joined the transformed brigade with the Fifth Illinois and Fourth Iowa
regiments, commanded by Col. Edward F. Winslow, Fourth Iowa.[1]

The brigade's first challenge occurred in northern Mississippi, where
their mission was to extradite rolling stock for the Mississippi Central and
the Mississippi and Tennessee Railroads. The destruction of the Pearl River
railroad bridge during the Jackson campaign had isolated more than four
hundred locomotives and cars around Grenada and Water Valley, located
one hundred miles north of Jackson. The only Confederate troops available
to guard the four million dollars' worth of stock remained James R. Chalmers's Second Brigade, totaling less than fifteen hundred men at Grenada.

Federal authorities became aware of the stranded rolling stock in late
July and devised a plan to send engineering troops from Memphis to re-
build the rail lines, while Winslow's cavalry gathered all the abandoned
stock from Yazoo City northward to Grenada. The two Federal forces
would meet at Grenada and move the stock out of Confederate possession to Memphis, Tennessee.

Sherman prohibited the cavalry from confiscating items from Mississippians during the expedition. Instead, the army allotted Winslow
three thousand Confederate dollars to "provide liberally and fairly for

the wants of your command by paying" for food, horses, and supplies. Winslow implemented Grant's new policy toward Mississippians when he strictly prohibited any wandering from the column without permission from field officers. "It is all important that good order and discipline be observed on every occasion and at all times," declared Winslow. Skiles believed the enforcement of Grant's new policy to be the sole reason for the scout: "We are ordered on a scout. . . . [T]o show the citizens that we can be gentlemen & not Vandals, as represented, I think Grant is going to coax Mississippi back."[2]

Stephen Hurlbut sent sixteen hundred men under Lt. Col. Jesse J. Phillips to meet Winslow at Grenada and cooperate in moving the rail stock to Memphis. Winslow's expedition began at 4:30 A.M., Monday, 10 August, as eight hundred men rode out of their camps, with the Third Iowa in advance, followed by the Fifth Illinois (Companies A, B, F, and K, under Farnan), and the Fourth Iowa regiments. The commander permitted only the best conditioned soldiers and horses to accompany the column and disallowed any wagons, trains, or ambulances. The sick, weak, and injured men that remained in camp silently watched their comrades leave from the confines of their hospital beds. No cheering hordes followed the cavalry as they started out that hot summer morning.

The Fifth carried rations for only four days in their haversacks, along with ample supplies of ammunition for their Cosmopolitan carbines and their newly acquired Sharps carbines and service revolvers. Weighing in at eight pounds and firing only a single .52 caliber bullet, the breech-loader could be loaded and fired up to five shots a minute. Winslow anticipated trouble from William H. Jackson's cavalry, rumored to be at Brandon, and ordered the men to "attack promptly and resolutely, and so handle your forces that they cannot count your numbers." The horsemen traveled on the Lower Benton Road until the heat forced them to make camp, eighteen miles from Haynes' Bluff.[3]

The next morning, the men started early, before dawn and the sweltering sun. They passed through Mechanicsburg late in the morning, riding to within nine miles of Yazoo City. Winslow expected to find the promised Federal gunboats and transports when they rode into the city early Wednesday morning, 12 August, but the docks remained empty. A scout sent to Satartia returned with news that the expected boats had returned to Vicksburg with the soldiers' rations. Additional bad news arrived when Winslow learned that Jackson's cavalry was at Canton, only thirty miles southeast of Yazoo City. After conferring with his senior officers, who voted to return to Vicksburg due to the lack of rations, the

Iowan instead determined to continue to Grenada "so as to leave all the rebel cavalry well to the rear the first day." Leaving before dawn on 12 August, Winslow reached Rankin about midmorning, and after a short rest in the blistering heat, the bluecoats marched thirty miles to Harlan's Creek, eight miles from Lexington.[4]

Unknown to Winslow, Whitfield's cavalry, consisting of the Third, Sixth, and Ninth Texas Cavalry regiments, followed Winslow along the Artesian Springs Road. The Texans were only five hundred strong, and far behind their Federal rivals. Additional Confederate troops from Carrollton, the Sunflower Rangers, under Capt. A. M. Hostin, rode out to block Winslow from the north. Calvin Mann had routed these same Rangers, also known as the Sixth Battalion Mississippi Cavalry, during the Yazoo Pass expedition in February.[5]

Winslow reached the outskirts of Durant about noon on 13 August, where he detached Company G of the Fifth, who "Charged on the town & Captured a train & mail" heading south from Grenada. Capt. John H. Peters, Third Iowa, took control of the cars and engine. To ensure no more trains reached Confederate-held territory, Peters rode the engine to Box Creek and burned the rail bridge, confiscating another engine and ten more cars. Peters moved his ever-growing train back to Durant, where he connected with the rest of the cavalry.[6]

Winslow's men now had control of the rail line, and their march lay along its track. A five-hour march brought the men to West's Station, where they discovered additional engines and cars. A late summer rain began to fall, providing a needed reprieve from the heat, but Winslow intended to march through the night. Soon, though, the rain turned into "tremendous and prolonged thunder-storms . . . with floods of water." Skiles believed they "had the hardest rain storm I ever witnessed, it was so dark we could'nt see your hand before you, [and] our horses could'nt keep the road." The men had difficulty controlling their mounts from running into the brush, and they would "stop untill it would lightning." Visibility grew so poor, the horsemen "had to keep up a perpetual hallooing, in order to keep the road." Winslow realized the futility of further travel and bivouacked the troops at Jordan's Creek.[7]

After destroying the rail bridge over Jordan's Creek, the Federal column reached Vaiden well before noon on 16 August. Peters took six hours to organize the cars into trains and asked for volunteers from the cavalry to staff the crews. While at Vaiden, a southbound Confederate train chugged into the station, heading for Canton. When the engineer "saw us [the Federals]," explained Skiles, "they ran back & Escaped. [I]t had 3 C. S. soldiers,

& 3 Citizens." Winslow also sent a demolition team to Peachalala Creek to destroy the railroad bridge, so "the trains could not be carried off if we should be forced to abandon them temporarily." The Texans reached Durant in the evening, twenty four hours behind the Federal column, and then Vaiden the next day.[8]

Winslow rode through the night, destroying rail bridges, finally arriving at Winona about daybreak on the morning of 17 August. When the column passed through Winona, however, they learned Texas scouts had fired the northern bridge the previous day. The Federal column's delay at Vaiden allowed a few of Whitfield's scouts to bypass the cavalry and ride north to destroy the bridge. This action crushed Winslow's hope of successfully rescuing the rolling stock, for the captured cars were now trapped below Winona.[9]

Abandoning the stock, Winslow reached Duck Hill before noon, skirmishing along the way with horsemen of the Sunflower Rangers, who delighted in hampering Winslow's progress. The Texans never encountered Winslow's cavalry in force, but one small group of Ninth Texas Cavalry scouts engaged the Federal advance at Duck Hill before retreating toward Greensborough. Winslow's column now had unhampered access to Grenada.[10]

Meanwhile, Phillips's column entered Grenada from Tennessee about 3:30 on 17 August. With no word from Winslow, Phillips destroyed all the cars and engines in town. The long billowing clouds of destruction from Phillips's fire guided Winslow to Grenada. The Vicksburg cavalry arrived by eight at night, and Winslow assumed command of all Federal forces. Skiles celebrated his twenty-first birthday "by helping take Grenada. . . . [W]e had considerable fun on the road."[11]

Winslow marched toward Memphis early in the morning of 19 August, passing through Oakland, then Panola, where Rebel guerrillas disputed their crossing of the Tallahatchie on the evening of 20 August. Once over the river, Kentucky native John Turner, Co. F, encountered four guerrillas who "jumped out of the brush & fired at him[,] putting 9 buck shot through 1 leg & 1 through the other & killing his horse & wounding a negro."[12] Past Senatobia, Winslow's and Phillips's columns parted.

On the twenty-first, the Vicksburg cavalry crossed the Cold Water without any difficulty, but at Hernando, known as a "guerrilla haunt," scouts reported Confederates posted on the north bank of a secondary stream of the river. Winslow ordered the Third Iowa to make a forward demonstration against the Rebels. Farnan, with three companies from the Fifth and two of the Third Iowa (supported by one company of the

Fifth), moved downriver half a mile to flank the Rebels. The Iowans kept the Confederates busy for an hour and a half while Farnan's men, now dismounted, moved west of their location. Due to "the indiscretion of some of [Farnan's] command[,] the alarm was given, . . . and the enemy in front retreated with some loss, just as the flanking party came in sight." The Fifth, under continual fire from all sides, sustained some casualties, including the death of Indiana native Isaac Jones, Co. B.[13]

Winslow's men repaired the ferry, while a detachment unsuccessfully pursued the Rebels. Continuing forward, the column reached Memphis on 23 August after marching 265 miles and routing the Rebels three times. The Iowan proudly boasted of his men's behavior and reported that the horsemen "did not commit any excesses; did not enter one house from camp to Grenada, except on duty, and the property was respected." This behavior, the prairie boys believed, confused the local farmers, who assumed the well-behaved soldiers to be Confederates in new uniforms. Skiles even related an incident where the Fifth, as advance guards, had stopped at a plantation and told the proprietor that they needed provisions. Believing he addressed Confederate soldiers, the old man promptly gathered sheep, hogs, and beef cattle and offered his mill to the Illinoisans to grind some flour. After baking their bread, the prairie boys told the old man who "we were, he did'nt believe it for along while, untill he saw our flag. [H]e slipped out the back door & that was the last we saw of him." Even the Confederate soldiers commented on the Federals' behavior, admitting that "they didn't take time to rob a house."[14]

The command bivouacked at Memphis for six days, giving the boys time to explore the town. Tennessee's largest city did not impress Skiles, who described it to his parents as "a hard looking place" with "poorer streets, poorer building[s] . . . [that] are full of holes."[15] The horsemen reached their camp at Haynes' Bluff on the last day of August. Winslow's men failed to fulfill their main goal of rescuing the rolling stock, but they did strike a major blow to the Mississippi transportation system and disrupted the Confederate rail system in Mississippi for several months.

The men had little time to enjoy their most recent pay in early September at Camp Sherman before Winslow had them back in the saddle as escorts for infantry forage trains. The prairie boys provided both mounted and dismounted details, due to the poor condition of their horses. The lack of mounts put such a strain on the regiment that Seley allowed only one horse per soldier, assigning surplus animals to dismounted cavalrymen. The boys also had fun on a couple of unsuccessful scouting trips that centered on hunting down Rebels, "riding hard all day, going through

1 of our blockaded roads, & through brush, & swamps, & up & down hills almost perpendicular in order to surprise" Rebels around Birdsong's Ferry. On 22 September, one hundred Illinoisans joined men from the Fourth Iowa for a scout along the west bank of the Big Black River. There the Federals flushed several Confederates "in their shirt tails" from a farmhouse. These bushwhackers "had been troubling our pickets at night," and the Illinoisans chased down and captured three Rebels, along with their horses and arms.[16]

At the end of September, Winslow's brigade saddled up for a minor movement to destroy a couple of Rebel cavalry camps around Vernon. The Confederates ventured out periodically to commit depredations, gathering cattle and slaves from the Yazoo valley. With so few cavalrymen available due to illnesses, Sherman augmented the troops with foot soldiers from Joseph R. Cockerill's and Ralph P. Buckland's infantries. Sherman also used the move to screen the removal of his infantry to Chattanooga.[17]

Only nine hundred cavalrymen from the Fourth Iowa, the Fourth, Fifth, and Eleventh Illinois, and the Tenth Missouri Cavalry regiments, with two mountain howitzers, participated in Winslow's expedition. The regiment, under Seley, contributed 225 men from the various companies. Sherman ordered Winslow to "strike the enemy, who is hovering between Vernon and Yazoo City." Sherman also reverted to the old policy toward civilians when he ordered Winslow to confiscate "freely on the cornfields," and to take all the wagons, carriages, and horses the cavalrymen could use while on the road.[18]

The countryside teemed with Rebel scouting parties, and Whitfield quickly learned that the Federal cavalry were on the move on 27 September. Leaving Camp Sherman, the cavalrymen crossed the Big Black at Messenger's Ferry, where they picked up Cockerill's brigade as they moved down the Bridgeport Road. Winslow's horsemen reached Brownsville around dawn the next day and were met by shots from fifty guns of the Ninth Texas. A few cannon shots from the First Illinois Light Artillery spurred the Texans toward Livingston. The dust of the dry roads coated horse and rider in suffocating layers as the men rode sixteen miles to Whitfield's camp south of Vernon. Light but continuous skirmishing kept the Federals from reaching the site before Whitfield abandoned camp. In the afternoon, Winslow moved toward Beattie's Bluff, heading for the ford nine miles from Vernon. Confederates appeared on the eastern edge of every major crossroad but retired on the Federals' approach. The lack of a ferry and the poor condition of the crossing at the bluff forced

Winslow to move farther north to Moore's Ford, taking the Federals closer to Canton, where Loring's infantry camped.[19]

The closeness of additional Confederate troops in the area induced Winslow to leave the main road, sending his troopers through woods and fields. This tactic confused Whitfield's Texans but also postponed the bluecoats' arrival at the ford till ten at night. Winslow crossed the river but left behind Company G of the Fifth with one howitzer to guard the crossing. After moving about a mile east, Winslow dismounted and bivouacked for the night just above the river's flood plain.

On learning that the Federals had crossed the river, the Ninth Texas and part of Edward Croft's Columbus, Georgia Battery headed for Moore's Ford. Before sunrise on 29 September, the Texans began feeling for the Federals, but the prairie boys had concealed themselves "among the trees and underbrush at a little distance from the bank" of the river. A sharp engagement broke out, but Company G "returned the fire so brisk that they did not care to try it again." Unable to locate the Fifth in the thick brush, the Texans waited until daylight before advancing. Company G let loose "a shower of our Sharps long blue pills [bullets], a physic that was liable to draw some of their entails out," but the Texans planted Croft's four guns and opened on them with "shell, grape, & Cannister." The shells damaged the Federal howitzer and broke the leg of a mule, but otherwise the shells fell "too high to do damage" to cavalrymen. Texans and Confederate newspapers reported that the Fifth fled quickly, leaving behind regimental colors and seven horses with accoutrements. Confederates reported many Illinoisans wounded and one killed, but the Fifth's regimental reports record no loss.[20]

On hearing Croft's guns, bugles sounded in the Federal camp, and Winslow sent the Fourth Illinois to reinforce Company G. On the way toward the river, the Fourth ran into the retreating Fifth, with Texans close on their heels. Winslow ordered the Illinoisans to the front of the column, while the Fourth served as rear guard. A running skirmish continued until the Federals moved through Benton, where Winslow halted, placing his men in line of battle. Not wanting to face a positioned brigade, the Texans turned back and fled toward the Big Black River.

The next morning, Winslow started early, moving south on the Valley Road. Near Mechanicsburg, the Texans tried to cut off the bluecoats "by crossing the creek at a ford lower down & getting ahead of us, but we didn't stick our heads into the lion[']s mouth without having the means of prying it open." Buckland's infantry arrived at the crossing to thwart an attack, causing the Confederates to retreat eastward. From Mechanicsburg to their main camp, Winslow's cavalry experienced easy riding, with no opposition from any Confederate adversaries. The expedition destroyed fifty stands of arms and bagged one hundred horses, fifty mules, eight prisoners from the Third Texas Cavalry, and one ambulance.[21]

The horsemen returned to a much-diminished army, as Sherman's First, Second, and Fourth Divisions of the Fifteenth Corps left Vicksburg for Memphis, en route to Chattanooga to relieve the besieged William S. Rosecrans. The Third Division, Fifteenth Corps, under James M. Tuttle, remained at Vicksburg, as did James B. McPherson's Seventeenth Corps, minus the Second Division, which joined Sherman in October. McPherson now commanded forces in the District of Vicksburg, with Winslow's cavalry brigade joining the Fifteenth Corps.

Braxton Bragg's victory at Chickamauga, Georgia, on 19–20 September against Rosecrans triggered Confederate authorities to redeploy Mississippi cavalry. Their new leader, Stephen D. Lee, took soldiers from Samuel Ferguson's, Lawrence Ross's, and Chalmers's cavalry brigades to harass Sherman's forces on their way to Chattanooga. By early October, fewer than ten thousand Confederate troops were left to challenge the Vicksburg garrison, including Jackson's four thousand cavalry. Wirt Adams, temporarily in command of the Cosby's brigade, was stationed at Brownsville. The brigade consisted of Robert C. Wood's Mississippi Cavalry, the Second and Twenty-Eighth Mississippi, John G. Ballentine's Mississippi Cavalry, Junius Y. Webb's Louisiana Cavalry, and Houston King's Missouri Artillery. Whitfield's brigade, headquartered at Livingston, contained the Third, Sixth, Ninth, and Twenty-Seventh Texas Cavalry regiments, plus Edward Croft's Columbus, Georgia Battery, under Alfred Young. John L. Logan, temporarily attached to Jackson's division at Raymond, included the consolidated Eleventh/Seventeenth Arkansas Mounted Infantry, the Fourteenth Confederate States Cavalry, the Ninth Louisiana Cavalry and Ninth Tennessee Cavalry Battalion, the Fourth Mississippi Cavalry, and Calvit Roberts's Seven Stars Artillery. The Confederate cavalry was bolstered by Loring's infantry at Canton, comprised of soldiers from John Adams's, Abraham Buford's, and Winfield S. Featherston's brigades.[22]

To curtail any further transference of Confederate troops into Tennessee to hinder the movement of Sherman's reinforcements, Grant ordered McPherson to make a demonstration toward Canton, Mississippi, "to create the impression that the Ohio and Mississippi Railroad was in danger." Grant wanted the Federal cavalry under Winslow to threaten east of Canton, toward Columbus, a vital transportation hub in northeast Mississippi. This move, Grant believed, would cause Johnston to hold all available forces in Mississippi to protect the vital rail line, allowing Sherman easy movement toward Chattanooga.[23]

Winslow's horsemen contained fifteen hundred men from the Fifth, Fourth, and Eleventh Illinois, Fourth Iowa, and Tenth Missouri Cavalry regiments. The Fifth, under Farnan, sent men from Companies B, C, F, G, H, and M. For the first time under Winslow, the cavalry commanded their own artillery: two brass 12-pounder James rifled cannon under the experienced Peter Joyce, Tenth Missouri Cavalry. Rising in the dark quiet of a mid-October morning, the men moved out at 5:30 A.M., reaching the Big Black River at Messenger's Ferry as the October sun rose over the darkened tree line. The prairie boys spearheaded the Federal cavalry, followed by James M. Tuttle and John A. Logan's infantry divisions. At Queen's Hill Church, Winslow took a cavalry detachment toward Bolton, reconnoitering for any signs of Confederate activity. Despite their scout, Winslow failed to discover any indication that Logan's Confederate cavalry camped a few miles south of Bolton. Logan's Rebels followed Winslow's wake on the afternoon of 15 October, heading for Brownsville to unite with Wirt Adams's cavalry at the Charles Catlett plantation, four miles east of the town. Simultaneously, Whitfield moved his forces south from Vernon to unite with Adams and Logan. To assist the Rebel cavalry movements, Adams deployed a welcoming party of sharpshooters in Brownsville to slow the Federals' progress.[24]

Winslow reached Brownsville around noon, hours before the infantry. Skirmishing with the enemy began immediately: As the Fifth's advance reached the outskirts of town, Adams's fifty sharpshooters opened fire on the Illinoisans. The prairie boys "charged the rebels with two companies of our reg." Roe described the fighting as desperate, but the Fifth managed to drive Adams's troopers through town. Once the cavalrymen secured Brownsville, Winslow dismounted his men, allowing the soldiers to feed their horses, and awaited orders from McPherson, who soon arrived.[25]

Winslow moved out about four in the afternoon, riding northeast on the Livingston Road, again with the prairie boys in advance. One mile north of Brownsville, the Fifth clashed with Companies C, D, and H of the Twenty-Eighth Mississippi Cavalry and Companies B and F of Ballentine's Cavalry Battalion. Capt. Kendall Peniwell, with Company B in advance and the rest of the regiment in support, charged the Mississippians, driving them about a mile back to their main column, located across a fork in the road. At this point, Kendall "found the rebs too strong & fell back followed by them." The Illinoisans came under "severe volleys of the enemy" that drove them into confusion; Winslow and Mumford rallied the terrified cavalrymen. As the Illinoisans again formed across the road, Winslow ordered the other cavalry regiments into position. The Rebs advanced "in column and line, attacking desperately." The Rebels "came up within 20 yards of" Company G, which had formed across the road, and according to Skiles, " [they] had to stop." One Reb rode up and fired at the company "& hallooed to the rest [of the Rebs] to come on & kill the d—m—d sons of bitches." One Federal spy, as Skiles called him, shot at the Rebel's head but missed. The Confederate then pulled his own revolver, but the spy quickly fired a second time and "shot him dead." After a severe skirmish of about fifteen minutes, Adams withdrew his men. The Federal cavalry pursued for about two more miles without further incident. The horsemen bivouacked north of Brownsville, the infantry south of town.[26]

As the Federals rested, Logan's brigade of Rebel cavalry traveled throughout the night from Raymond to Brownsville, arriving about daylight on 16 October. The two Confederate forces met at the Catlett plantation, a few miles past the forks in the road where the two opposing forces had clashed the previous night. Adams already had his men in position along the ridge west of Bogue Chitto Creek when McPherson advanced. Logan deployed the majority of his troops to the left of Adams's soldiers and placed Griffith's Arkansas dismounted infantry in a skirt of woods in the advance of his main line. A squadron of cavalry armed with short Enfield rifles supported Griffith, with skirmishers already feeling for the Federals' advance. Logan placed the Seven Stars Battery in for action.[27]

McPherson advanced toward Canton in the predawn hours of 16 October. At the forks in the road, the infantry and McPherson took the Livingston Road, running northeast toward Canton. Winslow, with the Missourians in advance, took the eastern road, toward Clinton. The Fourth and Fifth Illinois provided scouts. Riding warily down the road, Winslow soon heard from the prairie boys, who reported Adams's and Logan's Confederates massed across the road, about four miles from the forks.

Suspecting the superiority of Confederate numbers, Winslow did not bring on a full engagement but skirmished lightly with Logan's dismounted Arkansans infantry. About ten in the morning, Logan pushed his troops forward, only to receive orders from Adams to redeploy on the east bank of Bogue Chitto Creek, by Catlett's house. This protected the Confederates' rear and right flank, providing a position on the hills bordering the creek far superior to their first defensive line on the west bank.[28]

Winslow, unable to gain an advantage, called for assistance from the infantry. McPherson sent in Jasper A. Maltby's brigade with Battery D,

First Illinois Light Artillery, while Mortimer D. Leggett's infantry moved by a plantation road to get in the rear of the Confederates. After a wet crossing, the Federal horsemen reformed their line, with the prairie boys occupying the extreme left, in a strip of woods. The Fifth barely had time to get settled before Logan sent forth Thomas R. Stockdale's cavalry, who charged the Illinoisans "so impetuously that a part of the fighting was hand-to-hand." After this short but severe engagement, McPherson determined the country unsuitable for cavalry movements and withdrew Winslow's men, sending them on a mission to flank the Confederates.[29]

Meanwhile, Jackson joined Adams and Logan at the Catlett house. About two in the afternoon, the Confederate cavalry leader received unconfirmed information that another Federal column marched toward Yazoo City. Jackson sent Logan in pursuit of the fictitious troops, while Adams's men maintained their present position to hold off the Federal infantry.

Winslow's flanking movement began early in the afternoon. He left the Missourians and their artillery with the infantry at Catlett's, while four other regiments moved out on the Canton Road. Heading north toward Livingston around 2:00 P.M., the horse soldiers passed Leggett and Manning F. Force's infantry, who fell in behind the cavalry. Winslow's troops rode hard until they reached the Vernon-Livingston-Canton crossroads, where they discovered Whitfield's Texans in line of battle. Whitfield had left Vernon early that morning, heading for a rendezvous with Adams and Logan. On learning of Winslow's movement, Whitfield deployed his Texans at the A. B. Treadwell plantation, astride the Canton Road on the east bank of the Bogue Chitto Creek. The Confederates held "a splendid position," supported with guns from Croft's Georgia Battery.[30]

Light skirmishing commenced between the two forces, and Winslow soon realized the superiority of Whitfield's position. Force's troops responded to Winslow's request for support, and they quickly surged across the Bogue Chitto Creek, securing the east bank, and falling into line of battle. When Logan arrived on his way to intercept the fictional second Federal movement, Whitfield's combined forces left Force stranded on the east bank of the creek. The approaching darkness put an end to the fighting.

About midnight, Winslow ordered Companies F and G, under Farnan, to scout the left flank of the Confederate line. Farnan quickly ran into and captured a Confederate picket post of the Third Texas Cavalry, capturing eleven men and Lt. Frank Henderson. While the Fifth brought in their captives, Wirt Adams withdrew his men from the Catlett plantation, heading north to reinforce Whitfield and Logan. Adams's troops reached the Treadwell Plantation around daybreak on 17 October.[31]

Dawn witnessed McPherson redeploying his troops for a united assault against Whitfield and Logan. After a left flank movement by Winslow, Jackson sent Logan's brigade to Livingston, who took a strong position astride the Canton Road, in the hills about a mile west of town. When Force's and Leggett's troops advanced, Jackson's forces redeployed: Adams to the Madisonville Road and Whitfield on the Canton Road.

Believing he had the Rebels in retreat, McPherson ordered Leggett and Winslow to pursue the Rebels, then rendezvous at Robinson's Mills, a mile west of Livingston. Near Robinson's Mills, Winslow again became entangled with the ubiquitous Texans of Whitfield's brigade, who supported the right of Logan's forces. This time, the Rebels shelled Winslow's troopers with guns from Roberts's Seven Stars and Croft's Georgia artillery. The cavalry experienced another occasion when the men came under the heaviest fire while awaiting orders. Here they were most vulnerable, clearly in the range of the Confederate guns, but unable to deploy and find better protection than the rails from nearby fences. At this point, Winslow called for assistance, and Leggett sent forward Battery L, Second Illinois Light Artillery, causing the Confederates to retire. Darkness quelled any attempt at a Federal pursuit.[32]

That evening, McPherson received false information that Rebels from Grenada reinforced Loring, giving the Confederates an advantage. This prompted McPherson to end his campaign and issue orders for the troops to return to Vicksburg. By 5:00 A.M. the next morning, McPherson's infantry headed south on the Livingston Road, while Winslow's cavalrymen moved forward to engage the Confederates and screen the infantry's retreat. Moving about one and a half miles east, the Federal horsemen found Whitfield's and Logan's forces in line of battle, supported with three pieces of artillery from Croft's and Robert's batteries. The Third Texas and Stockdale's Mississippians moved forward to crush the Federal horsemen. Light skirmishing continued along the line until about noon, when Winslow ordered his cavalry to retire.[33]

Following the infantry on the Livingston Road, Winslow's men served as rear guard of the foot soldiers. The slow retreat of the infantry allowed Felix Dumonteil's Fourteenth Confederate Cavalry to make "frequent dashes upon the rear and flanks" of the Federal cavalry, who appeared to "find a sort of delight" in tormenting the Federal horse soldiers. Winslow's troopers, however, fought back, "ambush[ing] them 3 times[,] killing & wounding several each time, & every time our men wheeled & fired we could see some of them throw up their arms, yell & fall from their horses."[34]

Logan shadowed the Federal column, wanting to inflict as much damage as possible, "hoping to cut off his [Federal] cavalry or wagon train." Anticipating trouble on 19 October, Winslow sent the Fifth to the cavalry's right flank to guard the wagons. Skiles served as the regiment's vidette, hidden "on a hill in an open field." He saw the "rebs in the brush half a mile distant," probably from Dumonteil's and James H. Akin's cavalry. Skiles's position became untenable when a Rebel "came up within 300 yards & fired 6 fair shots at me, one bullet dident miss my head a foot[.] I could feel the wind of it in my face." The private witnessed five more Confederates join his closest adversary, and he "fell back, as we had orders to go. [W]e had orders not to fire or I would have made him git." The prairie boys could not resist though, and before leaving gave the Rebs "a parting salute that made them move. [O]ur [S]harps rifles shoot 900 yards." Logan's opportunity to ambush the wagons failed, as the Federal cavalry kept "close up to the train." Logan followed the Federal column until it crossed the Big Black River Bridge. McPherson's Canton expedition ended before accomplishing Grant's set goals.[35]

McPherson blamed the failure of the expedition, in part, on Winslow's handling of the cavalry. Though he considered the Iowan a good officer, McPherson believed Winslow lacked "spirit and dash." The cavalry's horses even reflected the men's timidity; the horses often "turn[ed] around involuntarily and [broke] for the rear as soon as a cannon shot [was] fired." McPherson deemed a lack of quality subordinate officers as the cavalry's weakness. In defense of Winslow, Confederate cavalry outnumbered his men for the entire expedition. The Iowan often faced two and sometimes three brigades of cavalry, supported by qualified and experienced artillerists. Winslow had only two 12-pound James rifled cannon, while the Confederates had a variety of artillery, including 12-pound Napoleons and 12-pound howitzers. Though the other cavalry regiments had vastly greater experience under cannon fire, this would have been the Fifth's second encounter under enemy artillery. The regiment initially panicked during the first barrage but soon rallied under Mumford and other officers. Winslow's loss seemed small, considering the odds against him, with only four men killed and missing, and eight men wounded. The Texans took twenty-four-year-old Sgt. Francis M. Easton, Co. A, prisoner at Brownsville; two other prairie boys received light wounds.[36]

By the end of October, John Mann returned to his duties as commissary for the regiment. His time at home on sick furlough had improved his health, and he felt "the glow of Youth in my blood again." Mann left home with a heavy heart, though, for his daughter Grace suffered from "an affiction of the Spine," which the lieutenant considered "very Serious." He asked Farnan, who was then leaving to return to Illinois on furlough, to check his daughter, and "give [his wife, Nancy,] a prescription for her," while he was home. Farnan eventually diagnosed Grace with a type of rheumatism and determined she "requires care and time to restore her" health. Being separated from his family at this sensitive time caused much anxiety for the lieutenant, and Mann desperately wanted "A Letter from [Nancy]," which "would relieve me much just now."[37]

On his return to camp, the Randolph County Ranger assisted in changing camp locations, from the Big Black River to Clear Creek, on the Bridgeport Road. The move, which coincided with the reduction of troops for Grant's battle at Chattanooga, drew all the Federal lines closer to the city, with the cavalry camp nine miles out. The regiment brigaded with the Eleventh Illinois.

Packard also returned from his sick furlough. After paying a six-dollar fare for transport aboard the steamer *J. C. Swan*, the lieutenant left Helena, arriving at Vicksburg on 5 November. While in town, the lieutenant met with Captain Withers and learned of the new camp location. Packard expressed his gratitude for the valuable information. "I was very glad of it for we Should have taken the [railroad] carrs for the Big Black." The cavalrymen rented horses in Vicksburg, costing them another five dollars each, and rode out of town as rain fell in torrents. Though the lieutenant still bore the sallow, yellow skin characteristic of liver damage from malaria, Packard believed he had regained his health. A few of Packard's friends still suffered from their own bouts with malaria, but the lieutenant believed he returned to a much healthier regiment. Thadeus's duty remained light throughout November, but he performed "all the duty I am able to volunterily work on Pay Rolls." Within a month, Packard informed Jennie that he "could not See So Much Yellow in my face now," and that he was finally on the mend. After finally mustering in as a lieutenant, Packard "went to the Pay Master," and after much maligning, the lieutenant finally received his pay of $523—the first earnings he had received for nine months.[38]

The paroled Brookhaven raiders also returned to the regiment throughout November as their personal parolee exchanges became available. Many of the men had spent their time since their release from capture at the parolee camp in St. Louis, though a few managed to obtain furloughs and return home for an extended visit.

For the next six weeks, the cavalry entered a period of relative quiet, with an occasional scouting party to the Big Black River. Roe confided to his wife, Celina, "We are Camped here in comfortable quarters and the Rebels do not molest us or we them." The cavalry spent most of their time building winter shanties and stables for their horses. Mann built a brick chimney to keep his and Thomas Barnfield's tent comfortable and warm through the cold, wet Mississippi winter. Packard, with the help of his black servant Ned, erected stables for his prized horses Black Bess and Charlie Edwards and also constructed a cook shanty for their mess. The men used oak sheeting from "an Old deserted Rebel Out House" and built an "Old[-]fashioned fireplace" for cooking. The mess's cooks, Oscar and his wife, Harriett, received a rack in one corner "and [were] as proud as Cuffey with a new rut." The cooks had been married in camp earlier in the year. They produced fine meals for the boys, who lived on "Corn bread, Potatoes, Ham & good Coffee with milk, [and] apple Butter."[39]

During this period, the cavalry's horses suffered for want of decent grain from the government, subsisting on cane and grasses the soldiers gathered outside their campgrounds. "Our horses are suffering for food and no remedy for grain is not to be had in Vicksburg. . . . Steamboats appear to be so scarce that the Gov't is not able to get the forage brought down the River. If the horses do not get more grain they will soon be unfit for duty," wrote an impassioned Mann. Morning reports throughout the fall recorded the weakened condition of the mounts, and by mid-November, the horses had become unserviceable. A few soldiers lost their mounts on scouts due to their poor condition. The animals suffered for six weeks, from the first of October to mid-November, when the commissary department at Vicksburg received two barges of hay and fourteen hundred sacks of grain for more than three thousand horses and mules at the garrison. The problem, McPherson learned, was the immense need for forage and grain in the Army of the Cumberland, besieged at Chattanooga. The horses did not get the needed nutrition until December, when they began to eat "hay along with oats and corn."[40]

To help relieve the drastic needs of the cavalry in the west, Grant placed William Sooy Smith as chief of cavalry for the Military Division of the Mississippi. Smith's main duty, outlined by Grant, was to "supply all deficiencies in arms, equipments, and horses" as quickly as possible, to enable the cavalry for active service. Smith's greatest challenge centered on acquiring good quality horses for the mounted arm of the service; many believed purchasing private mounts from the cavalrymen and placing the animals under government control would remedy this situation. The Fifth Illinois entered the service as a self-mounted regiment, with the men supplying their own horses and equipment; for this they received forty cents a day from the government. Officials believed the end to this practice would "cut off a fruitful source of fraud and stop the practice of horse stealing in these regiments." McPherson agreed and issued General Orders No. 49 to the regiment at the end of December, officially announcing to the men of the government's intention to purchase their animals.[41]

Psychological attrition among the prairie boys, caused by poor health, the lack of horses, and inferior regimental leadership, proved a hindrance in the government's goal to reenlist soldiers before their original enlistments expired. Inducements began in June 1863 but greatly increased in mid-December, a few weeks before the deadline outlined in General Orders Nos. 191, 216, 305, and 376. The army offered to men who had been in the service at least nine months a bounty and bonus amounting to $402, plus a thirty-day furlough if they reenlisted for the remainder of the war. If one-half of a regiment reenlisted, it would henceforth be designated a volunteer veteran organization, with the men adding special service chevrons to their uniforms. The rewards offered by the government held no enticement for Mann, who believed the furloughs would "have the reverse effect. No man of spirit will allow himself to be driven into a re-enlistment to get a chance to go home when 8 or 10 months more will end his present term of enlistment and then he can stay at home." Surprisingly, the lieutenant had little to write on the subject of reenlistment, for he considered himself "too far advanced in life to serve three years more in the army unless the necessity was great, and I do not think it is sufficient to justify me in enlisting again." Mann remained anxious "to return to my family again and quit the pursuit of war."[42]

McPherson's order to purchase cavalry horses held crucial importance for those prairie boys who pondered whether to reenlist as a volunteer veteran regiment. The men did not want to give up their privilege as a self-mounted unit, nor did they want to lose the extra pay for the horses and equipments. Skiles conveyed to his parents the regiment's response: "In the heat of the excitement [to reenlist] there came an Order to have our horses appraised & branded, the enlisting stopped, & those that had, withdrew their names, the boys swore, the officers winced & talked & wrote to Gov. Yates & the war department, our horses are appraised . . . but not branded, we have not heard anything Official about them yet, from the war department."[43]

Though some soldiers mistreated their mounts, many considered their horses valuable assets to their service. On many occasions horsemen relied on their animals to return them safely to Federal lines. During one such incident in late December, Packard had to lead his men back to camp from a forage expedition during a pouring thunderstorm. The darkness was so complete that he "trusted Mostly to My horse. I Shal[l] always like a horse better than Ever after [my] army life is Over." The lieutenant could not understand why soldiers mistreated their animals, for "they have more intelegence then Some Men, and I pity the poor animal when it has to perform Such awful hard work that they are called on to perform in the Service, and a Soldier that does not take good care of his horse, is not a good Soldier and does not deserve the name [of] a Man."[44]

With the threat of losing their horses, the prairie boys reversed their tendency to reenlist: "Our Neighbor Regiment the 11 Ill Cavalry are about to leave on a furlough and recruit and I expect the 4th Iowa Cavalry to go Soon. But turning the Boys['] Horses Over to the Goverment has put a Veto on the reenlisting Scheme in the bloody 5th and Many have Scratched their names off of the roll!" Mann believed the government had the "power & right to change the Status of the Regt at any time," but added he did not think it was for the best. "The change is demoralising to the command and is thereby working evil," he added. Roe alleged the "Government [broke] the . . . Contract with us," and hoped that "the proposed Branding of Horses will never be carried out."[45]

Capt. Samuel Wilson, Co. D, enlisted the aid of Governor Yates, by requesting that he "look to our Rights [of] the Solders." The captain believed that if the government "has no more use for us as an independent Regiment, all they have to do is to muster us out of the Service." They would rather be mustered out, than have the status of the regiment changed. "We are in the field and can Do nothing but Submit to orders as all good Soldiers Should do." Wilson reassured the governor that his men would "Remain true to the union" but requested the governor support the soldiers' rights "under our [original] enlistment and muster."[46]

By 18 December, the line officers of the regiment met to discuss their options in becoming a veteran organization. The topic of discussion focused on "devising some way to get Majors Seley & Mumford to leave the Reg't so that the officers would make the attempt to reenlist the Reg't in the veteran Service." None of the company officers, and few of the men, wanted another three years under either of the field officers. The next evening, the same committee passed resolutions asking Seley to resign immediately, and "a committee was appointed to wait upon him and present the resolution as well as make any explanation necessary." When presented with the officers' determinations, Seley "said he did not intend to go into the Veteran Service, and therefore he had not done anything to get [the] Soldiers to reenlist." The major announced he would resign as soon as he got his affairs in order. Packard believed "time will tell what the Bloody 5th will do."[47]

Few Fifth men wished to reenlist, despite governmental inducements. Many had seen at least one of their friends die from disease while in the service, and they had no trust in the military medical department. The thought of another hellish summer in the Southern climate frightened the men more than Rebel bullets. The problems with the regiment's command, their separation from loved ones, boredom, poor living conditions, and anxiety about their civilian lives caused these patriots to long for the Illinois prairies and home.

In the meantime, the boys spent the month of November on "Picket & Fatigue duty," with foraging expeditions thrown in for excitement. "Most of the leaves had fallen and only the Magnolia & Holly Berch retained their luxurient summer foliage," as the boys rode out one morning heading for Mechanicsburg, accompanied by three regiments of infantry "as an escort for the train." Skiles "had considerable fun . . . shooting hogs[;] you would have thought we were having a young battle." The hogs ran free in the cornfields and had become "very plenty and fat," and "nearly every wagon had four or five, big hogs" to quench the cavalrymen's appetite. "[T]he poultry suffered the same fate." After filling 125 wagons full of corn, chickens, and hogs, the foraging expedition headed back to camp.[48]

The prairie boys spent December chasing Wirt Adams's cavalry in southern Mississippi. A two-hundred-man detachment of the Fifth (Companies L, M, C, and G), under Farnan, joined units from the Fourth Iowa, Tenth Missouri, and Fourth Illinois Cavalries, plus two infantry regiments for the expedition to Natchez. Packard led twenty-five men from Company C, his first expedition since returning to the regiment. Walter P. Gresham commanded the entire force, while Martin R. M. Wallace, Fourth Illinois, directed the horsemen, who were ordered to "disperse and capture" the Rebels.[49]

Embarking on transports at Vicksburg on 4 December, anticipation put the men in good spirits: "We did not know where nor did We Care much if they would Only give us Some fighting to do." Disembarking at Natchez, the cavalry moved through the countryside to Washington, where they met Bernard G. Farrar and mounted men from the Thirteenth Missouri Infantry. Gresham gave Farrar command of the entire cavalry force and ordered the mounted troops to Ellis Cliffs, where it was rumored Adams and Wood's First Mississippi Cavalry planned to obstruct the navigation on the Mississippi River with artillery.[50]

Farrar's cavalry pursued "the Reer Guard of Reb Genl Wart Adams . . . command, and We Pursued them very closely all day" Monday, 6 December. The horsemen moved through the undeveloped countryside, heading southwest toward the river, where they hoped to attack Adams's rear on the Kingston Road, trapping him between the Homochitto and Mississippi Rivers. The cavalry rode well past dark, finally emerging on the road to Ellis Cliffs directly in the rear of the Rebels. The Fifth provided various squads to serve as pickets. Packard, with Company C, lay near the forks in the road, while Capt. Benjamin Hopkins took members from Companies D and G onto another road, very near the Rebel camp. Establishing a picket within four hundred yards of the Rebels, Jack of Clubs, as the boys called the captain, "Sang Out who is there[?] [and] they answer[e]d a Friend." When Hopkins identified the friends as Confederates, Jack told his enemy to "hold on til Morning and we will fight You." Both sides exchanged pleasantries with one another "til after Midnight."[51]

At daybreak, Adams sent forth the "Eleventh Arkansas Regiment, dismounted and deployed . . . and [lobbed] a few artillery shots" into the Federals posted along the crest of a ridge east of the waterway. Farrar, afraid Gresham's infantry could not reach supporting distance before Adams made a general advance, called a retreat. Finally having Adams in a vulnerable position after months of fighting the Mississippi horsemen, the Illinoisans did not take well to the retreat. "We were Commanded to Right About. I never," Packard complained, "felt meaner in My life[,] So Mad and Shagrinned to Make a retreet for the first time in My war Career[,] but it is true discretion was the better part of valor there and then." Many men, including Packard, initially refused to obey, and he "was quite Severly reprimanded [for] not prom[p]tly Obeying the Order. I had Mad[e] up My Mind to stay with them, if all would do the Same and fight!" The Federals retreated, with the rear guard skirmishing with the Fourteenth Confederate and Stockdale's cavalry, until they made contact with Gresham. Forming his troops into line of battle, Gresham waited for an attack, but the Rebels had retreated.[52]

While at Natchez, Farnan led the Fifth on a scout to "remoove a Gurrilla band that was prowling and firing into Our Transports" by Rodney, Mississippi. The men found only a "Small force which we Charged and Mooved them heavy with our Carbines." Farnan pursued until dark without encountering any other enemy forces. After lying on their horses all night, the morning greeted the Illinoisans with a heavy downpour, making the scout that much more miserable. Packard's huge "Cavalry Boots held enough water to drownd a Small Man. My Pant being inside of course" did not help. On the scout's return to Natchez, the men "saw nothing but Cattle and Horses running over the fields in Squads" and reunited with the brigade without further incident. After a few more days of scouting around Natchez, Gresham loaded his troops onto transports and the men arrived back in Vicksburg on the night of 16 December, during another heavy downpour. The Fifth detachment tried to reach their main camp, but "Rain! Mud! and water leg deep," along with a swollen creek and washed out bridges, forced the returning scouts to stay "in the Cold Mud all night." They finally reached their shanties the next day; the Illinoisans thrilled to find packages and letters from home awaiting their return. Packard found "a God! Send . . . from My dear Ones. The . . . brandy Came in just at the right time for I had been roughing it So long on [the] hard back of a Sow belly that My whole System was deranged. . . . So this will help me Out wonderfully." The goodies in the package reminded Packard of home and his beloved Jennie, whom he missed desperately, and considered "the true Source of all his happiness and joys."[53]

On returning, regimental officers immediately confronted the prairie boys as to their intentions about reenlisting. Within a few days, various generals and colonels addressed the men, calling on their patriotism to move them to stay with the army until the war ended. Sgt. James Bennett (1827–95) believed "a portion of each company [would] remain firm in the determination to "'go it, horse or no horse.'" Bennett, himself a newly enlisted veteran, believed "the results have exceeded the most sanguine expectations, and the enthusiasm of the men . . . equals that which characterized the uprising of the sturdy yeomany at the breaking out of the rebellion." Reenlistment, according to the lieutenant, had "unite[d] the army as a fraternity—a band of brothers whose hearts beat in unison and whose *one* purpose will be to make common cause with the armed rebels." Enthusiasm ran high, and soldiers heard repeatedly as they walked through the camps, "Are you a veteran?" and with "an affirmative response never fail[ed] to elecit a hearty 'all right' or 'bully for you.'" By 5 January, over half of the regiment had reenlisted, and the Illinoisans earned the designation of a veteran organization. Francis Wheelock, who recorded the veterans of Company C, lamented that he "cannot raise ¾ Co;" though he was saved at the "11th hour" when Alonzo Payne reenlisted. The regiment's new designation as a veteran organization permitted the men to receive a new colonel in May 1864; without the designation, Seley would have remained in control of the regiment.[54]

The regiment reenlisted three hundred and fifty soldiers as veterans. Companies H (45), B (35), G (33), L (32), and C (31) had over thirty men sign on for another three years. Companies A (19) and I (14) secured the fewest reenlistments. Capt. John Nelson of Company H bragged to the *Nashville Journal* that almost all his men had reenlisted and that his company could be truly called a veteran company. Contrary to his promises to resign, Seley remained with the regiment, as did Mumford and Farnan. Most of the Fifth diarists refused to reenlist, mainly due to health concerns. Malaria symptoms still plagued Mann and Packard, who constantly fretted about their health. Skiles, who had favored reenlisting in October, changed his mind after the fiasco with the regiment's horses. He originally planned to "serve out this term," recuperate at home, "then if my Country needs me & I am able, I will go." Skiles believed that "if a Government is not worth fighting for, it is not a fit protection for us when we are there." By December, the private had no desire to remain in the service. "I will come home when my time is out," he informed his parents, "and stay as long as I please, with no paper in my pocket, headed with, 'To all whom it may concern.' [A]nd if I dont get back within the specified time, have to be taken back as a deserter."[55]

Roe reassured his wife of his intentions: "I want you to be perfectly satisfied on that subject [reenlistment]. If I live until my present term of enlistment expires I will go home to stay. I will not again take the field on any conditions." John Burke never regained his strength, but he did reenlist and remained with the regiment until his mustering out in October 1865.[56]

Christmas came and went in camp just like any other day. This year, however, some of the men celebrated with special dinners. Roe enjoyed a can of peaches, but neither Packard nor Mann even mentioned the holiday in their private missives. Skiles explained to his parents his "happy Christmas," which he experienced after serving on picket: "had a splendid dinner, corned beef & good hard crackers, & goose wine, for supper the same, with the addition of a bellogna sausage, & some coffee." A few in the regiment decided to create some mischief on Christmas Eve. "[S]ome of the boys amused themselves" by filling "some canteens with [gun]powder & set them off." This was followed by "a loud report." Winslow failed to appreciate the festivities: "the bugle sounded the assembly, [and] we marched out on the parade ground." Mann considered Winslow "very foolish" for "paying any attention to the <u>fun</u> that the 'boys' intended" Christmas Eve. The colonel's action "done no good but much harm rendering the Reg't insubordinate and angry," announced Mann. Seley ordered the men to quarters for the night, and any "Caught running about [were] to be arrested by the guards, & kept in Custody till morning."[57]

Mann ended his year with optimism and hope for a quick end to the war. "The war progresses slowly but surely and the Rebles are fast failing in their stupenduous attempt to destroy our Gov't. I had little thought of being in the army so long when I first enlisted, but it seems to be a necessity ordered by Providence that war has been prolonged through rebel obstinacy that Slavery should be destroyed."[58]

Skiles thought "there is a very good prospect of peace before long." The Rebels "have stopped lying so much, and are whining and growling among themselves," showing much "dissatisfaction . . . in the way things are progressing." The Christian County private observed that the Southerners had "lost nearly every thing they had, and will soon loose what they have left, if they don[']t stop. . . . I think another year will see the end" of the war.[59]

The Fifth spent a very cold January patrolling the Vicksburg countryside and standing picket. The health of the regiment improved, except during a brief period when camp fever hit the men during the middle of the month. Company C lost all its commissioned officers within days: "F[rancis] A. W[heelock] lay Squirming and Muttering with an Ague Chill on one side [of the tent] and the Captain [Withers] on the Other, and to tell the truth, I don't feel well myself," confessed Packard. Picket duty became torture as the lieutenant suffered with a "chilly and Feverish Something like the Typhoid," but the boys "built Me a good fire under a large Magnolia tree," where Packard "counted the long night hours." Fever again left the McLean County clerk feeling "prety lonesome," and wanting to "[kick] off these Shackles and be free to go where I Cannot . . . hear this Eternal Clanking of Arms." He longed to travel to a "lonely Isle," where only "God and [him]self" occupied the place, but his duty overwhelmed his personal needs, and he concluded, "as long as this War lasts Some body has got to Stay with the Boys."[60]

Many men spent their leisure time whittling rings, pipes, and stars out of wood from the Pemberton/Grant oak, the place where the Vicksburg garrison had surrendered to Federal authorities. Sgt. James Bennett would present a "pen-holder" made from the "surrender oak" to the *Crawford County Argus* in 1864. Mann spent the month designing a silk flag he promised the Randolph Rangers when they reenlisted. Nancy and the Randolph County Ladies Union League created the banner and presented it to the boys when they returned to Illinois on furlough in March 1864. Mann requested that the flag not cost more than twenty dollars and pleaded with Nancy to attend to the details "for my sake as well as the brave men in Co 'K.'" Inscriptions on the flag highlighted two of Company K's engagements: Yazoo Pass and Mechanicsburg.[61]

Despite the lack of influence from the company's officers, the Randolph County Rangers reenlisted, believing it was best to remain together, and "after twelve or fifteen of the Co[mpany] re-enlisted, then many others joined to Keep 'K' together." The boys believed they would only be sacrificing another year to the service.[62]

The regiment also received several recruits to fill the void left by those men who had left the service due to illness, death, or disability. One hundred and fifty-three new recruits joined the regiment in December and January, with the majority mustering in Companies F and K. The new recruits did not inspire confidence in Wheelock, who claimed the boys "under Size," who "don[']t look to be worth the Bounty paid." By the end of January, the regiment numbered 714, the highest count since 1862.[63]

Toward the end of the month, one hundred Illinoisans from Companies D, C, and B, with the Fourth Iowa and a forage train of one hundred wagons, left on a two-day forage trip. The excursion seemed a futile exercise until twelve miles from camp, when the cavalry came upon the advance of the Ninth Texas Cavalry. The two sides exchanged fire, severely wounding one Texan in the thigh, and "mortally scaring the other, who fled as upon the wings of the wind." As the cavalry passed the wounded Texan on the side of the road, he expressed his sentiments as "an uncompromising rebel," who believed the Southern people to be right in their fight. The Fifth admired their adversary's "pluck, but depreciated his judgment." The soldiers transported the injured Texan to a local farmhouse, but when the farmer refused to provide aid to the Rebel, Farnan, a physician, treated his wounds and made him "as comfortable as circumstances would admit."[64]

The Illinoisans filled the wagons with corn, pork, mutton, sweet potatoes, and "such other things as the soldier, long familiar with 'hard tack' and 'sow belly,' considers a rare treat." The return trip witnessed some skirmishing between the cavalry's rear guard and the Sixth and Ninth Texans, but no one else went missing or was injured.[65]

The last few days of January witnessed the men preparing for the next significant expedition to Meridian, Mississippi. Mann and the commissary department worked for three days preparing and issuing rations for the men of the regiment. Each soldier carried twenty-three days' rations plus one hundred rounds of ammunition. All the Illinois diarists participated in the grueling expedition across Mississippi to Meridian.

Lt. Col. Benjamin L. Wiley raised the Fifth Illinois in the fall of 1861. Portrait by Karen Curry.

Postwar image of Lt. Col. Thomas Alders Apperson. Portrait by Karen Curry.

Lt. Col. Abel H. Seley. Abraham
Lincoln Presidential Library and Museum.

Postwar image of Capt. Francis
A. Wheelock, Co. C. Abraham
Lincoln Presidential Library and Museum.

Mexican War–era image
of George W. McConkey,
Co. E, 1846. Courtesy of Frank
Crawford.

Rev. John W. Woods,
the regiment's spiritual
leader, spent more time
with freedmen than his
charges. Abraham Lincoln
Presidential Library and
Museum.

Maj. Horace P. Mumford
became a sought-after
field commander in 1864.
Courtesy of Frank Crawford.

Pvt. William A. Skiles,
Co. G, holding a
Lefaucheux pistol in
1862. Christian County
Genealogical Society,
Taylorville, Illinois.

Dr. William A. Watts, one of sixteen physicians in the regiment. Randy Beck Collection.

Capt. Benjamin B. Hopkins, Co. G, became one of the regiment's most reliable leaders. Courtesy of Ron Coddington.

Bvt. Brig. Gen. John McConnell became the regiment's third commander in 1864. Abraham Lincoln Presidential Library and Museum.

Capt. Thomas Dean, Co. F, died from an unspecified disease in 1864. Randy Beck Collection.

7

THE GRAND RAID
February to March 1864

After several days of intense preparation, 375 men from the Fifth Illinois marched out of their Clear Creek camp at six in the morning of 3 February, with Company C of the regiment in advance. Seley commanded the men that remained in camp, while Farnan led the Fifth detachment in Sherman's Meridian expedition. John Mann rode with the commissary wagons, while Packard, who remained ill, "mustered up [his] Temper and Courage to the Sticking point" and accompanied Company C. Captain Withers, who "don[']t feel so awful bad now," also decided to participate, even "if He had to Start in the ambulance." Left behind due to illness was a disappointed Francis Wheelock, who had "the bules on account of not being able to go." Wheelock, "Still [Spinning] & grunting" from his fever and large doses of quinine, remained in his sickbed. Roe and Skiles also stayed in camp, with the latter suffering from a severe case of sore eyes. With the cavalry hampered by the lack of serviceable mounts, only fourteen hundred cavalrymen participated in the campaign, but despite their small numbers, they played a significant role. The Eleventh Illinois, Fourth Iowa, and Tenth Missouri Cavalry regiments also joined Winslow's brigade. The Missourians brought along their two James rifled cannon and two mountain howitzers, under Peter Joyce. The four guns added "valuable weight to the brigade."[1]

Sherman's forces from Vicksburg consisted of two army corps, amounting to 26,847 men, with sixty-six pieces of artillery. The Sixteenth Corps under Hurlbut contained James M. Tuttle's First Division, Andrew J. Smith's Third Division, and James C. Veatch's Fourth Division. McPherson commanded Alexander Chambers's Third Brigade, First Division, Mortimer D. Leggett's Third Division, and Marcellus M. Crocker's Fourth Division of the Seventeenth Corps. Another cavalry column, under William

Sooy Smith, with seven thousand mounted bluecoats, left Memphis on 1 February with instructions to tackle and destroy the railroad on its way to Meridian. Sherman planned to meet Smith in eastern Mississippi nine days later; unfortunately, Smith's role in the campaign would be negligible. Sherman hoped to destroy the railroad at Meridian and eastward, and to effect as much destruction as possible on the Confederate infrastructure in Mississippi. Many scholars believed the Meridian campaign witnessed the fruition of Sherman's total war policy, but Winslow's cavalry, especially the Fifth Illinois, were longtime proponents of this type of warfare. A return to the philosophy of civilian property confiscation and destruction appealed to the prairie boys.

Meridian, where three railroads intersected, was a valuable Confederate strategic point, lying roughly between the Mississippi capital of Jackson and the cannon foundry and manufacturing center of Selma, Alabama. It served as a storage and distribution center for not just the industrial products of Selma, but for grain and cattle from the fertile Big Black River region to the immediate north. The city's destruction would severely constrict the Confederate infrastructure in Mississippi and Alabama. To oppose Sherman's thrust into Mississippi, the Confederates relied on Leonidas Polk, who took command of the Army of the Mississippi in December 1863. Within a month, Polk restructured his command in the newly created Department of Alabama, Mississippi, and East Louisiana. He also reorganized his cavalry into two districts: northern Mississippi and western Tennessee under Nathan Bedford Forrest, with Stephen D. Lee retaining command of central and southern Mississippi and east Louisiana. Lee's cavalry, under William H. Jackson, remained a formidable opponent of the Federal forces in Vicksburg.

Jackson's four cavalry brigades confronted Sherman's forces on the march. His brigade commanders had changed since the last time Winslow's cavalry confronted them. Lawrence Ross now led the Texans in the Second Brigade, which guarded the Yazoo River and the Mississippi Central Railroad at Benton. Peter Starke commanded Cosby's (First) brigade, which headquartered at Brownsville and watched the crossings of the Big Black River opposite Vicksburg. Wirt Adams, who now led John Logan's brigade, contained almost eight hundred effectives and had moved from Natchez to Raymond in late January. Regiments in Samuel Ferguson's brigade played a pivotal role in the upcoming campaign, including R. G. Earle's Second Alabama Cavalry, Robert O. Perrin's Mississippi Cavalry, and John Waties's South Carolina Battery.[2]

Lt. Addison Harvey's company of twenty-three cavalry scouts played an essential part in the Confederates' defense. Polk also had at his immediate command two divisions of infantry, numbering close to 7,250 men. Loring's division remained at Canton, while French headquartered his troops at Brandon, and Polk at Meridian. Polk would underutilize his infantry against Sherman's forces during the Meridian campaign.

Bundled against the viscous cold, the Fifth gladly left "this Sick Camp" at Clear Creek, where "Huge Stenches boath Animal and human" make the air "almost unbearable." Heading toward the Big Black River, the Federal cavalry crossed a rickety pontoon bridge on the main Jackson Road, which sank under the cavalry's wagon trains. Engineers took most of the afternoon to repair the damaged bridge. Winslow, meanwhile, "push[ed] forward rapidly and secure[d] the bridge across Baker's Creek, near Champion's Hill." Within a few miles of the bridge, the cavalry, with the Fourth Iowa in the van, followed by the prairie boys, exchanged lead with Harvey's band of Confederate scouts, who fought delaying actions to allow Adams's and Starke's forces to establish lines west of Champion's Hill. Arriving at Baker's Creek late in the afternoon, the horsemen secured the bridge and settled in for the night.[3]

Bugles sounded early in both the infantry and cavalry camps on 4 February. The men woke to a cold, heavily frosted dawn. After a quick breakfast, Winslow's cavalry rode down the Raymond Road, with the Tenth Missouri in the advance. On their second day of the march, the cavalry protected McPherson's right flank as it moved east on the Jackson Road. Crocker's division spearheaded the Federal infantry column and soon ran into Wood's Mississippians deployed across the Jackson Road near Champion's Hill. A lively skirmish ensued.

Adams's main line of resistance, however, remained at Bolton: Winslow's position on the Raymond Road threatened the Confederate left flank. To meet this threat, Adams sent Dumonteil's Fourteenth Cavalry on a flanking movement down the Bolton Road, to the junction of the Raymond Road. Scouts from Dumonteil's cavalry met Winslow's advance; skirmishing continued for several hours, holding Winslow in place.

Unknown to the Iowan, Adams also sent Stockdale's Mississippians to reinforce Dumonteil. As Winslow's troops forced their "way along the main road," battling Dumonteil, the Mississippians hit the cavalry's left flank, hanging unprotected in a field. Winslow immediately placed the exposed companies into line of battle, facing the Mississippians, while the Iowan sent his rear cavalry regiment to "oblique to the left," to met the Mississippians' threat. The Federals successfully repulsed both attacks,

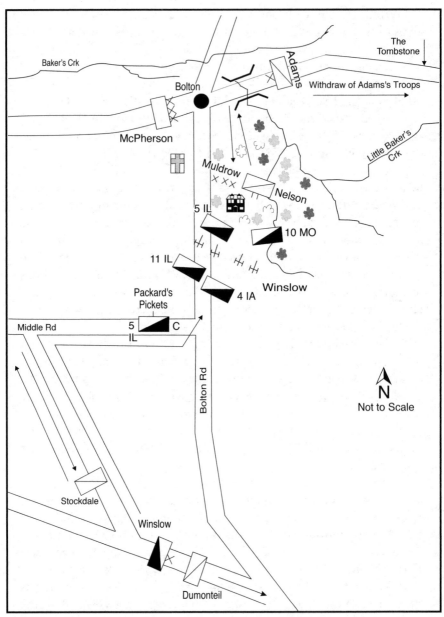

Baker's Crk

The Tombstone

Bolton

Adams

Withdraw of Adams's Troops

McPherson

Little Baker's Crk

Muldrow
x x x

5 IL

Nelson

10 MO

11 IL

Winslow

4 IA

Packard's
Pickets

Middle Rd

5
IL

C

Bolton Rd

N
Not to Scale

Stockdale

Winslow

Dumonteil

Map 7.1. Skirmish at Walton plantation, 4 February 1864, three P.M.

sending Dumonteil back to the junction of the Bolton-Raymond Road, and the Mississippians north on the country lane that led to the Bolton Road. Winslow followed in the Mississippians' wake, taking the same country lane that bypassed Dumonteil's position.[4]

Moving to the Bolton Road, Winslow rested his men at the junction of the two thoroughfares, while Packard with two companies of Fifth established a picket post on Middle Road. They remained there for almost an hour, then heard the cavalry's bugles sounding for the advance. Packard's men jumped on their mounts and rode to the Bolton Road, where they encountered a small squad of Dumonteil's cavalry firing into the rear of Winslow's column. Packard had his men return "a Sharp fire and Checked their progress."[5]

As Winslow made his way north to juncture with McPherson at Bolton, the Federal infantry continued to push back the Mississippians. By sheer weight of numbers, Crocker's troops forced the Rebels back until they hit the forks of the Jackson and Bolton Roads, just west of Baker's Creek. At this point, the Federals struck Adams's main line of resistance about three o'clock in the afternoon. As the infantry pressured Adams's front, Winslow's troopers, coming north on the Bolton Road, slammed the Confederate left flank consisting of Stockdale and Robert C. Wood's Mississippians anchored at the Walton plantation, just west of the waterway.

The sudden attack on two fronts caused Adams to withdraw his troops to the east bank of Baker's Creek. Using Akin's Ninth Tennessee to cover his front, Adams sent ninety men from Thomas Nelson's Georgia Cavalry and Capt. A. Muldrow's Company E, Wood's Mississippians, to deal with the threat to his left flank. The Confederates formed in line "on the farther side of an opening, among scattered trees" and "Opend the fight in Great Confidence." Winslow responded with his "Flying artillery of Steel Guns," causing Nelson and Muldrow to fall back as the Federal cavalry pushed forward. With the dismounted Tenth Missouri in the advance and the Fifth out as skirmishers, they soon warmly engaged the Georgians and Mississippians. The Fifth had charged the Georgians at Mechanicsburg in June the previous year and had easily routed them.[6]

The Illinoisans' and Missourians' charge came on strong and, with the Missouri howitzers in support, drove the Confederates out of the woods, "forcing them to fall back from [their] chosen positions." Shots from Confederate artillery east of Baker's Creek checked the midwesterners' charge, but not before the prairie boys thrashed the Georgians, sending them to their main line behind Baker's Creek. After routing the Confederates, Winslow rode north to connect with Sherman. Around

four in the afternoon, Adams withdrew his men to the Thomas plantation, a mile east of his line along the waterway. The Fifth sustained only
one injured during the day's fighting.[7]

On their way to camp, Packard witnessed for the first time Federal
and Confederate surgeons working side by side. "Each One had his table
at the Side of a Lane," and as Packard rode by, he "had a glimpse of the
desacting Knife and the howl of the poor Boys as off went a leg or arm."
After "honoring [the] Colors" of the fallen, the cavalry silently rode onto
Bolton and bivouacked in the field west of Baker's Creek.[8]

In the meantime, Polk passed command of the field troops to his subordinate Loring. The new commander immediately ordered French to
lead the troops at Jackson for quick movement toward the Alabama
border, and to send all public stores east to Morton. Loring concentrated
his forces at Canton and ordered the Third Mississippi Infantry of Featherston's brigade to Jackson. Ferguson's cavalry headed toward Clinton,
arriving early in the morning of Friday, 5 February.[9]

"'To horse' was sounded at daylight" on Friday morning, and the order
was "received by a shout from 20 thousand" soldiers in the Federal camps
so loud that people heard it miles away. By six in the morning, Winslow
rode out at the head of McPherson's column moving east toward Clinton.
Along the way, Mann witnessed "a man lazing by the road with his head
shot off. He belonged to our infantry." Winslow pushed the Confederate
cavalry ahead of the Federal tide; the "army looked splendid with their
bright arms glistening in the morning sun." At the Woodman plantation,
Winslow turned his men south, taking a country lane to the Raymond-
Clinton Road. Hurlbut's Sixteenth Corps moved down the Bridgeport
Road, coming in from the west, while Leggett's division drove in from
the north. Sherman's army created a pinching movement, squeezing the
Confederates from three sides, and forcing them to either confront or
retreat toward Jackson.[10]

The Federal cavalry reached Clinton about noon, simultaneously with
the Seventeenth Corps. Lee's cavalry fell back in strong position, to a
high hill called the Tombstone, with an open field separating the two
foes, astride the Jackson Road, two miles from Clinton and five miles
from the capital.

Winslow formed his men in the open valley to the west of the Tombstone. The Federal horsemen took a terrible pounding from Croft's and
Waties's batteries, and "the flash of Cannon and bursting Shell were the
order of the hour." Shots from Rebel artillery made a horrific sight, but
the "'Whistling Angels' passed over and around" the horsemen "without

further harm than wounding 2 or 3 horses." Mann, who stood near the commissary trains, had a close encounter when a Confederate shell struck a birch tree near him. The unexploded shell fell at his feet, and a frightened lieutenant admitted, "the <u>Rebs</u> threw them well."[11]

Sherman arrived on the scene and directed McPherson and Winslow to flank the Rebels. Winslow spearheaded the movement and headed south, riding through dense woods and open fields to the "Mississippi Springs upper road," completely flanking the Confederates. At Sharkey's residence, the column rode over the Lynch Creek Bridge and emerged on the southwestern outskirts of the state capital. To the east lay the Confederate fortifications the men had seen last July during their first visit to Jackson. To the north, the men witnessed an incredible sight, where open fields and a gentle slope led the men's eyes to a ridge that held the Jackson Road. The setting sun glinted off hundreds of rifles in the hands of Confederate cavalry as they quickly withdrew into town and away from Hurlbut's advancing hordes. Their column stretched for three miles and moved by fours. Winslow's appearance disrupted Confederate plans to hold the town until stores and soldiers safely crossed the Pearl River.[12]

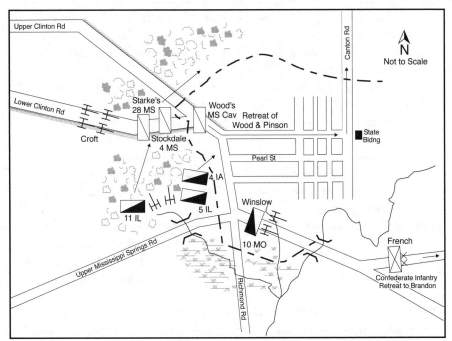

Map 7.2. Winslow's attack on the retreating Confederate cavalry outside Jackson at sunset on 5 February 1864.

With McPherson's infantry within supporting distance, Winslow did not wait for orders but moved to attack the retreating Confederate cavalry. Winslow targeted Stockdale's Mississippians, acting as rear guard. Unseen by the Rebels, the dismounted Fourth Iowa positioned to the north of the Upper Mississippi Springs Road, partially concealed by small trees and bushes. Next, the Eleventh Illinois came forward, mounted and to the left of the Iowans, ready to charge the column's rear. Joyce's two James rifles, set up just past Lynch Creek, blasted a hole in the column, killing three, while a second shot exploded near the Rebels. This threw Stockdale into confusion and into the shelter of the woods north of the Clinton-Jackson Road. To save his rear guard, Adams moved Wood's Mississippians back for support.[13]

With the Confederate column vulnerable, Winslow ordered the Eleventh Illinois to charge at the column's weak point, while the Iowans ran toward the gap in the fortifications. The Tenth Missouri followed the Iowans, while the Fifth brought up the rear. The charge broke the Confederates' forward momentum, scattering Wood and Stockdale's cavalry, cutting them off from safe haven across the Pearl. Heading through town, Wood, accompanied by Pinson's First Mississippians, which guarded the fortifications, escaped Jackson on State Street, riding furiously to the Canton Road. The two Illinois regiments, with the Eleventh in advance, entered the city about 5:00 P.M. "Their demonian yells were heard on the east bank of the Pearl river."[14]

As Winslow's forces entered Jackson, the last of the Confederate infantry evacuated the capital, passing over the Pearl River. To quell the ensuing madness that enveloped the city, Winslow directed Farnan with the Fifth and Fourth Iowa to secure the city's north and south approaches, and they dispersed throughout the city. Winslow also "direct[ed] the battery [James rifled] to occupy the hill commanding" Jackson, while he took the howitzers and the Tenth Missouri on a mission to save the Pearl River Bridge. After getting lost in the rapidly falling darkness, Winslow reached the bridge just as French's division cut loose the west bank moorings. A few shots from the Missourians followed by some well-aimed shells from the howitzers sent French's men retreating through the underbrush of the eastern bank. The Federal Pioneer Corps spent the next day repairing the pontoon bridge across the Pearl River.[15]

Farnan sent Packard with Company C on guard one mile in the timber out on the Clinton-Jackson Road. Complete darkness had fallen, and many landowners "refus[ed] to light up their places of abode at night," with the Federal army roaming the countryside. Confusion and disorder swept through both armies, with many not knowing how the lines had changed during the day's fighting. A lost Confederate scouting party, possibly Harvey's scouts, leisurely approached Packard's videttes. When the Illinoisans shouted for their surrender, the Rebels "fired and Wheeled to run," but not before Federal bullets wounded and unhorsed one cavalryman, who became "a prisoner of War."[16]

Sgt. James G. Bennett, Co. F, witnessed the "different expressions of the citizens and manner" in which they received the "'cruel invaders.'" Landowners, whom Bennett called the "'chivalry[,]' received us with sullen indifference," while those with foreign roots "seemed more communicative and expressed their delight" with the Yankees. The slaves, many of whom had only heard of others gaining their freedom, became "particularly jubilant," announcing they were "glad to see you alls . . . accompanied by the everlasting yah!, yah!, yah!"[17]

Early Saturday morning, 6 February, Winslow gathered his various detachments together for a reconnaissance toward Canton to ascertain the location of the Rebel cavalry. As the Fifth rode through the ill-fated city, the emotional scene elicited a strong response from Mann: "The scene was exciting. Woman (few men were to be seen) were trying to save their houses and property from the flames. Some were crying[,] while others were laughing. Children, little Boys & Girls, Slaves, young & old, were looking on the wild Scene of confusion & excitement with amazement and wonder. This fine City—the seat of fashion, wealth, empire, and refinement for the south was in ruins. All her splendor was gone. . . . A fearful reward for her treason."[18]

Winslow rode north on the Canton Road, strewn with evidence of the Confederates' rapid retreat: wagons, ambulances, and other property abandoned along the roadside. The Fifth took the advance, with Company C, under Packard, out as skirmishers. Three miles past the capital, the prairie boys encountered pickets from "Wort Addamses Mounted Infantry." Light skirmishing continued for about five miles, until they found Adams's forces lined up in a skirt of timber, "[w]here they Seamed determined to hold their ground." Packard dismounted his men, who then pushed the Rebs through the woods and over a bridge double quick, where Adams's men reluctantly retired. At a nearby barn, the cavalry partook of the owner's corn, each man filling his bags with the mainstay. There, the boys fed their horses, remounted, then rode out about five miles. With Starke in position by Hanging Moss Creek, Winslow turned the brigade back toward Jackson, with Company C serving as rear guard. They bivouacked at the insane asylum until 7:00 A.M. the next day.[19]

Sherman's third conquest of Jackson lasted less than one day. As the Confederate infantry passed safely over the Pearl River heading for Morton, Adams's, Ferguson's, and Starke's brigades remained east of the river "to operate on the flanks and rear of the [Federals]." Loring's infantry stayed well north of occupied Jackson, moving from Canton to Madisonville on 5 February, to cross the Pearl at Cullum's Crossing, preserving the pontoon bridge for Lee's wagons. By nine the next evening, Loring, too, headed east for Morton. On 7 February, Lee recalled Ross from the Yazoo Valley, requesting the Texan rejoin his forces east of the Pearl. Even with all the redirection, the only Confederate cavalry operating east of the river consisted of a forty-man detachment of the Fourth Mississippi Cavalry on conscript duty at Brandon, under C. C. Wilbourn, and sixty cavalrymen from the First Mississippi Cavalry. The Mississippians had the daunting task of hindering Sherman's entire column as they moved east toward Morton.[20]

Sunday dawned frosty and ice cold for the troops. Winslow's cavalry saddled up and marched out by eight in the morning. While riding through the doomed capital, John Mann passed the private residence that had quartered his brother and the Brookhaven raiders in June 1863. The cavalry crossed the Pearl after A. J. Smith's and Milton Montgomery's divisions. James H. Howe's infantry was the last over the river, destroying the pontoon bridge behind them.[21]

Riding through swampy, poor land, strewn with scraggly pine trees, Winslow's soldiers rode the rear of the Federal column until they hit the forks leading to Brandon. Here Sherman divided his army: the cavalry took the Upper Brandon Road, to screen the left flank of the infantry column, which moved on the Wire Road, a few miles south. Lucius M. Rose's forces spearheaded the infantry.

As was customary with the cavalry, they scavenged as they moved through the countryside, where they "[g]ot plenty of forage for our horses and meat[,] chickens & Corn," from the many plantations that dotted the countryside. Farnan explained, "the boys would be firing on the Rebs in the advance of our Brigade, while the rear would be gobbling chickens, hams, &c." Wilbourn spent most of his efforts delaying the Federal infantry, though a few scouts pestered Winslow's cavalry. Mann noted in his diary, "The enemy did not annoy us much to day."[22]

Rose's men hit Brandon first, pushing Wilbourn through the town, and capturing the Confederate adjutant at headquarters. By the time Winslow arrived at the Rankin County seat, Rose had moved the main Rebel resistance several miles east of Brandon: French toward Hillsborough, while Loring occupied Morton. The Federal cavalry spent their time in the town destroying several houses, where Mann observed the "citizens are much frightened [with] many . . . leaving their houses and fleeing upon our approach." After passing through and exchanging lead with a couple of Rebel scouts, Winslow's forces bivouacked three miles east of Brandon.[23]

During the night of 7 February, the various Confederate infantry and cavalry units converged on Morton. Lee's cavalry moved into northern Rankin County after crossing at Smith's Ferry and Cullum's Crossing early 8 February. Ferguson moved to cover Loring's front at Morton. Lee rode with Adams's brigade, heading southeast from the upper Pearl River crossing to operate against the Federal infantry's flanks. Jackson rode with Starke southward toward Brandon and Pelahatchie to get behind the Federal column and work on its rear guard. When the Federals moved out early the next morning, Wilbourn's cavalry was still the only force available to Loring at Morton to delay Sherman. Fearing for his small cavalry force, Loring implored Lee to send his forces to attack Sherman's front, flank, and rear.[24]

Winslow broke camp at six in the morning on 8 February. Without delay, the Iowan threw out flankers on both sides of the Wire Road to cover the infantry column as it moved toward Morton and immediately encountered resistance. "The enemy fell back steadily and slowly," with all of Winslow's regiments taking their shot at Wilbourn's "very small" force at various times during the day. When resistance became stubborn, Winslow dismounted his men, allowing the cavalry to skirmish in the pine-covered terrain. By dismounting, the Federals got "under cover," allowing the cavalry to move about with greater facility, and where the Confederates "invariably got the worst of it."[25]

Late in the afternoon, Wilbourn's Mississippians made a stand on the summit of a hill, directly in front of a small house inhabited by a large family. During the firing, the mother of the family, herself a widow, was shot and instantly killed. When the prairie boys reached the house, they found her six children, the oldest girl at twelve years, surrounding their fallen mother. Farnan sent Mann to the nearest neighbor to enlist aid for the family. The Federal officers from Sherman's and McPherson's headquarters and from the cavalry created a "generous fund" for the family, the money being "left with a kind-hearted neighbor." As the long shadows of a late winter afternoon fell over the stately pines, the winter darkness quickly engulfed Sherman's army. Winslow bivouacked his weary troopers by Line Creek, three miles west of Morton. A steady stream of Rebel deserters "much disheartened by fatigue, short rations[,] and the gloomy prospects of a [hard] course" entered the Federal camps.[26]

With the arrival of Francis M. Cockrell's brigade of French's division, Loring now had over twenty thousand infantry and artillery to oppose Sherman at Morton. Declaring Sherman too strong, however, Loring abandoned his line after dark on 8 February and headed for Newton, via Hillsborough. Confederate bands serenaded the two forces to cover the sound of the army's retreat.[27]

The horsemen saddled up shortly before daybreak Tuesday, 9 February, the weather cooperating with warm dry air. Finding the earthworks empty, Winslow pursued the retreating Rebels only to run into the vanguard of Ferguson's cavalry, which arrived just before sunrise. With McPherson's infantry in close support, Ferguson found it "impossible to get between him and General Polk's rear" and withdrew his command to Hillsborough. The cavalry skirmished with a squadron from Ferguson's cavalry for seven miles, until they made camp at the Coulan plantation on Shockalo Creek. Along the way they "found the road Strewn with broken down Waggons Camp & Garrison Equipage[,] Guns[,] and any amount thrown down by the Rebels Soldiers and heavy Gun Carriages left in their hurry."[28]

Meanwhile, Stephen Lee redeployed his troops. Leaving Ferguson to deal with Sherman's column, Lee headed for Garlandville, while his other

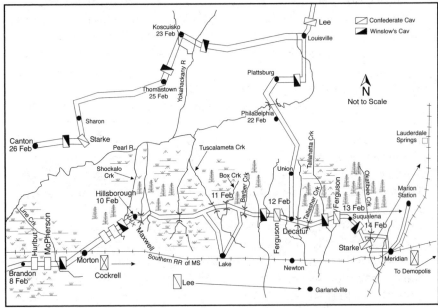

Map 7.3. Brandon to Meridian to Canton, 10 February to 26 February 1864, during Sherman's Meridian campaign.

horsemen moved to protect the Mobile and Ohio Railroad. By one in the morning of 10 February, Ferguson had moved to Newton, but left behind a small command under Lt. Col. William L. Maxwell, of Ballentine's regiment in command at Hillsborough.[29]

Winslow's horse soldiers saddled up by daybreak on Wednesday, 10 February, with the "'Bloody 5th' in the advance," moving through a pine-covered landscape. Within a mile of camp, the prairie boys skirmished with Maxwell's rear guard, who kept up a "constant fire" for five miles. At Hillsborough, Maxwell lodged his men behind fences and old buildings, "[i]ntending to Make a Stand here." Farnan, seeing Maxwell dug in, dismounted a battalion of men and "Mooved Steadily on into Town." Maxwell held his ground, but the Rebels' "obstinacy caused 11 of their braves to fall pierced by [U]nion bullets." The Fifth defied "Volley after voley," but not one man received a wound. After a thirty-minute exchange of bullets, Maxwell withdrew his men from the "poor dilapidated old town[,] on a poor situation and in a poor piney country." The area contained "Millions of Ackers of pine Woods[,] . . . the trees So large and tall and Open that we could March an Armey through it with Ease." Winslow moved to Hontokalo Creek, where they camped for the night.[30]

The following day turned into a nightmare as the Federals entered an area of low river bottoms with swampy, narrow roads and bisected with numerous marshes and creeks of the Young Warrior River. Winslow screened the advance of the Sixteenth Corps when they broke camp on the Tallabogue Creek, two miles east of Hillsborough. Maxwell delayed Winslow's progress by burning bridges at every crossing: Hontokalo, Tuscalameta, Box, Barber, and Conahatta Creeks. The Pioneer Corps corduroyed the roads and rebuilt bridges through the Tuscalameta swamp, keeping Sherman's army steadily moving east. At five in the afternoon, Winslow finally crossed the Conahatta, camping on the east bank, only eight miles from Decatur. Hurlbut's Sixteenth Corps camped opposite Winslow. By the time McPherson's troops moved forward, the Sixteenth Corps had destroyed the corduroyed roads, and the Seventeenth Corps trudged along in ankle-deep mud. They made it only as far as the Tuscalameta Creek. To ease wear and tear on the roads, Sherman reduced the number of wagons per regiment and sent all sick and injured to the wagon train. Sherman ordered the infantry to carry five days' worth of provisions; the cavalry, however, found "plenty of corn, fodder, meat, &c" from the countryside to fill their empty stomachs.[31]

Later the same day, Polk finally came to the realization that Sherman targeted Meridian not Mobile. He directed Loring to check the progress of the Federal column, possibly at Decatur, to allow evacuation of stores at Meridian. Ferguson moved from the vicinity of Newton to "get between General Loring's rear and the enemy's advance, then near Decatur," which he reached by a difficult night march, arriving on the morning of 12 February. Adams remained at Newton; Starke four miles south of the town.[32]

February 12 dawned cold, with a bitter wind bristling through the pine trees. Pioneer companies prepared the roads for the day's march, cutting down pines and laying three thousand feet of wooden roadway before the columns moved out. Winslow's troops, acting as the advance for Smith's Third Division, left their camp about eight in the morning. Fighting the cold and the condition of the roads, the Federal cavalry pushed through Decatur and rode effortlessly until they encountered Ferguson's scouts three miles west of the Chunky Creek. With the Fifth in advance, Winslow forced the Confederates through the almost impenetrable underbrush to Pachuta Creek by late in the afternoon, "by flanking every position [Ferguson] took." Confederate bullets wounded Amers Nicholson, Co. E, who lingered in the hospital until his death in April 1864.[33]

Winslow bivouacked just east of the Chunky, a tributary of Pascagoula River, about five in the evening. The cavalry had experienced a hard day of riding and skirmishing for fifteen miles, but the "troops [were] in fine spirits" and ready for a rest. Many Federal cavalrymen realized for the first time that "the enemy are not going to fight" *en force.*[34]

The Confederate infantry continued to retreat in the face of Sherman's overwhelming army. With Lee's cavalry the only forces between the infantry and the Federal army, Ferguson's horsemen spent their time on delaying actions produced by fire and axe. Winslow had his men in the saddle early in the morning of 13 February, but they only moved about a mile before encountering another burned bridge. The cavalry laid in camp until noon, watching and assisting the Pioneer Corps in bridging Tallasher Creek. With the overpass completed, Winslow spearheaded the eastward movement, skirmishing almost continuously with Ferguson on the Decatur-Meridian Road. Toward late afternoon, the Rebels fired "a heavy volley . . . but not a man hurt." Ferguson's delaying actions and obstructions became so effective, the general "found it impracticable to make a stand at any point in rear of me . . . in case of a flank movement." As a result, the Federals pushed Ferguson to within ten miles of Meridian. Just before sunset, the cavalry entered an area of untamed forest covering rough hills, uninhabitable and with poor forage. Here the Iowan determined to make camp, but Sherman ordered his cavalry back in the saddle to continue riding through the night, to allow the army to pass through the poor terrain quickly.[35]

Winslow's weary men resaddled their mounts and set off toward Meridian with the Fourth Iowa in advance, Hurlbut's corps in support. The Fourth Iowa encountered Perrin's Mississippians near Tallahatta Creek. The Iowans moved through "fell[ed] trees, . . . but we passed through it all without trouble and drove them from their camp and killed 3 of them." After running "from tree, to tree, & hill, to hill," and always gaining ground," Perrin's Mississippians finally retreated, leaving Big Mountain about midnight.[36]

Winslow drove the Rebels about five miles; "the Skirmishing was sharp and severe" through the low country east of the hills to Suqualena. The outnumbered Confederate cavalry formed in two lines across the road, with one line behind the other, securing their flanks in the woods bordering the road. Heading down the avenue, Winslow ordered his advance to attack the Rebel front line. Considering the lateness of the hour and the darkness the cavalry endured, it was not surprising that Ferguson's second line fired into his first, sending his weary cavalrymen into confusion, and breaking up his defensive lines. The Rebel cavalry withdrew, while Winslow established camp ten miles from Meridian.[37]

Sherman's objective, Meridian, was a relatively small town, located near the junction of the Mobile and Ohio and Vicksburg and Montgomery Railroads, making the city a major rail center. In 1862, the Confederates completed a line linking Meridian with Selma, Alabama, together with telegraph wires connecting Mississippi with the rest of the Confederacy on the east coast. The Confederate government established an arsenal, military hospital, and prisoner of war stockade and turned Meridian into a major transportation hub for the region. After the fall of Jackson, Meridian became the headquarters of the Mississippi chief of ordinance and the Confederate pay and department quartermasters. With Sherman's army now in striking distance, Polk rushed to save what was left of the Confederacy in Mississippi and ship it east into Alabama. The day ended with the Meridian streets full of frantic men, wagons, and excited horses and mules, as people strove to leave the doomed city.

February 14 dawned to an early spring day: warm, with a hint of rain in the air. Spirits remained high in Winslow's cavalry, the soldiers pleased at the prospect that they would spearhead the movement toward Meridian. Winslow moved out on the Marion Road at Suqualena Creek about daylight—the Fifth proudly served as the cavalry's advance as the column moved south. The Rebel cavalry had been busy during the night obstructing the avenue with felled timber and burning bridges over major arteries.

At Okatibee Creek, the Fifth confronted another bridge destroyed by the "flying Rebels." Winslow sent back for the Pioneer Corps and, with the help of "Genl Hurlburts 'Sappers & Miners', . . . Construct[ed] the bridge." Winslow, anxious for the cavalry to have its day, built another bridge with the long arms of a cotton press and other timbers. The structure bore the weight of the horses and men only if they crossed at carefully spaced intervals. Once the men were over, the work detail strengthened the bridge and brought over the four Tenth Missouri guns. "Col Winselow Built a temporary [bridge] . . . to cross the Cavalry On, which beat the Infantry bad, leaving the Infantry to finish their Structure," Packard proudly declared.[38]

Winslow moved his men up the hill that served as the east bank of the Okatibee. They expected resistance from the Rebels, but Starke had relieved Ferguson of command, and withdrawn Ferguson's exhausted troops from the earthworks. Starke placed his dismounted forces on the Meridian Road and waited for the Federal cavalry.

After receiving complaints from Farnan about the Fifth's lack of opportunity to fight, Winslow placed the regiment in the advance. Two miles west of Meridian at the Meridian-Demopolis Road, the Fifth came "onto a heavy force of Skirmishers Secreeted in Ambush, which opened on Our advance." The prairie boys faced Pinson's First Mississippians deployed astride the road, with a mounted squadron of the Twenty-Eighth Mississippi north of the thoroughfare near a hospital for support. Farnan dismounted and deployed his men as skirmishers, with Captain Withers taking command of the right flank, and Packard the left. The Mississippians produced a "galling cross fire, . . . but on we went with Such a furious fire from the whole Regiment" that the prairie boys drove them "from Every Log Stump and fence and trees." Winslow then ordered the whole line to charge, supported by the Tenth Missouri Battery.[39]

The Fifth pushed Pinson to the rear of the Twenty-Eighth Mississippians, who in turn exchanged shots with the Illinoisans. Starke's regiment then gave way to the rear of Ballentine's mounted Mississippians and reformed in line waiting the Federals' charge. Packard's excitement for the moment was conveyed in his memoirs: "It was a Magnificent Charge! And One I never will forget to See the Excitement of the Men and Office[rs] after we turned their tail too. [T]o See their flying horizontal Coattails will never be forgotten by [every] Soldier in the Bloody 5th that day."[40]

In the midst of the Fifth's triumph, the infantry tried to steal their glory. A rivalry existed between the mounted and foot soldiers of the army, each side bragging it would enter Meridian first. As the Illinoisans engaged one of their most hated adversaries, Gen. Andrew J. Smith of the Third Division, Sixteenth Corps, rode to Farnan demanding he halt his men to let Smith's "Indianians & Iowans charge at them!" A determined Farnan replied, "I believe this Cavalry would Charge the 'Gates of Hell' if I tell them. [T]hey like it!" Smith rode back to his men in disgust. During the charge, the prairie boys captured a number of prisoners, including a staff member of Ferguson's brigade.[41]

The Illinoisans' ferocity forced Starke to withdraw his brigade, and reform in line on the west side of the railroad, but not before mortally wounding Robert R. Kelley, from Co. I. Starke made "an obstinate defense" at an old barracks, but Farnan's prairie boys and shells from the Tenth Missouri Battery "drove them out in confusion." The old Virginian finally saw the futility of his position and withdrew his men to Lauderdale Springs. "The boys made this old pine clad hills echo and echo with the shouts of victory. . . . It would have," Mann insisted to Nancy, "done you good to hear the shout of triumph . . . they sent up to Heavens." The cry "was returned along the whole . . . column as far as ear could hear[,] perhaps a distance of ten miles."[42]

The way was now clear to Meridian, "[e]ach brave Man" having "done his best to be the first to get into" the "Objective Point." Winslow remounted his brigade, still with the "Bloody 5th" in advance, and headed toward the town at a gallop. The Fifth entered their prize first, at three in the afternoon, "with loud Shouts of victory." When Sherman received word of Winslow's triumph, he replied, "'Well done for the Cavalry,'" which sent another "Shout of joy" along the line. Once the infantry entered Meridian, Winslow ordered his tired horsemen to camp, three miles out on the Demopolis Road, at the plantation of McLamore, "a notorious secessionist." There the men found plenty of victuals, especially sweet potatoes, which they roasted over old pine logs as they waited for the rest of Sherman's army to enter Meridian.[43]

The army's first full day in Meridian turned cold and rainy, with temperatures around freezing. In their camp two miles west of town, the Federal horsemen and their mounts rested in a heavy downpour. As Lee observed, the Federals "kept quiet . . . about Meridian" during their first day of occupation. The innovative Illinoisans built shelters from "plank[s] taken from the barn and out building[s] on the plantations." The old owner was "much shocked at the bad conduct of the [Y]ankees in tearing up his houses to make shelter." McLamore, confronting the horsemen, threw his hands toward the heavens and exclaimed, "Can human Beings act so[?]"[44]

The Confederates, meanwhile, were on the move. Polk retreated with his infantry toward Demopolis, Alabama, reaching the east bank of the Tombigbee River on 17 February. Starke, Adams, and Ferguson hovered around Old Marion, while Ross's brigade arrived at Marion Station from Yazoo City.

On 16 February, Winslow screened the eastern approaches to the city, following Smith's division on the Demopolis Road as it destroyed the Selma railroad. Skirmishing continued between Winslow's and Starke's troops around Old Marion, where Winslow made camp for the night near Smith's division. Farnan sent Companies B and C out on picket, where Rebel pickets constantly fired on their videttes.

The sacking and burning of Meridian continued the following day, which dawned extremely cold, with heavy frost and ice over the landscape. Federal infantry destroyed the railroad lines at Chunky Station, Quitman, and Enterprise, including the trestlework and bridges, while Winslow remained at Old Marion. During the day, the Tenth Missouri Cavalry burned the home of an old Presbyterian preacher by the name of Phillips. According to Mann, Phillips had preached treason from his pulpit, and as a result, the Missourians exacted revenge. Fate, however, and gallantry got in the way. Phillips's daughter, whom Mann described as "a heroine, smiling through her tears," implored the Illinoisans to help save her household property. Men from the Randolph County Rangers "turned out almost en mass" and, together with other Egyptians, "saved most of their goods." Many of the boys "expressed regret that the house was burned, on account of the Brave[-]hearted Minister[']s Daughter."[45]

A layer of snow and extremely cold temperatures greeted the soldiers on 18 February. The mounted arm of Sherman's army remained in camp and "tried to make ourselves comfortable by keeping up large fires and making barriars against the cold north wind." During the day, citizens and slaves visited the boys. During one encounter, an old slave asked advice about whether or not to accompany the Federals back to Vicksburg, stating he would be unable to walk that far. The boys assured him his "day of jubilee . . . was near at hand" and advised the elderly man to remain at home a little while longer.[46]

The frosty morning air of February 19 witnessed Winslow's cavalry riding to Lauderdale Springs to destroy the town and railroad property. With Lee and Forrest's cavalry roaming around the countryside, the column remained cautious, but they easily reached Lauderdale without incident. The mounted arm burnt "all the public buildings including the station house, water tank, and Confederate warehouse for corn." The Fifth also found two members of their regiment "wounded prisoners at Lockhart Hospital," who had been recovering there for some months. The cavalry also captured a number of Confederate soldiers, including a corporal who dressed "finer . . . than most of our Com officers."[47]

While at Lauderdale, Winslow sent scouting parties in every direction, with hopes of locating Sooy Smith's cavalry column or news of his whereabouts. The scouts also reported the nearby presence of Ferguson's and Ross's brigades, which sent Winslow to deploy on the "crest of a ridge running at a right angle with the road." Rebels eventually fired on the pickets but quickly halted the attack. The troops had a very "hard day's travel (30 miles)" in "very cold weather—as cold as any day this winter. . . . Hard, cold days work for the 5th," according to Mann.[48]

The men welcomed the news of Sherman's plan to march his army back to Vicksburg. Hurlbut, followed by Winslow, would move from Marion toward Union and Hillsborough; the same route they had taken to Meridian. Sherman wanted all burning and destruction to cease, unless ordered by a commanding officer. He expected the return trip to be slow, methodical, and cautious. He did not anticipate any danger, because most of Lee's cavalry hovered between Macon and Starkville. Lee left only Perrin's Mississippians near Meridian in case Sherman made a retrograde move toward Demopolis.

By seven in the morning of 20 February, Winslow's column rode out of Marion. The day started warmer and much more pleasant than the previous week. Fruit trees blossomed, filling the air with fragrance, lifting the spirits of hundreds of exhausted soldiers. Veatch's division served as the van of the Sixteenth Corps, with Winslow guarding the rear of the column as they headed out on the Louisville Road. By this time, the entire army was without rations. Mann, with his counterparts in the Tenth Missouri and Fourth Iowa, searched the countryside for edible commodities, but they passed through "Poor pine country" and found little forage.[49]

Resuming the search the next morning, Mann and his foraging party found victuals three miles from the cavalry's campground. They filled the wagons full of "meat, meal, bacon," from a rich planter who happened also to be a Confederate conscription agent by the name of John Tinsley. Mann, ever the gatherer of stories, learned from a widow how Tinsley had destroyed her house when she refused to disclose the location of her son, a recent deserter from the Rebel army. The agent used bloodhounds to hunt down the poor soldier-boys, often his own neighbors; the dogs' teeth "catching and tearing them" to pieces. As they continued their march, the Randolph County merchant learned from a farmwoman the names of local secessionists who "were active in corrupting men for the Southern army." She insisted the lieutenant keep her information quiet, for if "her neighbors heard a word of what she told [him,] that her house would be burned and everything she had" would be lost.[50]

Though the cavalry ate the dust of the army's column, they had it easier than the exhausted and battered foot soldiers. "O! heavens what a dirty Set of Sore feet[,] hundred[s] Stragling [infantry] in the reer. Many of Our Boys take pity on them and dismount and offer the[m] a ride to help their fellow Soldiers along," declared the softhearted Packard. The return trip would be agonizing for the foot soldiers, who walked on blistered feet in cold, slimy mud, often without socks or shoes.[51]

At Decatur on the morning of 22 February, Winslow's brigade moved north heading for Union, to find Sooy Smith, the missing cavalry leader. They quickly passed through Philadelphia, burning bridges over the Pearl River and secondary creeks. At the J. W. Atkin plantation, they found "storehouses filled with corn and other provisions" contributed by local farmers to the Rebel cause. The farmer begged the cavalry to take only the storehouse provisions, but Winslow's men helped themselves to everything, including the household supplies. The boys "foraged with Spirit and energy" and loaded up with corn, bacon, sugar, salt, hams, turkeys, chickens, flour, meal, and honey. Considering the boys had been without rations, the plantation supplies helped the men survive for another twenty-four hours.[52]

After scouts returned without any news of Smith's column, Winslow turned west at Louisville on the morning of 23 February. The column moved through "broken & hilly" terrain, containing "less pine and more oak timbers." They reached Plattsburg in the early morning, and then Centre in the afternoon, crossing the Yockanockany, "a swampy ugly creek," destroying the bridge after they passed. Winslow finally camped within seven miles of Kosciusko. The Illinoisans, again without rations, foraged through the countryside finding "plenty of Corn, Meal and Ham! [and] Rye Coffee."[53]

Marching at daylight, the boys moved through a countryside populated with "fine [and] well improved plantations." Winslow reached Kosciusko by nine in the morning despite some light skirmishing with small bodies of Confederate cavalry throughout the day. At Kosciusko, the boys found merchants "selling out . . . their scanty supply of goods." Packard found a tobacco store and "[e]ach man helped him Self to a Supply of fine tobacco." Winslow reached the Canton Road on 24 February, sending a detachment toward the city to connect with Sherman. As the cavalry awaited orders, they established camp at a government plantation where they found plenty of "Corn and fodder and a nice find in Sweet Hams."[54]

The next day, Winslow continued through Thomastown, an old dilapidated town with few inhabitants and vacant houses. At Sharon, every bit the opposite of Thomastown, the houses and people showed "every appearance of luxury & wealth." At this point in their journey, the cavalry shared the road with slaves laden with supplies, whose Canton owners had sent them away from the Federal invaders. Unfortunately, they did not know of Winslow's journey southwest, and the cavalrymen captured "large numbers of horses, mules, oxen[,] wagons, & carriages." The soldiers also "gobbled up great numbers of negroes and stock as [the planters] attempted to hide it in their haste to escape." Mann, with over two years experience with property confiscation, believed he had never seen "such a day[']s work in the way of capturing property," with the regiment gaining seven six-mule teams loaded with bacon, meal, and sugar; five ox teams; and cattle. In all, the cavalry bagged six hundred new mounts for their use. Baggage hampered the cavalry's progress, but they arrived within two miles of Canton by that evening, allowing them to communicate with Sherman.[55]

The Fifth were unable to curb their delight at finding "very rich . . . plantations well stocked with property." At one such place, the regiment "gobbled a planter with his teams & Slaves," as well as removing the wagons from the planter's possession. The Southerner believed the Federals would also force his slaves from him, but Mann replied they would not, though the slaves were "'just as free as you are and can do as they please.'" Pleading with his chattel to remain at the plantation, the slaves recognized their day of jubilee and "came along with the Yankees, [as] freemen." Mann issued "rations to about 500 slaves" that accompanied the regiment into the Federal lines.[56]

Sherman determined to keep the army at Canton to await news of the Memphis cavalry while he rode to Vicksburg. After placing Hurlbut in command of the army, Sherman chose the Fourth Iowa Cavalry, which was ready for its veterans' furloughs, as his escort back to the city. Winslow accompanied his regiment, placing Col. Lucien H. Kerr, Eleventh Illinois Cavalry, in command of the brigade. The Federal horsemen held the area between the Pearl and Big Black Rivers and were responsible for scouting a twenty-mile area daily.

Cold and rain greeted the Federal horsemen on the morning of February 29 as they shielded a large foraging train moving on the Sharon

Road. Mann, along to acquire victuals, took possession of a planter's mill to grind up all the regimental corn, when Starke's brigade attacked, and the lieutenant "could see the flash of our guns from the mill door and the smoke of the Rebel Guns on an adjoining plantation." Starke sent a detachment "off on my right to attack his flank," but no opportunity arose, while several dismounted Federal cavalry battalions skirmished with Starke on the Sharon Road. With an additional dismounted battalion joining the foray, the Federal cavalry pushed Starke through the woods and into the open fields beyond. Seeing Adams's brigade in the distance, the Tenth Missouri lobbed a few shells, which "dismounted some of them, and hastened the departure of the rest." With the arrival of infantry from Force's and Maltby's brigades at the intersection of the Shoccoe and Ratliff's Ferry Roads, Starke was "compelled to fall back before a greatly superior force."[57]

Returning to camp, the Fifth received their marching orders for the following day. Excitement ran through the regiment, as the men "want to get to camp and hear from home once more." The army marched out to face a cold and rainy day, with the cavalry serving as rear guard to the infantry and the Fifth as the rear guard of the cavalry. Company C brought up the rear, which gave Packard a magnificent view of the column: "This was One of the Grandes[t] Sights I ever beheld[,] 15,000 men all in line of March[.] Cavalry[,] Infantry & Artillary[,] Bands playing[,] Drums Beating and Colors flying. And all the Cavalry Singing 'Old John Brown['s Body].'" Most of the day the boys spent waiting for the infantry to move out, and as a result, Starke's cavalry skirmished with Company C throughout the day, wounding several McLean County boys during the fighting. The cavalry marched slowly through "a cold tedious day & night," keeping warm by "fires [that] were Kept up [by] burning all the fences near the road as well as all the fences around the fine yards and gardens in Canton." They made only eight miles enduring the bitter cold of the first day's march.[58]

Packard described the movement on 1 March as "the Hardes[t] days work" he had ever performed in his life. "If I were to live a thousand Years I shall nere forget it or do more to save the life of my Men under my Command." Packard never described the fighting his company did during the march, but he believed his company should get some credit: "no man on this green Earth will ever know the vigilent fighting performed by Old Co. C that day, and no Man will Ever give us the Credit really due us."[59]

The second of March began with Rebel artillery lobbing shells into the ranks of the Federal cavalry just after sunrise. Farnan had command of the brigade, as Kerr had become ill on the march. The Tenth Missouri guns answered Starke's artillery with shot and shell, which "drove them behind a forest of timber." This allowed Farnan to form his line on a high hill, but Starke again opened with his artillery, and "we could see the flash of their guns and the flash of the shell very plain falling short ½ mile [but] not one Shell ever reached where we were drawn up in line of battle." Farnan withdrew, continuing to follow the infantry column, but the Virginian continued his pursuit. While trying to cross the Bogue Chitto Creek at Livingston, Starke pressed the rear guard to the point that the Tenth Missouri charged the Rebel advance guard "with such spirit & fury," driving them back and allowing the cavalry to cross in safety. At Green Hill, the highest point in the area, Joyce planted his artillery, and when the Rebels "got within range [we] opened upon them forcing them to retire." The Federal cavalry remained on the hill and established camp for the night.[60]

The evening lull, after a day of fierce fighting, brought out the quixotic in Mann. The splendid view from the hill summit, with "the setting sun in the west—the flash and roar of our guns—the long line of rebel skirmishers in the dim distance—the curling smoke as it quietly rose from the negro houses up the valley miles away—the sweet musick from our guns—sweet to the soldiers all combined to render the scene truly interesting & splendid."[61]

At sunrise on 3 March, the cavalry moved out, with the Fifth in advance. Starke had retreated during the night, and the boys spent a quiet day marching toward Vicksburg, arriving back at camp on the river about three in the afternoon the following day. The weary, dirt-covered Fifth entered camp "a worn down Set of Soldiers and Horses," but the boys who had remained behind received them with "shouts of joy." The horse soldiers looked just as ragged as the infantry; the only difference was the cavalry still wore their boots. Packard had been afraid he would arrive in camp naked. "I have lost a part of my coat and tore my pants Skirmishing in the brush, in this Godforsaken Country! but I [s]hall live through it all," he informed his wife, so "do not worry about me." The men found a month's worth of mail waiting for them in camp—a richly deserved welcome-home gift.[62]

Each side had opposing opinions about the expedition's goals. The Confederates, especially Polk, believed he had kept Sherman out of Alabama. Despite Sherman's destruction of miles of rail line, the Confederates deprived him "entirely of the rolling-stock . . . [and] the use of all the valuable stores[,] which had been accumulated at the depots."[63]

Considering Sherman's main goal had been Meridian and the destruction of the Confederacy's infrastructure and military resources in Mississippi, his campaign proved a success. Confederate reports indicate the Federals destroyed fifty-four bridges and at least seventy-six miles of track and needed to replace thousands of iron crossties on the Southern, Alabama and Mississippi and the Mobile and Ohio Railroads. Unfortunately, the Confederates repaired the Mobile and Ohio and the road east by 1 April. Work on the Southern, however, proceeded more slowly, with most of the track staying out of commission until June.[64]

The cavalry, under Winslow, showed their worth, as the Iowan "handled his cavalry brigade with skill and success." They spearheaded the army for most of the march, often battling Lee's cavalry without infantry assistance. The horsemen also captured and secured Meridian, a first for the mounted arm of Sherman's forces. The Fifth participated in three pitched battles: Jackson, Hillsborough, and Meridian, and were the first troops into Meridian. According to James Bennett, Co. F, "the expedition proved a complete success—everything being accomplished that was demanded, rumor to the contrary notwithstanding." The regiment lost two men killed, one wounded, and Henry Rose, Co. C, taken prisoner, while the remainder of the cavalry suffered eight killed, twenty-four wounded, and eight missing.[65]

"'Prepare to pucker,' to 'hunt your holes' and pull your hole in after you—ye pseudo patriots," warned James Bennett. With the regiment back from the Meridian campaign, the Fifth veterans were heading home for their hard-earned furloughs. The boys expected to "pay their respects" to "those detestable 'aiders' and 'abettors'" back home," who have labored to bring the army and its operations into disrepute."[66]

On 7 March, the Illinois veterans received orders for their thirty-day furloughs, each company choosing the officer to escort the veterans home. Francis Wheelock won the popular vote to escort the Company C veterans, beating Packard by thirteen votes. As the lieutenants made out the necessary muster rolls, the captains arranged transportation for their men at Vicksburg. After receiving their pay on 11 March, the veterans turned in their arms, except pistols, and received vouchers for their horses. With the men packed and ready to go, and "Homeward Bound" on their minds, the veterans became anxious when seven days later they still lingered in camp. On 17 March, orders finally arrived for the men to start north, and at 4:30 in the afternoon, the veterans rode for the Vicksburg docks. Packard reluctantly watched his friends and regimental mates board the steamer *Von Phal*, "all in the best of Spirits of hope and desires." The men had "very poor lodgings" overnight, not leaving Vicksburg until 3:00 the next afternoon. McPherson and his staff accompanied the Illinoisans and "treated the Boys to a drink all round," and despite the liquor, the boys behaved well.[67]

The spirits flowed quite easily during the entire northern trip, taken mostly to ward off the cold, but no one became inebriated or disorderly. On 22 March, the steamer pulled into Cairo, where the men hoped to find comfort and heat in railcars heading north. Unfortunately, the scarcity of cars forced the soldiers to board another steamer for St. Louis. After another cold night plying the waters, the boys pulled into the East St. Louis dock the next morning; all disembarked, and immediately "nearly the whole Regt [got] drunk." In mid-afternoon, the officers received orders to cross into St. Louis, and after a dinner provided by local women and a serenade of band music, the veterans boarded a ferry and recrossed the river to Alton, Illinois. After two years of active service, the men finally returned to the Prairie State. At Alton, they boarded rail cars to arrive at Springfield before daylight on 24 March.[68]

Company F, under Capt. William Wagenseller, boarded cars for Crawford County and, along the way, received "grand jubilee[s] at Hebron, Robinson and Palestine." In return, James Bennett presented the citizens with an emblem he had carved out of magnolia. The "emblem represents the United States by unified hands," with the constitution symbolized by a scroll, both images topped a shield. Bennett also carved the following words: "The Constitution, the Union, and the Laws. Presented to the *loyal* citizens of Crawford county by the Veterans of Co. F 5th Ills Cavalry."[69]

The boys of Company F were so enamored with their excellent treatment while on furlough that Wagenseller found time when he returned to the Fifth's camp in May to send an appreciative note to the *Crawford County Argus*. "We will never forget the enthusiastic feeling and generous welcome we met with every where we went, and particularly the delightful interest the ladies took" in their comfort. When the reality of war would again press on the boys, "while we are out here fighting for the rights of man," the captain believed the boys would remember "the generous[-] hearted welcome we received from the ladies of old Crawford." Those days at home would remain "bright spots in the history of our lives . . . and when this cruel war is over[,] our prayer shall ever be for the choicest blessings of Heaven to rest on our true-hearted friends in old Crawford."[70]

The citizens of Coles County treated the Company C veterans to fine dinners and parties to welcome them back home. On 28 March,

Wheelock, Withers, and the rest of the veterans attended a supper spon-
sored by the "Citizens of Bloomington" at the Ashley House. Withers
received a sash, while the citizens honored Wheelock and Packard with
sabers. Though Packard languished away at Vicksburg, he sent his acceptance speech via company comrades. Being especially humbled by
the "generous donors," the lieutenant found "words are to[o] weak[,] to[o]
powerless to Express," his gratitude. "This sword," Packard vowed, shall
"always be held by me as Scared, a token of united hearts toward Your
fellow Soldier, the Whol[e] union and Your God." The Union remained
inseparable "now and forever," and he would only "unsheath this glitter-
ing Steele" for lawful purposes.[71]

Washington County gave tribute to her soldiers on 21 April. The men
from Company H considered "it a lasting honor," and they praised the
citizens "for the interest they took" on the soldiers' behalf. The county
presented the company with money raised for the "glorious cause of the
sick and wounded soldiers of the army." Not only did the prairie boys
"esteem them for the noble efforts they made in our behalf," but also the
boys in blue would remember the good citizens "in our prayers."[72]

By 26 April, the fun had ended, as the men reported to Camp Butler,
though many snuck out of camp to spend their money in Springfield. The
Fifth at Camp Butler had the run of the place, for Farnan still had not
appeared and no one commanded the regiment. James Bennett observed
that "some [of the men] were cooking and eating, others taking a quiet
snooze in the bunks . . . there another writing while still another who being 'upon the war path' was swaggering up and down the isle endeavoring
by word and gesture to convince the world at large he was 'some if not
more.' Another class who love to 'trip the light fantastic' . . . had [started]
a 'stag dance,' and was 'whirling through . . . the dance.'"[73]

Veterans from Companies F and C finally left Camp Butler on 29 April,
taking a Great Western rail car for Cairo. At Jimtown (Riverton), Cham-
paign County, the train ran the track, but fortunately, no one sustained
any injuries. Decatur found the boys catching a Central Illinois train
south, making very "Slow time," and expecting a very hard overnight's
ride. Reaching Cairo at nine in the morning, the soldiers suffered through
a six-hour layover before boarding the steamer for Memphis, grateful to
finally "leave this filthy hole (Cairo)." After boarding the *Belle Memphis*,
the boys headed for Dixie, passing Fort Pillow on 1 May, just weeks after
Nathan Bedford Forrest's attack. "Naught but a scene of melancholy desolation here presented itself: no human being was to be seen. The buildings all burned," described Bennett, "fort dismantled, and the garrison

murdered or removed." The boys witnessed a "few carrion birds perched upon a lonely tree or lazily hovering over the scene of butchery."[74]

John Mann and the men from Company K had an easier trip, leaving Chester on 3 May on the steamer *Hillman*. They arrived at Cairo in less than twelve hours, after sharing their ride south with Gen. Frank P. Blair. At the river city, Mann called upon Wiley, David L. Phillips, and Hurlbut to discuss Republican politics and the Copperheads in Illinois. The lieutenant believed Wiley unfit for command, but he admired the Quaker's politics and moral fiber. After a few hours of conversation, Mann, with his thirty-eight charges from Company K, boarded the steamer *W. R. Arthur* just before noon on 4 May. The steamer made good time, discharging its passengers in Memphis at midnight.[75]

After another cold night on the water, Wheelock and Company C pulled into Memphis late in the afternoon on the first day of May. Disembarking the next morning, the company officers searched in vain for transportation to Vicksburg. The men spent the next few days "Loafing about Memphis," while others "bivouacked upon the wharf, under sheds, in shanties &C," but the "most refined officers and many of the 'fair haired' class of soldiers betook themselves to the hotels." Others visited fellow Illinoisans recovering in Memphis hospitals, including William Skiles, who convalesced with red eyes, and caught up on a month's worth of regimental news. With the veterans finally reunited on 5 May, the Fifth received orders to board the steamer *James Watson*, with much excitement. Leaving Memphis the next day, they reached Helena about noon. The men surveyed the town from the hurricane deck, prompting Bennett to recall "the sufferings we had endured . . . for it was here that we passed through the worst afflictions we . . . endure[d] in the service of our country. There in those rugged hills many of our messmates and comrades in arms found their resting place." Bennett's melancholy lasted until he lost sight of the Arkansas shore. The steamer finally pulled into the Vicksburg dock late in the night of 7 May, and the veterans disembarked healthier and in better spirits.[76]

8

GARRISON DUTY
March to December 1864

Spring witnessed many changes in the Army of the Tennessee in command and troop structure. On 9 March, Grant received the commission of lieutenant general and command of all Union forces, prompting Sherman's promotion to the Military Division of Mississippi. McPherson expected the action in Mississippi to "be little else except guerrilla fighting and cavalry raids on the Mississippi River," which spurred his request to leave Vicksburg. By the end of March, McPherson led the Department and Army of the Tennessee.[1]

After Meridian, Sherman's goals shifted to the capture or destruction of Johnston's army at Dalton, Georgia, but Vicksburg remained important in the overall Federal plans in the Western theater. The Federals still believed "the river Mississippi must be held sacred," but Vicksburg became only a garrison after March 1864, with the main force following Sherman east. The Ohioan believed the Confederates would be unable to attack the Gibraltar with anything but "marauding cavalry," but their actions "can in nowise influence the course of the grand war."[2]

While the veterans enjoyed their furloughs in Illinois, Seley had maintained command of the nonveterans at Vicksburg. Despite the reenlistment of over half the men (351 out of 627 present for duty), earning the designation as a veteran regiment, the major believed the Fifth had not reached elite status. Seley called for more reenlistments, reminding the men of their patriotism and the hardships they had already endured, but at this time the men "can now see [their] way to victory, peace and a speedy reconstruction of our glorious union. . . . The enemies of our country," concluded the major, "have been driven back into a very small compass." Nothing remained but "to give them the last final blow under these bright auspices for a speedy termination of the war." The major requested the soldiers to "all join in this matter, heart and soul," for only a few more reenlistments would make the Fifth a veteran organization. Seley believed that if they all worked "for the good of the service," the regiment would get their new colonel, John McConnell, as a "permanent commander." McConnell, claimed Seley, would "stick by us through thick and thin," but only if the Fifth became a veteran organization. "Let us all go in as a band of veterans and let peace, harmony, and the good of the service be our motto for evermore."[3]

In early April, word reached the Fifth's camp of the war being waged between civilians and Union soldiers in Illinois. As the Fifth veterans celebrated their homecoming in March, veterans from the Fifty-Fourth Illinois Infantry battled Copperheads and Democrats in Charleston, Coles County. When the firing ended, nine men had lost their lives, including six Union soldiers. What became known as the Charleston Riot epitomized the ill feelings and mistrust between men who supported Copperhead doctrines and Union soldiers.

The incident in Charleston "makes us all hot," declared Packard. The umbrage the prairie boys felt towards the Copperheads resulted in another letter-writing campaign denouncing their activities and doctrines. Rev. John Woods eloquently expressed the regiment's sentiments when he wrote of "our martyred soldiers" at Charleston. He believed that Copperheads were "determined to embarrass the Government and aid the rebellion," and the brutal murder at Charleston indicated what "is predetermined against this country." Though quiet now blanketed the prairies of Illinois, Woods warned that "those who were Copperheads the day of the murder . . . are just as base now as they were then," and they waited for "a favorable opportunity to deal a worse blow." Woods called on all patriots to "show your devotion to the flag of your country. Never let it fall and you will survive the mournful event."[4]

The spring of 1864 witnessed a renewed effort on the part of the Copperheads to undermine the Radical Republican's attempt to make the Emancipation Proclamation a permanent law. In March 1864, Lyman Trumbull presented a proposition to the Senate to amend the Constitution to prohibit slavery in the United States. December also witnessed Lincoln declaring he would grant amnesty to any Confederate who took the Oath of Allegiance. Many Egyptians saw these two measures as illustrations of the coercive powers of the Lincoln administration.

The Senate passed Trumbull's amendment, but the House of Representatives brought the measure to a halt in the spring and changed the entire character of the debate after Ohio congressman Alexander Long reached the floor. In what Mumford labeled a proclamation of treason in Congress, Long advocated on 8 April the recognition of the Confederacy and denounced the continuation of the war, claiming it violated the Constitution. Though other Democrats failed to support Long's claim, Benjamin Harris of Maryland defended his fellow congressman's right to free speech and endorsed the unconstitutionality of the war. Newspapers carried extensive coverage of both speeches, and soon the men of the Fifth learned of the "detestable traitors in [C]ongress."[5]

The prairie boys met at Vicksburg to express "our indignation" and "utter contempt," with "Long, Harris . . . and their like, who have of late been proclaiming treason so boldly in Congress." Long's and Harris's speeches, the soldiers contended, were a "direct insult and stigma to every soldier who is now fighting in the ranks of our army," and the Fifth men warned the Copperheads "that a day of retribution is coming." The regiment urged fellow Illinoisans to "discard all friendship, sympathy and affiliation," with those who spoke out against the war.[6]

"We, as soldiers of the United States army," addressed "those low contemptible, vile and venomous traitors, Long, Harris . . . and members of the detestable and loathsome gang of copperheads," and those who "so heartily oppose all measures on the part of our government for the vigorous prosecution of the war" in resolutions passed by the Fifth on 25 April. The prairie boys wanted Congress to expel Copperheads by banishing them into the Confederacy or confining them to military prisons "until the end of the war." The Fifth also wanted the Copperheads to know that their actions and words against the war "has not the least tendency to discourage us." The more the Copperheads voiced their objections, the more determined the Fifth was "to fight this thing out to the bitter end, and if extermination is necessary, then let our watchword be extermination of traitors in front and rear, for conquer and subdue the rebellion we will."[7]

William Skiles, in Overton hospital at Memphis, felt angry enough to write to his parents after hearing of the riot at Charleston. "<u>Insurrection in Illinois</u>," inquired the private, "it looks nice don[']t it[?]" The state's reputation as a lair for Copperheads made the private "allmost ashamed, to claim to belong to an Illinois Reg. [T]hey say (<u>Illinois men</u>, vollunteer, don[']t let it be said, your state had to draft men, to fight rebels)." While "truley loyal men are down here fighting to squash the rebellion, the authorities of the state, allow them blackhearted, cowardly, low-lived, ignorant, thickheaded, Secesh-Copperheads, to organize right under their noses." These men "destroy[ed], & disgrace[d], our homes, with no resistance," and the private "would ten times rather kill one of them, than a full blooded Secesh."[8]

Other bad news reached the Fifth when they learned that their service had degenerated to garrison duty, relegated "to fight[ing] Bush Whackers with thes[e] green Conscripts." Packard believed the sixty-seven new recruits too inexperienced to deal with the seasoned Confederates: "it is not [right] to place One in Command of these fresh fallows just off of Pudding and Milk from the Prairie to fight these prowling Gurrillas." The prairie boys had several one- and two-day scouts throughout the month of April, mostly working their way along the Big Black River, looking for Texans.[9]

During the 2 April scout to the Yazoo River bottom, Packard commanded his rookies to be on the lookout for the Third and Ninth Texas. Nothing of note occurred on the scout until around dusk, when the Fifth ran into a "Small force [of] rebels," and "took a running Skirmish After them, in the Woods." The McLean County recruits captured several Texans, and each side had one killed and one wounded.[10]

Company C's skirmish with the Texans was the regiment's last encounter. Jackson's cavalry moved to Grenada, while Ross's Texans left for the upcoming spring campaign against Sherman in Georgia. Wirt Adams remained behind in Mississippi and commanded the Fourteenth Confederate Cavalry, the Eleventh Arkansas Mounted Infantry, Stockdale's Fourth Mississippi, Robert C. Wood's Mississippi regiment, the Ninth Tennessee Battalion, and Calvit Roberts's Mississippi Battery. The brigade headquartered at Canton. Adams tasked his brigade with the destruction of the illegal cotton trade between civilians and the Federal government.[11]

April found the Fifth's camp at Bovina Station, "on the Rail Road from Vicksburg to Jackson to Supply the place and do duty of a whole Division." The men enjoyed the new surroundings offered by a one-thousand-acre plantation, the camp situated "in a beautiful[,] Secluded[,] fine timber," on a little eminence, with Clear Creek rushing in the rear of the camp. The rising slope "from Black River back on the Rail Road as far as the Eye Can reach" witnessed a never-ending sea of dirty white tents.[12]

Some nonveterans spent most of April suffering through picket duty; others visited friends in nearby Illinois regiments, while the majority protected the cotton speculators on the local plantations. Many farmers tried desperately to plant cotton for Federal trade, but the "Rebels are striving to twart them in their efforts by killing them & their colored hands & stealing their Mules &c. And they have been somewhat successful," remarked Roe.[13]

On 22 April, Adams's cavalry made a dash on the cotton enterprises near the Fifth's camp. They stole the speculators' mules and their "fine Sixteen Shooters they held for Self protection." Roe related ghastly stories to his wife of Rebel atrocities practiced on cotton planters and African American soldiers. According to the New Jersey physician, Rebels kidnapped a local farmer in mid-April, made the poor man dig his own grave, then "shot him & put him in it and covered him up." Rebels also kidnapped a Federal hospital steward by the name of Rose and "cut both of his ears off close to his head." The sergeant believed the Rebels were more "savage & ferocious than the most barbarous savages & I am fully satisfied that a large proportion of those blood thirsty & murderous wretches will have to be exterminated. They are unfit to live."[14]

As the warm Southern spring spread across Mississippi, the Fifth brigaded with the Second Wisconsin and the Eleventh Illinois Cavalry regiments, under Mumford. Except for these two white regiments, the Fifth spent the next ten months serving with African American infantry, cavalry, and artillery, which would "hereafter enter so largely into the means of defense to the river" and Vicksburg. Included with the Fifth's brigade was the Third United States Colored Cavalry (USCC), raised mostly from freed slaves in Mississippi and Tennessee in October 1863, and officered by Col. Embury Osband, entering Federal service in April. The month also brought Henry W. Slocum to command of the District of Vicksburg, while John McArthur led the troops at the Vicksburg post.[15]

Spring also witnessed the fruition of Grant's plan of simultaneous attacks on Robert E. Lee's and Joseph Johnston's armies. The Vicksburg cavalry served as distractions for Wirt Adams, to prevent Confederate troops from infiltrating northern Mississippi and Tennessee to wreck Sherman's supply lines. General Orders No. 10 sent five regiments of infantry, Mumford's cavalry brigade, and two artillery batteries, under John McArthur, to Yazoo City. Mumford commanded 550 horsemen from the Fifth and Eleventh Illinois and Second Wisconsin, and one hundred men from Third USCC regiments, under Maj. Jeremiah Cook. This would be the prairie boys' first fighting experience with African American soldiers. Capt. Alexander Jessop led 225 men from the Fifth.[16]

Mumford's cavalry saddled up by five in the morning of 4 May, all the soldiers "too glad to exchange the march, with a fair prospect of a fight, for the irksome, monotonous duties of camp." Packard found the expedition an excellent distraction that kept the boys "from drink and mischief." The columns rode out heading in the direction of Messenger's Ferry and then turned northwest toward Oak Ridge. After marching sixteen miles, McArthur bivouacked for the night.[17]

An unseasonably warm spring day dawned on 5 May as the troops headed for Mechanicsburg. The cavalry had some "sharp fighting and considerable skirmishing" with troopers from the Eleventh and Seventeenth Arkansas of Hinchie P. Mabry's cavalry brigade. Mumford's horsemen met Mabry's attack and drove the "rebs in every direction," wounding several and taking a few prisoners. After pushing the Arkansans eastward and crossing the Big Black River, the troops reached Mechanicsburg and Satartia on 6 May.[18]

Trying to beat the early spring heat, McArthur saddled up by four the next morning, heading east toward Benton. The Third USCC advanced and immediately skirmished with Arkansas mounted infantry, resulting in the retreat of the Confederates toward Benton. Another flanking movement and a frontal attack by the Third at Benton sent the Arkansans retreating through town, followed closely by the Third. Lawrence P. Hay, Co. D, praised the Third's charge, believing they "fought with great courage. There is no discount on the [T]hird U.S. colored cavalry."[19]

The Third's pursuit quickly became a Federal retreat when they contacted four Rebel cannon posted on an adjacent hill. William Bolton immediately unlimbered four Rodmans from Battery L, Second Illinois Light Artillery, to a frontal position, and a lively artillery duel followed. The rest of Mumford's cavalry organized behind Bolton's artillery, with the Fifth's Company C in the advance. Packard, who suffered during the skirmish from another malarial shake, "had the Ague nearly Scared out of Me by the Rebel Shells[,] which was thrown around Co. C in [caissons]." The Rebels held a strong position in a large field, with their artillery posted on the edge of a piece of timber. The guns had excellent range on the cavalry forces.[20]

Despite his illness, Packard stood with his company: "One Shell Came Scooping along and took two legs on One Side of a horse off next to Me and wounded two Men behind me." The shell then buried itself in the ground without exploding. The lieutenant's benediction soon followed: "Oh! how thankful it Makes a Soldier feel to See them light into the Earth and Keep Still." The McLean County clerk believed if the shell had exploded "I[,] with many of My Comrads would have been blown to attoms."[21]

Rebel and Bolton's artillery dueled for four hours, Packard describing it as the "'Grandest Artillary Duel' of the Campaign." Bolton's guns found their range, disabling one Rebel cannon. The Seventh Ohio guns soon joined the fight but took a quick pounding. Packard watched as one artilleryman wheeled his gun into position, his head "taken off by a Shell and rolled down a bank under My horse[']s feet [while] his body Still Sat on his gun." The lieutenant "cast One Sickening glance" and then "attend[ed] to my duty with all my 'might mind and Strength.'" The Federal infantry came forward and formed in line of battle, prompting Mabry to "[throw] up the Sponge with heavy loss on their part."[22]

Mumford's cavalry mounted up, with the Third out front, and pushed the Rebels five miles, until Mabry found suitable ground to make a stand. A flanking movement by the Third drove the Rebels from their position. Mumford pressed the Confederates for six miles on the old Lexington Road, taking several prisoners.

McArthur recalled Mumford's cavalry, and the Federals returned to Benton after dark, establishing camp where Mabry had set his battery during the battle. Packard believed the place unsuitable for even a one-night camp: "the ruts w[ere] drenched with blood and the trees was bespaterd with the bodyes of Men who fought to Conquer or die wortheyer of a better Cause." Packard and some Company C boys searched the battlefield picking up "Several pieces of Rebel Sculls bones just at the forks of the Benton & Canton Roads." The McLean County boys had been so excited with their finds, one private presented a piece of skull to McArthur, who "took it and put it in his vest pocket and never Spoke or Smiled" of the incident.[23]

On 12 May, Mumford's horsemen successfully destroyed Moore's ferry on the Big Black River, despite the Mississippians' attempt to thwart their activities. The following day, Adams's horsemen contested Mumford's movement at Luce's plantation, five miles southeast of Benton. Here, Adams "endeavored to test our strength." The cavalry became hotly engaged in an open field on the Picken's Road, and McArthur sent forward infantry and a battery of artillery. A flank movement by Mumford, and some well-aimed cannon shots, dislodged Adams. After a lively contest in which McArthur claimed "my cavalry and artillery behav[ed] handsomely and [fought] keenly," the Rebels reluctantly withdrew. On the evening of 13 May, McArthur camped near Vaughan, where the troops destroyed the depot and a portion of the rail track.[24]

That same evening, McArthur sent Mumford's cavalry to destroy the railroad bridge over the Big Black. The Crawford County editor handled "his men with great skill and bravery" and fought off repeated attacks from Company K, Wood's cavalry, under Capt. William S. Yerger, and two companies of Mabry's brigade, which guarded the bridge. Trudging through knee-deep swamps along the riverbank, Mumford's horsemen destroyed the bridge's trestlework, despite the fire from Stockdale's men on the eastern bank. Adams claimed to have driven off the Federals with heavy loss, but the only noted casualties in the Fifth were David Mason (1842–1925), Co. K, and Rice Hedsil (1844–64), Co. F. Captain Jessop, who commanded the Fifth during the fight at the bridge, "acted with a great deal of skill, caution and bravery, being foremost in the fight." As a result, Mumford's cavalry "won laurels and praise from the Commanders of the expedition" for their fighting at the bridge and Benton. Sgt. Lawrence Hay, Co. D, described Mumford as a commander who "handled his men with great skill and bravery, always in the advance, cheering his men onward to victory. Maj. H. P. Mumford is quite a young man and one of the most promising young officers of the war."[25]

With Adams's withdrawal to the east bank of the Big Black River, McArthur easily returned to Vicksburg on 21 May. The Fifth arrived back at camp looking "a good deal worse" from their exertions on the expedition. Packard, who would not participate in another military campaign, returned weak from malarial chills. With his morale lacking, he found great comfort in letters from his wife, Jennie. "The letters I now have before me," wrote an impassioned Packard, "are So full of the Soul and Spirit of goodness. They are like Angel Whispers to Me, and I would be stoney hearted indeed did I not appreciate them."[26]

The object of the expedition remained a mystery to the soldiers who participated. Hay heard from the "knowing ones" that the raid was considered "to be the most successful raid that has ever been conducted through Mississippi." The boys destroyed "thousands and tens of thousands of dollars worth of cotton, corn, machine shops, grist mills, stations and rail roads . . . and tore up the Southern Confederacy generally." Another soldier attributed the expedition to a "disease called in this climate 'cotton of the brain.'" He believed if cotton had been the object of the expedition then "it turned out badly for the projector, for very little of the 'staple' was to be found or was captured."[27]

McArthur believed his actions demonstrated that the Federals still had sufficient force at Vicksburg to "move into the interior when desired." The movement also allowed hundreds of recruits in the garrison to gain valuable fighting skills, "increasing their morale and giving them a prestige that cannot be overestimated to troops first brought under fire."[28]

When the veterans and the expedition returned to the Fifth's camp, they discovered the regiment lacked provisions: "no tents, no horses, every thing looks very discouraging in [the] 5th Cav.," with hard times hitting the recruits and veterans. John Burke explained to his sister Ellen, "our reg has been filled up with recruits this winter[,] and we have not drawn

Equipments for them yet so that leaves us in rather a poor fix just at present." In addition, the veterans had to contend with the depression of again leaving their families and home: "Boys look rather blue after [coming] from home," noticed Francis Wheelock. Upon their immediate return, the officers learned that John McConnell would join the regiment as the Fifth's new colonel, despite Seley's belief to the contrary. According to John Mann, the commissioned officers did not accept McConnell's commission with ease: "Many of the officers are talking of resigning in consequence of the appointment of Col McConne[ll]. They think . . . it a wrong upon the Regiment."[29]

The new colonel arrived at Vicksburg to a very cool reception on 27 May. The regiment's senior officers "received him very cordially," while the soldiers showed respect and courtesy. The Illinoisans failed to honor their new commander with cheers or hoorahs. Mann, of course, grumbled the loudest about the new commander: "Had he been a man of proper self respect[,] he would not have received the Commission, well knowing that it was not in accordance with the rule of the [W]ar Dep't to allow citizens to be promoted over those in the Service."[30]

Originally from New York, the McConnell family moved to Sangamon County, Illinois, establishing Woodside Farms in 1840, one of the most progressive establishments in the state. The family held hundreds of acres of land in and around the state capital and developed one of the first lines of Merino sheep in Illinois. When the war began in 1861, McConnell, a dedicated Republican, raised Company C, Third Illinois Cavalry, and soon held the position of major in the regiment. His work and "daring bravery" at Pea Ridge won him accolades, but McConnell's commission to the Fifth was pure political favor; neither Sherman nor Grant recommended him for the position or even knew of his previous service. Sherman preferred to have the regiment commanded by competent majors, instead of trusting to an unknown. Even the men of the Fifth expected the command to go to one of their own; yet Yates defied custom, sending not only an outsider, but also a civilian, to a command position. Despite the controversy of his appointment, the Sangamon County farmer brought more battlefield experience to the regiment than any of the Fifth's previous commanders. He would quickly earn the respect and admiration of the majority of the soldiers in the Fifth.[31]

When the regiment received three months' pay in late May, the prairie boys took the opportunity to get drunk on beer and whiskey every day. In response, McConnell issued General Orders No. 1, forbidding the sale of spirituous liquors in the regiment. Many diarists "thank[ed] the Lord" for the order. The new colonel "arrested, <u>tied & gaged by force</u>" Alexander Miller (1842–1917), Edgar Mott (1843–98), John Givens (1838–1923), and Cornelius O'Conner, who eventually spent May through October in military prison. When that punishment proved a worthless lesson, McConnell tied John Haligan (1843–84) and A. C. Tigner (1842–1916), to a post until they repented. Many believed "Drunkeness is fearfully on the increase," and the regiment faced ruin if the intoxication was "not stopped soon." Wheelock considered McConnell's first order a move in the right direction and believed that the "Regt improved very much Since Col. McConnell took command." He considered the colonel a "[very] good man."[32]

Only a few of the officers held a contesting opinion of the new colonel. McConnell's remarks during the regiment's first dress parade did not impress Mann. "I am not flattered by his appearance or remarks as to his capacity to manage the Reg't." The day after McConnell took office, Farnan sent in his resignation, claiming that a civilian had been appointed over the line officers, but the War Department refused it. Within a week, Mann recorded that several commissioned officers prepared to resign, claiming "they are not willing to serve under Col McConnell and Majors Seley & Mumford." Mann complained loudly of the "state of affairs" within the regiment, but no one resigned until late 1864, when health issues took precedence over regimental logistics.[33]

After settling into his new office, McConnell recommended Seley for the rank of lieutenant colonel, which had been vacant since Apperson's departure the previous October. Seley's promotion could not have been achieved without McConnell's recommendation, proving to Mann that the new colonel was already "in the interest and control of Seley and Mumford." Despite Mann's belief that Seley was "totally unfit for any Commissioned office," and that "[n]othing worse could have been done for the Reg't or Service," Seley had successfully managed the regiment for almost a year before McConnell's arrival. No other diarist complained about Seley's management style or command ability, though many entries contained criticisms about the major's fondness for whiskey. With Seley's promotion, Farnan moved up to first major and Mumford to second major. The position of third major remained unfilled until 1865.[34]

The men rejoiced over the many rumors that spread around the camps about Grant's advance and battle in the Wilderness. The "Hills and valeys ring with Shouts that Came from the Soul" at the "Success of Our Noble God Given Lieut Genl Grant." Grant failed to defeat Lee, but he also did not retreat after the battle, which many soldiers considered a victory. Mann recorded his excitement: "An <u>Extra</u> from Cairo paper . . . reports Gen Grant

fighting Lee for three days and Sherman advancing upon Johnston. Hope to
hear of great Union victories." By 13 May, the men heard the glorious news:
"[Grant] has defeated the traitor Lee in a pitched battle [Spotsylvania] and
is pursuing him towards Richmond. God grant that his successes may be
continued untill the rebels are compelled to submit." The lieutenant believed the prospect of peace seemed imminent: "Peace, sweet smiling peace,
will then soon spread her wings over our united and happy country."[35]

John Burke, who returned from an extended sick leave due to malaria
in late May, hoped the good news from Grant and Sherman signaled "the
beginning of the end of this rebellion." Burke had great confidence in
Grant and Sherman, and believed "that they are the right kind of men to
end this war." The private knew the two generals would "not lay around
all Summer within cannon shot of the rebs without fighting them and
hard knocks is just what it is going to take to wind up this affair."[36]

A great religious revival swept through military camps in both armies in
early spring, including the Federal camps at Vicksburg. Despite Mann's
belief in his fellow soldiers' immorality, many in the regiment converted
to Christ. Roe expressed his enthusiasm for the renewed religious fervor
to his wife, Celina: "I say it is soul cheering to the true friend of Man—to
see those brave & Patriotic men Striving to obtain an inheritance that is
incorruptible & that fardeth not away eternally in the Heavens an endless
life of bliss at the right hand of God."[37]

The regiment's religious leader, Rev. John Woods, rejoined the regiment
in April, after spending the previous year in Helena, as assistant super-
intendent of contraband. Woods held his first sermon on 29 May, just at
sunset, in an orchard by the camp. Attendance increased throughout the
summer, and by late June, Mann commented that he "never witnessed a
more orderly or attentive meeting since being in the army," with at least
twenty men desiring "to turn to the Saviour." McConnell's pledge to attend service every Sunday with the boys may have contributed to the
growing interest in worship.[38]

In July, the prairie boys exulted at Woods's suggestion to create a regimental church, for "many have expressed a strong desire to seek the Saviour and attend Devine Service regularly." The men organized a committee to draft a constitution for its government. Though Mann disapproved
of Woods and considered him vain and lacking talent as a preacher, he
believed the regiment needed divine guidance. Wheelock, on the other
hand, believed Woods, who preached "in every prayer meeting at night,"
presented a good sermon. Within a week, the men organized a Christian

association with Henry Gilbreath, Mann, Wallace Tuthill, and Arthur Sloan (1843–1915), from Company K, being some of its initial members. "God bless the work begun in this Reg't for it is needed," professed the devout Lieutenant Mann.[39]

Two trends characterized the regiment for the remainder of its service. January began the worst year for the regiment's health, even surpassing their first six months at Helena in the number of deaths from disease. In 1862, the regiment lost ninety-one men to disease, sixty-seven men in 1863, but 1864 witnessed 179 men succumb to illness at Vicksburg. Packard, stricken with malarial chills since the Jackson campaign, took another sick leave on 3 June and did not return for several weeks. The McLean County clerk would not die of his illness, but the recurring ma-larial episodes, with liver damage, prevented him from writing in his diary after 24 May. His last entries expressed his great concern for his health amid the complaints of fever and chills, which he believed he contracted during the Meridian expedition. He would never again pick up his pen during his service to record his war experiences.[40]

The year began with smallpox hitting the recruits and malarial chills paralyzing the veterans. The Meridian campaign devastated the health of almost all who participated and sent soldiers on sick furloughs to recover at home; many who stayed on active service would be hampered with poor health the rest of their lives. May witnessed the beginning of the warm season in Mississippi, and the arrival of the mosquito challenged the health of all stationed at the Vicksburg garrison. The regiment's morn-ing reports mentioned sickness on the increase throughout the summer, with one clerk in July observing "sickness [as] common as hard-tack and sow-belly." In early July, even Farnan received a twenty-day leave to "save life or prevent permanent disability," from chronic diarrhea.[41]

Sickness and death permeated the ranks to such an extent in the late summer that the men often neglected the funerals of fellow soldiers. In August, when Lt. Jacob Baker, Co. M, succumbed to illness, the inter-ment, according to Wheelock, was "very much neglected." Wheelock considered the poor attendance a "disgrace to the Comdg Officer of [the] Regt also the Capt of the Company M," to the extent that he felt soiled. Wheelock described Baker as a "good honest Christian man," who had been with the regiment since 1861 and deserved respect from those who had served under him. Within a few days, Wheelock attended another funeral and had the unpleasant task of writing to the widow of Edwin W. Butts, to inform her of the man's sudden death from an unknown illness.

Wheelock had known Butts in Bloomington and considered the sergeant "a true friend and a good Soldier."[42]

The other source of discord developed in late 1863, when cavalry horses became scarce due to neglect, glanders, battle fatigue, and lack of forage. To control the situation, the government confiscated the men's horses in January but provided mounts to the soldiers from government corrals in Memphis. Quantity, however, did not increase, and in spring 1864, Burke lamented, "we have not Horses enough for more than one[-]third of the men[,] not more than half enough arms." By June 1864, Burke believed the regiment was "now in the poorest fix that it was ever in."[43]

In early May, the Illinoisans became despondent over the rumor of their eventual dismounting and the prospect of serving as infantry. The men immediately announced they would not serve as foot soldiers. William Skiles complained to his father about the possibility of becoming "a webfooted Infantryman. . . . I did'nt enlist in infantry, therefore, I aint agoing to do their duty. I am not agoing to learn their drill, (which is entirely new to us) just for 3 . . . months [more service]." Despite all his bluster, Skiles served as dismounted cavalry until September. Poor health and the lack of horses lessened the men's enthusiasm for war, and many wanted to leave the service for civilian life.[44]

Wheelock lamented, "no horses, no horses . . . [the] men Seem lost without them." In May, the regiment mustered 855 men and officers, with only 203 healthy horses for the entire regiment. Within a month, McConnell transferred all the serviceable horses and their equipment from the Second and Third Battalions to the First Battalion, containing companies A, B, C, and D. Notwithstanding, the First Battalion did not receive enough animals to mount its forces: 192 horses for 281 men present for duty. The unmounted portion of the regiment remained available for fatigue and camp duty while those with serviceable horses held active service. Wheelock, whose Company C retained their mounts, considered this a "good arrangement." In late June, McConnell proceeded to St. Louis to procure animals for the regiment: eight hundred horses for an aggregate of 1,024 men and officers. The colonel did not return to Vicksburg until late August after traveling through Missouri purchasing mounts, but the quantity remained insufficient.[45]

In late June, word reached Sherman in Georgia of the Confederates' attempt to complete the repairs of the Mississippi Central Railroad Bridge over the Pearl River at Jackson. Sherman expected Slocum to send out weekly expeditions against the railroad to curtail any restoration operations. The Ohioan considered the bridge of great importance: It "is worth more to the Confederacy than all the population of Vicksburg." The general expected Slocum not only to destroy the rail bridge, but also to patrol the area between Brookhaven, Jackson, and Canton to "keep [the Confederacy] busy and from re-enforcing Lee and Johnston."[46]

On 1 July, Slocum left Vicksburg to execute Sherman's orders to destroy the Pearl River Bridge. The force contained twenty-two hundred infantry, Bolton's Second Illinois Light Artillery, with Mumford commanding six hundred horsemen from the Fifth and Eleventh Illinois, Second Wisconsin, and Third USCC regiments. Only the Fifth's First Battalion accompanied the expedition, commanded by Lt. Gordon Webster: forty-two men from Company A, thirty men from Company B under Lt. Clement March, and thirty-five men from Company D. Since all of Company C's line officers were too ill to participate or listed as witnesses for the court-martial of Mott, Miller, Givens, and O'Conner, Lt. Robert N. Jessop from Company M commanded forty-four men from Company C during the expedition.[47]

Slocum's column crossed the Big Black River on the morning of 3 July, reaching Champion's Hill by mid-afternoon and Clinton by noon on Independence Day, where they bivouacked. As the summer shadows lengthened in late afternoon, a large cavalry force from Adams's division took a position east of Clinton on the Jackson Road.

Dawn on 5 July witnessed Mumford and the infantry easily pushing Frank P. Powers's mounted Mississippi infantry and John S. Scott's First Louisiana Cavalry through Jackson. When Adams's horsemen retreated on the Canton Road, city officials sent Slocum a flag of truce, begging the general not to shell the capital, for it was devoid of any Rebel troops. That afternoon, Slocum moved his forces into Jackson and destroyed the bridge over the Pearl River. According to Confederate sources, however, Slocum "did no damage in Jackson to railroad or telegraph."[48]

The Federal forces stayed in the capital until 4:00 P.M. on 6 July and then began their retrograde march to Vicksburg. At the junction of Clinton and Canton Roads, just three miles into their march, Mumford encountered Scott, Powers and the newly arrived Samuel J. Gholson's cavalry with T. W. Ham and Thomas C. Ashcroft's Mississippi Cavalry, posted by Lodam Creek. Mumford immediately sent for the Second Wisconsin to form in line of battle before the Rebel batteries, while the major sent Company B from the Third to serve as pickets. While the Wisconsinites withstood the artillery barrage from James A. Owens's Arkansas Battery, the African American troops encountered Ham and Ashcroft's Mississippi cavalry in strong force. The Third USCC "withstood the first shock of the battle" but soon faltered. Mumford sent in both Illinois cavalry regiments as reinforcements, which became quickly engaged, and "a desperate cavalry fight ensued." During the fighting German-born Charles Wise, Co. B, received a fatal wound. First Lt. Clement March also received wounds, but his injuries sent him to the general hospital.[49]

With the Rebels posted along the crest of a hill, Mumford "with his cavalry attacked them with great spirit, and held them in check" until the Forty-Sixth Illinoisans and Bolton's artillery arrived. The two forces kept up a brisk fire until the gloom of night ended hostilities.[50]

Four hundred men from William L. Lowry's Mississippi regiment broke the morning stillness of 7 July when they charged the men of Company A of the Fifth as they stood picket on the Clinton Road. The Cumberland County soldiers "handsomely repulsed" the Mississippians, "shot as long as amunition lasted[;] then they 'went in' & clubbed [with] their guns." Company A inflicted severe losses on Gholson's men, including wounding Gholson, killing several, and taking fifty prisoners. The fight became general, but after three hours, Slocum moved forward, leaving the dead and wounded on the battlefields. Slocum's Federals arrived back in their camps on 9 July, fatigued and worn out with the constant fighting during the march. Mumford's cavalry lost six killed and seventeen wounded, with the Fifth sustaining one killed and five wounded.[51]

Stories spread of the gallant fighting conducted by the Third USCC. Skiles praised the men's combat abilities, and in a letter to his parents, the private lauded their efforts: "[T]here is one Reg of Negro <u>Cavalry</u> here, which I am most happy to say, is no disgrace to that branch of the service." Their work on the expedition started rumors about the black soldiers' reputation for taking no prisoners, "all that falls into their hands, need expect no mercy, & they [Rebels] are afraid of them too." Skiles declared, "they fight like so many devils." Roe boasted to his wife, Celina, "The Blacks make the best of soldiers[;] they exhibit no symptoms of cowardice whatever." Roe did not accompany the expedition to Pearl River, but he heard that when the "Blacks was ordered to charge the enemy[,] they done so with the ferosity of Tigers. They asked no quarter and Celina they gave none."[52]

Brig. Gen. Elias Dennis, who accompanied the expedition, had nothing but praise for Mumford's handling of the cavalry during the fighting. The regiment, it seemed, finally had an aggressive commander who understood battle tactics. In a letter to Jesse K. Dubois, Dennis extolled Mumford's abilities:

> In the late expedition from Vicksburg the Major had command of
> the entire cavalry forces, composed of parts of four regiments. When

I say to you that he handled his command as well, and done better
fighting than any cavalry officer I have met with in Mississippi, it
will be endorsed by all the old officers who were with the late raids.
Maj. Gen. Slocum was so well pleased and satisfied with him and the
good discipline of his command that he continued him in command,
notwithstanding his superiors were present with the expedition.[53]

While Mumford's cavalry battled it out against Adams, the Second
and Third Battalions of the Fifth remained at camp, suffering through
guard and picket duty. Wheelock grumbled that he spent a very dull, quiet
Independence Day, where his holiday lacked "even . . . a glass of Lemonade
to drink." Roe spent a rousing time listening to the "booming of Cannon[,]
good Patriotic songs and music[,] Patriotic Prayers and Orations." The
men also watched as soldiers raised a monument on the grounds where
Pemberton surrendered to Grant one year ago. Others found celebration
in whiskey and spent the day creating havoc in a drunken state. Mann did
not participate in any celebration but spent the day considering the war
and "hope[d] to celebrate the next 'fourth' at home in peace."[54]

As the sick lists increased, the regiment lost Farnan to chronic diarrhea. He initially left on a twenty-day leave of absence on 10 July, but his
health never improved at home. Additional medical certificates, obtained
from doctors in Randolph County in August and September, kept him
away from the regiment until the War Department accepted his resignation in October 1864. When Mann watched his old commander, who "was
quite sick," leave for Illinois in July, he did not expect to see the major with
the regiment again. The boys also lost their second major when Mumford
finally left on his veteran furlough on 25 July.[55]

Late summer also witnessed the death of Capt. Thomas J. Dean, Co.
F, who died of an unspecified disease in September. The popular captain
entered the service as a private in 1861 and rose to lieutenant and finally
captain of his company in July 1864. A native Hoosier, Dean lived in
Robinson prior to the war and had married Laura Blakely in April 1864
during his veteran's furlough. The marriage hit the local newspaper, who
described Dean as being "captivated" by Laura, a "fair young Union lady,
. . . and had to surrender to the rites of matrimony." The new bride became a grieving widow, receiving her husband's remains, shipped back
from Vicksburg by his friends and fellow soldiers. Within a month, the
young woman, who was also pregnant, received a widow's pension. To
the *Crawford County Argus*, Dean's friends sent a poem written by the
captain just before his death. His thoughts and words expressed the feelings of many soldiers during the war.

But once more I hope to meet them / When my soldier's life is o'er
/ And in love to greet them, / As I have in days before. . . .

In the bloody tide of battle / It may be my fate to fall / Though I'm
proud that I responded To my country's call. . . .

Fate has so decreed that I should leave my home / Far, far away, yet
oft I see / Things that remind me of my home, And make me
think of loving ones at HOME![56]

In late August, the regiment received back into their ranks with great
adulation William Berry, who had been captured during the Brookhaven
raid of June 1863. Berry escaped from Confederate custody twice. After
spending months at Libby prison, Berry eluded Confederate authorities
during a transfer to Macon, Georgia, but Rebels recaptured him after a few
days of freedom. As he neared Federally held territory on his second attempt in Georgia, Berry, who had disguised himself as a Rebel, became ill
and convalesced with a Confederate family. He contacted Federal cavalry
when they came within four miles of the house. After Berry returned to
Federal lines, he received an extended furlough due to his poor treatment
in prison. He finally rejoined his Company L comrades on 24 August, to
cheers and well wishes.[57]

When he returned, McConnell made Berry "chief of scouts" of a special
force consisting of selected men from the Fifth. Scouts included Cpl. William N. Dawson and Langston Richards from Co. B; Charles K. Peifer, Co.
C; Jesse Cannon and Thomas D. Hedspeth of Co. D; Samuel Whipple, Co.
G; William F. Smith, Co. I; Isaac Castell, Co. K; and John L. Berry, John
L. Dow, and James H. Hogue from Berry's Company L. The government
furnished each scout with Sharps carbines and revolvers, and each rode
a quality mount.[58]

The prairie boys' enmity toward their dismounting increased when
the regiment received orders in August to turn all their horses over to
the Eleventh Illinois Cavalry; something Wheelock considered "a Serious
joke on the 5th." The men objected to the transfer, talked mutiny, but soon
learned that the army had disbanded and dismounted the Mississippi
Marine Brigade. The Fifth received the marines' horses: "good news comes
to our relief." Eventually the prairie boys supplemented the horses with
those obtained from McConnell and those confiscated from area plantations: "the Boys have a 'high Old time'" legally pilfering from the locals.[59]

Summer also witnessed a shortage of good food and rations, causing
the men to complain quite loudly about John Mann, their commissary. By

early July, the regiment lacked meat, and many of the officers condemned Mann "for not keeping up the supply," whereas the lieutenant blamed the men for "wasting their rations." Mann complained in his diary about the lack of food: "[I] have never saw the Reg't so scarce of rations as they are at present." Meat remained scarce until 16 July; in the meantime, the officers grumbled to Seley that they received deficiencies in their company rations. Seley, in turn, berated and threatened Mann. The Randolph County lieutenant believed his feud with Seley prompted the complaints, and that the colonel would use this to remove him from office.[60]

The lack of rations, combined with the high cost of food from area markets, caused great consternation among the men. "We get tired [of] living on the same diet," Roe complained, "and we are necessarily obliged to buy some Articles of food—& every thing is very high." Eggs cost half a dollar for a dozen, potatoes almost ten dollars a barrel, almost two dollars for a dozen ears of corn, with coffee a dollar a pound, and common chewing tobacco over a dollar for a box. When the boys got desperate for food, they would run the pickets and "go out in the Country & get some fruit & vegetables, Apples, Peaches, Pears, Figs, Corn, Cabbage, Potatoes, Watermelons & muskmelons." Unfortunately, the days of unadulterated foraging had run its course, and fresh meat continued scarce. "Chickens & hogs," declared Skiles, "are among the things that were. [N]one to be seen this side of Big Black."[61]

In late September, N. J. T. Dana, who now commanded the District of Vicksburg, ordered a number of raids against Confederate partisan bands operating between Bolivar and Tunica Bend, along Deer Creek. The men served this month-long expedition under their new brigade commander, Embury Osband, Third USCC. Mumford returned from his furlough to command a three-hundred-man detachment of the Fifth; this was the first time since the Meridian campaign that all companies participated in an expedition. The Illinoisans boarded the steamer *B. J. Adams* during the night of 21 September, accompanied by Osband. The prairie boys reached Bolivar Landing two days later, disembarked, then rode south in the direction of Egg Point, where they rendezvoused with a detachment of the Third USCC. The Fifth captured "3 of the enemy's most important scouts," as they moved south. The only fighting the Fifth experienced was against Osband's lack of sobriety. Mumford, risking a charge of mutiny, instructed the regiment to disregard the colonel's orders until he sobered.[62]

When the Fifth arrived back at camp, Mumford received orders to escort forty-two nonveterans from Companies E and F to Springfield for their mustering out in October. The nonveterans started on their way home "'rejoicing'" on 3 October. Jonas Roe, who accompanied Mumford to Springfield, mustered out of the service on 17 October. Weeks prior to leaving the regiment, his wife, Celina, feared Jonas would not be discharged, but Roe promised his wife, "I will get out as soon as I can Legally," sometime in September or October. Also leaving the regiment in October was Thadeus Packard, whose resignation was finally accepted on 29 October, based on Dr. Ensey's diagnosis of chronic hepatitis, caused by a severe case of malaria. Ensey called Packard "much debilitated and entirely useless to the Service" and believed that "a change in climate is necessary for his recovery."[63]

Mann tried to resign for three months because of poor health. Seley finally acquiesced and endorsed the resignation, but not without consequences to the lieutenant. Mann left the service on 15 October based on Seley's recommendation: "This Officer is of no earthly use to the service, being sick most of the time, and when well worthless. I would earnestly reccommend the acceptance of this Resignation as the service would be materially benefitted thereby." With McConnell absent from the regiment, Osband not only endorsed Seley's recommendation but also replied that Mann "should not be permitted to remain in it [the army] an hour." Since Mann resigned, he was not given a dishonorable discharge; Seley's words also remained in Mann's records, and the lieutenant spent years trying to rescue his reputation. In early 1865, the lieutenant started a letter-writing campaign, even writing to Secretary of War Edwin M. Stanton requesting an honorable discharge, "for I would rather die in the Service than receive a Dishonorable discharge." Not fully understanding the weight of Seley's sanction, Mann not only wanted his record expunged but requested the position of major in a "Colored Cav Regiment," since his health had improved. His efforts caused a reevaluation of his dismissal, but McConnell upheld Seley's recommendation, as did Washburn. John Mann's record remained tarnished, whether justified or not.[64]

No sooner had Osband's troopers returned to camp from Deer Creek than they received additional orders to saddle up for an expedition to Rodney and Fayette. A false report of Confederate troop buildup near Rodney prompted Dana to send out a two-pronged attack consisting of Osband's cavalry and 525 infantry and artillery under Col. Charles A. Gilchrist. Osband's troops consisted of eleven hundred men from the Eleventh Illinois, Second Wisconsin, and Third USCC, and three hundred men from all companies in the Fifth, with four guns from the Twenty-Sixth Ohio Light Artillery. Records do not indicate who commanded the

Fifth's detachment, but it was probably Captain McConkey, who served as senior company officer.[65]

Osband and Gilchrist's troops embarked on transports on the night of 29 September, arriving at Bruinsburg about 4:00 A.M. of the next day. Once on land, the cavalry quickly moved through twenty-seven miles of countryside, reaching the vicinity of Port Gibson by four in the afternoon. The Fifth served as advance guards, and as the regiment moved toward town, McConkey ordered his Illinoisans to "advance at a gallop ... in columns of twos instead of fours," arriving at the town well ahead of the column. The Coles County captain divided the men into squads and "sent about the streets in quest of the enemy." Veteran Cpl. Jacob W. Hale, Co. F, soon found himself and his four-man squad "surrounded by several times their number, and they were compelled to either surrender or break through the rebel lines." Sgt. James Bennett ordered his men to charge, and the boys immediately spurred their horses forward. Capt. Joseph T. Cobb's Texans fired, hitting Hale in the left breast and Bennett in the left leg. The ball from Hale's wound lodged within his body, killing him within a few minutes. The men of Company F, who described Hale as "a good soldier and an agreeable messmate," buried him "as decently as the circumstances" permitted after the skirmish. Bennett received just a slight wound, which did not prohibit him from duty.[66]

The Fifth ran into thirty men from Cobb's Texas (Black River) Scouts, "just drunk enough to render them reckless." With the rest of the Fifth close behind, the prairie boys quickly dispatched the Texans, killing two. Osband, who had just arrived with the rest of the column, did not pursue Cobb due to the fagged condition of the horses. The troops from Vicksburg camped in town.[67]

Osband reached Rodney by late in the afternoon of 1 October, and Fayette the next day. On 3 October, the troops moved at daylight, and after a short skirmish with Captain Boyd's Rebels, the column reached Natchez about one in the afternoon, accompanied by hundreds of confiscated cattle, sheep, mules, and horses. Osband reported to Dana, who had arrived at Natchez two days earlier.

Dana wanted to strike any Confederates in the interior of southeast Mississippi, including Scott's Louisiana forces at Woodville and Liberty, a Confederate commissary depot. Dana supplemented Osband's original force with a detachment from the Fourth Illinois Cavalry stationed at Natchez. Col. Loren Kent, with the Twenty-Ninth Illinois Infantry, and Col. Bernard Farrar commanded two separate infantry detachments, their movements designed to support and secure Osband's route. On the evening of 4 October, transports moved Osband and Kent's troops to Tunica Bend. The combined force marched northward to Pickneyville, where they parted: Kent toward Fort Adams, where the gunboats and transports awaited, while Osband marched toward Woodville.

After leaving Kent's infantry, the horsemen rode rapidly down the muddy Woodville Road, reaching their destination late in the afternoon of 5 October. Rain masked Osband's approach, and he quickly sent his forces forward to surround Woodville. After securing their positions, Companies A and C of the Fifth and the Third USCC charged into town, surprising the Confederates. The prairie boys captured twelve prisoners, including the quartermaster, and one caisson, some military stores, and twelve wagons with their teams.[68]

After leaving a small provost guard in town, Osband moved half a mile south of the village on the Woodville and Sligo Road and established camp. During the night, the colonel received word from a freedman that Daniel Gober's East Louisiana Cavalry and three cannon from Eugene Holmes's Louisiana artillery camped at Edward McGehee's plantation, on the Whitestown Road, two miles southwest of the Federal camp. Learning of Osband's occupation of Woodville, Gober awaited Captain McKowen's reinforcements, but before the captain arrived, Osband attacked, early in the morning of 6 October.[69]

Before light even reached the sky, the Federal horsemen cautiously moved out. As they neared Gober's camp, Osband sent the Fifth and Third cavalries with a section of Company K, Second Illinois Artillery, under Major Cook, to the left. The Eleventh Illinois and Second Wisconsin, plus a section from the Twenty-Sixth Ohio Battery, commanded by Osband, moved around toward the right.

Fearful that Cook's column would turn his right flank and sever his line of retreat down the Whitestown Road, Gober sent forward Holmes's Louisiana artillery, with the Louisiana cavalry in support. His troops rested between two bridges, just north of the McGehee house, his left spanning the Bayou Sara Road, while his right extended to a small plantation bridge that connected the field to the plantation. Holmes's gunners blasted away at Cook's column, peppering the Third and Fifth with shot and shell. Gober's cavalry charged but was quickly repulsed by the Third horsemen.[70]

As the Third moved toward the left along the Bayou Sara Road, the Second Illinois Battery opened their artillery at about one thousand yards, while the prairie boys pressed Gober's forces from the front. Cook swung around, moved over the plantation bridge, and gained the rear of the artillery, charged "them with sabres and drove the gunners, drivers and all, from their guns and horses . . . right on to the Fifth Illinois Cavalry, . . . who captured them."[71]

According to James Bennett, the regiment "bore an honorable part" in the skirmish, but he was aggravated to discover that newspaper accounts credited the Third USCC as the captors of Holmes's artillery. Bennett claimed the Third approached Holmes's cannon from the rear, while the Fifth "approached the battery from the front." The sergeant believed "equal honor is due *all* the forces engaged upon that occasion. . . . [I]t may seem a matter of small importance to whom the palm is given, but the faithful soldier is chagrined to see his well earned laurels placed upon the brows of the undeserving and it is too often that he is thus despoiled of his rights by a contemptible set of lickspittle reporters."[72]

The Fifth captured one 12-pound howitzer and two 6-pound smooth bores, and Capt. Eugene Holmes, from the Louisiana battery. No one in the Fifth was wounded or killed. Gober claimed to have lost thirty captured, six killed, and three wounded. After the thirty-minute battle, the Federals officers helped themselves to breakfast at the McGehee homestead and then burned the Southerner's house and outbuildings. Osband camped that night a few miles from Fort Adams.[73]

A scout toward Woodville on 8 October resulted in a short skirmish with Scott's cavalry, but Osband found the area devoid of any large Rebel force. The Fifth arrived back in camp at Vicksburg on 11 October, without further incident of note. The prairie boys considered the expedition to have been "eminently successful," and their easy victories proved that the "Southern Confederacy is about 'played out' in these parts."[74]

A charged political climate awaited the Fifth when they returned to camp in October. The two major political parties had nominated their presidential candidates, and the camp rang with speculation about the upcoming election. Believing Lincoln could not win the 1864 election, a splinter group within the Republicans broke away from the main party and nominated John C. Fremont. The conservative Republicans joined forces with War Democrats and created the National Union Party, which nominated Lincoln for president and Andrew Johnson as vice president. When the Peace Democrats and Copperheads met in Chicago for their national convention in August, peace remained the party's creed, and they touted the war as a failure that destroyed the Union. The Peace Democrats rallied around their cry that they were the watchful guardians of the Constitution, and nominated George B. McClellan (Little Mac).

Skiles, whose father disliked Lincoln, warned his father of the evils of remaining neutral. "Little Mack," explained Skiles, "claims to be a war democrat, though he has not shown what he is now. [H]e allows the war democrats, to think so & the Peace men to think him a peace man." He was a man, Skiles believed who would soon show "his true colors." Once again, the Christian County private begged his father to "vote against him [McClellan], for a man that is not a loyal man is a disloyal man. [T]herefore if you do not use all your power against the Copper nominee, you are helping them by not killing a Copperhead vote." Lincoln was the man to reunite the country for "he has been tried, & we know what he will do." A vote for Lincoln would prove that Skiles's father loved his country and wanted the war to end, while "Mack[']s election [was] the rebs only hope & resort." Skiles informed his father that if he mustered out before election day, he would "cast all the votes I can for Old <u>Abe</u>," for "I am an Abolitionist." Unfortunately, Skiles mustered out of the service on 8 November, missing the election by only a few days.[75]

McClellan's nomination insulted many Fifth Illinoisans. Called a "contemptible place-hunter," the ex-general seemed to epitomize the derision the soldiers felt toward "the traitorous copperhead peace sneaks up north." In several letters to the *Crawford County Argus*, Mumford requested that the Illinois people "[a]bolish your copperhead doctrines—go for a vigorous prosecution of the war to the bitter end, and we [the soldiers] will say 'bully for you!' 'Long may you wave.'"[76]

Mumford accused the Copperheads of acts that "weaken our government, and our army which is laboring so zealously and so ardently for a glorious and permanent termination of our troubles." Surprise and anger greeted the major when he learned that people who had "expressed such strong Union sentiments" at the beginning of the war now supported "that traitorous gang of copperheads," solely because Lincoln had emancipated the slaves. Illinois soldiers, Mumford allowed, were "no lover[s] of the negro," but they learned early in the war that "the abolition of slavery was the heaviest blow the rebellion ever received" and was the "only chance for a permanent and complete settlement of our present difficulties." The major believed that Copperheads remained foolish uninformed people who thought that the Federal armies should not have interfered with slavery.

But is there an honest thinking man, who keeps himself posted, going to presume for a moment that we could fight the battles of this war and not interfere with the institution of slavery? That we could march into the country of these men who had made war upon our flag and government, and meet them in battle array . . . [and] not interfere with this race of men called negroes . . . [whom we found to be] our warm friends . . . whose hearts were as deeply set in the object of our efforts as our own.[77]

The major's editorial eloquence, and his Democratic Party affiliation, prompted the National Union Party in Illinois to nominate him for state senate. His adopted county of Crawford supported Mumford's nomination: "we think no better choice could at this time be made for the position. . . . He is a good speaker, and speaks boldly and fearlessly, handling secession sympathisers without gloves; . . . he will make a most able representative in our State Senate." Unfortunately, Mumford learned he was constitutionally ineligible for that office, being only twenty-four years of age. The major, however, continued to labor for the Union cause.[78]

While at Springfield canvassing for the party, Mumford suffered severely from dysentery, and "after lingering ten or twelve days" with fever, he died. The regiment, his political allies, and his friends in Illinois found it difficult "to lose so brave and good an officer—so noble a young man—who had so many bright prospects for the future." On 23 October, a military escort carried the body to the Illinois State House, with the services being attended by Jesse K. Dubois, Col. Hall Wilson, and Secretary of State O. M. Hatch.[79]

When word arrived at Vicksburg of the major's death, shock paralyzed both his troops and the commanding officers. Osband called a meeting of all cavalry officers to pay homage to Mumford. McConnell, Maj. Charles E. Johnson, Eleventh Illinois Cavalry, Maj. William Woods of the Second Wisconsin, and Maj. Jeremiah B. Cook, Third USCC served on the committee to draft resolutions concerning the late major. The committee expressed "heartfelt sorrow" at the loss of "our brother officer and friend," with whose death his associates lost "a kind, generous and honorable friend, and his country a true, noble and valuable defender." The officers recognized Mumford, "whom all loved," as "brave almost to a fault, capable, self-possessed, of untiring energy, and deeply in earnest in putting down this atrocious rebellion." The officers believed his death constituted a loss to the regiment and the military service, "in which none promised greater usefulness." The committee resolved to wear the "usual badge of mourning" for thirty days and sent a copy of the resolutions to Mumford's mother in Ohio, and to Vicksburg, Illinois, and Tennessee newspapers. The regiment mourned the death of their major and attended funeral services conducted by Reverend Woods, who conveyed an "exc[e]llent effort," in praising the late Mumford. With Farnan gone, and Mumford dead, the regiment was "entirely without a Major," lamented Thomas H. Barnfield.[80]

In August, McConnell recommended Capt. William Withers for major. At that time, Withers remained the only original captain left in the

First Battalion, and McConnell considered him "one of the very best Officers of this Regt. . . . A good disciplinarian, always ready and willing to
do his duty and his whole duty." The men serving under him in Company
C respected Withers and considered him one of the best in the regiment.
By October, however, Withers still had not received the major's commission, and the captain proceeded to Springfield for mustering out. He
had been ill for months, spending more time in the hospital than with
his men. The bereaved captain had also lost his wife in July 1863 to illness, leaving his four small children in Illinois with relatives. When he
left Vicksburg on the last day of October, he did not even bid "his best
friends 'Adieu,'" injuring his fellow officers, especially his first lieutenant,
Francis Wheelock. "Never were my feelings more hurt than on this oc-
cation, after Serving with him as a Solider for more than 3 years, he has
left me in this unkind manner." Yates finally issued Withers's commission
in late December, but the captain never returned to the regiment, which
remained without a major until August 1865.[81]

During the fall of 1864, the men focused their efforts on maintain-
ing their health. Illness, mostly fevers, ran rampant through the ranks,
with 274 men in the hospital or on furlough in September, and thirty
dying of disease. October witnessed 239 prairie boys in the hospital with
almost 12 percent succumbing to their illnesses. Others, like Skiles, suffered through relapses of malaria in their tents, treating their symptoms
with "Ayers Ague Cure, (1 bottle) blue mass, & castor Oil." The numbers
rose again in November to 140 men listed sick, with twenty dying, while
December witnessed eleven of the fifty-four men dying from disease.
Wheelock blamed the lack of quality shelter as the cause of much sickness: "I feel the late cold Storm has been more than our men can bare
with Such miserable Shelter, without much Sickness & Some loss of life.
May God help the poor Soldiers." Many considered their filthy and inadequate quarters to be the cause of the increase in sickness, but even
after the soldiers received new pup tents, the health of the regiment did
not improve. The army forbad the men to build winter quarters until
mid-November, and officers believed they delayed because "the White
Cavalry will be ordered away from here Soon—to go up into Tennessee;
. . . we are not needed Here [Vicksburg]."[82]

The prairie boys spent long hours discussing the upcoming presidential election. Many knew that with Lincoln's reelection the Rebels' "last
hope of success is blighted," because the president's "policy will speedily
end the rebellion." The election was "no ordinary political contest," but a
"struggle for the existence of free government." The Illinois boys wanted
desperately to vote, but the state legislature had failed to amend the state's

constitution in 1862 to allow soldier enfranchisement. The Illinoisans never doubted Lincoln's reelection: "[T]hink Old Abe[']s prospects are good & improving, it will be a time of grate rejoicing to us Soldiers if Abraham is re-elected. I am very Sanguine he will be." While convalescing in the officers' hospital at Vicksburg, Francis Wheelock participated in an impromptu mock election, with Lincoln receiving 95 percent of the votes.[83]

When word finally reached the Vicksburg troops of Lincoln's reelection, celebrations ran through the ranks. "We could not do much for Old Abe's Election," declared Barnfield. "But when it comes to firing Salutes[,] there[']s not many places can make a louder noise than Vixburg. . . . Speeches, Toasts, Songs, Music from the Band . . . are the Order of the day and in the Afternoon a Salute of 100 Guns from those Monster Guns at [F]ort Rawlings."[84]

With McConnell absent from camp in early November, liquor flowed easily, and the boys "report[ed] a number of Officers in 5th Cavalry very much under the influence [of] Liquor." Wheelock, who liked to imbibe occasionally, thought any officer publicly drunk was "a disgrace to any Regt," who "aught to be discharged [from] the Service." A drunken spree on the evening of 16 November caused the death of Lt. Maurice Dee, Eleventh Illinois Cavalry. Dee, together with his friend Capt. Alexander Jessop, served on Osband's staff and had been drinking socially, "without any thought of excess." The party turned dangerous when Jessop propositioned Dee that he could shoot a tin goblet off Dee's head. Knowing that Jessop was an "unerring pistol shot," Dee agreed and positioned himself against the wall with the goblet on his head. Just as Jessop was about to fire, Dee straightened his back, causing "a difference of about two inches in his height." Jessop did not see the movement before he pulled the trigger, and the shot crashed through the lieutenant's neck, killing him instantly. Jessop, knowing he had just killed his best friend, tried to commit suicide with the same pistol. Observers quickly disarmed Jessop, and he was placed under arrest for murder. The captain's trial began on 19 November, ending with an acquittal for Jessop and a ruling of accidental death.[85]

Towards the end of November, the Fifth participated in Osband's raid against the Mississippi Central Railroad above Canton, to cut supply lines for John B. Hood's Army of Tennessee, then stationed at Spring Hill, Tennessee. Dana tasked Osband's forces with the destruction of the newly rebuilt Way's Bluff Bridge and the railroad, but he also wanted the Vicksburg troops to serve as a diversion for John W. Davidson's forces heading toward the Mobile and Ohio between Meridian and Mobile, Alabama.

Moving out from Vicksburg at daybreak on 23 November, the Fifth contributed two hundred men from all companies, under the command of McConnell, his first field assignment with the prairie boys. Osband's forces numbered twenty-two hundred men, including forces from the Fifth and Eleventh Illinois, Second Wisconsin, and Third USCC. Thomas Barnfield believed the cavalry was "plentifully Sup[p]lied—with Whiskey for the Trip."[86]

The following day found the Federal forces striking the Benton Road at Oak Ridge. The troops knew nothing of their destination, only surmising that the road north was "a blind on the Rebs," according to Wheelock, who found the movement a "mystery to me." The troops traveled "Steady & hard all day" and, except for a few halts, reached Wesley Church, six miles south of Mechanicsburg, late in the afternoon. Wheelock, newly promoted to captain of Company C, recorded sighting a few scouts from Capt. Samuel Henderson's company.[87]

The men saddled up before dawn on 26 November, moving towards Benton over "fine Roads, fair count[r]y, [and] pass[ing] through Mechanicksberg," where Wheelock noted the dilapidated look of the "war[-]worn Town." Four miles short of Benton, Osband ordered the troops to stop and camp. After unsaddling and settling in for the night, Osband ordered the Fifth's First Battalion to move their camp a quarter of a mile east, causing outrage from the men, who were "all tired, hungry, Sleepy & Cross." Wheelock believed Osband would "march any Set of men & horses to death."[88]

Another day of pleasant marching witnessed the troopers passing through Benton, reaching Vaughan Station at half past noon. Here Osband sent Cook with detachments from the Third to the Way's Bluff Bridge, where the cavalry destroyed the stockade and set fire to the bridge. While Cook tackled the Rebels at the bridge, McConnell with the Fifth tore up and burned one mile of Mississippi Central rail track, "bending every rail and throwing away the chairs." As Wheelock's squad struggled with a portion of track, the lieutenant caught his leg when a portion of rail track fell back, severely injuring his ankle. Company C boys took Wheelock, unable to remain in command, to a local planter's house, where he received medical care from the women of the plantation. After depositing the lieutenant, the boys set fire to the planter's carriage house, terrifying the women and Wheelock, who believed the main house was in danger from the flames. Once the regiment extinguished the fire, the ladies gladly serenaded Wheelock with "nothing but Secesh Songs" and claimed the Confederacy would establish its independence. "Poor deluded creatures will never See that day," declared the captain. When Wheelock and the boys returned to camp, they confiscated all the planter's hams and chickens, sugar and molasses, and mules.[89]

McConnell, with the Fifth and Eleventh Illinois, moved toward Goodman on 29 November. With one battalion from the Fifth, McConnell attacked an equal number of Rebels at the wagon road bridge near the town, driving the Confederates across the river. The boys set fire to the tollhouse and bridge, but as they left the area, a patrol of Arkansas mounted infantry, under Lt. B. B. Chism, arrived and aided the local inhabitants in putting out the fires before the bridge became too damaged. The Fifth also burned thirteen hundred bales of cotton and large amounts of corn and wheat, as well as two train engines and four cars. The boys were quite "delighted with the Col. (McConnele) in the field," despite the fact that the bridge had been saved by civilians.[90]

The next morning, Osband turned his column back toward Yazoo City, with the injured Wheelock riding in an ambulance. When the column reached the city just after noon, the boys transferred Wheelock to the steamer *Shenango*, which had just arrived carrying rations for the men. While resting his men on the last day of November, Osband learned that Confederate reinforcements under Griffith had blockaded all western roads leading into Yazoo City, essentially blocking Osband's retreat toward Vicksburg. Aided by the navy, the commander shifted his troops to the west bank of the Yazoo River by the morning of 2 December. The men continued marching down the west bank, halting near the mouth of the Big Sunflower to await transports to ferry them to Vicksburg.

Wheelock, on board the *Shenango*, left for Vicksburg as soon as the Federal troops reached the west bank. As the *Shenango* neared the mouth of Short Creek, sixty sharpshooters from Jones's scouts fired on the transport. A few volleys from those onboard and a shell from the accompanying gunboat dislodged the scouts, but not before Alabama native Levi Johnson, Co. H received fatal wounds. The private lingered four days, finally dying from his wounds on 4 December. Wheelock, with his injured ankle, and now suffering from malarial chills and fever, had been safely ensconced in quarters and remained out of danger. Osband's troops finally reached their Vicksburg camps on the night of 6 December.[91]

Prior to Osband's Yazoo City raid, Dana had moved all his effective cavalry at Natchez to Vicksburg, as part of his ploy to deceive the Confederates into believing the Federals' target was Jackson, Mississippi. On 5 December, Dana sent Companies A, B, C, D, E, and H of the Fifth, under Capt. George McConkey, to protect Natchez. The problems with alcohol followed the regiment to the river city, with the post commander requesting a "Sober Capt for 'Picquet Officer,'" when Captain Peniwell got so "Drunk he did'nt Know how to relieve his men" from picket duty and "left them out 2 or three days." McConkey, however, had no sober officers to fulfill the request.[92]

Capt. Francis Wheelock, still in the hospital at Vicksburg due to his injured ankle and fever, did not accompany his company to the famous city. Within a day of the transfer, Wheelock felt the strain of being left behind: "company gone, very lonesome, had the blues, out of my head." News arrived from his brother Lt. Clarendon Wheelock that the boys had arrived safely and "like[d] the place very much, had a plenty of lumber to build Quarters," and that everyone anticipated the captain's return soon. Finally, McConnell released Wheelock and ordered him to Natchez on 22 December, but not before the captain spent a "dull, quiet—gloomy Christmas." After settling his hospital bill of twenty-three dollars, Wheelock boarded transports and arrived at Natchez three days after Christmas. Accompanying the captain was Seley, who had been ordered to command the Natchez detachment.[93]

The boys at Vicksburg spent a very somber holiday in their winter quarters. Barnfield with his messmates, William Berry, James Nesbit, and Henry Caldwell (who had been reinstated to captain in late 1863) elected "to Have a Turkey for Christmas Dinner," the first they had had in four years. Barnfield remained reflective about the holidays in a letter to his best friend, John Mann: "You up North will have a very Happy time, I presume; down here it will be quite different and yet we may as well be Happy. I used to think I would forego the present for the Sake of the future. I have said to myself 'Well by Next Christmas I will be at Home Where I can be Happy!' but Christmas comes & I was farther from Home than ever."[94]

As 1864 drew to a close, Wheelock spent the last days at Natchez, in a reflective mood about the war, his family, and his life. He credited his life to "Divine providince" which had "vouchsafed to Us, deliverance from the many dangers which have beset us, and has led us through an Ocean of difficulties to the end of another Year." The last day also brought news of Sherman's successful march to and capture of Savannah, Georgia, on 22 December. Wheelock noted his reaction: "Upon Victory: The most cheering news reaches us from all quarters. . . . The [C]onfederacy is crumbling, our prospects for a Speedy, Successfull, and victorious ending of this civil war was never better, or more bright, than now. The coming year of 1865 may it be Signalized by the restoration of peace to our Suffering country. . . . May God forgive all passed Sins & direct and bless us in all future time."[95]

9

SOON THIS CRUEL WAR WILL CLOSE
January to October 1865

As the last year of the war opened, the regiment remained separated: Companies A, B, C, D, E, and H garrisoned at Natchez, while Companies F, G, I, K, L, and M held Vicksburg. The historic river port in southern Mississippi became as boring as the Gibraltar, with "picket and fatigue duty order of the day." Though the Union's "prospects for the Surpresion of this rebelion Seems brightning" in the new year, the soldiers wanted "this cruel war . . . over So we could return to our homes and live in peace the rest of our days." The prairie boys longed to see their families and home, but not before they saved the Union: "a thing half done is never done," declared Sgt. Alonzo Payne, Co. C. All dreamed of a time "when we will have our own way about things and not bee bound down under this military Law.[1]

Old habits resurfaced, and the boys quickly fell into their familiar pattern of drinking and lazing around, with nothing better to do than to create mischief. Payne witnessed many soldiers disciplined for delinquent behavior by their captains. On the first day of January, "Ben Smith [was] tied up by the thumbs by order of Capt [Francis Wheelock] for dishonesty and neglect of duty." Five days later, the "Boys on a Spree[.] Some tied up for abusive Language." He also recorded seeing an officer of the regiment so drunk he could not find headquarters. "Many is the man that has bin ruined by the cursed Stuff [liquor]." The sergeant believed that if he ever enlisted again he "Shall not go with Such whisky loveing fellows as Stands at the head of our Regiment."[2]

On 7 January, John W. Davidson, commander of the District of Natchez, issued Special Orders No. 2, which placed the Fifth on active field service. Eight days later, the prairie boys received orders to reunite at Memphis. Immediate departure and quick transport of the Fifth became top priority, and steamboat captains retained orders to make no unnecessary landings to allow the "complet[tion] [of] the passage in the fewest hours."[3]

The Fifth's move to Memphis was to participate in Dana's effort to drive "off the guerrilla and partisan bands under [Isaac F.] Harrison and [Stephen D.] Lee that now infest the upper parishes of Louisiana between the Washita [Ouachita] and Mississippi Rivers." Starting in mid-December 1864, Edward Canby, commanding the Military Division of West Mississippi, instructed Dana to send an expedition into northern Louisiana and southeastern Arkansas, but Dana postponed the movement until he received more cavalry. Within a month, Dana acquired the Fifth and Twelfth Illinois, Eleventh New York, and Osband's cavalry brigades, which the general believed would give him a large enough reservoir to select the needed three thousand effectives for the expected arduous journey.[4]

During the first quarter of 1865, Federal authorities still feared that Trans-Mississippi troops would cross the Mississippi River to reinforce the decimated Army of Tennessee under John Bell Hood. The Federal army staged repeated raids into southern Arkansas and northern Louisiana to keep the Rebels off-balance and drive Confederate forces away from the river. Canby and Dana hunted specifically for Harrison's troops, including the Third, Fourth, and Fifth Louisiana Cavalry regiments, stationed near Monroe and Oak Ridge, Louisiana, operating between the Ouachita and Mississippi Rivers.

Just before moving to Memphis, the prairie boys lost another soldier to disease. David Perrine had joined his older brother William (1839–1914) in Company F in April 1864. Six months later, William mustered out, leaving his twenty-two-year-old brother to carry on in the company. Harrison Sears (1824–1903), a blacksmith for the company, wrote to David's father on 12 January, expressing his and the company's grief at the loss of one so young:

> With grief and sorrow I seat myself to pen you a few lines to let you know of David's death. . . . He had been poorly all summer, but I thought he had regained his health, and he looked as well and hardy as any of the boys. . . . I saw him the day before he was taken sick—he was in as good spirits as I ever saw him. But death is abroad in the land, and called him to exchange a world of trouble for one of happiness. I regret his loss very much. I feel as if I had lost a friend, and so I have, and so have you; and his wife has lost more than this world can restore to her.[5]

On 19 January, the Natchez boys loaded all their gear: "[H]ere it comes[,] dig out of this you five horse Cavalry[;] this is not the place for you," declared a joyful Payne. The horsemen packed up and quickly embarked on the *Autocrat*, "[g]lad to get away from Genl Davidson" at Natchez. Even Francis Wheelock, who left the hospital in mid-January, readied to leave Natchez, though "his ankle not much better[,] is in a bad fix." The captain feared he would "be a criple," the rest of his life.[6]

Leaving at 4:00 P.M., the boys, "all gay and happy," arrived at Vicksburg the next morning. Despite their orders, the Illinoisans left their transport and "had a run round town, looking for old friends." They also learned that the rest of the regiment left for Memphis the previous day. After refueling, the *Autocrat* left Vicksburg on the evening of the twentieth. A heavy, cold fog crept over the river, and the boats becalmed near the river's edge, creating "a very unpleasant trip" for those onboard and causing some to wonder whether they would "get to Memphis in a weak." The trip quickly denigrated into a slow, tedious journey, despite the orders for quick movement. The fog finally broke on 23 January, but the temperature dropped by the time the transports reached Helena; the wet cold penetrating those left exposed on the deck. After a short stop to refuel, the steamers crept upriver where the frozen soldiers woke to find themselves "laying at the warf at Memphis."[7]

After disembarking early in the morning of 24 January, the men "move[d] out to the vacated quarters of Second New Jersey Cavalry." Payne described their insufficient shelters as a rough place, where he believed they would "freeze to death if we Stay here." Despite the paucity of adequate lodgings against the cold and snow, the boys had again reunited, becoming a full regiment, and many "hope[d] we will Stay together as long as we are Soldiering."[8]

Much to the disappointment of the men, the Fifth joined the newly organized cavalry division under Embury Osband at Memphis. Many believed "Col E D Osband is determined to have a Star and we have to make it for him." The proposed Arkansas expedition consisted of 2,621 men in three brigades from Osband's division. The Fifth Illinois (349) joined John P. C. Shanks's brigade, along with men from Seventh Indiana and the First Mississippi Mounted Rifles.[9]

Seley, with the Fifth, reached the docks by four in the afternoon on 26 January and viewed the sight of fourteen steamers waiting for the horsemen. The men carried all their rations on their horses and pack mules but were not permitted to carry any camp equipage or tents. The prairie boys boarded the *Maria Denning*, all bundled against a morning as "cold as thunder." Payne believed "we are going to have a good trip[.] I hope So[.] Some thinks it is going [to be] a Splendid Expedition."[10]

Two days later, the transports docked at Eunice, six miles above Gaines Landing, Arkansas. As daylight brightened the extremely cold winter morning of 29 January, Osband's division moved down the west bank of Mason's Lake, until they hit Bayou Mason, where Osband struck off in a southwesterly direction toward Bayou Bartholomew. Those who had previously served in Arkansas dreaded another expedition into the marshy Mississippi River swamps in winter. The area contained backwater bayous, rivers, streams, and creeks overflowing with freezing slush and rainwater. After six or seven miles, the column hit an almost impassable swamp, where the boys "have a mudy time[,] every boddy mad an all wet and mudy." Moving through the waterlogged ground was slow and treacherous and soon the column scattered far and wide, as the frozen men searched in vain for solid ground to transverse the bog. After trudging through the slushy muck for twelve miles, the Federal column finally reached Bayou Bartholomew, where they found considerable corn for forage at the Belzer plantation. "The boys go in heavy on hams, chickens and sausage," remembered Payne. Osband ordered the rear brigade to gather enough for dinner and morning, and then the column rode another four miles to the next plantation. The roadway worsened, the mud thickened, and several pack mules were abandoned due to exhaustion or miring down in the mud. With the loss of the mules, the Illinoisans lost their rations, "so now for rough times."[11]

Another cold morning greeted the horsemen as they marched down the eastern bank of Bayou Bartholomew. Though the roads became easier, they marched through very unsettled country that Payne described as the "poor part of God[']s Creation." When the column camped that night at Holloway's Ferry, malarial chills hit Alonzo Payne, and he began to wonder at the purpose of their suffering: "what the object is I canot tell[.] Thare is no boddy of rebels in this country."[12]

The Fifth's First Battalion, under Kendall Peniwell, held the advance when they saddled up before dawn on the last day of January. Rumors reached Osband that Confederates loaded corn on the transport *Jim Barkman* at Poplar Bluff for their troops stationed at Camden. Osband sent a detachment of the Fifth at a "rapid gait, to intercept and capture her." The Illinoisans seized not only the small steamer, but also her crew, taking about nineteen Rebels prisoners. They also destroyed Confederate supplies and a flourmill at Poplar Bluff. Companies B and C held picket for the night, under the command of Payne and Peniwell. While standing guard in the cold remote countryside, a disguised Rebel "come fooling around our post with a blew coat on." The boys took off after the impostor and, after a short half-mile chase, captured the man. The Southerner insisted he was a citizen, but the Illinoisans identified him as a militia captain and placed him in custody.[13]

The environment and the landscape conspired to create the worst circumstances for a cavalry march, with torrents of rain on 1 February turning the roads to frozen slush. The men saddled up by daylight, and the cold, penetrating rain followed them as they moved along the bayou to Knox's Ferry. Not knowing the extent of the swamps, Osband took the road to Bastrop and camped just past Great Mills. The night air echoed with the soldiers' complaints: "Still rainy canot find a place to lay down[.] [R]ained all night all as wet as can be[.] [H]orses nee deep in the mud. This is our fine trip we w[ere] expecting." The men's three-day rations ran out, and with the loss of the additional rations on pack mules, the frozen prairie boys camped that night on empty stomachs.[14]

Another cold, leaden day greeted the horsemen as they scouted for A. J. McNeill's eight hundred men rumored to be at Oak Ridge. Osband sent a two-hundred-man detachment of the Fifth, under McConkey, to Monroe, where they chased about forty Rebels through town. The Confederates had even cleared out all the government stores moving them across the Ouachita River. With the fun of the chase over, the boys returned to Bastrop late at night "all wet and tired."[15]

Much to the delight of the soldiers, Osband started the return trip at daylight on 3 February. They marched up the west bank of Bayou Bartholomew to Point Pleasant, the weather remained blistering cold, but the rain had thankfully stopped. The Fifth, as well as other regiments, suffered empty stomachs: "[A]ll out of Bread and Coffe[e] So for Some hungry times it canot be helped." All the boys carried with them for comfort and warmth were woolen blankets as frozen and wet as the soldiers.[16]

As a cloudy, frozen dawn broke over the First Battalion of the Fifth Illinois in the advance, the men moved out, northeast toward Hamburg. The roads steadily worsened, and sleet battered both the horses and their riders. The day remained bone-penetrating cold, as the men slowly trudged through swollen, partially frozen streams and muck so thick, horses and mules disappeared in it. Soon the horsemen and their mounts looked as glacial as the landscape. Osband continued pushing the men for twenty-eight miles, finally reaching the Louisiana state line late in the afternoon, where he made camp for the night. Nothing of interest happened during the day, the men more interested in finding food than in locating Rebels, though they did "pick up a johny every little while." Payne considered it one of their most difficult days: "have a bad time all hungry and

wet[.] [T]his is the worst time I have Seen Since I have bin in the Survice."
Through his suffering, the McLean County sergeant could not comprehend
the reason for the expedition: "I canot See the point of marching through
this country as thare is know rebs to be Seen in this country."[17]

Misty, freezing rain pelted the bodies of the soldiers as they slept in
frozen clothes they had not removed or changed for over a week, their feet
so swollen in their water-soaked leather boots that they could not remove
them. "Drownded out last night[;] all in a bad fix this morning," remarked
a Fifth soldier. Instead of finding comfort in warm fires, the horsemen
faced a flooded and frozen countryside, where the roads disappeared
under slush and ice. The front of the column moved easily through the
wet ground, reaching Hamburg in the evening of 5 February.[18]

The rear guard, consisting of the Fifth, however, trudged through
"perfect quicksand," with the roads providing no footing whatsoever for
man or horse. Hours passed as the cavalrymen pushed and pulled their
exhausted mounts through the frozen slush; incentive for continuing
was found in the bodies of dead African Americans who had died of
exposure the previous night. Finding some purchase, the Fifth camped
for the night, reaching Hamburg the next day.[19]

Traveling through swollen streams and sloughs the next day, the Fifth
had "the worst time I have Seen yet," declared one horseman. Finally succumbing to exhaustion at sunset, the men camped in the swamp, with
hardly a "dry spot large enough for a man to lie down on." With no food
for either the horses or soldiers, one prairie boy believed this was the
"poorest time in the poorest country I ever See[n]. If this is the country
we are fighting for[,] I believe I don[']t want any in mine[.] [L]et them
have the cursed place."[20]

A swollen Bayou Bartholomew greeted the men on 9 February. Men
and horses plunged into the frozen mixture and swam to the opposite
bank: Thankful that they were a few hundred yards closer to home. Osband gave the men time to build fires to dry their clothes and warm their
cold-ravaged bodies at Hughes's plantation. Reaching Gaines Landing
the next day, the men unsaddled their horses and drew "some hard tack
and pork, cut sharp sticks and roast it over the fire, and swear that we
never eat a better meal." The men "Thank [G]od we are on the Banks of
the Mississippi river once again."[21]

Osband's soldiers looked ravaged; men so completely worn out, some
soldiers believed they would not recuperate for months. All the hardship
on the march seemed for naught, as the expedition achieved "no honor,
glory or profit. We lost more horses than we captured, some of our pack

mules, and almost all our rations." The loss of men was slight with only one man killed, two captured, and seven left sick in Bastrop. Osband did not accomplish his goal to destroy Harrison's command, as the Federals found the area devoid of any large-scale Confederate troops, the countryside so desolate and barren of supplies and forage that even a small force could not successfully exist.[22]

On the expedition's return to Memphis, the regiment lost many of its favorite and most talented company officers due to the expiration of their services. The erosion began in 1864 when Capt. Samuel Wilson, Co. D, mustered out at the end of December. Seley recommended Robert Toler (1834–1912), from Clay City, as Wilson's replacement, with Lawrence P. Hay as first lieutenant. William Watts, a soldier "worthy of promotion" became chief surgeon with Charles B. Kendall (1837–90) as his first assistant; many welcomed the loss of the inebriated John Ensey. Company A's Captain Culler mustered out on 9 January, to be replaced with Gordon Webster, "one of the most efficient Officers" at Natchez. Company B lost Kendall Peniwell and Clement March and with no one to fill the leadership position, Jacob Stifal (1838–1903), Co. F, commanded the men. Company E also lost their first lieutenant, Joseph Ewing, and Captain McConkey requested the promotion of Francis M. Webb to fill the vacancy in the company. The captain considered Webb "the best Sergt in the Co. and one amongst the best in the Redgt," who often commanded the company and in so doing "has proven himself comp[e]tent, and reliable." McConkey considered Webb's promotion "an act of justice" to a soldier who had served so faithfully for over three years.[23]

James Nesbit, "one of the most efficient officers of the Regiment," received command of Company K in February, only to die from disease seven months later. James K. Brown replaced Capt. James Balch, Co. I, in March 1865. Balch had succumbed to a severe cold, which he believed he developed during the Woodville, Mississippi, scout in November 1864. The cold was actually tuberculosis, and the disease incapacitated Balch to the point of making him unable to support his small family when he became a civilian. A government pension helped Balch's family, but his inability to work plunged the veteran into poverty. When Balch died in 1869 from tuberculosis, his wife received a widow's pension.[24]

Capt. Francis Wheelock, Co. C, left on a leave of absence in February because of his damaged ankle; the furlough continued through March. Wheelock finally received an honorable discharge at the end of April. Francis spent the rest of 1865 recuperating, but his injury never fully healed, fulfilling his fear of being "a cripple for life, necessitating the use of crutches." Wheelock's disability never diminished his unwavering spirit, and he eventually owned and operated one of the most successful grocery stores in McLean, Illinois.[25]

In May, his brother Clarendon Wheelock naturally stepped in as captain of the Normal Cavalry Company. Sergeant Payne worked his way up through the ranks, finally receiving the commission to first lieutenant. Payne had not expected the promotion, and when McConnell offered it to him after a lengthy conversation in the colonel's tent, he decided it was "not a bad position to be in[,] if a fellow comes up to his duty—And unless he does he is not worth a cent." Payne eventually received a promotion to captain of Company D in early October 1865.[26]

Memphis did not provide any relief for the men: Rain, sleet, and cold permeated their skimpy shelters. The privates worked "geting out boards for quarters[;] prehaps we will get in quarters before Spring." The horses still lacked accommodations: the stock "Shake and Shiver all day and night." A few weeks into February, one soldier noted that many horses had "allready died being chilled to death in the cold rain."[27]

The rest of February proved arduous for the boys, "roughing it with no quarters, except temporary plank sheds," through the last of the winter cold. The men stayed on active duty, some doing "double duty," in camp while others left on numerous short scouts to the interior. Seley sent Cpl. Nathan Fitts (1833–91), and Lewis Stiff (1844–1923) and Joseph Dunn (1842–1922), Co. F, upriver to guard a stranded steamboat twenty miles below Cairo. A skirmish with partisans left Stiff with a thigh wound that sent him to the hospital at Memphis until he received a disability discharge in May for his wound. The rough service also led to the increase of desertions within the regiment, a trend that steadily increased throughout 1865. William N. Dawson, once considered an excellent soldier and chosen to be part of William Berry's scouts, William R. Cothim, and John O'Brien unofficially left the regiment in January.[28]

C. C. Washburn assumed command of the forces at Memphis on 4 March. The Second Arkansas also joined the First Brigade under Shanks with the Fifth Illinois and Seventh Indiana, and the First Mississippi Mounted Rifles; the cavalry at Memphis now being designated Cavalry Division, District of West Tennessee.

In February, plans solidified concerning the Federal attack on D. H. Maury's ten thousand Confederate troops at Mobile Bay, Alabama. Federal forces began their movement in early March, and the Fifth Illinois served with Shanks's cavalry in western Tennessee as a distraction against the Memphis and Charleston Railroad.

On the first of March, the regiment received orders for the ten-day demonstration. The men packed their rations and horses and were ready to depart when the Fifth's officers determined that the scout did not leave until the next day. The soldiers believed the source of this constant confusion in orders lay with the incompetent, drunken officers: "Some how we can never recieve an order correct," lamented Payne; "it is the cause every one Seems to be down on the [F]ifth because we have Such officers I Supose and not much wonder they are drunk all the time and [does] not look to the interus of the men one bit."[29]

The Memphis cavalry was tasked with the destruction of the Memphis and Charleston Railroad and telegraph lines, and all supplies that could be used by the Rebels. Shanks's three thousand forces included three brigades, with 348 men of the Fifth Illinois serving in the First Brigade with the Second Arkansas and Seventh Indiana Cavalry regiments. This expedition began as dismally as the Fifth's trip into southern Arkansas in February: under torrents of rain that caused the roads to deteriorate quickly under horse hooves. Payne, who remained in camp, pitied the "boys that is going out as their clothing is not good and they will Some of them Suffer with the cold." The horses, already weak from the trip into Arkansas and the cold weather, contended with knee-deep mud, where "they Seem to Sink down all at once," while marching.[30]

Rain, flooded roads, and waterways followed Shanks's column to Germantown on 2 March, and at Mount Pleasant the next day. After driving a small squad of Rebels across the Coldwater River, the horsemen snatched a few Confederates from a conscription camp at Ripley, but the area seemed devoid of any large-scale force of Rebels. Shanks sent Seley with the Fifth and Fourth Illinois to Booneville to damage the Mobile and Ohio Railroad to Baldwyn, but Seley discovered the railroad already destroyed by the flooded waters. Furthermore, Seley learned that the citizens honored the February agreement between Generals Nathan Bedford Forrest and George Thomas to use the railroad for strictly nonmilitary purposes. Seley believed that "under these circumstances I did not feel justified in destroying the road." Seley moved out early in the morning of 8 March, arriving at Ripley by late afternoon. The march was uneventful except for the pursuit of three mounted Rebels and the capture of two of them. The trip continued to be hard on both the men and horses, with the regiment losing twenty of the latter, but they also captured eight mules and six other horses. Shanks praised Seley's handling of the detachment and gave him credit for "the promptness with which he moved . . . through the worst of roads with a scarcity of forage."[31]

Taking into account the condition of the roads, the inhospitable weather, and the lack of food, Shanks turned his forces west, entering Memphis around midnight on 11 March. Despite the harsh conditions, Payne reported "boys [return] all in good health." The expedition accomplished nothing of any consequence, except the capture of sixteen Confederates and ninety-five horses and mules.[32]

Warm weather finally visited the Memphis camps in mid-March, giving everyone a much-needed boost of optimism. One prairie boy daydreamed of the farm life he had left behind: "I Should like to be with them [farmers.] I can plow as well as the best of them and love to do it." Four days later, the cold resurfaced, plunging the temperatures below freezing again. The "wind blew from the west like great guns. . . . [V]ery hard bad times on both man and beast," bemoaned Payne. "It Seems as we are to be left here all the Time without any Quarters to live in and not much wonder as all our officers is drunk all the time."[33]

The prairie boys spent days erecting wooden shelters but many believed "our work is all for nothing [and] I think we will leave about the time we get them done." The boys subsisted "from hand to mouth[,] not much to eat." Rations remained so poor they could eat "10 days all in two days." Payne blamed the scarcity on the avarice of men: "thare is a Screw loose Some place. Uncle Sam provides enough and maintains[;] we Shall have it but by Some means we do not get our dues. Some one is puting it in his pocket."[34]

Skimpy shelters, low rations, cold, wet weather, and general war weariness caused the prairie boys to get "out of patience and don't care a cuss for nothing." One prairie boy declared he was "tired of Soldiering in this way[;] we have to be kicked around from one place to another, and ever[y] little cuss that has a pair of Shoulder Straps on is ordering a fellow a round." The boys had issues with the upper echelon of the army at Memphis, especially "Some of those poor little fellows that thinks they rank Genl Grant." In mid-March, Clarendon Wheelock brought in some nice "ham meat" for his messmates, and with an issuance of clothing, the boys in Company C were "all well satisfyed" for a little while, at least.[35]

To assist the people of western Tennessee in their return to the Union, the Federal government ordered the cessation of all raids, impressments, and foraging on "people who are peaceably inclined" in and around Memphis. Washburn also encouraged refugees to return to their old homes, and hire freedmen to assist in planting, only after the authorities determined that they would treat the workers with respect and kindness and would pay an appropriate rate. To this end, Washburn also received orders to occupy and repair the Mobile and Charleston Railroad, as far as La Grange "to restore confidence to the people of West Tennessee." The war in Tennessee was winding down, and the Federal government pushed toward the restoration of civil government in the state.[36]

On 19 March, Shanks received orders to move the First Brigade to White's Station, then Germantown, to guard and assist the Pioneer Corps with the repairs on the railroad. The commissary finally provided all camp and garrison equipage the men of the brigade needed to secure their comfort. Leaving the Fifth at White's, the rest of the brigade followed the construction train toward Collierville. The horsemen's movements were governed by the progress of the repairs along the Mobile and Charleston.[37]

Detachments came and went from White Station to the Fifth's main camp over the next couple of weeks. Payne relieved Wheelock at White Station near the end of March, so the lieutenant could attend to company business in the city. Payne had not left camp for weeks, and the prospect of active service brightened his spirits. "[G]lad I am a going out as I want to See the country and see the boys," declared Payne. Camp life provided "no place for me whare I can have no fun Shut up close all the time." The brilliant spring day made "the country looks nice but the inhabitance looks bad. They are a poor class of people and have farmed out their country." The McLean County soldier did not know whether the inhabitants would "Submit to the laws of The United States" but hoped they would obey.[38]

The Federal forces in western Tennessee considered the countryside a conquered territory, but many Confederate partisan bands still roamed about, inflicting damage whenever possible. Capt. Clinton "Clubfoot" Dewitt Fort, Co. G, Second Missouri Cavalry, caused great concern for the prairie boys along the Memphis and Charleston Railroad. Fort's scouts had been associated with Stephen Lee until March 1865 when Fort began "acting without authority," his troops thereafter labeled guerillas by the Federal army. On 3 April, Company D, Seventh Indiana, confronted Fort's troopers, twelve miles from Lafayette, where the Hoosiers received the brunt of the attack, leaving many dead and wounded. The Fifth, sent out as reinforcements, brought in the causalities. Eleven days later, Fort and his guerillas ambushed thirty-five men from the Eleventh New York on the Pigeon Roost Road, then struck again on 18 April, six miles from Germantown. Fort also struck the Fifth Illinois in mid-April, leaving four men from Company M missing: Benjamin R. Craw, Levi Branch, William Jerdan, and Richard Feather. All four managed to escape and return to the regiment within two days.[39]

Despite Fort's persistence, Federal work on the railroad continued. Part of the Fifth remained at Memphis under Lyman Clark, while the active portion, under Seley, guarded the rail line near Lafayette, thirty-five miles east of the city. Repairs on the rail line reached Wolf River, with brigade headquarters at Moscow.

April witnessed spring weather taking hold in southwestern Tennessee. The warm air brought the men out for daily drill, and camp life seemed idyllic for the prairie boys of McLean County: "[W]e have battallion drill by Capt [James H.] Woods [Co. F] all pass of[f] lively [time]. [C]ome in have Su[p]per beans hard tack & coffe[e]. This is quite a nice place every thing looks nice. [T]he grass is growing fine. [O]ur horses runs around camp loose [and] gets all They want to eat."[40]

Amid this idyllic setting, the men heard the gratifying news of the fall of Richmond on 2 April, followed a week later by Robert E. Lee's surrender to Ulysses S. Grant, and the capture of Mobile on 12 April. One Illinoisan "hope[d] how Soon this thing winds up. I am tierd of Soldiering and willing to quit. I have enough glory and honor to return to civil life." In North Carolina, the Fifth Illinois' old nemesis Joseph E. Johnston surrendered to Sherman on 26 April. In Memphis, the authorities on 17 April issued General Orders No. 45, declaring that any Confederate that continued to fight in the District of West Tennessee did so "from a spirit of pure malice and revenge or for purposes of robbery and plunder." Authorities considered these men guerillas and murderers, whom they would treat not as prisoners of war, but who would be held for "trial as felons and common enemies of mankind." The Fifth continued to work in and around Memphis rounding up guerillas and instilling peace to the civilians of the state.[41]

The celebration and good spirits of the men ended on 15 April, when news of the assassination of Abraham Lincoln reached Memphis and the outlying posts. Washburn ordered all officers to wear the usual badge of mourning on the left arm for thirty days, businesses closed down, and a funeral gun fired at every half hour from sunrise to sunset. The military in Memphis, including the Fifth, participated in a funeral procession four days later, which began at ten in the morning on Union Street. The men donned their best uniforms, groomed their horses, and "attend[ed] the [mock] funeral of President Lincoln[,] a day that will be long remembered." To minimize the hostile interaction between the Federal military and returning Confederate citizens and soldiers, Federal authorities curtailed any passes to soldiers bound for Memphis.[42]

As the eastern Union armies demobilized, the Fifth remained stationed at Memphis, along the Memphis and Charleston Railroad. On 17 May, the regiment reunited after receiving orders to occupy La Grange. The female college in town provided ample and sufficient quarters for many of the officers and men. Payne noted that many "rebs are coming in every day and being paroled. The war is over and they Seem very kind—all are willing to quit." The town, according to Payne, seemed "quite a nice place but is torn to pieces prety well." He believed the civilian population welcomed the Federals who were there to protect their property. Many had already started new enterprises in town and "are doing fine. [La Grange] will be a lively little town in a Short time."[43]

A small detachment, under Captain Wood, Co. F, moved to Senatobia, Mississippi, to guard the railroad. Seley commanded another detachment, consisting of men from Companies C, I, and M at Jackson, Tennessee, where they arrived in the afternoon of 24 May. Seley took possession of the city hotel, where he set up an office to receive the surrender of Confederate soldiers. "[T]hare is plenty of them here all willing to stop fighting," declared one cavalryman, "which we have no Objections to ourselvs." Some found the sight of so many Rebels mingling with the Federals unnerving, but they "Seem to be good fellows and treat us well." Many Rebels still held strong opinions against the Federal government, but others were "willing to quit their fighting and come under the laws of the old Government."[44]

With the town ruined by war, businesses lacked sufficient supplies to feed the detachment and horses. Lieutenant Payne commanded a small force sent back to La Grange for supplies. During his travels, the lieutenant noted that people seemed to be willing to put the war behind them, "to work to try and make a living." He hoped the men would stay at home and attend to their farms, for their homes and fields badly needed tending. The trip made the lieutenant yearn for the Prairie State: "think I would go to Memphis and take the first boat for Cairo. Thare get on train and go home and Stay with the girl I left behind me. I think perhaps I can go Some day before long. I Shall be glad to See the day come when we can all go home."[45]

The regiment received 114 recruits from the Eleventh Illinois Cavalry, and the regiment's aggregate soared to 715 men, the highest total since January 1865. The recruits joined the regiment on 1 June and were distributed throughout the companies, on a needed basis. Despite this influx of new men, the regiment received orders to consolidate to seven companies eight days later. Company A absorbed men from Company L, under Berry, with John Dow as first lieutenant. Company C now contained men from Company D, under Wheelock and Payne. Company K became Company D under Nesbit and William C. Addison. Company E remained the same, with McConkey still its captain. Company F absorbed men from Company M, commanded by Alexander Jessop and Ridley McCall. Company G retained its designation with Sam McConnell and Alexander Pittenger commanding. Capt. James K. Brown commanded the new Company B, which combined Company H with Company I. The old Company B mustered only twenty-three soldiers in June and was broken up, with its remaining men assigned to other companies and its commissioned and noncommissioned officers mustered out of the service. Though the regiment did consolidate, each company continued to fill out morning reports, and all twelve companies appeared on the regimental returns for July. No returns exist for August through October 1865.[46]

Early June witnessed the seven companies of the Fifth spread along the railroads at La Grange, Senatobia, and Jackson. Each detachment guarded the line and accepted the Oath of Allegiance from Confederate soldiers. On 9 June, orders went out to reunite the regiment as quickly as possible at La Grange, with movement toward Memphis anticipated. Many hoped they would be mustered out of the service and sent home; instead the prairie boys would become part of a horrendous expedition into Texas to counteract any Confederate involvement with the French-backed Mexican government.

In 1861, France, Britain, and Spain agreed to force payment of debts owed to them by the government of Mexico. Napoleon III, emperor of France, however, slyly persuaded Maximilian (Ferdinand Maximilian Joseph), House of Hapsburg, to become emperor of Mexico, superseding the tripartite agreement between the three superpowers. As a result, Britain and Spain withdrew, giving France free reign in Mexico. With the help of French arms, a small governing minority offered the throne to Maximilian in April 1864. To the United States, the French involvement in Mexico violated the Monroe Doctrine, but being in the midst of a civil war, the Federal government was unable to take any action against France. With the end of the war, Philip H. Sheridan moved fifty-two thousand troops to Texas, including ninety-five hundred cavalry from the Western theater, to counteract any Confederate connection with the French. The Fifth Illinois, Seventh Indiana, Twelfth Illinois, and Second Wisconsin moved south, instead of mustering out and heading north toward home.

On 8 June, Sheridan ordered the Memphis cavalry to Shreveport, Louisiana. Before McConnell could move his troops from La Grange, however, he received orders to send a small detachment east along the Memphis and Charleston toward Pocahontas, seventy-five miles east of Memphis. For the next eleven days, McConnell's fifty men patrolled the rail line, guarding the Pioneer Corps as they repaired it to Pocahontas. The last detachment arrived in Memphis on 19 June.[47]

It was at this point that the men learned they reunited not for mustering out, but for a movement toward Texas. All the prairie boys wanted out of the service: "Think of Texas and weap, whare the Sun has no mercy on a poor fellow atall." Next summer, declared one war-weary soldier, "I am going to be at home raising corn & hogs. Thats what will Suit me. . . . [E]very body wants to get out [of] the army." Many soldiers took control of their own destiny. As the regiment organized for its move to Texas, fifty-one men deserted between 22 June and 6 July, the day the Fifth left Memphis. Eight veterans who had been part of the regiment since 1861 unofficially left for home: William H. Barcus, Jesse Cannon, Thomas Ross, John Brown, Thomas W. Wiley, Archibald C. Tigner, William H. Warren, and Joseph Hakin. Thirteen other deserters had been transfers from the Eleventh Illinois Cavalry; the remaining deserters had served with the Fifth for less than two years. The old Company D lost the most men at eleven desertions on 23 June, while Company E lost twelve on the day the regiment left Memphis.[48]

By the time McConnell reached Memphis, the Eleventh New York, Seventh Indiana, and Twelfth Illinois had steamed downriver to Shreveport, Louisiana. Before the Fifth boarded, they received new Sharps carbine rifles and quality horses. On 3 July, the regiment boarded the steamers *Idahoe* and *Carrie*, leaving the Memphis docks three days later.[49]

Onboard the hot, overcrowded transports, the prairie boys steamed downriver, passing Helena, Vicksburg, and Natchez. Just north of Fort Adams, the men saw a change in the water: Dull, brownish red, soil-laden water flowed into the Mississippi from the Red River, their destination. The Red River was barely navigable in spring, but in late summer, when the Fifth rode its waters, the river remained low and sluggish. The heat became oppressive as the tall trees lining the red banks cut off any breezes the men would have felt onboard. Their only relief was targeting alligators with their new Sharps, from the decks of the steamers.

The transports twisted and turned through the narrow, clogged waterway. After eight days onboard, the troops finally reached Alexandria on 11 July. The regiment disembarked and established camp below the burned-out town. The residents had partially rebuilt the town after A. J. Smith set Alexandria ablaze when the Federals withdrew in May 1864. A few small, one-story cottages replaced the once-thriving town of five hundred. Low, flat countryside bordered Alexandria, and the smell of rank, decomposing vegetation rose from the banks. The hot, tepid air and stagnant water of hundreds of boggy bayous created an oasis for mosquitoes. Clouds of bloodsuckers, including gallinippers (large flying insects that gave a painful bite) enveloped the men when they landed.

The Fifth joined the Twelfth Illinois and Seventh Indiana in the First Brigade of George A. Custer's division of cavalry reorganizing at Alexandria. The Second Brigade contained the First Iowa and the Second Wisconsin Cavalry regiments. At Alexandria, all regiments, except the Fifth, refitted with Spencer carbines and new horses, but all the men lacked camp and garrison equipment and adequate clothing. Medical supplies, especially the much-needed quinine, remained scarce for the soldiers, though the officers had ample supply.[50]

Elizabeth Bacon Custer, wife of the general, recorded a diary during her husband's command in Louisiana and Texas. The Fifth's distress at their extended service meshed with the feelings of all the cavalrymen at Alexandria. Libbie described the men as "[t]ired out with the long service, weary with an uncomfortable journey by river from Memphis, sweltering under a Gulf-coast sun, under orders to go farther and farther from home when the war was over, the one desire was, to be mustered out and released from a service that became irksome and baleful when a prospect of crushing the enemy no longer existed."[51]

As soon as the army settled at Alexandria, the prairie boys' discontent demonstrated in men deserting in squads and platoons. On several occasions, Custer called out the entire command to prevent whole companies and regiments from leaving their post.

General Custer's inability to understand the volunteers' plight further exasperated this disgruntlement. Being regular army, Custer handled the men as professional soldiers. His regulations and orders reflected this treatment, and the volunteers considered the general a tyrant, who had no sympathy for the common soldier. Their plight made worse by the menial tasks Custer demanded the men perform for him and his wife. At the end of July, Custer sentenced two men to death but commuted one sentence to imprisonment. Fellow cavalry shot the condemned soldier, and Custer ordered every man in the command to file past the body. Many considered the soldier's execution a violation of military law that required the secretary of war and the president's review of death sentences, as outlined in Article 65 of the Articles of War.[52]

Fifteen men from the Fifth deserted while stationed at the burnt-out town of Alexandria. In total, from June to the regiment's mustering out in October, seventy-five men abandoned their commitment to the service. It is certain that the men's extended service contributed significantly to the prairie boys' motives for desertion, as did the transfer of unwilling recruits from the Eleventh Illinois Cavalry.

The malarial content of Alexandria's countryside, poor water, and poor rations created a very unhealthy environment for all the cavalrymen. Regimental surgeons sent requests for medical supplies, especially quinine, but "the necessary required amount could not be obtained," forcing surgeon Charles Lothrop, First Iowa Cavalry, to purchase quinine from unregulated sources. In July, the Fifth Illinois had 105 men and officers sick, out of a 666-man aggregate, and unable to perform duties. Almost 16 percent of the regiment remained out of commission, but only three men died of disease while at Alexandria.[53]

Throughout the year, McConnell sought to promote men for field office. Capt. George McConkey received a major's commission in August 1865. McConnell recommended Alexander Jessop's promotion over McConkey, even though the Company E captain ranked Jessop by ten days. McConnell stressed Jessop's experience and called him "one of the best disciplinarian[s] in this Dpt and most certainly in this Regiment." Though the colonel considered McConkey a decent and "efficient Officer," he believed Jessop was one of his best commanding officers and "a Gentleman of fine abilities in every way." On 8 August, McConnell received three majors' commissions, for McConkey, Jessop, and Lyman Clark. McConkey would be the only one mustered and given the rank of major. The other two, though promoted, mustered out of the service as captains.[54]

On 7 August, Custer issued his field orders for the march to Hempstead, allowing only three days' rations in the men's haversacks for a three-hundred-mile trip, and only fifteen pounds of forage for their horses. Before leaving Alexandria, Custer issued General Orders No. 15, explaining the conditions of the march. He expected the cavalrymen to march in columns of four, without the usual interval between companies, squadrons, and regiments. Since the troops marched through an area "beyond the control of the Government . . . and it being desirable to cultivate the most friendly feelings with the inhabitants," Custer forbad any unauthorized absence from the column and strictly prohibited any foraging along the route. Custer believed the men could obtain "all needed supplies . . . from the supply train," though all knew that sufficient provisions had not reached the men before the march. Many dismounted cavalrymen marched on foot at the rear of the brigade, subject to the inhalation of the dust along the march. Custer threatened any soldier's unauthorized absence from the column with dismounting.[55]

Custer also reiterated his General Orders No. 2, dated 24 June, against unauthorized foraging. Any "luckless wight . . . caught plundering or foraging off the 'chivalry'" would receive prompt and severe punishment in the form of head shaving and twenty-five lashes on the soldier's back. These punishments would be performed without the benefit of a court martial, which violated military regulations. James Bennett considered these "rigorous measures" wise, "for while they restrain the wayward, they only affect the orderly soldier for the better."[56]

Reveille sounded at two in the morning of 9 August, arousing three thousand men for the march to Hempstead. Custer had his column moving within two hours. A full moon shone down on the men and horses, and the men sent up a "hearty shout" as they left the burnt-out city behind them. During the first few hours, the column's march paralleled the Red River, as they rode through abandoned sugar and cotton plantations. Soon the column headed southwest, over a road "skirted on either side with hedges" twelve feet tall. When the sun rose, the heat turned oppressive, and the roads dried, coated with about one foot of fine dust and sand. The grime covered the men and got into their lungs and mouths and ears. One soldier described fellow cavalrymen as looking like they were "living sand-heaps." Within fifteen miles, the column struck a bluff at the edge of a level plain, which overlooked a forest of pines. The column made twenty-five miles their first day and camped in a "beautiful pine grove."[57]

At night, the cold air sent shivers over the poorly dressed soldiers, who had very little camp equipment to keep the cold at bay. Buglers again called reveille at two, with the column heading out by four in the morning to beat the heat. The cavalrymen marched through a forest of giant pines, populated with abundant deer and wild game. Custer moved his men eleven miles, camping near a good source of water, the countryside so flat that the men could see miles into the distance in all directions. During the next several days, the column marched through a world with "[p]ines before us, pines behind us, pines on each side of us, nothing but pines."[58]

August 11 found the column at Annacoco Creek, where the men found abundant, clear, potable water. Custer issued rations for the first time to his men, and they spent the night drawing food, getting less than two hours' sleep before the bugle sounded at two. Custer reached Sabine River the next day, the men crossing at Bevil's Ferry, and into the Lone Star State.

Texas resembled western Louisiana during the first two days, with tall pines, scarce water, and hot, dusty roads. The men passed Cow Creek, then Jasper, finally camping on the Neches River, fifteen miles from the confluence with the Angelina. On 17 August, the column forded the Angelina but waited impatiently for the pontoon across the Neches. The river bisected a countryside covered in tall pine forests, inhabited with deer, snakes, mosquitoes, chiggers, and ticks. The men enjoyed the "usual luxury of being bitten almost to death by the infernal bugs" during the night.[59]

Over the next few days, the cavalrymen rode "out of woods, into the woods, and through the woods, and camped, God only knows where." Water being so scarce, the men dug holes in dry runs to catch enough to fill their canteens. Finally reaching the Trinity on 20 August, the column forded the waterway, camping on the river's western bank. The boys named it Camp Rattlesnake for the dozens of poisonous vipers found in the area. One cautious soldier believed he could not put a foot down "without waking up some old rusty looking snake."[60]

After crossing the Trinity River, the boys discovered a much-improved countryside, dotted with working plantations and farmhouses. James Bennett described the area as a "very rich land, where corn, cotton, fruit and garden vegetables grew luxuriantly." The prairie boys were glad to see large prairies that "afford great facilities for stock raising," though "the soil is said to be less productive than in some other localities." Custer's ban against soldiers stealing or buying supplies did not preclude the general from purchasing eggs and butter from willing farmers. This heightened the animosity the men felt toward their general. Finally reaching the three forks of the San Jacinto on 22 August, the men easily forded the waterways, after taking their fill of the fresh water. The next day, Custer passed through Danville and Montgomery and, much to the delight of the Illinoisans, reached the prairies of Texas. Hundreds of cattle grazed on the tall prairie grasses, but Custer forbad the men from killing any beeves, although they had been on half rations for days. At Cypress City, the men awaited rations they expected to arrive via the Texas Central Railroad; however, none materialized. The men marched at midnight on empty stomachs, heading toward Hempstead, twenty-seven miles away. Finally after marching three hundred miles in sixteen days, the worn-out, dirty, starving midwesterners reached Hempstead on 26 August. When the men arrived, their clothes hung in tatters, and they were nearly starving."[61]

On arrival, McConnell learned that the army had brevetted him a brigadier general, based on his "gallant and meritorious services during the war." Political motivation gained McConnell his commission, for the colonel had done nothing in his year with the Fifth Illinois to warrant this promotion, serving only once with his regiment in the field.[62]

The Fifth's fortunes did not improve at Hempstead, nor did those of the other cavalry regiments. Shortly after arriving, hunger forced Twelfth

Illinois and Seventh Indiana soldiers to slaughter cattle belonging to one of the few Union men in Texas. Custer took the theft as a personal affront to the dignity of the command and punished the offenders with shaved heads and forty lashes. None of the men had been brought before a court martial, and the lashing violated army regulations that abolished flogging in 1861. Many commanding officers protested "the brutal and illegal order," but Custer carried out the sentence, earning the "lasting hatred of every decent man in his command."[63]

Custer settled his men at Leonard W. Groce's Leido plantation in Austin County, where the men shared the countryside with "centipedes, tarrantulas, stinging lizards, alligators, horned frogs, chameleons and venomous serpents, and 'varmints' innumerable." The large plantation provided a clean, wide, and deep creek for the men's drinking water. Quality food, however, remained scarce, with the men receiving inadequate supplies of hairy hogs' jowls and wormy hard bread, supplemented with corn stolen from their horses' supplies. Custer and his family, however, dined on "milk, vegetables, roast of mutton, jelly and other things," plus deer Custer killed during many of his hunting trips.[64]

Finally, after days of poor food, and complaints from commanding officers, Custer ordered the inspection of the rations on 10 September. Regimental and brigade commissaries were ordered to destroy defective rations and issue "good quality" food. Within a few days, commissaries were issuing fresh beef to the men every Wednesday and Saturday, relieving the men's hunger, if only just a little.[65]

The Fifth spent September on fatigue, camp, and stable guard duty. Morale and discipline markedly slipped. Custer charged Thomas H. Weaver, Co. I, with mutiny and "conduct prejudicial to good order and military discipline" on 19 September. The private received a forfeit of pay for a month and was "confined [to] hard labor under . . . the provost marshal" for sixty days.[66]

McConnell finally had enough of Custer's action, and in correspondence with Illinois Adjutant General Haynie, the Fifth's colonel requested the prairie boys' mustering out, for there was "but little use for their services here [Texas]." Within ten days, McConnell received orders for the regiment's release from military service, thus ending the tyrannical command of Custer for the Fifth Illinois. Surprisingly, McConnell received requests from some of the Randolph Rangers for their mustering out in Texas, for the men had "a view to remaining in the country." Since all mustering out was in the control of the states, McConnell could not fulfill their requests.[67]

On 6 October, more than five hundred war-weary, sun-burnt, mosquito-ravaged men from the Fifth turned in their camp equipment and made their farewells to their horses, friends, and fellow soldiers. The prairie boys boarded cattle cars on the old Houston and Texas Railroad, arriving at Houston the next day. From Houston, the men rode steamers to Galveston and then transferred to the ocean steamer *Clinton* for New Orleans. As they rode north on the Mississippi, the river they helped to open and secure for the Union, the veterans reflected on their four years of service. As rookies, they had aided the Army of the Southwest in the invasion and occupation of Missouri and Arkansas. Posting at Helena, one of the most insalubrious stations in the Union, the Federal army had relied heavily on the mobile arm of the blue-clad cavalry, with the horsemen gaining more time in the field than the infantry at Helena. The Fifth Illinois, Fifth Kansas, First Indiana, Fourth Iowa, and Second Wisconsin shared the same service, and they quickly became adept at fighting and counteracting the guerrilla tactics of Confederate cavalry. Here, the Illinoisans gained their soubriquet as the bloody Fifth, after participating in some of the most bitter fighting against Texas cavalry and Arkansas civilians during the war.

The hard service performed at Helena weaned out the weakest soldiers and most inept officers, with the regiment losing two hundred men to disease, wounds, or disability discharges. The prairie boys' second year of service had witnessed the loss of most of the original line officers to disease, debility, or war weariness, which weakened the regiment's cohesion. Compared with other cavalry regiments serving at Helena, the Fifth Illinois' loss to disease equaled the numbers dying in the Second Wisconsin and the Fifth Kansas, indicating the environment and lack of discipline had equal influence on mortality.

With the loss of Colonel Wilson, and under the leadership of Wiley in early 1863, anarchy had reigned throughout the companies, and the regiment's penchant for drunken behavior, stealing, and vengeance warfare preceded their move to Mississippi. Leaving behind the Fifth Kansas and First Indiana, the Fifth joined the Fourth Iowa and Second Wisconsin in Grant's army at Vicksburg.

Using their knowledge of guerrilla fighting, the regiment had routed Confederate cavalry during the charge at Mechanicsburg but quickly learned this style would not work well in Mississippi. After numerous scouts, the regiment adapted to fighting in the traditional army style: in line behind defenses, and usually under artillery fire, where they did not perform well. Losing Wiley, then Apperson, the regiment fell under the command of Seley, a man of questionable morality, and liquor easily flowed through the regiment. It was through the leadership of Captains McConkey, Withers, Wheelock, Caldwell, Mumford, Jessop, Hopkins, and Balch that the men found pride and valor on the battlefields in Mississippi and Louisiana, securing those states for the Union. Despite the Fifth's obvious problems, including lack of leadership, the regiment participated and fought in major postsiege movements to Jackson, Canton, Grenada, and Yazoo City, often spearheading the Federal column. Even with the lack of quality regimental officers, over 350 men reenlisted for the duration of the war, securing the Fifth's status as a veteran organization.

Their exceptional service during Sherman's Meridian campaign, however, failed to alter the regiment's abysmal reputation, and the army relegated the men's third year to garrison duty with the Second Wisconsin, as the rest of the army accompanied Sherman to Atlanta. Disease, wounds, and debility claimed 245 men while the regiment was stationed at the Gibraltar, thinning the ranks more quickly than the diseases at Helena. Their last eight months at Vicksburg allowed the regiment to serve with black troops, fighting side-by-side with soldiers they had at one time considered lesser beings. Despite their culturally engrained hatred and suspicion, the Fifth learned to respect the black soldier as fighting companions and men.

Continuing their northern journey at war's end, the weary veterans onboard the steamer *Clinton* docked at Memphis in mid-October. Here the regiment had watched the war end, helping their recent enemies return to a normal life. At the Cairo wharf, the soldiers boarded rail cars for Springfield, Illinois, arriving at the capital on 18 October. Reporting to Camp Butler on 27 October 1865, the men of the Fifth Illinois finally mustered out of the service. On 9 November 1865, the *Crawford County Argus* announced the prairie boys' arrival in Illinois: "The boys from this county belonging to the 5th cavalry, arrived at home on last Thursday and Friday [2–3 November] all of them being well." Of the 1,845 men who had entered military service with the Fifth, only 1,427 men survived the challenges of war, but all the survivors were transformed by their military experiences. Final statistics for the regiment include eleven killed in action, sixteen died of wounds, five of which were accidental, 386 succumbed to disease, one suicide, and four men drowned. The regiment lost more men to disease than other cavalry regiments in the same army but had a much lower rate of men dying in action. The Second Wisconsin, serving with the prairie boys for almost four years, had equal numbers: twenty-four killed in action with 284 dying of disease. A total of 227 Fifth men received disability discharges for wounds or disease contracted during military service. The regiment witnessed sixteen men dishonorably discharged or dismissed, and 125 men deserted their post during the war. The regiment never received the accolades that other Illinois regiments gained, but the sacrifices the soldiers made helped reunite the country and end slavery, which made every prairie boy proud of their service.[68]

The Fifth veterans now confronted the adjustment to civilian life: new jobs, relocation, recovering their health or failing to, economic readjustment, and the healing of personal relationships strained by four years of absence. The boys from the prairie who fought and saved the Union would now become the people who forged modern American society and culture. Many Fifth veterans moved west of the Mississippi River, homesteading in Kansas, Nebraska, Colorado, Utah, and the Dakotas. Others became the entrepreneurs who brought an agrarian nation into the industrial revolution and forged the basis of our contemporary economy. Many prairie boys stayed in Illinois and developed the small family farms of the Midwest, creating the grain belt that spread from Illinois through the western grasslands in the late nineteenth century. Others lacked the ability to adjust to their civilian lives, due to physical and mental disability, and many were lost to the historical record. The challenges the veterans faced in the postwar era became a story unto itself and will be addressed in another volume.

NOTES

BIBLIOGRAPHY

INDEX

NOTES

1. The Politics of War, August 1861 to February 1862

1. McConkey to Yates, 16 June 1863, Woods to Yates, 9 April 1863, Fifth Illinois Cavalry, Administrative Files on Civil War Companies and Regiments, RS 301.018, Illinois State Archives, Springfield, Illinois (hereafter cited as Administrative Files); Thadeus B. Packard Diary, 1 June 1863, Reminiscences, MS. BV, Thadeus B. Packard Papers, ALPL (hereafter cited as Packard Diary).

2. John Moses, *Illinois Historical and Statistical. . . .* (Chicago: Fergus, 1892), 2:1208–9. All 1860 voting statistics taken from Moses.

3. Allen Johnson, *Stephen A. Douglas: A Study in American Politics* (New York: Macmillan, 1908), 478.

4. *The War of the Rebellion: A Compilation of the Official Records of the Union and Confederate Armies in the War of the Rebellion* (Washington, DC: GPO, 1880–1901), ser. 3, 1:67–69 (hereafter cited as *OR*); Illinois Adjutant General, *Report of the Adjutant General of the State of Illinois* (Springfield: Phillips Bros. State Printers, 1900), 1:5, 11, 14.

5. Illinois Adjutant General, *Report*, 1:15; Frank L. Klement, *The Copperheads in the Middle West* (Chicago: Univ. of Chicago Press, 1960), 30. Updegraff was never mustered, and his military record lacked all demographic information; even his age and nativity were not recorded.

6. "G.O. 177," 4 September 1861, Benjamin L. Wiley Papers, Collection 99, Special Collections, Morris Library, Southern Illinois University Carbondale (hereafter cited as Wiley Papers), "Colonel Ben L. Wiley," *Carbondale Free Press*, 12 December 1890. David Phillips hosted Lincoln in Jonesboro during the 1858 senatorial debate with Stephen Douglas.

7. "Colonel Ben L. Wiley," *Carbondale Free Press*, 12 December 1890.

8. Helen Edith Sheppley, "Camp Butler in the Civil War Days," *Journal of the Illinois State Historical Society*, 25, no. 4 (January 1933): 289.

9. "John Apperson," "Thomas Apperson," Eighth Census of the United States of Population and Housing, 1860, Cumberland County, IL, Microfilm M653, Roll 172: 118, 698, Washington, DC: NARA, Heritage Quest Online, ProQuest, 1999–2011, http://persi.heritagequestonline.com (hereafter cited as 1860 PS; all census material from Heritage Quest unless otherwise noted); "Apperson, Thomas A.," State of Illinois, Illinois Public Land Purchase Records [database on-line], Provo, UT: Ancestry.com Operations Inc, 1999, http://www.Ancestry.com; Mumford to Yates, 10 April 1863, McConkey to Fuller, 16 June 1863,

Administrative Files; "Apperson, T. A.," Masons of Wabash Lodge No. 179, transcribed by Kim Torp, http://genealogytrails.com/ill/coles/mason3.html.

10. The database of Fifth soldiers consisted of 1845 entries, but only 562 were linked with real estate and personal property values: 437 for the original regiment and 125 for later recruits. Comparisons were done only between original enlistees, since later recruits were difficult to identify in the 1860 census.

11. "Abel H. Seeley," 1860 PS Marion County, IL, Roll 207: 804; Packard Diary, 22 August 1862; Mumford to Yates, 11 April 1863, Administrative Files.

12. John P. Mann Diary, 19 October 1861, typescript (hereafter TS), John P. Mann Papers, Collection 111, Special Collections, Morris Library, Southern Illinois University Carbondale; Packard Diary, 5 October 1862.

13. David Hackett Fischer, *Albion's Seed. Four British Folkways in America* (New York: Oxford Univ. Press, 1989), 687.

14. J. G. Bennett, "Our Army Correspondence," CCA, 4 February 1864, 2.

15. Mann Diary, 26 October 1861, TS.

16. *Counties of Cumberland, Jasper, and Richland, Illinois. Historical and Biographical* (Chicago: F. A. Battey, 1884), 266–67; "Charles Neecwanger," 1860 PS Cumberland County, IL, Roll 172: 767.

17. "E. W. Pearson," 1860 PS Cumberland County, IL, Roll 172: 859.

18. Webster to Fuller, 27 May 1863, McConnell to Fuller, 30 October 1864, Administrative Files; "Lyman Clark," "Gordon Webster," 1860 PS Cumberland County, IL, Roll 172: 705, 744.

19. "Thomas McKee," 1860 PS Coles and Crawford Counties, IL, Roll 171: 82; Packard Diary, 1 April 1862. Pairings were based on the place of residence, surname, age, census information, and material from first-person accounts.

20. Packard Diary, 19 September 1861; "Election Certification," 14 September 1861, Co. C, Administrative Files.

21. *History of Ray County, Missouri* (St. Louis: Missouri Historical Co., 1881), 710-11; *The History of McLean County, Illinois. . . .* (Chicago: W. Le Baron Jr., 1879), 398; Franklin W. Scott, *Newspapers and Periodicals of Illinois 1814–1879* (Chicago: Illinois State Historical Library, 1910), 29; "W. P. Withers," 1860 PS McLean County, IL, Roll 204: 539; Apperson to Fuller, 20 July 1863, McConnell to Fuller, 2 August 1864, Administrative Files.

22. Francis A. Wheelock Diary, passim, Francis A. Wheelock Papers, SC 16467, ALPL; "A Notable Figure. Death of Capt. F. A. Wheelock," *Daily Pantagraph*, 13 February 1904.

23. Packard Diary, 3 March 1862; "Thaddeus Packard," "William Packard," 1860 PS McLean County, IL, Roll 204: 650.

24. Packard Diary, 6 October 1861, 23 March 1864.

25. Due to restrictions on the Alonzo Payne diary, only a transcription was available for use, and that could not be photocopied. Molly Kennedy, a researcher in Springfield, Illinois, type-copied the Payne transcription in December 2007. Alonzo G. Payne Diary, passim, TS, Alonzo Payne Papers, SC 1152, ALPL. A Civil War–era photograph of Payne is available at http://www.findagrave.com/cgi-bin/fg.cgi?page=gr&GRid=31922187.

26. "GO 5," 26 September 1861, ROB, Fifth Illinois Cavalry, Records of the Adjutant General's Office, 1780s–1917, Record Group 94, NARA, Washington, DC (hereafter cited as Records AGO).

27. Mann Diary, 24, 25 October 1861, 6 February 1862, TS. Of the 1,318 men who reported their marital status, 62.5 percent or 825 remained bachelors, 481 were married, 12 were widowers, with 236 claiming children. Most men had only one child, though two men had ten or more offspring.

28. Mann Diary, 30 September, 21 October 1861, TS; "SO 8," 26 September 1861, "SO 9," 27 September 1861, "SO 102," 11 October 1861, ROB, Records AGO.

29. Mann Diary, 2, 12 October 1861, TS.

30. Ibid, 9 October, 9 November 1861, TS.

31. Packard Diary, 20, 27 October 1861.

32. US, War Dept., *Revised Regulations for the Army of the United States, 1861* (Philadelphia: W. Childs, 1862), 525–26.

33. Jonas H. Roe to Celina Roe, 13 October 1861, Jonas H. Roe Papers, 1861–1864, SC 1837, ALPL; "SO 24," 7 November 1861, ROB, Records AGO; Mann Diary, 26 November 1861, TS; Janet B. Hewett, ed. *Supplement to the Official Records of the Union and Confederate Armies* (Wilmington, NC: Broadfoot, 1995), pt. 2, 7:543.

34. *History of Wayne and Clay Counties, Illinois* (Chicago: Globe, 1884), pt. 1: 174; "H. A. Organ," 1860 PS Wayne and White Counties, IL, Roll 236: 302; Wiley to Fuller, 9 April 1863, Administrative Files.

35. "Court Martial of Col. Updegraff—The Charges Against Him," CT, 28 October 1861, 2; Skiles to Parents, 30 September 1861, William A. Skiles Letters, Christian County Historical Society, Taylorville, IL.

36. Mann Diary, 18 October 1861, TS; Skiles to Parents, 30 September 1861, Skiles Letters.

37. "SO 17," 22 October 1861, ROB, Records AGO; "Petition to His Excellency Gov. Yates," 7 December 1861, Administrative Files.

38. *History Wayne and Clay Counties, Illinois*, pt. 1: 78, pt. 3: 116–17; "S. J. R. Willson," 1860 PS Wayne and White Counties, IL, Roll 236: 30. Ten Mexican War veterans became commissioned officers of the Fifth; three held noncommissioned status. Samuel served in the Third Infantry with John J. Adams, Calvin Schell, and Thomas Williams.

39. "Calvin Schell," "L. P. Hay," 1860 PS Wayne and White Counties, IL, Roll 236: 291; *History of Wayne and Clay Counties, Illinois*, pt. 3: 51–52; Packard Diary, 19 February 1862.

40. "Election Results," 25 September 1861, Administrative Files.

41. Newton Bateman and Paul Selby, *Historical Encyclopedia of Illinois and History of Coles County* (Chicago: Munsell, 1906), 831; William H. Perrin, *The History of Coles County, Illinois* (Chicago: W. Le Baron, 1879), 250, 452; "G. W. McConkey," 1860 PS Coles and Crawford County, IL, Roll 171: 9.

42. "SO 2," 14 October 1861, ROB, Records AGO; Perrin, *The History of Coles County*, 557; "John W. Woods," 1860 PS Coles and Crawford County, IL, Roll 171: 34; Mann Diary, 29 September 1861.

43. Mumford to T. S. Mathers, 4 September 1861, Administrative Files; Scott, *Newspapers and Periodicals of Illinois*, 297.

44. "Francis M. Dorothy," "William Wagenseller," 1860 PS Coles and Crawford County, IL, Roll 171: 375, 568; George W. Wagenseller, *The History of the Wagenseller Family in America with Kindred Branches* (Middleburgh, PA: Wagenseller, 1898), 59–60.

45. "Election Results," 2 November 1861, Co. G, Administrative Files.

46. "Wm N. Elliott," 1860 PS Shelby and Schuyler County, IL, Roll 228: 398; "A. H. Smith," 1860 PS Pike County, IL, Roll 219: 451.

47. Skiles to Parents, 7 September 1863, Skiles Letters.

48. Pease to Fuller, 14 December 1861; Apperson to Dubois, 25 May 1863, Administrative Files.

49. "B. Jenkins," "E. S. Norfolk," "John F. Smith," 1860 PS Cumberland County, IL, Roll 172: 758, 858, 730.

50. Mann Diary, 9, 11 September, 30 November 1861, TS.

51. Phillips to Yates, 29 October 1861, Mumford to Fuller, 22 January 1864, Administrative Files; E. J. Montague, *A Directory, Business Mirror, and Historical Sketches of Randolph County* (Alton, IL: Courier Steam Book, 1859), 159, 160; Mann Diary, 17 October 1861. A postwar image of Farnan is available at http://barbaras.org/ayres/farnan_james2.jpg.

52. *Portrait and Biographical Record of Randolph, Jackson, Perry, and Monroe Counties, Illinois* (Chicago: Biographical Publishing Co., 1894), 309, 310; "C. J. Childs," 1860 PS Randolph County, IL, Roll 221: 972.

53. "Petition to Governor of the State of Illinois," n.d., Administrative Files; *Portrait and Biographical Record of Randolph, Jackson, Perry, and Monroe Counties Illinois*, 441–42; "Calvin A. Mann," 1860 PS Randolph County, IL, Roll 221: 1019; "Dr. C. A Mann Dies in Kansas," *Chester Herald Tribune*, 24 April 1902, 1.

54. Mann Diary, 6 December 1861, TS; Montague, *A Directory, Business Mirror*, 199, 201.

55. "John Preston Mann Dead," *Chester Herald Tribune*, 5 March 1908, 1.

56. Burke to Ellen E. Hudson, 23 January 1862, John W. Burke Letters, 1862–1864, John W. Burke Papers, 89–21, ALPL.

57. Mann Diary, 30 November 1861. For more information on the Fifth's flag, see "Civil War Flags of Illinois," John Schmale, ed., Mahomet, IL, 1998–2001, http://civil-war.com/searchpages/result.asp?Name=005th&category=Cavalry&Submit=Search+for+Flags.

58. Apperson to Dubois, 25 May 1863, Administrative Files; "Henry D. Caldwell," 1860 PS Edgar, Edwards, and Effingham County, IL, Roll 176: 1038; Caldwell Family History, pp. 1–2, Jean Adams Personal Family Files, El Paso, Texas. Twenty-six men had previous Civil War service, of which five gained commissions in the Fifth.

59. "Captain William N. Berry Biography," Maurice Krueger, ed., *Memorial and Biographical Record; an Illustrated Compendium of Biography, Containing a Compendium of Local Biography, including Biographical Sketches of Prominent Old Settlers and Representative Citizens of South Dakota* (Chicago: G. A. Ogle 1899), 826–29, http://files.usgwarchives.org/sd/biography/memor99/berry-w.txt. Berry's military record is a bit confusing. He supposedly fought in the battle at Fredericktown in October 1861, but his muster roll indicated he enlisted in the Fifth in September 1861, but he was not present for duty until February 1862. Notes attached to his record indicate he transferred to the Fifth in February 1862. "Muster Roll," September 1861 to February 1862, William N. Berry Military Service Record, Compiled Service Records of Volunteer Union Soldiers, Fifth Illinois Cavalry, Records of the Adjutant General's Office, 1780s–1918, Record Group 94, NARA, Washington, DC (hereafter cited as CSR).

60. "Robert Schell," 1860 PS Wayne and White Counties IL, Roll 236: 304; Xenia to Editor, 28 November 1861, PP, 2; *History Wayne and Clay Counties, Illinois,* pt. 1, 191. Baker served as a private in Co. D, First Illinois Infantry during the Mexican War. Robert Schell was related to Calvin Schell of Company D.

61. "Regimental Return," February 1863, Wilson to Yates, 12 October 1862, Administrative Files; "Alexander Jessups," 1860 PS Wayne and White County, IL, Roll 236: 227.

62. Roe to Celina, 13 October 1861, Roe Papers; "Dr. Jonas H. Roe History," Eric Feagan, ed., 2001–2011, http://civilwarletters.150m.com/Copyright_2001 /JonasRoe_history.html. A Civil War-era photograph of Roe is available on the website.

63. "SO 211," 29 October 1861, ROB, Records AGO; Mann to Nancy, 3 November 1861, TS, Mann Papers.

64. Mann Diary, 2 November 1861, TS; Roe to Celina, 13 October 1861, Roe Papers.

65. Mann Diary, 17, 22, 24 November 1861, TS.

66. "GO 248," 12 December 1861, ROB, Records AGO.

67. PP, 27 February 1862, 2; Mann Diary, 15 December 1861, TS; Mann to Nancy, 18 December 1861, TS, Mann Papers.

68. *Passenger Lists of Vessels Arriving at New York, New York, 1820–1897,* Records of the US Customs Service, Record Group 36, Microfilm Roll 237, List 533, NARA, Washington, DC; "Wilson, Hall," Illinois Public Domain Land Tract Sales Database, Illinois State Archives Databases, http://www.ilsos.gov/GenealogyMWeb/ landsrch.html; C. S. Williams, *Williams' Springfield Directory, City Guide, and Business Mirror for 1860–61* (Springfield: Johnson and Bradford, 1869), 143; PP, 27 February 1862, 2; "GO 3," 17 December 1861, ROB, Records AGO; *History Wayne and Clay Counties, Illinois,* pt. 1: 191.

69. Mann Diary, 26 December 1861, 1 January 1862, TS; Packard Diary, 12 January 1862.

70. Richard Rainsforth, "Camp Butler near Springfield, Jan. 17, '62," *Belleville Democrat,* 25 January 1862, 2.

71. "Special Notices," PP, 17 October 1861, 2; Mann to Nancy, 3 November 1861, TS, Mann Papers.

72. Wilson to Fuller, 26 January 1863, Administrative Files.

73. Roe to Celina, 10 December 1861, Roe Papers. Ten other men died while at Camp Butler: Henry Brothers, Ezekiel McDaniel, William Orrison, Samuel P. Little, Owen Cravens, Patrick Fry, Edwin N. Fulfer, John Jones, James A. Smith, and Jefferson Slow.

74. Mann to Nancy, 10 November 1861, TS, Mann Papers; United States, War Dept., *1861 Revised Army Regulations,* 21.

75. Mann Diary, 11, 16 February 1862, TS; Packard Diary, 17 February 1862.

76. Mann Diary, 13, 18 February 1862, TS; "Announcement," *Mattoon Independent Gazette,* 22 February 1862, 2.

77. Mann Diary, 18 February 1862, TS; Skiles to Parents, 19 February 1862, Skiles Letters.

78. "Camp Butler near Springfield," *Belleville Democrat,* 25 January 1862; "Morning Reports," Co. E, February 1862, Records AGO; "Deserter Shot," MG, 29 July 1863, 2.

2. The Springtime of War, March to July 1862

1. Mann Diary, 21 February 1862, TS; PP, 27 February 1862, 2. Surgeon Higgins's last morning report for the Fifth listed thirty-one men in the hospital when the regiment left Camp Butler. "Morning Report of Surgeons," 19 February 1862, Thomas Madison Reece Papers, 1857–1876, Box 1, Folder 2, ALPL.
2. "Payment Schedule," Co. E Order Books, Records AGO; Wilson to Yates, 28 February 1862, Administrative Files; Mann Diary, 2 March 1862, TS; Skiles to Parents, 13 March 1862, Skiles Letters.
3. "SO 190," 1 March 1862, ROB, Records AGO; *OR*, ser. 1, 8:579–80 (all references to series 1 unless otherwise noted).
4. Packard Diary, 3 March 1862.
5. Ibid, 7 March 1862.
6. Ibid, 7 March 1862.
7. *OR*, 13:391–92. Wiley, "Statement of Account," 24 January 1864, Wiley Papers; Packard Diary, 12 March 1862.
8. Packard Diary, 13, 14 March 1862.
9. Ibid, 18 March 1862. Glimpse and McLaughlin were bachelors from Bloomington. McLaughlin died of disease while on sick furlough in March 1864.
10. Mann Diary, 20 March 1862, TS; Packard Diary, 18 March 1862.
11. Packard Diary, 18 March 1862.
12. Mann to Nancy, 23 March 1862, TS, Mann Papers; Mann Diary, 26 March 1862, TS.
13. Mann to Nancy, 21 March 1862, TS, Mann Papers; Mann Diary, 20, 31 March 1862, TS.
14. Mann Diary, 26 March 1862, TS; Packard Diary, 27 March 1862.
15. Packard Diary, 28 March 1862.
16. Mann Diary, 28 March 1862, TS; Mann to Nancy, 21 March 1862, TS, Mann Papers.
17. Packard Diary, 28 March 1862; "GO 11," 29 March 1862, "SO 7," n.d., "SO 8," 30 March 1862, ROB, Records AGO; Mann Diary, 28, 30 March 1862, TS; Skiles to Parents, 16 July 1862, Skiles Letters. John Ludwickson identified the First Indiana guns as English Blakelys with a 2 9/10 inch caliber. John Ludwickson to Kohl, 5 November 2009, e-mail correspondence.
18. *OR*, 8:578–79, 626–27, 651, 657.
19. Mann Diary, 31 March, 1 April 1862, TS; Mann to Nancy, 30 March 1862, TS, Mann Papers; Packard Diary, 1 April 1862.
20. Packard Diary, 1 April 1862.
21. Ibid. Beath received a discharge in October 1862 for a hernia and became a carpenter in McLean County. Keeran reenlisted as a veteran in 1864, mustering out with the regiment in October 1865. "Beath, Edward E.," 1870 PS McLean County, IL, Roll 259: 535.
22. Skiles to Parents, 12 April 1862, Skiles Letters.
23. Packard Diary, 2 April 1862; *OR*, 8:657.
24. Robert I. Girardi and Nathaniel C. Hughes Jr., eds., *The Memoirs of Brigadier General William Passmore Carlin U.S.A.* (Lincoln: Univ. of Nebraska Press, 1999), 41.
25. Hewett, *Supplement OR*, pt. 2, 9:438, 11:11, 50:476; Lowell Wayne Patterson, ed., *Campaigns of the 38th Regiment of the Illinois Volunteer Infantry Company K,*

1861–1863: The Diary of William Elwood Patterson (Bowie, MD: Heritage, 1992), 5; *History of the Sixteenth Battery of Ohio Volunteer Light Artillery, U.S.A. from Enlistment, August 20, 1861 to Muster Out, August 2, 1865. Compiled from the Diaries of Comrades, the Best Recollections of Survivors, and Official Records* (N.p.: n.p., 1906), 14–15.

26. Packard Diary, 1 March, 10 April 1862.
27. Ibid, 10 April 1862; Mann Diary, 5 April 1862, TS.
28. Packard Diary, 3 April 1862; "RCD," Cos. C and G, 1862, Administrative Files. Jones survived his wound but died of disease at Helena. Brower received a disability discharge for an unknown ailment in December 1862.
29. Fischer, *Albion's Seed*, 767; Packard Diary, 6 April 1862.
30. Mann Diary, 6 April 1862, TS.
31. Packard Diary, 22 March, 10 April 1862; *OR*, 8:666, 672, 13:362.
32. Packard Diary, 13 April 1862; Frank Moore, ed. *Rebellion Record. A Diary of American Events* (New York: G. P. Putnam, 1862), 4:498–99; Skiles to Parents, 5 May 1862, Skiles Letters.
33. Mann Diary, 17, 19, 20 April 1862, TS.
34. Ibid, 21 April 1862, TS.
35. Packard Diary, 21 April 1862; Skiles to Parents, 5 May 1862, Skiles Letters; "Morning Report," Co. E, April 1862, Records AGO.
36. Mann Diary, 25 April 1862, TS; Packard Diary, 23 April 1862; "RCD," December 1862, Administrative Files.
37. "SO 25," 29 April 1862, ROB, Records AGO; Mann Diary, 30 April 1862, TS; Packard Diary, 1 May 1862.
38. Wilson to George, 25 December 1862, Col. Hall Wilson Military Service Record, CSR; Mann Diary, 6, 7, 26 May 1862, TS.
39. "RO 58," 26 May 1862, ROB, Records AGO; Mann Diary, 18 May 1862, TS.
40. Burke to Ellen E. Hudson, 8 May 1862, Burke Papers; Mann Diary, 12 May 1862, TS; Skiles to Parents, 14 June 1862, Skiles Letters. Typhoid caused the deaths of Jonathan Young, James Roberts, John F. Black, and John W. Adams. James McFarland, Joseph McManis, Joseph W. Estes, William H. Owen, and James W. Hall succumbed to an unspecified disease.
41. Apperson to Dubois, 23 May 1863, Pease to Fuller, 14 December 1861, Pease to Yates, 1 May 1862, Administrative Files; "Benj Glenn," 1860 PS Coles County, IL, Roll 171: 363; Perrin, *History Coles County Illinois*, 587.
42. Packard Diary, 23 April, 11 May 1862; Mann Diary, 1 May 1862, TS.
43. Mann Diary, 12, 19 May 1862, 14, 16 June 1862, TS.
44. *OR*, 13:30, 835.
45. Packard Diary, 18 June 1862.
46. Mann Diary, 9 May 1862, TS.
47. Ibid, 15, 21 May 1862, TS. Cullers became second lieutenant of Company A in July 1862.
48. Ibid, 20–21, 25 June 1862, TS. McQuiston, Gordon, and Boudonot hailed from Sparta; Morrison from Chester. McQuiston was an Ohio native and practiced farming. Indiana native Gordon was a forty-three-year-old unmarried farmer. Morrison practiced law. Boudonot died of accidental wounds in January 1863 at Helena.

49. Packard Diary, 18 June 1862.

50. Hewett, *Supplement OR*, pt. 2, 7:563; Packard Diary, 18 June 1862; Mann Diary, 31 May 1862; "SO 181," 24 May 1862, ROB, Records AGO.

51. Dula McLeod Baker, "History of Smithville School," *Lawrence County Historical Quarterly* 7, no. 3 (Summer 1984): 12.

52. Seley to Wilson, 18 June 1862, ROB, "Morning Reports," Co. F, June 1862, Records AGO.

53. *OR*, 13:126–27; Seley to Wilson, 18 June 1862, ROB, Records AGO.

54. *OR*, 13:126–27. *IL AGR* erroneously listed Mills as dying at Smithton, Kentucky, 12 June 1862; however, Company F's Morning Reports listed Mills as dying at Smithville. IL GAR, 7:669; "Morning Reports," Co. F, June 1862, Records AGO. After resigning, Dorothy moved to Clay City, Indiana, where he became a successful dry goods merchant. His wound continued to plague him and he applied for an invalid pension by 1880. "Dorothy, Francis," Tenth Census of the United States of Population and Housing, 1880, Clay County, IN, Roll 270: 559, Microfilm T9 (Washington, DC: NARA); "Dorothy, Francis M.," Co. F, Fifth Illinois Cavalry Index Card, Cert. 219.201, 21 April 1880, digital images from *Organization Index to Pension Files of Veterans Who Served Between 1861 and 1900*, T289, Washington, DC, http://www.footnote.com (all index card images of the Fifth Illinois Cavalry from Footnote.com unless otherwise noted; hereafter cited as PFI).

55. Mann Diary, 21, 23 June 1862, TS; *OR*, 13:126, 390–91.

56. "SO 217," 30 June 1862, ROB, Records AGO; *OR*, 13:448; "John F. Heath," Dewitt GenWeb Project, Dewitt County Illinois Obituaries H, The DeWitt County GenWeb Project Team, 2000–2010, http://dewitt.ilgenweb.net/obits-h.htm.

57. "Morning Reports," 18 June 1862, Co. C, 2 January 1863, Co. E, Records AGO; Mann Diary, 26 June 1862.

58. Mann Diary, 27 June 1862, TS.

59. Edward A. Davenport, *History of the Ninth Regiment Illinois Cavalry Volunteers* (Chicago: Donohue and Henneberry, 1888), 43.

60. Mann Diary, 2–4 July 1862, TS; Wiley, "Statement of Account," 24 January 1864, Wiley Papers.

61. Skiles to Parents, 16 July 1862, Skiles Letters.

62. Skiles to Parents, 16 July 1862, Skiles Letters; *OR*, 13:145. The battle of 7 July is variously known as the battle of Cache River, Round Hill, or Hill's Plantation. The battle was a very confusing affair, and modern interpretations fail to untangle the intricate play between all Union forces that claimed participation in the battle. Considering this would have been a major fight for the Fifth, it seems likely that their contribution was minimal, or the men would have elaborated as to their actions.

3. This Godforsaken Town, July to October 1862

1. Davenport, *Ninth Illinois Cavalry*, 46; "From Gen. Curtis' Army," CT, 5 August 1862, 2.

2. Mann Diary, 7, 8 July 1862, TS.

3. Ibid, 8 July 1862, TS.

4. Packard Diary, 21 July 1862; Burke to Ellen Hudson, 22 July 1862, Burke Papers.

5. Mann Diary, 9 July 1862, TS.

6. "SO 56," 10 July 1862, ROB, Records AGO.

7. Mann Diary, 11 July 1862, TS; Wiley to Emily, 14 July 1862, Ben Wiley Collection, 2003.064, John A. Logan Museum, Murphysboro, IL (hereafter cited as Ben Wiley Collection, JAL).

8. Mann Diary, 12 July 1862, TS; Burke to Ellen Hudson, 22 July 1862, Burke Papers.

9. Mann Diary, 12, 13 July 1862, TS.

10. Skiles to Parents, 16 July 1862, Skiles Letters; Roe to Celina, 12 July 1862, "Jonas H. Roe and Family," Eric Feagan, ed., Elf Junction, 2001–2011, http://civilwarletters.150m.com/Copyright_2001/JonasRoe_main.html (hereafter cited as Feagan Collection).

11. Mann Diary, 14, 15 July 1862, TS.

12. Burke to Ellen Hudson, 15, 22 July 1862, Burke Papers; Packard Diary, 21, 22 July 1862.

13. Packard Diary, 29 July 1862; Skiles to Parents, 2 August 1862, Skiles Letters.

14. Packard Diary, 20 July 1862.

15. Mann Diary, 17 July 1862, TS; Packard Diary, 21, 29 July 1862; OR, 13:477. William finally received a disability discharge in January 1863.

16. Mann Diary, 21, 26 July 1862, TS. Smith resigned from the Fifth in September 1862.

17. Packard Diary, 29 July 1862; Skiles to Parents, 8 September 1862, Skiles Letters.

18. Anne J. Bailey, *Between the Enemy and Texas: Parson's Texas Cavalry in the Civil War* (Fort Worth: Texas Christian Univ. Press, 1989), 83; Bailey, *In the Saddle with the Texans: Day by Day with Parsons's Cavalry Brigade, 1862–1865* (Abilene: McWhiney Foundation Press, 2004), 41.

19. OR, 13:203–4.

20. Ibid, 207; Mann Diary, 4, 6 August 1862, TS; Packard Diary, 6 August 1862.

21. OR, 13:206; Burke to Ellen Hudson, 20 August 1862, Burke Papers.

22. Mann Diary, 6 August 1862.

23. Mann Diary, 8, 9, 11 August 1862, TS; Burke to Ellen Hudson, 20 August 1862, Burke Papers; "William Pride," 1860 PS Monroe County, AR, Roll 46: 801.

24. Mann Diary, 12 August 1862, TS.

25. Burke to Ellen Hudson, 20 August 1862, Burke Papers; Mann Diary, 13 August 1862, TS.

26. Mann Diary, 14, 15, 16 August 1862, TS; "Francis P. Redmond," "B. Joel Lambert," 1860 PS Monroe County, AR, Roll 46: 810, 849.

27. Mann Diary, 16, 17 August 1862, TS.

28. Mann Diary, 20, 21 August 1862, TS; Wiley, "Statement of Account," Wiley Papers; Packard Diary, 22 August 1862. Being a close and personal friend of Wiley, it seems doubtful that Higgins circulated a petition against Wiley. Their friendship was so strong that Wiley named his fifth child Charles Higgins. Carl Wiley, "Makanda's Colonel Ben Wiley," *Illinois Magazine* 19 (May–June 1980): 19. For more information about the soldiers' plight at Helena and the Federal army's response, see my article "This Godforsaken Town: Death and Disease at Helena, Arkansas, 1862–1863," *Civil War History* 50, no. 2: 109–44.

29. OR, 13:608; Roe to Celina, 25 August 1862, Roe Papers.

30. "SO," 24 August 1862, ROB, Records AGO; Mann Diary, 25, 26 August 1862, TS; Packard Diary, 26 August 1862.

31. Packard Diary, 30 August 1862; Mann Diary, 28 August 1862, TS.

32. Packard Diary, 22 July, 6 August 1862.

33. Ibid, 1 September 1862. During the nineteenth century, malaria was called remittent fever, intermittent fever, congestive chills, ague, and bilious fever.

34. Mann Diary, 4 September 1862, TS; Skiles to Parents, 8 September 1862, Skiles Letters; Packard Diary, 6 September 1862. James Kavanaugh died of yellow fever. William Shumake and Henry James succumbed to congestive chills; John A. Williams, Lewis W. Redmon, Thomas Chandler of typhoid pneumonia; John Dennis and John Bowman died of chronic diarrhea; Basil Purdew of lung congestion; and Charles M. Griswold succumbed to inflammation of the brain. "RCD," Cos. D, E, L, and M, Records AGO.

35. Packard Diary, 17 August 1862. Calvin was detailed as assistant post surgeon on 28 July. Muster Roll, July-August 1862, Calvin A. Mann Military Service Record, CSR.

36. Packard Diary, 21, 27 September 1862. Debilitated after the war by his illness, Ingalls entered the Quincy Illinois Soldiers Home in 1898, after relying on an invalid pension for twelve years. "Ingalls, Francis P.," Co. C, Cert. 443.554, 15 May 1886, PFI; "Ingalls, Francis P.," No. 4424, 17 July 1898, ISSH DB.

37. Mann Diary, 10 September 1862, TS.

38. Mann Diary, 13 September 1862, TS.

39. Mann Diary, 13 September 1862, TS.

40. Wiley, "Statement of Account," 24 January 1864, Emily to Wiley, 1, 17, 21 July 1862, Wiley Papers.

41. Wiley to Seley, 11 September 1862, C. W. Higgins, "Certificate of Disability," 11 September 1862, Wiley Military Service Record, CSR.

42. Mann Diary, 27 August, 2, 20 September 1862, TS.

43. OR, 13:624-25; U.S. Congress, The Statues at Large, Treaties, and Proclamations of the United States of America (Boston: Little, Brown, 1863), 12:319, 589-92.

44. Mann Diary, 29, 30 September 1862, TS.

45. Packard Diary, 28 September 1862.

46. Jackson County, Illinois Circuit Court Records, Book H (May 1861–May 1868), Murphysboro, IL: 351, 405, 523, Murphysboro, IL.

47. "The Question of Negro Residence," Jonesboro Gazette, 10 May 1862; Emily to Wiley, 9 April 1863, Wiley Papers.

48. John Q. Anderson, comp., Campaigning with Parsons' Texas Cavalry Brigade, CSA. The War Journals and Letters of the Four Orr Brothers, 12th Texas Cavalry Regiment (Hillsboro, TX: Hill Junior College Press, 1967), 73.

49. Claborne McCalpin owned a $60,000 estate close to plantations owned by Lucius Polk, John A. Craig, and Isa M. Lamb. "Claborne McCalpin," 1860 PS Phillips County, AR, Roll 47: 366; Mann Diary, 23, 24, 27, 29 September 1862.

50. Packard Diary, 8 October 1862.

51. Ibid.

52. Mann Diary, 15 October 1862, TS.

53. "Order," 18 October 1862, ROB, Records AGO; Mann Diary, 19 October 1862, TS.

54. Mann Diary, 19 October 1862, TS.

55. Ibid.

56. Ibid.

57. Ibid.
58. Hewett, *Supplement OR*, pt. 1, 3:70, 72–74.
59. Ibid, pt. 1, 3:73.
60. Wilson and Seley were on medical leave; Farnan and Withers were recruiting in Illinois. Seley to L. D. Hubbard, 9 October 1862, Seley Military Service Record, CSR; "SO 277," 31 August 1862, "SO 314," 3 September 1862, ROB, Records AGO; Mann Diary, 16 October 1862.
61. Roe to Celina, 27 October 1862, Roe Papers; Mann to Nancy, 25 October 1862, TS, Mann Papers.
62. Roe to Celina, 27 October 1862, Roe Papers.
63. "RCD," December 1862, Cos. A, E, F, and M, "Regimental Return," February 1863, Administrative Files; "Joseph Voorhees," 1860 PS Coles and Crawford Counties, IL, Roll 171: 389; Hewett, *Supplement OR*, pt. 2, 7:549, 561, 563, 577. Voorhies's wife received compensation from the government for her loss. "Voorhies, Joseph T.," Co. F, Cert. 6.183, 127.725, 7 January 1863, PFI.
64. "RCD" December 1862, Co. G, Administrative Files. Adkins became a very successful farmer and stock dealer living in Lovington after the war. Roberts moved to Franklin County, Indiana. *Portrait and Biographical Record of Shelby and Moultrie Counties, Illinois* (Chicago: Biographical Publishing Co., 1891), 293. "Adkins, Rodney," 1870 PS Moultrie County, IL, Roll 264: 54; Adkins, Rodney," Co. A, Cert. 25.666, 2 July 1863, "Roberts, John W.," Co. G, Cert. 37.654, PFI.
65. Mann Diary, 22 October 1862; Hewett, *Supplement OR*, pt. 1, 3:73–74.
66. W. A. Crouch to wife, 26 October 1862, W. A. Crouch Papers, MC 550, Special Collections Division, University of Arkansas Libraries, Fayetteville.
67. Mann to Nancy, 25 October 1862, TS, Mann Papers. All companies were represented in the eighty-one men captured on 22 October 1862: A: 12; B: 7; C: 3; D: 8; E: 9; F: 7; G: 15; H: 3; I: 4; K: 3; L: 6; M: 4. "Regimental Returns," February 1863, "RCD" December 1862 to April 1863, Administrative Files.
68. Mann Diary, 22 October 1862, TS.
69. Ibid.
70. Ibid.
71. Mann to Nancy, 25 October 1862, TS, Mann Papers; Mann Diary, 23 October 1862, TS.
72. Mann Diary, 24 October 1862; Mumford to Yates, 10 April 1863, Administrative Files; "SO," 24 October 1862, ROB, Records AGO; "Charges and Specifications against Thomas A. Apperson 1st Major 5th Regt Ills Cav Vols.," Fourth Charge, Fourth Specification, p. 6, n.d., Apperson Military Service Record, CSR.
73. Mann Diary, 24 October 1862, TS.
74. Roe to Celina, 8 November 1862, Roe Papers; "Morning Reports," Cos. A-M, January to June 1863, Administrative Files; "SO 385," 23 December 1862, ROB, Records AGO.
75. Packard Diary, 26 October 1862; Ken Baumann, *Arming the Suckers, 1861–1865* (Dayton: Morningside House, 1989), 45; Bussey to Commanding Officer Fifth Illinois, 23 October 1862, ROB, Records AGO; Wilson to Fuller, 26 January 1863, Co. G, Administrative Files. Elliott returned to Shelby County and continued farming after the war. "Elliott, W. N.," 1870 PS Shelby Co., IL, Roll 277: 139.

76. Packard Diary, 26 October 1862; Wilson to Fuller, 26 January 1863, Administrative Files; *Portrait and Biographical Album of Pike and Calhoun Counties, Illinois* (Chicago: Biographical Publishing Co., 1891), 794; "Benjamin Hopkins," 1860 PS Pike County, IL, Roll 219: 261.

77. "Kendal B. Pennywell," "Clement March," 1860 PS Morgan and Moultrie Counties, IL, Roll 213: 969, 938.

78. O'Brien and Diefendorf, *General Orders of the War Department embracing the Years 1861, 1862, 1863*, 1:386–88; Mann Diary, 26 October 1862.

4. Under Grant's Command, November 1862 to May 1863

1. "RO 1," 16 September 1862, "RO," 26 September 1862, ROB, Records AGO.
2. *OR*, 17, pt. 1: 533.
3. Ibid, 534.
4. Ibid, 534–35. Griffith's cavalry brigade contained the First Texas Legion, Third and Sixth Texas Cavalries, and Francis McNally's four-gun battery.
5. Roe to Celina, 8 December 1862, Roe Papers.
6. Skiles to Parents, 10 December 1862, Skiles Letters.
7. *OR*, 17, pt. 2: 383, 410; 22, pt. 1: 809; Mann Diary, 6 January 1863, TS.
8. Mann Diary, 7 April 1863, TS.
9. Burke to Ellen Hudson, 30 December 1862, Burke Papers; *OR*, 22, pt. 1: 858–59.
10. Roe to Celina, 19 December 1862, Roe Papers.
11. Ibid.
12. Ibid.
13. Mann Diary, 25 December 1862, TS.
14. Mann to Nancy, 1 January 1863, Mann Papers.
15. Ibid. Neville was a medical student when he enlisted, finishing his education in the postwar years, and settling in Nebraska. "Neville, Joseph," 1900 PS Douglas Co., NE, Roll 925: 163.
16. Mann to Nancy, 1 January 1863, Mann Papers.
17. Mann Diary, 4, 6 January 1863, TS.
18. *OR*, 22, pt. 1: 855, 857.
19. "Order," 10 January 1863, ROB, Records AGO; Packard Diary, 12, 18 January 1863.
20. Mann Diary, 13 January 1862, TS.
21. "Letter from Lt. Cushman K. Davis, During Gorman's Expedition up the White River, Arkansas," *Twenty-Eighth Wisconsin Volunteer Infantry*, Kent A. Peterson, Webmaster, 2011 http://www.28thwisconsin.com/letters/cush_davis.html; August Bondi, *Personal Reminiscences*, chap. 4:20, TS, August Bondi Papers, 1884–1952, Series B, MF 1772, Kansas State Historical Society, Manuscripts Department, Center for Historical Research, Topeka, Kansas.
22. Mann Diary, 15, 23 January 1863, TS; Skiles to Parents, 6 February 1863, Skiles Letters.
23. Mann Diary, 15, 16 January 1863, TS.
24. Packard Diary, 15, 16 January 1863.
25. Mann to Nancy, 24 January 1863, Mann Papers.
26. Mann Diary, 20, 21 January 1863, TS.
27. Ibid, 23 January 1863, TS.

28. Packard Diary, 24 January 1863; Skiles to Parents, 6 February 1863, Skiles Letters.

29. *OR*, 22, pt. 1: 218–19; 22, pt. 2: 67; Bondi, *Personal Reminiscences*, chap. 4:21, TS.

30. *OR*, 24, pt. 3: 144.

31. Packard Diary, 22, 24, 25, 29 January 1863; Mann Diary, 1 February 1863, TS.

32. Childs returned to his medical practice in Randolph County. He received an invalid pension in 1879 for health issues related to his service. "Childs, Charles A.," Co. K, Cert. 187.025, 3 August 1879, PFI.

33. Wilson to George, 25 December 1862, Hall Wilson Military Service Record, CSR; Mann Diary, 2, 10 February 1863, TS. Wilson resumed his position in the state auditor's office. In 1869, he contracted pneumonia in February, and within a month, the malaria he had suffered at Helena resurfaced, and the paroxysmal episodes became too much for the once-vibrant officer. He died on 21 March, at thirty-eight years of age. The state closed its offices in honor of Wilson. The men of the Fifth thought so highly of their colonel, they named their Grand Army of the Republic Post 424 in Toledo after Wilson. "Death of Col. Hall Wilson," *Illinois State Journal* (Springfield), 22 March 1869, 3; "Funeral of Col. Hall Wilson," *Illinois State Register* (Springfield), 23 March 1869, 4.

34. Mann Diary, 2 February 1863, TS.

35. Ibid, 18 February 1863, TS.

36. Wiley to Fuller, 19 November 1862, 25 January 1863, 11 March 1863, "DO 29," 11 March 1863, Records AGO; Wiley to Stanton, 12 December 1862, Wiley Papers.

37. "SO 14," 7 March 1863, ROB, Records AGO.

38. "SO 116," 18 February 1863, ROB, Records AGO; Packard Diary, 8 March 1863.

39. Mann Diary, 5, 9 February 1863, TS.

40. *Helena Hospital Registers, Arkansas, 1862–1865*, 46:1, 10, 12, 14, 15, 16, 17, Records AGO, Record Group 94, NARA, Washington, DC (hereafter cited as HHR). James Duncleberger, Asbury J. Browning, John W. Stephens, Patrick McGraw, James M. Ward, William Dewease, and Willis Morris died of smallpox in 1863.

41. *OR*, 22, pt. 2: 110–11, 199; 24, pt. 3: 5–6, 7, 22; "SO 63," 4 March 1863, "SO 22," 6 March 1863, "GO 7," 14 March 1863, "GO 22," 2 April 1863, "GO 1," 9 April 1863, "SO 54," 9 April 1863, ROB, Records AGO.

42. Mann Diary, 14 February 1863, TS; Hewett, *Supplement OR*, pt. 2, 7:550, 553.

43. Edwin C. Bearss, *The Campaign for Vicksburg* (Dayton: Morningside House, 1985), 1:495; Flanders to Brother, 4 March 1863, George E. Flanders Papers, Civil War Letters 1861–1864, Microfilm Box 767, Kansas State Historical Society, Manuscripts Department, Center for Historical Research, Topeka, Kansas; Mann Diary, 18 February 1863, TS.

44. Mann Diary, 2 March 1863, TS; Mann to Nancy, 14 March 1863, Mann Papers.

45. Mann Diary, 2 March 1863, TS; Mann to Nancy, 14 March 1863, Mann Papers. Gordon, an unmarried farmer from Sparta, owned $3,000 in real estate and supported his mother and four siblings. "A. J. Gordon," 1860 PS Randolph County, IL, Roll 221: 840.

46. Mann Diary, 2 March 1863, TS; Mann to Nancy, 14 March 1863, Mann Papers. Jamison, Cashen, and Barnes all returned to Randolph County after the war. Barnes became a teacher; Jamison an engineer. "Barnes, Harrison R.," 1880 PS Randolph County, IL, Roll 244: 511, "Jamison, Alexander," 1880 PS Randolph County, IL, Roll 338: 164.

47. "Declaration for Original Invalid Pension," 7 February 1889, George W. Mc-Conkey, Pension Record 255.986, Military Pension and Bounty Land Warrant Records, 1775–1916, Records of the Veterans Administration, Record Group 15, NARA, Old Military and Civil Records Branch, Washington, DC (hereafter cited as Pension Records); Skiles to Parents, 2 March 1863, Skiles Letters.

48. Mann Diary, 5 March 1863, TS; Roe to Celina, 6 March 1863, Feagan Collection; Skiles to Parents, 2 March 1863, Skiles Letters.

49. "DO 29," 11 March 1863, ROB, Records AGO; Wiley to Fuller, 11 March 1863, Records AGO; Wiley to Emily, 20 February 1863, Ben Wiley Collection, JAL.

50. "GO 12," 2 March 1863, ROB, Records AGO; Skiles to Parents, 4 April 1863, Skiles Letters.

51. Packard Diary, 8 March 1863; Mann to Nancy, 11 March 1863, Mann Papers; Mann Diary, 7 March 1863, TS.

52. "DO 38," 21 March 1863, ROB, Records AGO; Packard Diary, 19 April 1863.

53. Packard Diary, 23 March 1863; Roe to Celina, 26 March 1863, Feagan Collection.

54. Roe to Celina, 26 March 1863, Feagan Collection; Packard Diary, 23 March 1863.

55. Packard Diary, 2 November 1862.

56. Ibid, 1, 5, 24 February 1863.

57. Mann to Nancy, 21 April 1863, Mann Papers.

58. Mann Diary, 19 March, 5, 14 April 1863, TS. Despite her infidelity, Thomas and Sarah remained married, moving to Rockwood, Randolph County by 1880. Williams sustained a gunshot wound in Mississippi in June 1863, gaining a disability discharge two months later. By December 1863, he received a government pension for his wounds, dying by 1888. "Williams, Thos.," 1880 PS Randolph County, IL, Roll 244: 510; "Williams, Thomas," Co. K, Cert. 23.468, 26 December 1863, PFI.

59. Mann to Nancy, 3 April 1863, TS, Mann Papers; Skiles to Parents, 4 April 1863, Skiles Letters.

60. OR, ser. 3, 5:118–21; Mann to Nancy, 9 April 1863, Mann Papers; Packard Diary, 24 February 1863; Wiley to Emily, 9 May 1863, Ben Wiley Collection, JAL.

61. Skiles to Parents, 6 October 1863, Skiles Letters.

62. R. M. Nelson, "Another Letter from the 5th Illinois," NJ, 17 April 1863, 3.

63. W. C., "Letter from a Soldier in the 5th Illinois Cavalry," NJ, 17 April 1863, 3.

64. Apperson, "Letter from Major Apperson," MG, 29 April 1863, 2.

65. G. Webster, "Editor Gazette," MG, 28 March 1863, 1.

66. Mann to Nancy, 14, 29 March 1863, Mann Papers.

67. Mann Diary, 20 February 1864.

68. Mann Diary, 20, 21, 24 February 1863, TS.

69. Rainforth, "Letter from the Fifth Illinois Cavalry," NJ, 29 May 1863, 3.

70. Packard Diary, 10, 19 February 1863.

71. Emily to Ben Wiley, 19, 26 April, 4 May 1863, Ben to Emily 3 April, 15 May 1863, Ben Wiley Collection, JAL.

72. Roe to Celina, 30 April 1863, Roe Papers; Packard Diary, 7 April 1863.

73. Mann Diary, 9, 18 April 1863, TS.

74. Ibid, 9 April 1863, TS.

75. Ibid, 11 April 1863, TS.

76. Ibid, 7 April 1863, TS; Apperson to Dubois, 25 May 1863, Administrative Files. Caldwell returned to his law practice in Effingham County. He received a disability pension by 1877. "Caldwell, Henry D.," Co. L, Cert. 164.966, 17 December 1877, PFI; "Caldwell, H. D.," 1880 PS Effingham Co., IL, Roll 205: 332.

77. "The Case of Captain Cox," NJ, 12 June 1863, 2; Mann Diary, 21 April 1863; "SO 163," 10 April 1866, Administrative Files. Cox became a clergyman after the war and moved to Oswego, Kansas, by 1870. "Cox, Joseph A.," 1870 PS Oswego Co., KS, Roll 436: 85.

78. Wiley to Fuller, 9 April 1863, "GO 42," 18 March 1863, Co. I Order Books, Apperson to Dubois, 23 May 1863, Administrative Files. Norfolk served Cumberland County as circuit clerk after the war. "Norfolk, Edward," 1870 PS Cumberland Co., IL, Roll 214:258. Glenn became a Kansan farmer by 1880. "Glenn, B. G.," 1880 PS Franklin Co., KS, Roll 381: 5.

79. Apperson to Dubois, 23 May 1863, Administrative Files; "J. A. Balch," 1860 PS Cumberland County, IL, Roll 172: 720.

80. Wiley to Fuller, 31 March 1863, 7 April 1863, Webster to Fuller, 27 May 1863, Administrative Files. Pierson continued his medical career after the war, serving communities in Indiana and Kansas. "Pierson, Edward," 1870 PS Marion County, IN, Roll 339: 566.

81. For a more thorough account of the actions during this expedition, see Rhonda M. Kohl, "Raising Thunder with the Secesh: Powell Clayton's Federal Cavalry at Taylor's Creek and Mount Vernon, Arkansas, May 11, 1863," *Arkansas Historical Quarterly* 64, no. 2 (Summer 2005): 146–70.

82. Burke to Ellen Hudson, 24 May 1863, Burke Papers; Major Buck Walton, *An Epitome of My Life. Civil War Reminiscences* (Austin: Waterloo Press, 1965), 55.

83. Mann to Nancy, 15 May 1863, Mann Papers; Hewett, *Supplement OR*, pt. 1, 4:126.

84. Roe to Celina, 15 May 1863, Roe Papers. Buck enlisted in Federal service at Helena and became a recruiting sergeant for the First Arkansas Colored Infantry.

85. "Interesting from Arkansas," *New York Herald*, 27 May 1863, 4; Mann Diary, 11 May 1863, TS.

86. Mann to Nancy, 15 May 1863, Mann Papers.

87. Mann Diary, 12 May 1863, TS.

88. Roe to Celina, 15 May 1863, Roe Papers; "Morning Reports," Co. B, May 1863, Records AGO. Richards farmed in Nilwood, Macoupin County. He reenlisted as a vet in 1864 and became part of a special scouting unit commanded by William Berry. After the war, Harrison became a stock dealer in South Dakota. "Harrison, Edwin," 1900 PS Hughes County, SD, Roll 1550: 235.

89. "SO 148," 29 May 1863, ROB, Records AGO; Mann Diary, 14, 27, 29 May 1863, TS; HHR, 46: 18. The regiment lost ninety-six men to disease, and 104 obtained disability discharges while stationed at Helena.

5. Redemption at Vicksburg, June to August 1863

1. Mann Diary, 28 May 1863, TS; *OR*, 24, pt. 3: 349, 362.
2. Mann Diary, 29 May 1863, TS; Baumann, *Arming the Suckers*, 45.
3. Mann Diary, 1 June 1863, TS; Packard Diary, 1, 4 June 1863.
4. Wiley, "Statement of Account," 24 January 1864, Wiley Papers; Burke to Ellen Hudson, 12 June 1863, Burke Papers.

5. *OR*, 24, pt. 3: 375. Brig. Gen. Frank Blair and Grant planned to send the cavalry under Col. Amory Johnson, until Wiley took command of the cavalry brigade at Haynes' Bluff. Johnson, however, did accompany the troops to Mechanicsburg, according to John Mann, and may have been there to command the strike force to the bridge. Mann Diary, 4 June 1863.

6. Thadeus Packard, "The Charge of the Fifth Illinois Cavalry," *Transactions of the McLean County Historical Society* 2 (1903): 397; Wiley to Emily, 2 June 1863, Ben Wiley Collection, JAL; *OR*, 52, pt. 1: 65–66; 24, pt. 3: 957–58.

7. Packard, "Charge of the Fifth Illinois Cavalry," 397.

8. Ibid, 397–98; Mann Diary, 5 June 1863, TS; "Williams, Thos.," 1880 PS Randolph County, IL, Roll 244: 510; "Williams, Thomas," Co. K, Cert. 23.468, 26 December 1863, PFI.

9. Burke to Ellen Hudson, 8 June 1863, Burke Papers; Packard, "Charge of the Fifth Illinois Cavalry," 398.

10. Wiley, "Statement of Account," Wiley Papers.

11. Packard Diary, 4 June 1863; Packard, "Charge of the Fifth Illinois Cavalry," 398–99; Mann Diary, 4 June 1863, TS; Mann to Nancy, 8, 13 June 1863, Mann Papers; "Charges and Specifications against Thomas A. Apperson, 1st Major, 5th Regt. Ills. Cav. Vols.," n.d., Apperson Military Service Record, CSR. Packard asserted Apperson's horse faltered while jumping the trench before the first Rebel line, but he also wrote that Withers led the charge, so the horse must have stumbled at the beginning of the attack. This is verified by Skiles's account, which claimed Apperson's horse fell and a captain took command. Skiles to Parents, 23 June 1863, Skiles Letters.

12. *OR*, 52, pt. 1: 65–66; Lewis F. Levy, "Two Years in Northern Prisons," *Confederate Veteran* 14 (January 1906): 122.

13. Packard, "Charge of the Fifth Illinois Cavalry," 399.

14. Ibid, 399; Mann Diary, 4 June 1863, TS; Packard Diary, 1 June 1863. Bradshaw mustered out in December 1864 only to die shortly thereafter, probably from disease he acquired during the war. His wife received a widow's pension in February 1866. "Bradshaw, Zenius," Co. M, Cert. 68.592, 14 February 1866, PFI.

15. Mann to Nancy, 8 June 1863, Mann Papers; Roe to Celina, 9 June 1863, Feagan Collection; *OR*, 52, pt. 1: 65–66.

16. Mann to Nancy, 13, 8 June 1863, Mann Papers; "Morning Reports," Co. K, June 1863, Records AGO. Thomas's widow received a pension by July 1863. "Thomas, Emanuel," Co. K, Cert. 17.985, 22 July 1863, PFI.

17. *OR*, 24, pt. 2: 441–42; Mann Diary, 4 June 1863, TS; Mann to Nancy, 13 June 1863, Mann Papers; Burke to Ellen Hudson, 8 June 1863, Burke Papers.

18. Skiles to Parents, 23 June 1863, Skiles Letters; Levy, "Two Years in Northern Prisons," 122.

19. Mann to Nancy, 8 June 1863, Mann Papers; Packard Diary, 1 June 1863; Burke to Ellen Hudson, 12 June 1863, Burke Papers.

20. Mann Diary, 4 June 1863, TS.

21. "S.O. 231," 23 May 1863, Wiley Papers; Wiley to Fuller, 13 June 1863, Records AGO.

22. Mann Diary, 13 June 1863, TS. In July 1864, Lincoln appointed Wiley commissioner of the Board of Enrollment for the Thirteenth Congressional District of Illinois at Cairo. Wiley returned to his Makanda orchard in May 1865 and

became the largest grower of farm produce in Jackson County. He maintained his seniority in the Illinois Republican Party, where he officiated as chairman of the 1868 Jackson County convention, presided as president of the committee on permanent organization, and served as a delegate to various state conventions. Despite his political standing within the party, elected office eluded Wiley, who lost in 1869 for Jackson County judge, in 1871 for the state legislature, in 1872 for the Fiftieth District senatorial seat, and in 1876 after a bitter run for the Eighteenth District Congressional seat. "Wiley, Ben L.," 1870 PS Jackson County, IL, Roll 232: 172; *Nonpopulation Schedules for Illinois, 1850–1880, 1870 United States Agricultural Census*, Jackson County, Makanda Precinct, IL, Roll 17: 3–4, Illinois State Archives; Illinois Secretary of State, Record of Election Returns, 1869, 1871, 1872, 1876, Illinois State Archives, Springfield; "Colonel Ben L. Wiley," obit, *Carbondale Free Press*, 12 December 1890.

23. Mann Diary, 16 June 1863, TS.

24. Woods to Yates, 9 April 1863, Administrative Files.

25. Mumford to Yates, 11 April 1863, Administrative Files.

26. Apperson to Fuller, 15 June 1863, Administrative Files.

27. Mann Diary, 23 June 1863, TS, Administrative Files.

28. Yates to Adjutant General [Fuller], 16 June 1863, Administrative Files; Klement, *Copperheads in the Middle West*, 30; Mann Diary, 5 July 1863, TS.

29. Mumford to Curtis, 9 December 1862, Apperson to Fuller, 20 July 1863, Administrative Files; "Court Martial Charges against Horace P. Mumford," 30 April 1863, Mumford Military Service Record, CSR.

30. "SO No. 5," 17 June 1863, ROB, Records AGO; Mann to Nancy, 13 June 1863, Mann Papers.

31. "SO No. 3," 21 June 1863, ROB, Records AGO; Mann to Nancy, 4 July 1863, Mann Papers.

32. Burke to Ellen Hudson, 11 August 1863, Burke Papers; Mann Diary, 23 June 1863, TS. A: John S. Webster; B: John A. Arrington, William Sylvester; C: Michael O'Neil, Cornelius O'Conner; E: Smith Lamm, Joseph Nicholson, Hiram Landrus; H: Sanders Earl; K: Calvin Mann, James Clendenin, Abner Hall, James McQuiston, Peter Parker, Robert Fulton, Charles Koehn, Samuel Jones, Henry Gilbreath, Isaac Castell, Jacob Hooker, Henry Stokes; L: William Berry, James Hogue, Lee Ray, Hiram Benefield, Samuel Hair, Norville Hughes, Samuel Parks, John Parks, Jerry York, Daniel Benifield, James Furre, James Berry, John Dow; M: Abraham Reese, William Sumpter, Franklin Russell, Ransom Miller, Hiram Johnson, and George Russell. The last soldier was either Joseph Osterman or Samuel Ellis.

33. Mann Diary, 22 June 1863, TS.

34. *OR*, 24, pt. 2: 513.

35. Ibid.

36. Dunbar Rowland, *Military History of Mississippi, 1803–1898* (1908; rpt., Spartanburg, SC: Reprint Co., 1978), 409.

37. *OR*, 24, pt. 2: 514–15; "Morning Report," Co. B, November 1863, Records AGO.

38. *OR*, 24, pt. 2: 515; "The Brookhaven Raiders," *Memphis Daily Appeal*, 4 July 1863, 2; "Morning Reports," Cos. A, K, C, E, B, and H, August-October 1863, Records AGO. O'Neil returned to Perry County as a farmer. His wounds gained

him an invalid pension by 1880. Webster became a merchant after the war, but his wounds caused difficulties until he was forced to live off a pension by 1872. "O'Neal, Michael," 1900 PS Perry Co., IL, Roll 335: 118; "O'Neil, Michael," Co. C, Cert. 240.237, 28 June 1880, "Webster, John S.," Co. A, Cert. 240.237, 21 December 1872, PFI; "Webster, John," 1870 PS Jo Daviess Co, IL, Roll 234: 6.

39. "Morning Reports," 2 February 1865, Co. K, Records AGO; "Muster Roll," "Memorandum from Prisoner of War Records," no. 125, Emily Mann to Lt. Col. W. T. Bennett, 5 December 1864, Calvin Mann Military Service Record, CSR; "Dr. C. A Mann Dies in Kansas," *Chester Herald Tribune*, 24 April 1902, 1.

40. Bailey, *Between the Enemy and Texas*, 140–41; Skiles to Parents, 5 July 1863, Skiles Letters.

41. Skiles to Parents, 5 July 1863, Skiles Letters; Mann to Nancy, 4 July 1863, Mann Papers; *OR*, 24, pt. 2: 517.

42. Mann to Nancy, 4 July 1863, Mann Papers, Skiles to Parents, 5 July 1863, Skiles Letters.

43. Mann Diary, 4 July 1863, TS.

44. *OR*, 24, pt. 3: 460, 461.

45. Mann Diary, 7, 14 July 1863, TS; Burke to Ellen Hudson, 11 August 1863, Burke Papers.

46. *OR*, 24, pt. 2: 551; Homer L. Kerr, ed. *Fighting with Ross' Texas Cavalry Brigade, C.S.A. The Diary of George L. Griscom, Adjutant, 9th Texas Cavalry Regiment* (Hillsboro, TX: Hill Junior College Press, 1976), 73.

47. *OR*, 24, pt. 2: 552.

48. Mann to Nancy, 15 July 1863, Mann Papers; Mann Diary, 7 July 1863, TS; Kerr, *Fighting with Ross' Texas Cavalry Brigade*, 73. King did not return to the regiment until June 1864. Unable to perform labor after the war, he relied on a disability pension by 1868. "King, Robert," Co. K, Cert. 93.947, 25 March 1868, PFI.

49. Mann Diary, 7 July 1863, TS.

50. William F. Scott, *The Story of a Cavalry Regiment. The Career of the Fourth Iowa Veteran Volunteers* (New York: G. P. Putnam Sons, 1893), 118; Burke to Ellen Hudson, 14 July 1863, Burke Papers.

51. Mann Diary, 10 July 1863, TS.

52. *OR*, 24, pt. 2: 552; "Our Suspension and Resumption—The Yankee Raid to Canton," *American Citizen*, 19 September 1863, p. 1.

53. Mann Diary, 12, 13, 17 July 1863, TS; Skiles to Parents, 9 August 1863, Skiles Letters.

54. "GO," 14 July 1863, ROB, Records AGO; *OR*, 24, pt. 3: 510–11, 515.

55. *OR*, 24, pt. 2: 660; Moore, "Colonel Bussy's Expedition," Document 138, Moore, *Rebellion Record*, 7:451–52.

56. *OR*, 24, pt. 2: 618.

57. Douglass Hale, *The Third Texas Cavalry in the Civil War* (Norman: Univ. of Oklahoma Press, 1993), 185–86; *OR*, 24, pt. 2: 553.

58. *OR*, 24, pt. 2: 553; Kerr, *Fighting with Ross' Texas Cavalry Brigade*, 75; Moore, *Rebellion Record*, 7:452.

59. *OR*, 24, pt. 2: 553.

60. "Our Suspension and Resumption—The Yankee Raid to Canton," 19 September 1863; *OR*, 24, pt. 2: 553–54.

61. Craig returned to the regiment in May 1864, McAllister in October 1863, and Willets in February 1865. "Morning Reports," Co. G, July 1863, October 1863, February 1864, May 1864, February 1865, Records AGO. McAllister farmed in Nebraska after the war. His imprisonment complicated his health, and he filed for an invalid pension in 1885, dying in 1921. William Thomas died in the Quincy Soldiers' Home in 1902. Craig farmed in Kansas by 1880, until he applied for an invalid pension in 1883, dying in 1910. Albert Willets moved to Ohio and Indiana after the war; he became an invalid in 1879. Melvin McAllister to RMK, 22 April 2007, e-mail correspondence; "Thomas, William R.," No. 4109, 24 June 1897, 4 December 1902, ISSH DB; "Craig, Thomas," 1880 PS Wilson County, KS, Roll 399: 137; "Craig, Thomas C.," Co. G, Cert. 287.778, 17 September 1883, "Willets, Albert," Co. G, Cert. 313.499, 26 December 1879, PFI.

62. Mann Diary, 14 July 1863, TS; Packard Diary, 9, 10 July 1863; Roe to Celina, 15 July 1863, Roe Collection.

63. *OR*, 24, pt. 3: 536, 544.

64. Packard Diary, 21, 22, June 1863, 1, 6 July 1863; Roe to Celina, 17 June 1863, Feagan Collection; Roe to Celina Roe, 15 July 1863, Roe Collection.

65. Packard Diary, 6, 8, 10 July 1863.

66. Ibid, 9, 10, 19, 25, 28 July 1863. Doctors used calomel as a purgative.

67. Ibid, 9, 10, 15, 31 August 1863, 19, 20, 29 September 1863, 29 October 1863.

68. Roe to Celina, 23 July 1863, Feagan Collection.

69. Mann Diary, 20, 21, July 1863, TS; Mann to Nancy, 5 July, 3 August 1863, Mann Papers.

70. Packard Diary, 1 August 1863; *OR*, 24, pt. 3: 554, 557; Mann to Nancy, 3, 16 August 1863, Mann Papers. Packard received his promotion in March 1863 but could not get paid his commissioned salary until he was mustered for his new office.

71. Mann to Nancy, 16, 31 August, 4 September 1863, Mann Papers.

72. Burke to Ellen Hudson, 11 August 1863, Burke Papers.

73. "Medical Certificate," 26 August 1863, Apperson Military Service Record, CSR; Skiles to Parents, 10 September 1863, Skiles Letters.

74. "Charges and Specifications against Thomas A. Apperson, 1st Major, 5th Regt. Ills. Cav. Vols.," n.d., Apperson Military Service Record, CSR; Seley to George W. Phatterton, 15 October 1863, Administrative Files; "SO No. 278," 10 October 1863, ROB, Records AGO.

Apperson returned to his farm in Neoga, Cumberland County. His once substantial real estate holdings dwindled to a mere $8,000 by 1870. The colonel continued his work with Masonic Lodge 179, served on the board of supervisors for Neoga Township from 1868 to 1874, and became a state delegate at the 1872 Republican convention. Apperson died of chronic diarrhea in 1879. The prairie boys honored their fallen leader by naming their Grand Army of the Republic Hall No. 202 in Neoga, Cumberland County, after Apperson. "Apperson, Thomas," 1870 PS Cumberland County, IL, Roll 214: 189; Charles A. Church, *History of the Republican Party in Illinois 1854–1912* (Rockford, IL: Wilson Bros., 1912), 114; "Thomas A. Apperson," Nonpopulation Census Schedules for Illinois, 1850–1880, Mortality Schedules 1880: Neoga, Cumberland County, IL, Roll 1133: 62; *Counties of Cumberland, Jasper and Richland, Illinois*, 145.

75. Mann to Nancy, 9 August 1863, Mann Papers; Seley to Yates, 15 October 1863, Farnan to Fuller, 7 August 1863, Administrative Files.

6. Winslow's Cavalry, August 1863 to January 1864

1. Skiles to Parents, 9 August 1863;, Skiles Letters; Mann Diary, 18 January 1864.
2. *OR*, 24, pt. 3: 582–83; "SO 3," 9 August 1863, ROB, Records AGO; Skiles to Parents, 9 August, 7 September 1863, Skiles Letters.
3. *OR*, 24, pt. 3: 582; Baumann, *Arming the Suckers*, 46.
4. Scott, *Story Cavalry Regiment*, 129.
5. Kerr, *Fighting with Ross' Texas Cavalry Brigade*, 78.
6. Skiles to Parents, 7 September 1863, Skiles Letters.
7. Scott, *Story Cavalry Regiment*, 131; Skiles to Parents, 7 September 1863, Skiles Letters.
8. Skiles to Parents, 7 September 1863, Skiles Letters; *OR*, 30, pt. 1: 9.
9. Kerr, *Fighting with Ross' Texas Cavalry Brigade*, 79.
10. W. Smith Cummins, "A Ruse that Worked Well in Mississippi," *Confederate Veteran* 20 (January 1913): 27.
11. Skiles to Parents, 7 September 1863, Skiles Letters.
12. Ibid; "Regimental Return," February 1864, Administrative Files. The Illinois adjutant general placed Turner's death on 19 August 1863, while the Fifth's regimental return states he died 1 February 1864.
13. Skiles to Parents, 7 September 1863, Skiles Letters; *OR*, 30, pt. 1: 9–10; Scott, *Story Cavalry Regiment*, 136–37; "Morning Report," Co. B, Records AGO.
14. *OR*, 30, pt. 1: 10; Skiles to Parents, 7 September 1863, Skiles Letters; Cummins, "A Ruse that Worked Well in Mississippi," 27.
15. Skiles to Parents, 10 September 1863, Skiles Letters.
16. Ibid, 6 October 1863.
17. *OR*, 30, pt. 3: 885.
18. Ibid, 885–87. The Fourth and Eleventh Illinois and the rest of the Tenth Missouri regiments arrived at Vicksburg on 18 September.
19. Phenius O. Avery, *History of the Fourth Illinois Cavalry Regiment* (Humboldt, NE: Enterprise, 1903), 146, 147.
20. Scott, *Story Cavalry Regiment*, 163; Skiles to Parents, 6 October 1863, Skiles Letters; William Forbes II, *Capt. Croft's Flying Artillery Battery Columbus, Georgia* (Dayton, OH: Morningside, 1993), 124; Kerr, *Fighting with Ross' Texas Brigade*, 82.
21. Skiles to Parents, 6 October 1863, Skiles Letters; *OR*, 30, pt. 2: 661.
22. *OR*, 30, pt. 4: 704, 717.
23. Simon, *Papers of Ulysses S. Grant*, 9:271; *OR*, 30, pt. 4: 233.
24. Scott, *Story Cavalry Regiment*, 167.
25. Skiles to Parents, 2 November 1863, Skiles Letters; Roe to Celina, 27 October 1863, Roe Papers.
26. Skiles to Parents, 2 November 1863, Skiles Letters; *OR*, 30, pt. 2: 810; Hewett, *Supplement OR*, pt. 2, 32:433, 436, 448, 281, 288.
27. *OR*, 30, pt. 2: 816.
28. Ibid.

29. Ibid; Scott, *Story Cavalry Regiment*, 168.
30. *OR*, 30, pt. 2: 810, 816; Forbes, *Capt. Croft's Flying Artillery Battery*, 128.
31. Hewett, *Supplement OR*, pt. 2, 67: 713; Skiles to Parents, 2 November 1863, Skiles Letters.
32. Forbes, *Capt. Croft's Flying Artillery Battery*, 129; Scott, *Story Cavalry Regiment*, 169–70.
33. *OR*, 30, pt. 2: 817.
34. Scott, *Story Cavalry Regiment*, 171–72; Skiles to Parents, 2 November 1863, Skiles Letters.
35. *OR*, 30, pt. 2: 817; Skiles to Parents, 2 November 1863, Skiles Letters.
36. *OR*, 31, pt. 1: 748–49; 30: pt. 2: 810–11; 31, pt. 3: 757; "Morning Report," Co. A, October, 1863, Records AGO. Francis Easton never returned to the regiment, and he disappeared from the historic record after his capture.
37. Mann to Nancy, 20, 24, 31 October 1863, Mann Papers.
38. Packard Diary, 5, 9, 20 November, 2 December 1863.
39. Roe to Celina, 23 November 1863, Feagan Collection; Mann Diary, 8, 9 November 1863, TS; Packard Diary, 20 November, 2, 23 December 1863.
40. Mann Diary, 17, 24, 30 November 1863, TS; "Morning Reports," October, November 1863, Records AGO; *OR*, 26, pt. 1: 907–9.
41. *OR*, 31, pt. 3: 122–23; 30, pt. 4: 472; "GO 49," 23 December 1863, ROB, Records AGO.
42. United States, Adjutant General's Office, *General Orders Affecting the Volunteer Force, 1863* (Washington, DC: GPO, 1864), 134–37, 149-50, 170, 195–96; Mann Diary, 6, 8, 16 December 1863, TS.
43. Skiles to Parents, 30 December 1863, Skiles Letters.
44. Packard Diary, 31 December 1863.
45. Ibid, 31 December 1863; Mann Diary, 23 December 1863, TS; Roe to Celina, 27 December 1863, Roe Papers.
46. Wilson to Yates, 31 December 1863, Administrative Files.
47. Mann Diary, 18, 19, 20 December 1863, TS; Packard Diary, 20 December 1863.
48. Skiles to Parents, 5 December 1863, Skiles Letters; Mann Diary, 1 December 1863, TS.
49. *OR*, 31, pt. 3: 337; "Morning Reports," Co. C, G, L, M, December 1863, Records AGO.
50. Packard Diary, 11 December 1863.
51. Ibid. Packard identified the "Jack of Clubs" as a Capt. Jack Young, but no one from the regiment held this name. Ben Hopkins, however, was known as the "Jack of Clubs," and he was also captain of Company G. Skiles to Parents, 4 April 1863, Skiles Letters.
52. *OR*, 31, pt. 1: 600–601; Packard Diary, 11 December 1863.
53. Packard Diary, 17 December 1863.
54. Bennett, "Our Army Correspondence," CCA, 21 January 1864, 1; 4 February 1864, 2; Wheelock Diary, 5 January 1864.
55. Nelson, "The Fifth Cavalry Letter," NJ, 29 January 1864, 2; Skiles to Parents, October 1863, 10 January 1864, Skiles Letters. The regiment had 627 men present for duty at the time of reenlistment. "Regimental Return," December 1863, Administrative Files.

56. Roe to Celina, 19 December 1863, Roe Papers.

   After marrying Mary Mann, niece of Calvin and John Mann, in 1866, Burke purchased sixteen hundred acres in Marshall County, Kansas. He lived in Kansas and became the house Democrat in 1909 and 1911 in the Sixty-Eighth District. Burke died in 1935 at the advanced age of ninety-four, one of seventeen Fifth veterans who lived past their ninth decade. "Burke, John," 1870 PS Marshall County, KS, Roll 438: 354; "J. W. Burke Dies. Long a Prominent Resident of Salina," *Salina Journal* (Salina, KS), 4 January 1935, 9, TS; "Kansas Legislators Past and Present, Boh–BZZ," Alphabetical Index of Kansas Legislators, State Library of Kansas, compiled by Rita Haley, Sherri Schulte, Donna Copeland, Bill Sowers and Lois Delfelder, http://www.kslib.info/legislators/membb3.html.

57. Roe to Celina, 27 December 1863, Roe Papers; Skiles to Parents, 30 December 1863, Skiles Letters; Mann Diary, 25 December 1863, TS.

58. Mann Diary, 31 December 1863, TS.

59. Skiles to Parents, 10 January 1864, Skiles Letters.

60. Packard Diary, 24, 28 January 1864.

61. "Serg't Jas G. Bennett . . . ," CCA, 7 April 1864, 3; Mann to Nancy, 8 January, 31 January 1864, Mann Papers. The Ladies League handled money claims for Illinois soldiers and their families, donated food to hospitals, and corresponded with wounded soldiers.

62. Mann to Nancy, 8 January 1864, Mann Papers.

63. "Regimental Return," December 1863, January 1864, Administrative Files; Wheelock Diary, 19 January 1864.

64. Bennett, "Our Army Correspondence," CCA, 18 February 1864, 1.

65. Ibid.

7. The Grand Raid, February to March 1864

1. Packard Diary, 30 January, 17 March 1864; Wheelock Diary, 3 February 1864; Scott, *Story Cavalry Regiment*, 188–89. A: Cullers with 50 men; B: March and 27; C: Withers with 45; D: 28; E: 48 men; F: Dean and 26; G: Hopkins with 30; H: Nelson with 20; K: Nesbit and 37; L: Caldwell with 24; M: Jessop with 30 men. "Morning Reports," February 1864, Records AGO.

2. *OR*, 32, pt. 1: 365, pt. 2: 585.

3. Packard Diary, 30 January 1864; *OR*, 32, pt. 1: 209, 372.

4. Scott, *Story Cavalry Regiment*, 190; *OR*, 32, pt. 1: 381, 372.

5. Packard Diary, 4 February 1864.

6. *OR*, 32, pt. 1: 372; Scott, *Story Cavalry Regiment*, 190; Packard Diary, 5 February 1864.

7. Mann Diary, 4 February 1864.

8. Packard Diary, 5 February 1864.

9. *OR*, 32, pt. 2: 671, 32, pt. 1: 379.

10. Mann Diary, 5 February 1864; *OR*, 32, pt. 1: 249.

11. Mann Diary, 5 February 1864.

12. *OR*, 32, pt. 1: 249; Scott, *Story Cavalry Regiment*, 191–92.

13. *OR*, 32, pt. 1: 373–74; Scott, *Story Cavalry Regiment*, 193.

14. *OR*, 32, pt. 1: 249; Packard Diary, 6 February 1864; Frank A. Montgomery, *Reminiscences of a Mississippian in Peace and War* (Cincinnati: Robert Clarke,

1901), 151; "The Third Fall of Jackson," *Memphis Daily Appeal*, 11 February 1864, 2.

15. *OR*, 32, pt. 1: 249; Scott, *Story Cavalry Regiment*, 195.

16. James Bennett, "Our Army Correspondence," CCA, 7 April 1864, 4; Packard Diary, 6 February 1864.

17. Bennett, "Our Army Correspondence," 7 April 1864.

18. Mann Diary, 6 February 1864.

19. Packard Diary, 7 February 1864; *OR*, 32, pt. 1: 376.

20. *OR*, 32, pt. 2: 677, 678, 679, 683, 684, 690, 32, pt. 1: 366. Correspondence indicates the Confederate cavalry crossed the Pearl north of Jackson.

21. Mann Diary, 7 February 1864.

22. Ibid.

23. Ibid.

24. *OR*, 32, pt. 2: 684, 690, 692, 693, 694, 32, pt. 1: 366, 369, 52, pt. 2: 609. No evidence exists to suggest Ballentine's and Stockdale's forces reached Morton and skirmished with Winslow on the early morning of 8 February as suggested by Bearss. More than likely, it was Wilbourn, for as of 8 February at 10:20 A.M., Loring still begged Lee for cavalry. Margie Riddle Bearss, *Sherman's Forgotten Campaign: The Meridian Expedition* (Baltimore: Gateway, 1987), 100.

25. Scott, *Story Cavalry Regiment*, 200; "The Great Mississippi Expedition," CT, 14 March 1864, 2; *OR*, 32, pt. 2: 694.

26. Mann Diary, 8, 9 February 1864; Scott, *Story Cavalry Regiment*, 200–201.

27. Bearss stated that Loring transferred command of the army to French based on this statement in French's autobiography: "This morning Loring placed the whole force present at my command to face about, form line of battle, and give the enemy a fight." Since no other primary source supports Bearss's claim, another interpretation would be that Loring ordered the troops under French's command to face about and give battle. The cavalry continued to receive orders from Loring and not French, and newspapers did not report a change in command. Bearss, *Sherman's Forgotten Campaign*, 108; Samuel G. French, *Two Wars: An Autobiography of Gen. Samuel G. French* (Nashville: Confederate Veteran, 1901), 188–89.

28. *OR*, 32, pt. 1: 216, 379–80; Packard Diary, 9 February 1864; Scott, *Story Cavalry Regiment*, 202. Bearss stated that Winslow made a bold dash at 5:00 P.M. on 8 February against the Rebel fortifications, but primary sources indicate no forward movement until the following morning. Bearss, *Sherman's Forgotten Campaign*, 108.

29. *OR*, 32, pt. 1: 380, 358, 52, pt. 2: 617–18.

30. Packard Diary, 10 February 1864; Mann Diary, 10 February 1864.

31. Mann Diary, 11 February 1864.

32. *OR*, 32, pt. 2: 718, 32, pt. 1: 380, 360.

33. Ibid, 32, pt. 2: 723, 32, pt. 1: 378; Packard Diary, 11 February 1864; "Regimental Return," May 1864, Administrative Files.

34. Mann Diary, 12 February 1864.

35. Ibid, 13 February 1864; *OR*, 32, pt. 2: 731.

36. Mann Diary, 13, 14 February 1864; *OR*, 32, pt. 2: 733.

37. Mann Diary, 14 February 1864; Scott, *Story Cavalry Regiment*, 204.

38. Packard Diary, 11 February 1864.
39. Ibid, 14 February 1864; *OR*, 32, pt. 1: 376; Scott, *Story Cavalry Regiment*, 205–6.
40. Packard Diary, 14 February 1864; *OR*, 32, pt. 1: 376.
41. Packard Diary, 14 February 1864.
42. Mann Diary, 14 February 1864; Mann to Nancy, 27 February 1864, Mann Collection; "Morning Reports," Co. I, February 1864, Records AGO.
43. Packard Diary, 14 February 1864; Mann Diary, 14 February 1864; *OR*, 32, pt. 1: 250.
44. Mann Diary, 15 February 1864.
45. Ibid, 17 February 1864.
46. Ibid, 18 February 1864.
47. Ibid, 19 February 1864.
48. Scott, *Story Cavalry Regiment*, 209–10; Mann Diary, 19 February 1864.
49. Mann Diary, 20 February 1864.
50. Ibid, 21 February 1864.
51. Packard Diary, 21 February 1864.
52. *OR*, 32, pt. 2: 448; Scott, *Story Cavalry Regiment*, 211; Mann to Nancy, 27 February 1864, Mann Collection.
53. Mann Diary, 23, 24 February 1864; Packard Diary, 23 February 1864.
54. Mann Diary, 24 February 1864; Packard Diary, 24 February 1864.
55. Mann Diary, 25 February 1864.
56. Ibid, 25 February 1864.
57. Ibid, 29 February 1864; *OR*, 32, pt. 1: 377; James Bennett, "Our Army Correspondence," CCA, 31 March 1864, 2.
58. Packard Diary, 27 February 1864; Mann to Nancy, 5 March 1864, Mann Collection.
59. Packard Diary, 2 March 1864.
60. Mann Diary, 2, 3 March 1864; Mann to Nancy, 5 March 1864, Mann Collection.
61. Mann to Nancy, 5 March 1864, Mann Collection.
62. Mann Diary, 4 March 1864; Packard Diary, 4 March, 27 February 1864.
63. *OR*, 32, pt. 1: 338.
64. Ibid, 344–45.
65. Ibid, 178, 193; Bennett, "Our Army Correspondence," 31 March 1864.
66. James Bennett, "Our Army Correspondence," CCA, 4 February 1864, 2.
67. "SO 63," 7 March 1864, ROB, Records AGO; Mann to Nancy, 11 March 1864, Mann Collection; Packard Diary, 20 March 1864; Wheelock Diary, 12, 17, 18, 19 March 1864.
68. Wheelock Diary, 20–25 March 1864.
69. Wagenseller, "Headqrs, Co. F, 5th Illinois Cav.," CCA, 2 June 1864, 1; "In Our Harried Notice," CCA, 5 May 1864, 3.
70. Wagenseller, "Headqrs, Co. F, 5th Illinois Cav."
71. Wheelock Diary, 28 March 1864; Packard Diary, 5 April 1864.
72. "Letter from Co. 'H,' 5th Cavalry," NJ, 22 September 1864.
73. James Bennett, "Our Army Correspondence," 2 June 1864, 1.
74. Ibid.
75. Mann Diary, 3, 4, 5, 6 May 1864.
76. Wheelock Diary, 1–5, 8 May 1864; Bennett, "Our Army Correspondence, 2 June 1864.

8. Garrison Duty, March to December 1864

1. *OR*, 32, pt. 3: 35–36, 60, 58, 87, 567.
2. Ibid., 34, 50.
3. Seley to Rodgers, 17 August 1864, Seley Military Service Record, CSR; Seley's Address to the Fifth Illinois Cavalry, 18 March 1864, Co. A Order Books, Records AGO.
4. Packard Diary, 6 April 1864; Woods, "For the Gazette. Communication," MG, 21 April 1864, 2.
5. Mumford, "Our Army Correspondence," CCA, 12 May 1864, 1.
6. Ibid.
7. Ibid.
8. Skiles to Parents, 4 April 1864, Skiles Letters.
9. Packard Diary, 2 April 1864.
10. Ibid.
11. *OR*, 32, pt. 3: 750, 605, 52, pt. 2: 651, 652.
12. Packard Diary, 6 April 1864.
13. Roe to Celina, 19 April 1864, Feagan Collection.
14. Packard Diary, 23 April 1864; Roe to Celina, 19 April 1864, Feagan Collection.
15. *OR*, 32, pt. 3: 325.
16. Ibid, 414, 479, 39, pt. 2: 14–15; Hay, "Letter from L. P. Hay," *Fairfield War Democrat*, 23 June 1864, 1; "GO 10," 27 April 1864, ROB, Records AGO.
17. "The Yazoo Expedition," CT, 4 June 1864, 1; Packard Diary, 3 May 1864. B: 7 led by Peniwell; C: 21 under Packard; D: 27 with Clark; E: 22 men; F: 28 under Wood; H: 11 men; I: 31 men; K: 24 commanded by Barnfield; L: 19 men; M: 11. "Morning Reports," Co. A–M, Records AGO.
18. Hay, "Letter from L. P. Hay," 23 June 1864.
19. Ibid; Rowland, *Military History of Mississippi*, 411.
20. Packard Diary, 22 May 1864; Edwin M. Main, *The Story of the Marches, Battles and Incidents of the Third United States Colored Cavalry* (1908; reprint, New York: Negro Universities Press, 1970), 167.
21. Packard Diary, 22 May 1864.
22. Ibid.
23. Ibid.
24. *OR*, 39, pt. 1: 7; "The Yazoo Expedition," CT.
25. Hay, "Letter from L. P. Hay," 23 June 1864; Rowland, *Military History of Mississippi*, 393, 412; *OR*, 39, pt. 1: 10–11; "Morning Report," Cos. K and F, May 1864, Records AGO. Mason moved to Gilliam County, Oregon, where he became a farm laborer after the war. He qualified for an invalid pension in 1878 and died in 1925. Rice convalesced at the Vicksburg general hospital until he died of disease in September 1864. "Mason, David," 1900 PS Gilliam County, OR, Roll 1347: 23; "Mason, David," Co. K, Cert. 168.128, 26 November 1878, PFI; "Regimental Return," September 1864, Administrative Files.
26. Mann Diary, 20 May 1864, TS; Packard Diary, 22 May 1864.
27. Hay, "Letter from L. P. Hay," 23 June 1864; "Soldier 5th ILL. Cav. Correspondence from Vicksburg," *Belleville Advocate*, 10 June 1864, 2.
28. *OR*, 39, pt. 1: 7–8.
29. Wheelock Diary, 8 May 1864; Burke to Ellen Hudson, 10 June 1864, Burke Papers; Mann Diary, 9 May 1864, TS.

30. Mann Diary, 27 May 1864.

31. "John McConnell," 1860 PS Sangamon County, IL, Roll 226: 35; Newton Bateman and Paul Shelby, ed., *Historical Encyclopedia of Illinois and History of Sangamon County* (Chicago: Munsell, 1912), 1:361; *OR*, 8: 264, 30, pt. 3: 227–28.

32. "GO 1," 6 June 1864, ROB, Records AGO; Wheelock Diary, 29–31 May, 1, 6, 18 June 1864; Mann Diary, 6 June 1864, TS; "Regimental Return," July–September 1864, Administrative Files. Miller moved to Kansas after the war. Mott returned to McLean County, married, became a laborer, and lived with his in-laws. Tigner deserted in July 1865 but returned to muster out in October 1865 as bugler. He lived in Nebraska and California after the war. *Journal of the Thirty-Sixth Annual Encampment of the Grand Army of the Republic* (Topeka: Kansas State Printing Office, 1917), 6; "Mott, Edger," 1880 PS McLean County, IL, Roll 230: 249; "Tignor, A. C.," 1880 Platte County, NE, Roll 754: 142.

33. Mann Diary, 30 May, 1, 8 June 1864, TS.

34. Ibid, 15 July 1864, TS.

35. Packard Diary, 22 May 1864; Mann Diary, 12, 13, 18 May 1864, TS.

36. Burke to Ellen Hudson, 10 June 1864, Burke Collection.

37. Roe to Celina, 14 March 1864, Feagan Collection.

38. "SO 93," 4 April 1863, ROB, Records AGO; Mann Diary, 26 June, 1864; Wheelock Diary, 5 June 1864.

39. Mann Diary, 17, 22, 24 July 1864; Wheelock Diary, 26 June 1864. Gilbreath, Sloan, and Tuthill all mustered out as sergeants and returned to Randolph County but later moved to Kansas. Gilbreath worked as a laborer in Ottawa. Sloan became a successful merchant in Saline, living near Capt. William Addison, a fellow Randolph Ranger. Tuthill entered the mercantile business in Saline County. He died in 1931. Woods returned to Mattoon and built Woods's Chapel in 1877, ten miles south of Mattoon. Perrin, *History of Coles County*, 557; "Gilbraith, Henry," 1870 PS Randolph County, IL, Roll 272: 276; "Gilbreath, Henry," 1900 PS Ottawa County, KS, Roll 494:119; "Sloan, Arthur C.," 1870 PS Saline County, KS, Roll 442: 21; "Tuthill, W. C.," 1900 PS Saline County, KS, Roll 498: 213.

40. Packard Diary, 22 May 1864.

41. "Morning Report," Co. F, 23 July 1864, "SO 65," 9 July 1864, ROB, Records AGO.

42. Wheelock Diary, 7, 17, 18 August 1864.

43. Burke to Ellen Hudson, 10 June 1864, Burke Papers.

44. Skiles to Parents, 31 May 1864, Skiles Letters.

45. Wheelock Diary, 12 May, 22 June 1864; "SO 16," 22 June 1864, "SO 54," 28 June 1864, "Regimental Return," May–June 1864, ROB, Records AGO; Mann to Nancy, 31 August 1864, Mann Collection.

46. *OR*, 39, pt. 2: 150–51.

47. *OR*, 39, pt. 1: 242–43; "Morning Reports," Cos. A, B, C, D, M, July 1864, Records AGO. The court found Mott, Miller, Givens, and O'Conner guilty of drunken misbehavior in June 1864, but Lincoln pardoned all four soldiers, and they returned to their company by 23 October 1864.

48. *OR*, 39, pt. 2: 690.

49. Main, *Third USCC*, 176; "Morning Reports," Co. B, 11, 15 July 1864, Records AGO.

50. Henry H. Woodbury, *Complete History of the 46th Illinois Veteran Volunteer Infantry* (Freeport, IL: Bailey and Ankeny, 1866), 66.

51. Skiles to Parents, 19 July 1864, Skiles Letters; Rowland, *Military History of Mississippi*, 524.

52. Skiles to Parents, 19 July 1864, Skiles Letters; Roe to Celina, 22 July 1864, Feagan Collection.

53. "State Senator Major Mumford," CCA, 25 August 1864, 2.

54. Wheelock Diary, 4 July 1864; Roe to Celina, 9 July 1864, Feagan Collection; Mann Diary, 4 July 1864, TS.

55. Mann Diary, 9, 10 July 1864, TS; "SO 345," 13 October 1864, "Surgeon Certificates," 17 October 1864, 18 August 1864, 7 September 1864, Farnan Military Service Record, CSR.

    Farnan returned to Randolph County and rebuilt his medical practice until 1870. His propensity for controversy, so evident during his service with the Fifth, embroiled him in numerous court cases during his civilian life. Lt. Charles Childs sued Farnan for libel and won, but the case was overturned in 1871 on a technicality. That year also witnessed Amelia Miller's accusation against Farnan for rape, which resulted in a pregnancy. The grand jury indicted Farnan on three counts of rape, assault, and pregnancy, but a later jury found the major not guilty beyond a reasonable doubt. The Millers' accusations ruined Farnan's reputation and his marriage. Farnan died in 1877, a free man, but ostracized by the people of Randolph County. He was only forty-seven years old. "James Farnan v. Charles J. Childs," http://barbaras.org/ayres/Farnan/libelcase1875.pdf; "Grand Jury Indictment," 16 January 1871, The People vs. James Farnan in the case of rape and bastardy, 2 March 1871, http://barbaras.org/ayres/farnan/James_Farnan_Case2.pdf; The People vs. James Farnan in the case of assault with intent to murder, 2 March 1871, http://barbaras.org/ayres/farnan/James_Farnan_Case3.pdf.

56. "Lieut. T. J. Dean," 7 April, 1864, "Poetry," 15 December 1864, CCA; "Dean, Thomas J.," Co. F, Cert. 71.175, 27 October 1864, Cert. 175.954, n.d., PFI.

57. "SO 113," 22 July 1864, "Memorandum from Prisoner of War Records," No. 408, Muster Roll, September–November 1864, Berry Military Service Records, CSR. In 1881, Berry purchased property near Lake Willow in what would become Clark County, South Dakota. He served in the seventeenth session of the Dakota territorial legislature in 1887, became Clark County's first postmaster, and served as a county commissioner. "Captain William N. Berry," Old Obituaries Transcriptions from My Grandmothers Scrapbook . . . Mostly Clark County, South Dakota, http://oldfamilyobits.blogspot.com/2008/06/captain-william-n-berry.html; "Captain William N. Berry," from *Memorial and biographical record; an illustrated compendium of biography, containing a compendium of local biography, including biographical sketches of prominent old settlers and representative citizens of South Dakota* (G. A. Ogle & Co., Chicago, 1899), 826–29, USGenWeb War Archives, http://files.usgwarchives.org/sd/biography/memor99/berry-w.txt.

58. "Regimental Return," September 1864, "SO 75," 21 September 1864, ROB, Records AGO.

59. Wheelock Diary, 10, 11, 20 August 1864.

60. Mann Diary, 10, 11, 16, 19 July 1864, TS.
61. Roe to Celina, 29 June 1864, Feagan Collection; Skiles to Parents, 19 July, 10 August 1864, Skiles Letters.
62. *OR*, 39, pt. 1: 572; Wheelock Diary, 23 September 1864.
63. "SO 138," 30 September 1864, ROB, Records AGO; Wheelock Diary, 3 October 1864; Roe to Celina, 29 August 1864, Feagan Collection; Packard to Lt. Col. W. T. Clark, 6 October, 1864, "Certificate of Disability," 7 October 1864, Packard Military Service Record, CSR. Roe and family moved to South Otter Creek, Greenwood County, Kansas, where Roe practiced farming and served as physician to neighbors. Roe's health never improved after his military service, and he entered the Western Health Reform Institute in Battle Creek, Michigan, for treatment in 1873 but died a few months later. "Dr. Jonas H. Roe Family History," by Colleen Rader Mapes, http://civilwarletters.150m.com/Copyright_2001/JonasRoe_history.html; "Roe, Jonas H.," 1870 PS Greenwood County, KS, Roll 434: 206.
    Packard returned to Bloomington weak from hepatitis and malaria, but he slowly healed and returned to carpentry. Thadeus lived near his brother William in Bloomington, and his life with Jennie looked bright, despite their inability to have children, possibly due to his hepatitis. By the late 1870s, however, the lieutenant's health deteriorated, and he received a disability pension from the government. Within ten years, Jennie and Thadeus were boarding with her aging parents, where he became a genealogy solicitor by 1900. Thadeus and Jennie spent the last decade of his life boarding with the Hardy family, where Thadeus wrote and published his exploits about the Civil War in the *McLean County Historical Society* journal. "Packard, Thadeus," 1870 PS McLean County, IL, Roll 258: 143, 144; "Packard, Thadeus B.," 1880 PS McLean County, IL, Roll 230: 173; "Packard, Thaddeus B.," 1900 PS McLean County, IL, Roll 322: 139; "Packard, T. B.," 1910 PS McLean County, IL, Roll 306: 51; "Packard, Thadeus B.," Co. C, Cert. 331.742, 15 December 1879, PFI.
64. Mann to Nancy, 9, 24 September 1864, Mann Collection; Mann to Stanton, 13 April 1865, "SO 232," 15 October 1864, "Resignation Endorsement," 15 September 1864, John P. Mann Military Service Record, CSR; Maj. Gen. Howard Endorsement, 6 May 1865, Col. John McConnell Endorsement, 29 May 1865, Letters Received & Endorsement Book, Records AGO.
    Mann received his license to practice law in 1870, and he became "a man who has made his influence and personality felt" in Randolph County, helping veterans with the pension process. There was nothing in his military file to indicate he had his dismissal reversed, but Mann did receive an invalid pension in 1891. "John Preston Mann Dead," *Chester Herald Tribune*, 5 March 1908, 1; "Mann, John P.," 1880 PS Randolph County, IL, Roll 244: 506, Co. K, 21 September 1891, Cert 763.501, PFI.
65. *OR*, 39, pt. 1: 569. A: Clark with 23 men; C: Wheelock with 23 men; E: 8 men under McConkey; F: Wood with 41 men; G: Elliott with 23 men; H: 22 men; K: Nesbit and 36 men; M: 18 under Ellis. "Morning Reports," Co. A, C, E, F, G, H, K, M, 28, 29 September 1864, Records AGO.
66. Bennett, "Our Army Correspondence," CCA, 10 November 1864, 2.
67. Ibid.

68. *OR*, 39, pt. 1: 831, 837; Bennett, "Our Army Correspondence," 10 November 1864.
69. Main, *Third USCC*, 186.
70. Ibid, 186; *OR*, 39, pt. 1: 458, 832.
71. Main, *Third USCC*, 187.
72. Bennett, "Our Army Correspondence," 10 November 1864.
73. Ibid; *OR*, 39, pt. 1: 458, 832, 833.
74. Bennett, "Our Army Correspondence," 10 November 1864.
75. WAS to Parents, 2 November, 19 July 1864, Skiles Letters. Skiles returned to his parents' house after the war and clerked in local stores. His biography stated he moved to Kansas on a homestead grant in 1871, but he remained in Christian County, leaving only after the death of his mother in 1887. Skiles farmed in Catlin, Marion County, Kansas, and by July 1890, he supplemented his income with an invalid pension. The private never married, and by 1910, William had moved back to Christian County and lived with his sister Sarah Salander until his death in 1916. His obit stated he died in Kansas, and may have been in the state visiting friends when he passed. Somewhat destitute at his death, he had no grave marker until the Veterans Administration provided one in the next century. William A. Skiles, *Letters to Home. A Collection of Letters of Civil War Union Soldier William A. Skiles September 1861 to November 1864, Christian County, Illinois* (Taylorville, Illinois: Christian County Historical Society, 1998), 1-2; "Body of Former Resident of City Arrives," *Taylorville Daily Breeze*, 31 July 1916, 4; "Skiles, Wm A.," 1880 PS Christian County, IL, Roll 181: 747; "Skiles, William A.," 1900 PS Marion County, KS, Roll 488: 21; "Skiles, W. A.," 1910 PS Christian County, IL, Roll 235: 43; "Skiles, William A.," 19 July 1890, Cert. 620.189, PFI.
76. Mumford, "Our Army Correspondence," CCA, 29 September, 6 October 1864, 1.
77. Ibid.
78. "State Senator Major Mumford," CCA, 25 August 1864, 2; "Death of Major Mumford," CCA, 13 November 1864, 2.
79. "From Springfield," CT, 29 October 1864, 1; "Death of Major Mumford," CCA, 13 November 1864.
80. "Death of Major H. P. Mumford," *Vicksburg Daily Herald*, 5 November 1864, 2; Wheelock Diary, 6 November 1864; Barnfield to Mann, 10 November 1864, Mann Collection.
81. McConnell to Fuller, 2 August 1864, 28 October 1864, McConnell to Haynie, 20 April 1865, Administrative Files; Wheelock Diary, 30 October 1864. Withers eventually moved to Caldwell County, Missouri, where he entered the hardware and agricultural implement trade. Poor health forced him to leave the mercantile business, and he purchased 230 acres in Ray County. He died in Oklahoma in 1898 but has a gravestone in Ray County. *History of Ray Country, Missouri* (St. Louis: Missouri Historical Co., 1881), 710; "Withers, W. P.," 1880 PS Ray County, MO, Roll 713:293–94; Findagrave Memorial 39521864, Knoxville Cemetery, Ray County, MO, http://www.findagrave.com (hereafter cited as Findagrave).
82. "Regimental Returns," September–December 1864, January 1865, Administrative Files; Skiles to Parents, 9 October 1864, Skiles Letters; Wheelock Diary, 4 November 1864; Barnfield to Mann, 16 November 1864, Mann Collection.

83. Woods, *Fairfield War Democrat*, 27 October 1864, 2; Wheelock Diary, 7 October, 8 November 1864.

84. Barnfield to Mann, 16 November 1864, Mann Collection.

85. Wheelock Diary, 13, 19 November 1864; R. L. Howard, *History of the 124th Regiment Illinois Infantry Volunteers, Otherwise Known as 'the Hundred and Two Dozen' from August, 1862 to August, 1865* (Springfield: H. W. Rokker, 1880), 254. Jessop remained in the service and became major of the regiment in August 1865.

86. Barnfield to Mann, 24 November 1864, Mann Collection. A: 16 men; B: 11 under Peniwell; C: 21 men under Wheelock; G: Sam McConnell with 24 men; H: Nelson with 20 men; I: Balch with 26 men; K: Nesbit with 26 men; L: Caldwell with 24 men; M: Ellis with 7 men. "Morning Reports," Cos. A–M, November 1864, Records AGO.

87. Wheelock Diary, 25 November 1864.

88. Ibid, 26 November 1864.

89. *OR*, 45, pt. 1: 782; Wheelock Diary, 25 November 1864.

90. *OR*, 45, pt. 1: 782, 785; Barnfield to Mann, 3 December 1864, Mann Collection.

91. *OR*, 45, pt. 1: 787, 783; Wheelock Diary, 2 December 1864. Levi Johnson, a twenty-three-year-old farmer, hailed from Nashville, Washington County.

92. "SO 80," 5 December 1864, ROB, "Morning Reports," Cos. B, C, E, Records AGO; Barnfield to Mann, 31 December 1864, Mann Collection.

93. Wheelock Diary, 6, 10, 25, 27 December 1864; "SO 85," 22 December 1864, "SO 87," 25 December 1864, ROB, Records AGO.

   Seley's postwar career was as mysterious as his regimental experience. He moved his family to California after the war, only to abandon his wife and three children by 1870. Seley, with his brother William and Edwin P. Martin, worked as contractors and builders in Wyoming. By 1880, Mary Seley listed herself as a widow in the San Francisco census, while her husband registered to vote in Sacramento the same year. Seley died in July 1886. The regiment last saw Seley in 1885 at their second annual reunion in Vandalia, Illinois. "Seeley, A. H.," 1870 PS Carbon County, WY, Roll 1748: 402; "Seley, Mary A.," 1880 PS San Francisco, CA, Roll 79: 311; "Abel Hildreth Seley," California, Voter Registers, 1866–1898, database online, Ancestry.com, Provo, UT; *Proceedings of the Second Annual Reunion of the Society of the Fifth Ills. Vet. Vol. Cav. Held at Vandalia, Illinois, October 6 and 7, 1885* (Neoga, IL: Neoga News Print, 1886), 1.

94. Barnfield to Mann, 11 December 1864, Mann Collection. Caldwell returned to his law practice in Effingham County. The diarrhea that plagued him during his service continued to deteriorate his health, until he was forced on an invalid pension in 1877. He received $10 a month for "disease of the abdominal viscera," which eventually killed him in 1902. "Caldwell, Henry D.," *Effingham County IL Archives Military Records. Effingham County Pensioners List 1883 Civilwar—Pension*, Deb Haines, contributor, USGenWeb Archives, http://files .usgwarchives.org/il/effingham/military/civilwar/pensions/effingha475nmt.txt. Barnfield moved to Lake County, California as a farmer and hardware store owner. He died in May 1920. "Barnfield, Thomas H.," 1900 PS Lake County, CA, Roll 88: 31.

95. Wheelock Diary, 29, 31 December 1864.

9. Soon This Cruel War Will Close, January to October 1865

1. "Morning Reports," Co. B, January 1865, Records AGO; Payne Diary, 4, 5, 8 January 1865, TS.
2. Payne Diary, 1, 6 January, 15 March 1865, TS.
3. *OR*, 48, pt. 1: 447–48; "SO 17," 18 January 1865, ROB, Records AGO.
4. *OR*, 41, pt. 4: 901, 951–52, 48, pt. 1: 544–45.
5. Sears, "Another Soldier Gone," CCA, 26 January 1865, 2. William settled in Cisne, Illinois, after the war. Sears became a farmer in Crawford County. "Sears, Harrison," 1870 PS Crawford County, IL, Roll 214: 72.
6. Payne Diary, 15, 19, 22 January 1865, TS.
7. "The 5th Illinois Cavalry," *Bloomington Pantagraph*, 27 February 1865, 1; Payne Diary, 21, 23 January 1865, TS.
8. Payne Diary, 24 January 1865, TS.
9. Ibid, 16 February 1865, TS; *OR*, 48, pt. 1: 68; "Morning Reports," Co. B–M, Records AGO.
10. Payne Diary, 25, 27 January 1865, TS.
11. Ibid, 29 January 1865, TS; "The 5th Illinois Cavalry," 27 February 1865.
12. Payne Diary, 30 January 1865, TS.
13. *OR*, 48, pt. 1: 69; Payne Diary, 31 January 1865, TS.
14. Payne Diary, 1 February 1865, TS.
15. *OR*, 48, pt. 1: 70; Payne Diary, 2 February 1865, TS.
16. Payne Diary, 3 February 1865, TS.
17. Ibid, 4 February 1865, TS.
18. Ibid, 5 February 1865, TS.
19. *OR*, 48, pt. 1: 70.
20. Payne Diary, 7 February 1865, TS; "The 5th Illinois Cavalry," 27 February 1865.
21. "The 5th Illinois Cavalry," 27 February 1865; Payne Diary, 10 February 1865, TS.
22. "The 5th Illinois Cavalry," 27 February 1865; *OR*, 48, pt. 1: 71, 625.
23. Seley to Fuller, 3 January 1865, McConnell to Haynie, 30 January 1865, Seley to McConnell, 17 January 1865, McConkey to McConnell, 19 February 1865, Administrative Files. Wilson returned to Wayne County and served as judge and deputy sheriff. March moved to Kansas, where he became a saloonkeeper. Cullers became a grocer in Texas. Hay returned to farming in Wayne County but relied on a $15 month pension by 1878, for an injury to his right leg and disease of the abdominal viscera. Watts returned to Wayne County and expanded his medical practice. Kendall moved to California, then Oregon, and practiced medicine. Stifal became a sawmill laborer after the war. Francis Webb became a Labette County, Kansas, farmer. *History of Wayne and Clay Counties*, pt. 3: 117; "March, Clement," 1870 PS Miami County, KS, Roll 439: 516; "Cullers, Jacob," 1880 PS Grayson County, TX, Roll 1306: 92; "Hay, Lawrence P.," "Watts, William," 1870 PS Wayne County, IL, Roll 288: 187, Roll 214: 161; "Hay, Lawrence P.," *Wayne County IL Archives Military Records. Wayne County Pensioners List 1883 Civilwar—Pension*, Diane Williams, contributor, USGenWeb Archives, http://files.usgwarchives.org/il/wayne/military/civilwar/pensions/wayne468nmt.txt; "Kendall, Charles Brockway," Sons of Union Veterans of the Civil War, National Graves Registration Database, 1995–2011, http://www.suvcwdb.org/home/ (hereafter cited as SUVCW Graves database);

"Stifal, Jacob," 1880 PS Cumberland County, IL, Roll 184: 514; "Webb, Francis M.," 1870 PS Labette County, KS, Roll 436: 96.

24. McConnell to Haynie, 6 February 1865, Administrative Files; "Civil War Pension Papers, From the Pension Record of Capt. James A. Balch," TS, Charles Brummel, contributor, Illinois Genealogy Trails, Coles County, Kim Torp, ed., 1998–2011, http://genealogytrails.com/ill/coles/page13.html.

25. "A Notable Figure. Death of Capt. F. A. Wheelock," *Bloomington Pantagraph*, 13 February 1904.

26. Payne Diary, 12 May 1865, TS.

27. Ibid, 18, 22 February, 4 March 1865, TS.

28. Bennett, "Army Correspondence, CCA, 23 February 1865, 2; "Morning Reports," Co. F, February 1865, "Regimental Return," January–February 1865, Records AGO. Stiff settled in Lawrence County and practiced farming. He received an invalid pension for his leg wound starting in 1876. Joseph Dunn moved to Alabama. "Stiff, Lewis M.," Co. F, 11 September 1876, Cert. 144.343, PFI; "Dunn, Joseph G.," SUVCW Graves database; "Stiff, Louis," 1870 PS Lawrence County, IL, Roll 224: 77.

29. Payne Diary, 2 March 1865, TS; "Morning Reports," Co. C, 2 March 1865, Records AGO.

30. Payne Diary, 3 March 1865, TS.

31. *OR*, 49, pt. 1: 77–78, 81–82.

32. Payne Diary, 11 March 1865, TS; *OR*, 49, pt. 1: 78.

33. Payne Diary, 12, 15, 16 March 1865, TS.

34. Ibid, 6, 8 March 1865, TS.

35. Ibid, 7, 9, 11, 12 March 1865, TS.

36. *OR*, 49, pt. 2: 106, 168–69.

37. Ibid, 30–31.

38. Payne Diary, 28, 31 March 1865, TS. Clarendon returned to McLean after the war and served as the town's constable, assessor, trustee, and deputy sheriff. *History of McLean County, Illinois*, 941–42.

39. *OR*, 49, pt. 2: 809; "Morning Report," Co. M, April 1865, ROB, Records AGO; Payne Diary, 3 April 1865, TS.

40. Payne Diary, 1 April 1865, TS.

41. Ibid, 27 March 1865, TS; *OR*, 49, pt. 2: 389.

42. *OR*, 49, pt. 2: 413; Payne Diary, 20 April 1865, TS; "GO 44," 17 April 1865, Co. A Order Books, Records AGO.

43. Payne Diary, 17, 19 May 1865, TS. Returning to his farm in Catlin after the war, Alonzo served on the school and town boards. Payne eventually opened a dry goods and grocery store under the name of Payne and Crutchley in the 1870s, but it failed during the decade's financial crisis. Kidney disease and prostate cancer forced Payne to apply for an invalid pension in 1890. H. W. Beckwith, *History of Vermilion County* (Chicago: H. H. Hill, 1879), 638; "Payne, Alonzo G." Co. C, 1 July 1890, Cert. 541.602, PFI.

44. Payne Diary, 22–24 May, 1, 5 June 1865, TS.

45. Ibid, 28, 31 May 1865, TS.

46. "SO 104," 26 June 1865, "SO 61," 26 June 1865, "Regimental Return," June 1865, Administrative Files.

47. "SO 130," 9 June 1865, "SO 137," 16 June 1864, "SO 98," 16 June 1865, ROB, Records AGO; *OR*, 48, pt. 2: 814.
48. Payne Diary, 21, 22, June 1865, TS. On 5 July 1884, Congress removed all unauthorized absence charges against soldiers who had maintained a good record during the war. The following Fifth soldiers had their desertion charges removed: John Brown (1912), William H. Barcus (1889), Thomas Ross (1889), John A. Williams (1904), and Seth Evans (1907). James Spaulding, who was listed as deserted on 6 July 1865, had actually been honorably discharged on 30 June 1865 to enter the United States Military Academy.
49. Baumann, *Arming the Suckers*, 46; *OR*, 48, pt. 2: 910.
50. Charles H. Lothrop, *A History of the First Regiment Iowa Cavalry Veteran Volunteers* (Lyons, IA: Beers and Eaton, 1890), 223, 225–26.
51. Elizabeth B. Custer, *Tenting on the Plains or General Custer in Kansas and Texas* (New York: Harper and Bros., 1895), 62–63.
52. Thomas S. Cogley, *History of the Seventh Indiana Cavalry* (La Porte, IN: Herald, 1876), 164, 165, 166; *1861 Revised Regulations for the Army*, 509.
53. Lothrop, *History of the First Regiment Iowa Cavalry*, 223; "Regimental Return," July 1865, Records AGO.
54. McConnell to Haynie, 20 April 1865, 1 June 1865, 8 September 1865, Administrative Files. McConkey filed a pension for an 1863 horse-related injury, but since he stayed on duty, there was no record of the injury, and the government denied his clam for many years. He did, however, qualify for a Mexican War pension. Alex Jessop moved back to his farm in Wayne County after the war, living next to his brother until 1920, when he moved to Boulder, Colorado. Clark became a clergyman and moved with his family to Massachusetts. George W. McConkey Civil War Pension File No. 346.305, Mexican War Pension File No. 11200, Pension Records; "Jessop, Alex S.," 1870 PS Wayne County, IL, Roll 288: 254; "Jessup, Alexander S.," 1920 PS Boulder County, CO, Roll 156: 168; "Clark, Lyman," 1880 PS Worcester County, MA, Roll 563: 463.
55. "FO 1," 7 August 1865, ROB, Records AGO; Lothrop, *History of the First Regiment Iowa Cavalry*, 220–22.
56. Lothrop, *History of the First Regiment Iowa Cavalry*, 219; James Bennett, "Our Army Correspondence," CCA, 28 September 1865, 2.
57. Cogley, *History of the Seventh Indiana Cavalry*, 167–68.
58. Ibid, 169.
59. Ibid, 172.
60. Ibid, 172.
61. Bennett, "Our Army Correspondence," 28 September 1865; Custer, *Tenting on the Plains*, 95; Cogley, *Seventh Indiana Cavalry*, 176. Bennett and his wife settled in Sullivan County, Indiana, where the sergeant became a wheelwright. "Bennett, James G.," 1880 PS Sullivan County, IN, Roll 313: 627.
62. "GO 133," 22 August 1865, McConnell Military Service Record, CSR.
63. "GO 2," 4 September 1865, ROB, Records AGO; Cogley, *History of the Seventh Indiana Cavalry*, 177.
64. Bennett, "Our Army Correspondence," 28 September 1865; Custer, *Tenting on the Plains*, 98, 102.

65. "SO 48," 10 September 1865, "Circular No. 32," 21 September 1865, ROB, Records AGO.

66. "GO 30," 19 September 1865, Co. I Order Books, Records AGO. Weaver mustered out with the regiment and became a laborer in Cumberland County. "Weaver, Thomas H.," 1870 PS Cumberland County, IL, Roll 214: 281.

67. McConnell to Haynie, 8 September 1865, Administrative Files; Addison to McConnell, 1 October 1865, Letters Received and Endorsement Book, Records AGO.

68. "Morning Report," Co. C, October 1865, Records AGO; "Local and Miscellany," CCA, 9 November 1865, 3.

BIBLIOGRAPHY

Manuscripts and Unpublished Sources

Abraham Lincoln Presidential Library, Springfield, Illinois
    Brown, Henry C. Diary, 1861–1862, Microfilm.
    Burke, John W. Letters, 1862–1864, SC 2387.
    Hussey, Fenton Andrew. Papers, SC 729.
    Packard, Thadeus B. Diary, 1861–1864, Reminiscences, MS.
    Payne, Alonzo G. Diary, TS, SC 1152.
    Reese, Thomas Madison. Papers, 1857–1876. Box 1, Folder 2.
    Roe, Jonas H. Papers, 1861–1864, SC 1837.
    Wheelock, Francis A. Diary, 1864, SC 1646.

Christian County Historical Society, Taylorville, Illinois
    Skiles, William A. Civil War Letters.

Illinois State Archives, Springfield
    Database of Soldiers' and Sailors' Home Residents (Quincy),
        1887–1916, (ISSH DB). http://www.cyberdriveillinois.
        com/departments/archives/quincyhome.html.
    Fifth Illinois Cavalry, Administrative Files on Civil
        War Companies and Regiments, RS 301.018.
    Illinois Public Domain Land Tract Sales Database, http://
        www.ilsos.gov/GenealogyMWeb/landsrch.html
    Illinois Public Land Purchase Records [database on-line]. Provo, UT:
        Ancestry.com Operations Inc., 1999, http://www.Ancestry.com.
    Illinois Secretary of State, Record of Election
        Returns, 1869, 1871, 1872, 1876.
    Illinois Statewide Marriage Index, 1763–1900, http://www.
        ilsos.gov/GenealogyMWeb/marrsrch.html.

Indiana Historical Society, Indianapolis
    Thurman Family Papers, M246.

Indiana State Archives, Indianapolis
    First Indiana Cavalry Regimental Correspondences. Microfilm.
    First Indiana Cavalry Regimental Order Books, New
        Harmony Manuscripts, Microfilm F415P, roll 19.

John A Logan Museum, Murphysboro, Illinois
    Ben Wiley Collection, Collection 2003.064.

Kansas State Historical Society, Topeka
     Bondi, August. *Personal Reminiscences of August Bondi,*
         August Bondi Papers, 1884–1952, Series B, MF 1772.
     Flanders, George E. Civil War Letters 1861–1864. Microfilm Box 767.

National Archives, Washington, DC.
     Compiled Service Records of Volunteer Union Soldiers,
         Fifth Illinois Cavalry, Records of the Adjutant
         General's Office, 1780s–1918, Record Group 94.
     Fifth Illinois Cavalry, Records of Movements and Activities of
         Volunteer Union Organizations, Records of the Adjutant
         General Office, 1780s–1917, Record Group 94.
     Helena Hospital Registers, Arkansas, vols. 45 and 46, 1862–1865.
         Records of the Adjutant General's Office, Record Group 94, National
         Archives and Records Administration, Washington, DC.
     Military Pension and Bounty Land Warrant Records, 1775–
         1916, Records of the Veterans Administration, Record
         Group 15, National Archives Records Branch, Old Military
         and Civil Records Branch, Washington, DC.
     Organization Index to Pension Files of Veterans Who Served
         Between 1861 and 1900, T289, Washington, DC.
     Passenger Lists of Vessels Arriving at New York, New
         York, 1820–1897, Records of the US Customs Service,
         Record Group 36, Microfilm Roll 237, List 533.

Private Collections
     Adams, Jean. Henry Caldwell Family History, Jean
         Adams Personal Family Files, El Paso, Texas.

Special Collections, Morris Library, Southern Illinois University–Carbondale
     Mann, John Preston. Papers, Collection 111.
     Wiley, Benjamin Ladd. Papers, Collection 99.

State Historical Society of Missouri, Columbia
     Hinrichs, Charles F. Papers, 1862–1902, C335, Western
         Historical Manuscript Collection.

United States Bureau of the Census, National Archives and Records Administration
     Eighth Census of the United States of Population
         and Housing, 1860. Microfilm M653.
     Fourteenth Census of the United States of Population
         and Housing, 1920. Microfilm T625.
     Ninth Census of the United States of Population
         and Housing, 1870. Microfilm M593.
     Seventh Census of the United States of Population
         and Housing, 1850. Microfilm M432.
     Tenth Census of the United States of Population
         and Housing, 1880. Microfilm T9.
     Thirteenth Census of the United States of Population
         and Housing, 1910. Microfilm T624.
     Twelfth Census of the United States of Population
         and Housing, 1900. Microfilm T623.

University of Arkansas, Fayetteville
Crouch, W. A. Papers, MC 550, Special Collections Division.

Newspapers

American Citizen, Canton, Mississippi.
Belleville Advocate, Belleville, Illinois.
Belleville Democrat, Belleville, Illinois.
Bloomington Pantagraph, Bloomington, Illinois.
Carbondale Free Press, Carbondale, Illinois.
Chicago Tribune, Chicago, Illinois.
Crawford Country Argus, Robinson, Illinois.
Du Quoin Tribune, Du Quoin, Illinois.
Fairfield War Democrat, Fairfield, Illinois.
Mattoon Gazette, Mattoon, Illinois.
Memphis Daily Appeal, Atlanta, Georgia.
Nashville Journal, Nashville, Illinois.
New York Times, New York.
New York Herald, New York.
Prairie Pioneer, Fairfield, Illinois.

Books and Articles

Anderson, John Q., comp. *Campaigning with Parsons' Texas Cavalry Brigade, CSA. The War Journals and Letters of the Four Orr Brothers, 12th Texas Cavalry Regiment*. Hillsboro, TX: Hill Junior College Press, 1967.

Avery, Phineas O. *History of the Fourth Illinois Cavalry Regiment*. Humboldt, NE: Enterprise, 1903.

Bahde, Thomas. "'Our Cause Is a Common One': Home Guards, Union Leagues, and Republican Citizenship in Illinois, 1861–1863." *Civil War History* 56, no. 1 (March 2010): 66–98.

Bailey, Anne J. *Between the Enemy and Texas: Parsons's Texas Cavalry in the Civil War*. Fort Worth: Texas Christian Univ. Press, 1989.

———. *In the Saddle with the Texans: Day-by-Day with Parsons's Cavalry Brigade, 1862–1865*. Abilene: McWhiney Foundation Press, 2004.

Baker, Dula McLeod. "History of Smithville School." *Lawrence County Historical Society Quarterly* 7, no. 3 (Summer 1984): 12–18.

Baker, Thomas H. "Refugee Newspaper: The Memphis *Daily Appeal*, 1862–1865." *Journal of Southern History* 29, no. 3 (August 1963): 326–44.

Barnes, Joseph K. *The Medical and Surgical History of the War of the Rebellion*. 6 vols. Washington, DC: GPO: 1870–88.

Barron, Samuel. *The Lone Star Defenders: A Chronicle of the Third Texas Cavalry, Ross' Brigade*. New York: Neale, 1908.

Bateman, Newton, and Paul Shelby, eds. *Historical Encyclopedia of Illinois and History of Coles County*. Chicago: Munsell, 1906.

———, eds. *Historical Encyclopedia of Illinois and History of Sangamon County*. 2 vols. Chicago: Munsell, 1912.

Baumann, Ken. *Arming the Suckers, 1861–1865. A Compilation of Illinois Civil War Weapons*. Dayton, OH: Morningside House, 1989.

Beall, Jonathan A. "'Won't We Never Get Out of This State?': Western Soldiers in Post–Civil War Texas, 1865–1866." MA thesis, Texas A&M Univ., 2004.

Bearss, Edwin C. *The Battle of Jackson, May 14, 1863/The Siege of Jackson*. Baltimore: Gateway, 1981.

———. *The Campaign for Vicksburg*. 3 vols. Dayton, OH: Morningside House, 1986.

———. "The Great Railroad Raid." *Annals of Iowa* 40, nos. 2–3 (1969): 147–60, 229: 39.

———. "Misfire in Mississippi: McPherson's Canton Expedition." *Civil War History* 8 (December 1962): 401–16.

Bearss, Margie Riddle. *Sherman's Forgotten Campaign: The Meridian Expedition*. Baltimore: Gateway, 1987.

Beckwith, H. W. *History of Vermilion County, Illinois.* . . . Chicago: H. H. Hill, 1879.

Behlendorff, Frederick. *History of the Thirteenth Illinois Cavalry Regiment Volunteers U.S. Army, from September 1861 to September 1865.* . . . Grand Rapids, MI: n.p., 1888.

Bennett, Stewart, and Barbara Tillery, eds. *The Struggle for the Life of the Republic: A Civil War Narrative by Brevet Major Charles Dana Miller, 76th Ohio Volunteer Infantry*. Kent, OH: Kent State Univ. Press, 2004.

Bergeron, Arthur W., Jr. *Guide to Louisiana Confederate Military Units, 1861–1865*. Baton Rouge: Louisiana Univ. Press, 1989.

Biographical and Historical Memoirs of Eastern Arkansas. . . . Chicago: Goodspeed, 1890.

Black, Robert C. *The Railroads of the Confederacy*. Chapel Hill: Univ. of North Carolina Press, 1952.

Brackett, Albert. "A Memorable March." *United Service* 4 (October 1890): 336–41.

Brown, Russell K. *To the Manor Born. The Life of General William H. T. Walker*. Athens: Univ. of Georgia Press, 1994.

Carroll, John M. *Custer in Texas: An Interrupted Narrative.* . . . New York: Sol Lewis, 1975.

The Century of Golden Years: Centennial History of McLean County, Illinois. Chicago: William LeBaron Jr., 1879.

The Chicago Copperhead Convention (August 29, 1864). . . . Washington, DC: Congressional Union Committee, 1864.

Christ, Mark, ed. *Rugged and Sublime: The Civil War in Arkansas*. Fayetteville: Univ. of Arkansas Press, 1994.

Church, Charles A. *History of the Republican Party in Illinois 1854–1912*. Rockford, IL: Wilson Bros., 1912.

Cogley, Thomas S. *History of the Seventh Indiana Cavalry.* . . . Laporte, IN: Herald, 1876.

Cole, Arthur Charles. *The Era of the Civil War*. Springfield: Illinois Centennial Commission, 1919.

Coleman, Charles H., and Paul H. Spence. "The Charleston Riot, March 28, 1864." *Journal of the Illinois State Historical Society* 33, no. 1 (March 1940): 7–56.

Connelley, William E. *A Standard History of Kansas and Kansans*. 5 vols. Chicago: Lewis, 1918.

Cooke, Philip St. George. *Cavalry Tactics*. Philadelphia: J. D. Lippincott, 1862.

Counties of Cumberland, Jasper and Richland, Illinois. Historical and Biographical. Chicago: F. A. Battey, 1884.

Cox, Florence M. A, ed. *Kiss Josey for Me!* Santa Ana: Friis-Pioneer, 1974.

Crabb, Martha L. All Afire to Fight. *The Untold Tale of the Civil War's Ninth Texas Cavalry*. New York: Post Road, 2000.

Crute, Joseph H., Jr. *Units of the Confederate States Army*. Midlothian, VA: Derwent, 1987.

Cryder, George R., and Stanley R. Millers, comps. *The American "War for the Union": A View from the Ranks. The Civil War Diaries of Corporal Charles E. Smith.* . . . Delaware, OH: Delaware County Historical Society, 1999.

Cummins, W. Smith. "A Ruse That Worked Well in Mississippi." *Confederate Veteran* 20 (January 1913): 27–28.

Curschmann, H. *Typhoid Fever and Typhus Fever*. Philadelphia, PA: W. B. Saunders, 1905.

Custer, Elizabeth B. *Tenting on the Plains, or General Custer in Kansas and Texas*. New York: Harper and Bros., 1895.

Dalton, Lawrence. *History of Randolph County, Arkansas*. Little Rock: Democrat Print and Lithographing, 1946.

Davenport, Edward A., ed. *History of the Ninth Regiment Illinois Cavalry Volunteers*. Chicago: Donohue and Henneberry, 1888.

Dougan, Michael B. *Confederate Arkansas. The People and Policies of a Frontier State in Wartime*. Tuscaloosa: Univ. of Alabama Press, 1976.

Duis, E. *The Good Old Times in McLean County, Illinois.* . . . Bloomington, IL: Leader Publishing and Printing House, 1874.

Dyer, Frederick. *A Compendium of the War of the Rebellion*. 3 vols. Des Moines: Dyer, 1908.

Eddy, T. M. *The Patriotism of Illinois.* . . . 2 vols. Chicago: Clarke, 1866.

Elliott, Isaac H., and Virgil G. Way. *History of the Thirty-Third Regiment Illinois Veteran Volunteer Infantry in the Civil War 22nd August, 1861, to 7th December, 1865.* . . . Gibson City, IL: The [Regimental] Association, 1902.

Fellman, Michael. *Inside War: The Guerilla Conflict in Missouri during the American Civil War*. New York: Oxford Univ. Press, 1989.

Field, Charles D. *Three Years in the Saddle from 1862 to 1865: Memoirs of Charles D. Field: Thrilling Stories of the War in Camp and on the Field of Battle*. Goldfield, LA: n.p., 1898.

Fischer, David Hackett. *Albion's Seed: Four British Folkways in America*. New York: Oxford Univ. Press, 1989.

Forbes, William II. *Capt. Croft's Flying Artillery Battery Columbus, Georgia*. Dayton, OH: Morningside, 1993.

Foster, Buck T. *Sherman's Mississippi Campaign*. Tuscaloosa: Univ. of Alabama Press, 2006.

French, Samuel G. *Two Wars: An Autobiography of Gen. Samuel G. French*. Nashville: Confederate Veteran, 1901.

Fry, Alice L. *Following the Fifth Kansas Cavalry*. Lebanon, MO: A. L. Fry, 1998.

Gardner, Harry, and A. G. Apperson. *History of Wabash Lodge No. 179, A. F. and A. Masons, Etna, Illinois, organized May 23, 1854*. Etna, IL: n.p. 1904.

Girardi, Robert I., and Nathaniel C. Hughes Jr. *The Memoirs of Brigadier General William Passmore Carlin U.S.A.* Lincoln: Univ. of Nebraska Press, 1999.

Gosnell, H. Allen. *Guns on the Western Water: The Story of the River Gunboats in the Civil War*. Baton Rouge: Louisiana State Univ. Press, 1993.

Grant, Ulysses S. *Personal Memoirs of U. S. Grant*. 2 vols. 1885–86. Reprint, New York: Konecky and Konecky, 1992.

Griffith, Paddy. *Battle Tactics of the Civil War.* New Haven: Yale Univ. Press, 1987.

Hale, Douglas. *The Third Texas Cavalry in the Civil War.* Norman: Univ. of Oklahoma Press, 1993.

Hammond, William A. *Military, Medical and Surgical Essays: Prepared for the United States Sanitary Commission, 1862–1864.* Philadelphia: J. B. Lippincott, 1864.

Harris, Benjamin G. *On the Resolution to Expel Mr. Long. Speech of Hon. Benjamin G. Harris of Maryland Delivered to the House of Representatives of the United States, April 9, 1864.* Washington, DC: Constitutional Union Office, 1864.

Hattaway, Herman, and Archer Jones. *How the North Won: A Military History of the Civil War.* Urbana: Univ. of Illinois Press, 1983.

Hearn, Chester G. *Ellet's Brigade: The Strangest Outfit of All.* Baton Rouge: Louisiana State Univ. Press, 2000.

Hess, Earl J. "Confiscation and the Northern War Effort: The Army of the Southwest at Helena." *Arkansas Historical Quarterly* 44, no. 1 (1985): 56–75.

Hewett, Janet B., ed. *Supplement to the Official Records of the Union and Confederate Armies.* Wilmington, NC: Broadfoot, 1994–2001.

The History of McLean County, Illinois: Portraits of Early Settlers and Prominent Men. Chicago: W. Le Baron Jr., 1879.

History of Pike County, Illinois. . . . Chicago: C. C. Chapman, 1880.

History of the Forty-Sixth Regiment Indiana Volunteer Infantry, September 1861 to September 1865. Logansport, IN: Wilson, Humphreys, 1888.

History of the Sixteenth Battery of Ohio Volunteer Light Artillery U. S.A. From Enlistment, August 20, 1861 to Muster Out, August 2, 1865. Compiled from the Diaries of Comrades, the Best Recollections of Survivors, and Official Records. N.p.: n.p., 1906.

History of Ray County, Missouri. . . . St. Louis: Missouri Historical Co., 1881.

History of Wayne and Clay Counties, Illinois. Chicago: Globe, 1884.

Hougland, James H. *Civil War Diary of James H. Hougland, Company G, 1st Indiana Cavalry for the Year 1862.* Bloomington, IN: Monroe County Civil War Centennial Commission and Monroe County Historical Society, 1962.

Howard, Richard L. *History of the 124th Regiment Illinois Infantry Volunteers, Otherwise Known as 'the Hundred and Two Dozen' from August, 1862 to August, 1865.* Springfield, IL: H. W. Rokker, 1880.

Illinois Adjutant General. *Report of the Adjutant General of the State of Illinois, 1861–1866.* 8 vols. Springfield: Baker, Bailhache, 1867.

———. *Roll of Honor. Record of Burial Places of Soldiers, Sailors, Marines, and Army Nurses of All the Wars in the United States Buried in the State of Illinois.* 2 vols. Springfield: N.p., 1929.

Jackson County, Illinois Circuit Court Records, Book H (May 1861–May 1868), Murphysboro, IL.

Johnston, Joseph E. *Narrative of Military Operations.* New York: D. Appleton, 1874.

Johnson, Allen. *Stephen A. Douglas: A Study in American Politics.* New York: McMillan, 1908.

Jones, Lottie E. *History of Vermilion County Illinois. . . .* 2 vols. Chicago: Pioneer, 1911.

Journal of the Thirty-Sixth Annual Encampment of the Grand Army of the Republic. Topeka: Kansas State Printing Office, 1917.

Kansas Adjutant General's Office. *Report of the Adjutant General of the State of Kansas.* 2 vols. Leavenworth, KS: Bulletin Co-Operative Printing, 1867.

Kerr, Homer L., ed. *Fighting with Ross' Texas Cavalry Brigade, C.S.A. The Diary of George L. Griscom, Adjutant, 9th Texas Cavalry Regiment.* Hillsboro, TX: Hill Junior College Press, 1976.

King, James T. *War Eagle: A Life of General Eugene A. Carr.* Lincoln: Univ. of Nebraska Press, 1963.

Klement, Frank L. *The Copperheads in the Middle West.* Chicago: Univ. of Chicago Press, 1960.

Kohl, Rhonda M. "Benjamin Ladd Wiley: Nineteenth-Century Entrepreneur and Politician." MA thesis, Southern Illinois Univ., Carbondale, IL, 1987.

———. "The Hard Lessons of War: The Fifth Illinois Cavalry at Helena, Arkansas." *Journal of the Illinois State Historical Society* 99 (Fall–Winter 2006–7): 185–210.

———. "Raising Thunder with the Secesh: Powell Clayton's Federal Cavalry at Taylor's Creek and Mount Vernon, Arkansas, May 11, 1863." *Arkansas Historical Quarterly* 64 (Summer 2005): 146–70.

———. "This God-Forsaken Town: Death and Disease at Helena, Arkansas 1862." *Civil War History* 50 (June 2004): 109–77.

Lawrence County Historical Society. *Mother of Counties: Lawrence County, Arkansas: History and Families.* Paducah, KY: Turner, 2001.

Lee, Stephen D. "Meridian Campaign." *Publications of the Mississippi Historical Society* 4 (1900): 37–48.

———. "Sherman's Expedition from Vicksburg to Meridian, Feb. 3, to March 6, 1864." *Southern Historical Society Papers* 32: 310–19.

Levy, Lewis F. "Two Years in Northern Prisons." *Confederate Veteran* 14 (January 1906): 122–24.

Lothrop, Charles C. *A History of the First Regiment Iowa Cavalry Veteran Volunteer....* Lyon, IA: Beers and Eaton, 1890.

Main, Edwin M. *The Story of the Marches, Battles and Incidents of the Third United States Colored Cavalry.* 1908. Reprint, New York: Negro Universities Press, 1970.

Marriage Records, Sangamon County, Illinois. Springfield: Sangamon County Genealogical Society, 1981.

Marshall, Albert O. *Army Life: From a Soldier's Journal: Incidents, Sketches, and Record of a Union Soldier's Army Life.* Joliet, IL: Chicago Legal News, 1884.

Massie, Melville. D. *Past and Present of Pike County, Illinois.* Chicago: S. J. Clarke, 1906.

Monks, William. *History of Southern Missouri and Northern Arkansas. . . .* West Plains, MO: West Plains Journal Co., 1907.

Montague, E. J. *A Directory, Business Mirror, and Historical Sketches of Randolph County.* Alton, IL: Courier Steam Book, 1859.

Montgomery, Frank A. *Reminiscences of a Mississippian in Peace and War.* Cincinnati: Robert Clarke, 1901.

Moore, Frank. ed. *Rebellion Record. A Diary of American Events. . . .* 11 vols. New York: G. P. Putnam, 1862–1868.

Moses, John. *Illinois Historical and Statistical. . . .* 2 vols. Chicago: Fergus, 1889–1892.

Nichols, Bruce. *Guerrilla Warfare in Civil War Missouri, 1862.* Jefferson, NC: Mc-
    Farland, 2004.
O'Brien, Thomas M., and Oliver Diefendorf. *General Orders of the War Depart-
    ment, Embracing the Years 1861, 1862, and 1863.* 2 vols. New York: Derby and
    Miller, 1864.
Packard, Thadeus B. "The Charge of the Fifth Illinois Cavalry." *Transactions of the
    McLean County Historical Society* 2 (1903): 395–400.
Patterson, Lowell Wayne, ed. *Campaigns of the 38th Regiment of the Illinois Volun-
    teer Infantry, Company K, 1861–1863: The Diary of William Elwood Patterson.*
    Bowie, MD: Heritage, 1992.
Perrin, William H., comp. *The History of Coles County, Illinois.* . . . Chicago: W. Le
    Baron, 1879.
Peterson, William S. "A History of Camp Butler, 1861–1866." *Illinois Historical Journal*
    82, no. 2 (1989): 74–92.
Piper, J. A. *Roster of Soldiers, Sailors and Marines of the War of 1812, the Mexican
    War, and the War of the Rebellion, Residing in Nebraska June 1, 1895.* York, NE:
    Nebraska Newspaper Union, 1895.
Ponder, Jerry. *History of Ripley County, Missouri.* Fairdealing, MO: J. Ponder, 1987.
———. *A History of the 15th Missouri Cavalry Regiment, CSA: 1862–1865.* Doniphan,
    MO: Ponder, 1994.
Portrait and Biographical Album of Coles County, Illinois. . . . Chicago: Chapman
    Bros., 1887.
Portrait and Biographical Album of Pike and Calhoun Counties, Illinois. . . . Chicago:
    Biographical Publishing Co., 1891.
Portrait and Biographical Album of Sangamon County, Illinois. Chicago: Chapman
    Bros., 1891.
*Portrait and Biographical Record of Randolph, Jackson, Perry, and Monroe Counties,
    Illinois.* . . . Chicago: Biographical Publishing Co., 1894.
Portrait and Biographical Record of Shelby and Moultrie Counties, Illinois. . . . Chi-
    cago: Biographical Publishing Co., 1891.
*Proceedings of the Second Annual Reunion of the Society of the Fifth Ills. Vet. Vol.
    Cav. Held at Vandalia, Illinois, October 6 and 7, 1885 and Constitution and
    By-Laws.* Neoga, IL: Neoga News Print, 1886.
Prosser, Zane Lee, and Shirley Patton Prosser, eds. *The Civil War Service of John
    Prosser of Spencer County, Indiana, Private, Company 'F,' 1st Regiment Indiana
    Cavalry.* Bethalto, IL: Z. L. Prosser, 1991.
Riley, Franklin L. "Extinct Towns and Villages in Mississippi." *Publications of the
    Mississippi Historical Society* 5 (1902): 311–83.
Roberts, Bobby, and Carl Moneyhon. *A Photographic History of Arkansas in the Civil
    War.* Fayetteville: Univ. of Arkansas Press, 1987.
Robinson, Doane. *History of South Dakota.* B. F. Bowen, 1904.
Rose, Victor M. *Ross' Texas Brigade.* 1881. Reprint, Kennesaw, GA: Continental
    Book, 1960.
Rowland, Dunbar. *Military History of Mississippi, 1803–1898.* 1908. Reprint, Spar-
    tanburg, SC: Reprint Co., 1978.
Sampson, Robert. "'Pretty Damned Warm Times': The 1864 Charleston Riot and 'the
    Inalienable Right of Revolution.'" *Illinois Historical Journal* 89, no. 2 (Summer
    1996): 99–116.

Scott, Franklin W. *Newspapers and Periodicals of Illinois 1814–1879*. Chicago: Illinois State Historical Library, 1910.

Scott, William F. *The Story of a Cavalry Regiment. The Career of the Fourth Iowa Veteran Volunteers from Kansas to Georgia, 1861–1865*. New York: G. P. Putnam Sons, 1893.

Scroggs, Jack B., and Donald E. Reynolds. "Arkansas and the Vicksburg Campaign." *Civil War History* 5, no. 4 (1959): 391–401.

Shea, William L. "The Confederate Defeat at Cache River." *Arkansas Historical Quarterly* 52, no. 2 (Summer 1993): 120–55.

Shea, William L., and Earl J. Hess. *Pea Ridge: Civil War Campaign in the West*. Chapel Hill: Univ. of North Carolina Press, 1992.

Sheppley, Helen Edith. "Camp Butler in the Civil War Days." *Journal of the Illinois State Historical Society* 25, no. 4 (January 1933): 285–317.

Sherman, William T. *Memoirs of William Tecumseh Sherman*. Bloomington: Indiana Univ. Press, 1957.

Sifakis, Stewart. *Compendium of the Confederate Armies*. 11 vols. New York: Facts on File, 1992–1995.

Simon, John Y, ed. *The Papers of Ulysses S. Grant*. 31 vols. Carbondale: Southern Illinois Univ. Press, 1967–2008.

Skiles, William A. *Letters to Home. A Collection of Letters of Civil War Union Soldier William A. Skiles September 1861 to November 1864, Christian County, Illinois*. Taylorville, Illinois: Christian County Historical Society, 1998.

Smith, Charles E. *The American War for the Union: A View from the Ranks. The Civil War Diaries of Corporal Charles E. Smith*. Delaware, OH: Delaware County Historical Society, 1999.

Smith, George W. *A History of Southern Illinois. . . .* 3 vols. Chicago: Lewis, 1912.

Smith, Thomas West. *The Story of a Cavalry Regiment: "Scott's 900," Eleventh New York Cavalry from the St. Lawrence River to the Gulf of Mexico, 1861–1865*. Chicago: Veterans Association, 1897.

Sperry Andrew F. *History of the 33d Iowa Infantry Volunteer Regiment, 1863–6*. Des Moines: Mills, 1866. Reprint, Fayetteville: Univ. of Arkansas Press, 1999.

Steiner, Paul. E. *Disease in the Civil War: Natural Biological Warfare in 1861–1865*. Springfield: Charles C. Thomas, 1968.

Sterling, Bob. "Discouragement, Weariness, and War Politics: Desertions from Illinois Regiments during the Civil War." *Illinois Historical Journal* 82, no. 4 (Winter 1989): 239–62.

Trumbull, Lyman. *Speech of Hon. Lyman Trumbull, of Illinois, on Amending the Constitution to Prohibit Slavery*. Washington, DC: L. Towers for the Union Congressional Committee, 1864.

United States, Adjutant General's Office. *General Orders Affecting the Volunteer Force, 1863*. Washington, DC: GPO, 1864.

United States Congress. *Journal of the House of Representatives of the United States: Being the First Session of the Thirty-Eighth Congress; Began and Held at the city of Washington, December 7, 1863 in the Eighty-Eighth Year of the Independence of the United States*. Washington, DC: GPO, 1863.

———. *The Statutes at Large, Treaties, and Proclamations of the United States of America*. Boston: Little, Brown, 1863.

The United States Magazine. New York: Charles B. Richardson, 1864.

United States, Naval War Records Office. *Official Records of the Union and Confederate Navies in the War of the Rebellion*. 30 vols. Washington, DC: GPO, 1894–1922.

United States, War Dept. *Revised Regulations for the Army of the United States, 1861.* Philadelphia: W. Childs, 1862.

Van Buren, W. H. *Report of a Committee Appointed by Resolution of the Sanitary Commission, to Prepare a Paper on the Use of Quinine as a Prophylactic against Malicious Diseases.* New York: W. C. Bryant, 1861.

Wagenseller, George W. *The History of the Wagenseller Family in America with Kindred Branches.* Middleburgh, PA: Wagenseller, 1898.

Walton, William M. *Major Buck Walton: An Epitome of My Life.* Civil War Reminiscences. Austin: Waterloo, 1965.

The War of the Rebellion: A Compilation of the Official Records of the Union and Confederate Armies in the War of the Rebellion. 130 vols. Washington, DC: GPO, 1880–1901.

West, Emmet C. *History and Reminiscences of the Second Wisconsin Cavalry Regiment.* 1904. Reprint, Rochester, MI: State Register Press, 1982.

White, John H. "Forgotten Cavalrymen: General Edward Francis Winslow, U.S. Volunteers." *Journal of the United States Cavalry Association* 25 (January 1915): 375–89.

Wiley, Carl. "Makanda's Colonel Ben Wiley." *Illinois Magazine* 19 (May–June 1980): 14–20.

Williams, C. S., comp. *Williams' Springfield Directory, City Guide, and Business Mirror for 1860–61.* Springfield: Johnson and Bradford, 1860.

Willison, Charles A. *Reminiscences of a Boy's Service with the 76th Ohio.* 1908. Reprint, Huntington, WV: Blue Acorn, 1995.

Winters, B., comp. *Springfield City Directory for 1857–'58.* Springfield: S. H. Jameson, 1857.

Winters, John D. *The Civil War in Louisiana.* Baton Rouge: Louisiana State Univ. Press, 1963.

Wolfe, Thomas J., ed. *A History of Sullivan County, Indiana. . . .* Chicago, New York: Lewis, 1909.

Woodbury, Henry H. *Complete History of the 46th Illinois Veteran Volunteer Infantry. . . .* Freeport, IL: Baily and Ankeny, 1866.

Woodward, Joseph J. *Outlines of the Chief Camp Diseases of the United States Armies.* 1863. Reprint, New York: Hafner, 1964.

Worley, Ted. R. "Helena on the Mississippi." *Arkansas Historical Quarterly* 13 (Spring 1954): 1–15.

Wyeth, John A. *That Devil Forrest: Life of General Nathan Bedford Forrest.* New York: Harper and Bros., 1959.

Zuber, William P. *My Eighty Years in Texas.* Austin: Univ. of Texas Press, 1971.

Internet Sources

"Alonzo Grimes Payne," "The Descendants of Prosper Payne," Miller-Malcolm Family Tree, http://miller-malcom-familytree.net/descendants_of_prosper_payne.html.

Civil War: Illinois, USGenWeb Archives Project, Jennifer Dorner, Coordinator. Illinois Civil War Pensions Project, 2009–2011, http://www.usgwarchives.net/pensions/civilwar/ilindex.htm.

Dewitt GenWeb Project, Dewitt County Illinois Obituaries H, The DeWitt County GenWeb Project Team, 2000–2010, http://dewitt.ilgenweb.net/obits-h.htm.

Effingham County IL Archives Military Records. Effingham County Pensioners List 1883Civilwar—Pension, Deb Haines, contributor, USGenWeb Archives, http://files.usgwarchives.org/il/effingham/military/civilwar/pensions/effingha475nmt.txt.

Feagan, Eric, ed. *Jonas H. Roe and Family*. Elf Junction, 2001–2010, http://civilwarletters.150m.com/Copyright_2001/JonasRoe_history.html.

Findagrave, Russ Dodge, administrator, http://www.findagrave.com.

Heritage Quest Online, ProQuest, 1999–2011, http://persi.heritagequestonline.com.

Illinois Genealogy Trails, Coles County, Kim Torp, ed., 1998–2011, http://genealogytrails.com/ill/coles/page13.html.

"James Farnan," Ayres Genealogy, Dr. James Farnan Court Cases, David Kidd, ed., http://barbaras.org/ayres/ayres.html.

"Kansas Legislators Past and Present," Boh-BZZ. Alphabetical Index of Kansas Legislators, State Library of Kansas, compiled by Rita Haley, Sherri Schulte, Donna Copeland, Bill Sowers and Lois Delfelder, http://www.kslib.info/legislators/membb3.html.

Krueger, Maurice. ed. *Memorial and Biographical Record; an Illustrated Compendium of Biography, Containing a Compendium of Local Biography, Including Biographical Sketches of Prominent Old Settlers and Representative Citizens of South Dakota*. Chicago: G. A. Ogle, 1899, http://files.usgwarchives.org/sd/biography/memor99/berry-w.txt.

Organization Index to Pension Files of Veterans Who Served Between 1861 and 1900, T289, Washington, DC http://www.footnote.com.

Schmale, John. ed. "Civil War Flags of Illinois," Mahomet, IL, 1998–2001, http://civil-war.com/searchpages/result.asp?Name=005th&category=Cavalry&Submit=Search+for+Flags.

Sons of Union Veterans of the Civil War, National Graves Registration Database, 1995–2011, http://www.suvcwdb.org/home/.

"Thos. A. Apperson," Wabash Lodge, No. 179, A. F. and A. M. Coles County, IL, transcribed by Kim Torp, 1998–2010, http://genealogytrails.com/ill/coles/mason3.html.

"Twenty-Eighth Wisconsin Volunteer Infantry, Letter from Lt. Cushman K. Davis During Gorman's Expedition up the White River, Arkansas," Kent A. Peterson, webmaster, 2011, http://www.28thwisconsin.com/letters/cush_davis.html.

Wayne County, IL, Archives Military Records. Wayne County Pensioners List 1883 Civilwar—Pension, Diane Williams, contributor, USGenWeb Archives, http://files.usgwarchives.org/il/wayne/military/civilwar/pensions/wayne468nmt.txt.

"Wiley C. Jones," *Goodspeed's Biographical and Historical Memoirs of Northeastern Arkansas, Lawrence County*, Arkansas GenWeb Project, Bill Couch, ed., 1996, http://www.couchgenweb.com/lawrence/law-h-1.htm.

INDEX

Adams, John, cavalry brigade: Mechanicsburg, Mississippi skirmish, 115–20, 149

Adams, Wirt, 134, 149–53, 159–60, 166–70, 172–75, 178, 182, 186, 195–96, 198–99, 205, 207

African American, 3, 10, 17, 69, 70, 102–3, 196, 205, 226; soldier recruitment, 106–7, 108; troops, First Arkansas Volunteers (African Descent), 128

Akin, James H., 154, 169. *See also under* Tennessee troops, Confederate

alcohol, 14, 41, 141, 200, 201, 207, 219

Anderson, Dick, plantation, 87

Apperson, Thomas, xv, 4, 6, 7, 14 17, 41–42, 44, 50, 51, 63, 67, 68, 100, 104, 105, 108–9, 122, 123, 125, 137, 140–41, 247n9, 262n11, 265n74; command, 65, 66, 108; McCalpin plantation, 75, 78, 80; Mechanicsburg expedition, 115, 116, 117, 119–20

Arkansas: Batesville, 32, 36, 45, 47, 48; Cotton Plant, 75, 100, 101, 110; Fort Hindman (Arkansas Post), 88, 90; Little Rock, 36, 45, 46, 48, 59, 80, 88, 91, 110; Old Town, 58, 73, 74, 75; Phillips County, 55, 59, 71, 85, 108, 110; St. Charles, 49, 66, 78, 89, 90

Arkansas, Federal troops, Second Cavalry, 228, 229

Arkansas troops, Confederate: Archibald Dobbin's Cavalry, 110; Eleventh/Seventeenth Mounted Infantry (John W. Griffith), 149, 151, 195, 219; Francis Chrisman's Cavalry, 59, 74; George W. Rutherford's Company, 75, 78; James A. Owens's Battery, 205; Samuel Corley's Company, 55, 74–76, 77–78, 80, 107

Baker, Conrad, 54, 85, 87, 94, 95

Baker, Jacob, 21, 23, 203

Balch, James A., 109, 131, 227, 242, 276n86

Barnfield, Thomas H., 20, 79, 80, 107, 139, 156, 215, 217, 218, 220, 271n17, 276n94

Beath, Edward W., 37, 65

Bennett, James G., 161, 163, 173, 188, 189, 190–91, 211, 213, 238, 239, 279n61

Berry, William N., 21, 140, 208, 220, 228, 233, 250n59, 273n57; Brookhaven raid, 125, 127

Breckinridge, John C., 114, 129

Brown, Harrison, 21, 87, 140

Brown, James K., 227, 234

Buckland, Ralph P., 147, 148

Burke, John W, 20, 43, 53, 56, 61, 85, 114, 120, 125, 130, 132, 138, 139–40, 162, 199–200, 202, 204, 268n56

Bussey, Cyrus R., 81, 85, 108, 124, 129–31, 132, 133–35, 142

Caldwell, Henry, 21, 48, 108, 220, 242, 261n76, 268n1, 276n86, 276n94

Camp Butler, Illinois, 5, 8, 11, 12, 14, 24, 58, 190, 242

Canton, Mississippi, 114, 120, 130, 132, 133, 134–35, 142, 143, 144, 148, 167, 170, 171, 173, 174, 175, 176, 185, 186, 195, 205, 217, 242; expedition to, 149–54

Rhonda M. Kohl earned a bachelor's degree in anthropology at Temple University and a master's in American history at Southern Illinois University. She is an independent researcher and writer living in southern Indiana and is currently exploring the experiences of the Fifth Illinois soldiers' wives during the war.